Explanatory Style

EXPLANATORY STYLE

Edited by

Gregory McClellan Buchanan
Martin E. P. Seligman
University of Pennsylvania

LEA LAWRENCE ERLBAUM ASSOCIATES, PUBLISHERS
1995 Hillsdale, New Jersey   Hove, UK

Lawrence Erlbaum Associates, Inc., Publishers
365 Broadway
Hillsdale, New Jersey 07642

Library of Congress Cataloging-in-Publication Data

Explanatory style / edited by Gregory McClellan Buchanan, Martin E. P.
  Seligman.
        p.   cm.
    Includes bibliographical references and indexes.
    ISBN 0-8058-0924-4
    1. Communication—Psychological aspects. 2. Explanation.
  I. Buchanan, Gregory McClellan. II. Seligman, Martin E. P.
  BF637.C45E93   1994
  153.7—dc20   94-1043
                                                        CIP

Books published by Lawrence Erlbaum Associates are printed on acid-free
paper, and their bindings are chosen for strength and durability.

Printed in the United States of America
10 9 8 7 6 5 4 3 2 1

We dedicate this volume to
Leslie Derek McClellan and
Irene Brown Seligman.

Contents

Acknowledgments

We wish to extend our thanks to Lawrence Erlbaum Associates, Publishers, and, in particular, Judith Amsel, for the preparation and care of this work. We would like to acknowledge our contributors Lyn Abramson, Lauren Alloy, Rob DeRubeis, Jane Eisner, Joan Girgus, Adele Hayes, Steve Hollon, Alice Luten, Gerald Metalsky, Sue Mineka, Susan Nolen-Hoeksema, Gabriele Oettingen, Chris Peterson, Cynthia Pury, Karen Reivich, David Rettew, Clive Robins, Peter Schulman, and Harold Zullow. We also acknowledge the significant contribution of Dr. Mary Anne Layden to the authorship of the Attributional Style Questionnaire (ASQ). Finally, we extend our gratitude to the countless researchers who have utilized the ASQ, CAVE technique, and other aspects of explanatory style in their work. It is the efforts of these many, many individuals that have collectively led to our understanding, curiosity, and excitement about this area.

Gregory McClellan Buchanan
Martin E. P. Seligman

1

▼▼▼▼▼▼▼

Explanatory Style: History and Evolution of the Field

Christopher Peterson
University of Michigan

Gregory McClellan Buchanan
Martin E. P. Seligman
University of Pennsylvania

A concern with explaining why events happened as they did no doubt predates recorded history. Explanations are an important aspect of most philosophical, religious, and scientific accounts, and are found in the most casual conversation and commentary as well. In the last 15 years, psychologists have become interested in the possibility that certain individuals habitually favor certain sorts of explanations over others. Evidence has accumulated that explanatory style indeed exists and relates to a variety of important outcomes, including health and happiness.

The purpose of this book is to review these lines of research, focusing on what we currently know and what we may know in the near future. In this chapter, we start the story by locating explanatory style in its historical context. The explanatory style tradition is both theoretical and empirical. We suspect that a large part of the popularity of explanatory style is due to this grounding in well-defined theory, on the one hand, and straightforward measures, on the other. Explanatory style has not been without its critics, however, and we discuss the shortcomings—both actual and perceived—as well.

DEFINING EXPLANATORY STYLE

The general definition of *explanatory style* is quite simple: It is one's tendency to offer similar sorts of explanations for different events. We can identify a style only by looking across different explanations; to the degree that individuals are consistent, we can sensibly speak of them as showing a style of explanation.

1

Complexity enters the picture when we decide just how we want to study explanatory style. Among the questions that must be posed, and subsequently answered, are:

1. What type of events interest us—those involving the self, or others; those that are good, bad, neutral, or ambivalent?
2. What type of explanations interest us—causal, teleological, moral, and so on?
3. What aspects of the explanations interest us—their literal content or their characterization in terms of abstract features?
4. What degree of consistency must be demonstrated before we identify it as a style?

As explanatory style research has been conducted, stances were taken on these issues and others, sometimes for explicit theoretical reasons, and sometimes for reasons of practicality or even for no good reason at all.

At present, when we refer to *explanatory style*, we mean more exactly the way that people explain the causes of bad or good events involving themselves along three dimensions. The first of these is the extent to which the explanation is internal ("It's me") versus external ("It's someone else"). The second is the stable ("It's going to last forever") versus the unstable ("It's short-lived") dimension. And the third is the global ("It's going to affect everything that happens to me") versus the specific ("It's only going to influence this") dimension.

We expect a degree of consistency across the explanations offered by individuals for different events, that is, we demand that these correlate at above-chance levels. But we do not expect perfect agreement, in part because explanatory style is but one of several influences on the actual causal explanations that people offer, and in part because the consistency of one's explanatory style appears to be an individual difference in its own right.

We have gone into this definition in some detail because explanatory style has become popular enough that other psychologists are questioning whether this particular definition is the best for all purposes. We gladly acknowledge that it may not be, and we encourage other researchers to look at explanations that do not entail causes; to consider explanations about other people; to study actual explanations rather than their abstract properties; to ascertain the simplicity or complexity of causal schemas; to study dimensions other than or in addition to internality, stability, and globality; and to study not the consistency of explanations but instead their waxing and waning. Indeed, we have explored some of these avenues ourselves, and we will do so further in the future.

We look forward to a fleshing out of the ways in which people make sense of themselves and their worlds. People no doubt have a variety of explanatory styles. A full catalogue of these styles, their origins and their consequences, would go a long way toward depicting human nature as seen from the vantage of explanatory style. At the present, however, explanatory style usually has the specific meaning we have offered.

THE ANTECEDENTS OF EXPLANATORY STYLE

Explanatory style has two ancestors. The one usually identified is the learned helplessness research tradition (Seligman, 1975), from which explanatory style emerged as a way of accounting for variation in individuals' responses to uncontrollable events (Abramson, Seligman, & Teasdale, 1978). We discuss this ancestor first because its importance lies in explaining the details of why explanatory style has been defined by our research group in the way that it has. The second ancestor is a long-standing tradition within psychology that concerns itself with individual differences in thoughts and beliefs, and how these influence motivation and emotion. Although we have not always explicitly acknowledged the origin of explanatory style in this broad tradition, it legitimizes the very notion of an explanatory style.

The Learned Helplessness Tradition

Learned helplessness was first recognized in an animal learning laboratory. Psychologists immobilized a dog and exposed it to a series of electric shocks—painful but not damaging—that could be neither avoided nor escaped. When, 24 hours later, the dog was placed in a situation in which electric shock could be terminated by a simple response, it sat there passively enduring the shock. This was in marked contrast to dogs in a control group that reacted vigorously to the shock and learned readily how to turn it off (Overmier & Seligman, 1967; Seligman & Maier, 1967).

These investigators proposed that the dog had learned to be helpless. In other words, when originally exposed to uncontrollable shock, it learned that nothing it did mattered. The shocks came and went independently of each and every one of the dog's behaviors. This learning of response–outcome independence was represented cognitively as an expectation of future helplessness that was generalized to new situations to produce a variety of deficits: motivational, cognitive, and emotional.

The deficits that follow in the wake of uncontrollability have come to be known as the *learned helplessness phenomenon*, and their cognitive explanation as the *learned helplessness model* (Maier & Seligman, 1976). Learned helplessness in animals continues to interest experimental psychologists, in large part because it provides an opportunity to investigate the interaction between mind and body (e.g., Peterson, Maier, & Seligman, 1993).

But psychologists interested in humans, and particularly human problems, were quick to see the parallels between learned helplessness as produced by uncontrollable events in the laboratory and maladaptive passivity as it exists in the real world. Thus, several lines of research looking at learned helplessness in people began. In one line of work, helplessness in people was produced in the laboratory much as it was in dogs, by exposing them to uncontrollable events and seeing the effects on their motivation, cognition, and emotion (e.g., Hiroto & Seligman, 1975). Unsolvable problems were usually substituted for uncontrollable electric shocks, but the critical aspects of the phenomenon remained: Following uncontrollability, people showed a variety of deficits.

In another line of work, researchers proposed various failures of adaptation as analogous to learned helplessness and investigated the similarity between these failures and learned helplessness on various fronts. Especially provocative and popular was Seligman's (1974) proposal that reactive depression and learned helplessness shared critical features, such as causes, symptoms, consequences, treatments, and preventions.

As these lines of work were pursued, it became clear—in both cases—that the learned helplessness model was an oversimplification when applied to people. Most generally, it failed to account for the range of reactions that people displayed in response to uncontrollable events (see reviews by Miller & Norman, 1979; Roth, 1980; Wortman & Brehm, 1975). Some people indeed showed pervasive deficits, as the model hypothesized, that were general across time and situation, whereas others did not. Further, failures of adaptation that the learned helplessness model was supposed to explain, such as depression, were sometimes characterized by a striking loss of self-esteem, about which the model was silent.

In an attempt to resolve these discrepancies, Abramson et al. (1978) reformulated the helplessness model as it applied to people. The contrary findings could all be explained by proposing that when people encounter an uncontrollable event, they ask themselves why it happened. The nature of their answer—the causal explanation they entertain—sets the parameters for the helplessness that follows. If their causal attribution is stable, then induced helplessness is long-lasting; if unstable, then it is transient. If their causal attribution is global, then subsequent helplessness is manifest across a variety of situations; if specific, then it is correspondingly circumscribed. Finally, if the causal attribution is internal, the individual's self-esteem takes a tumble following uncontrollability; if external, self-esteem is left intact.

The attributional reformulation of helplessness theory left the original model in place, because uncontrollable events were still hypothesized to produce deficits when they gave rise to an expectation of future response-outcome independence. However, the nature of these deficits was now said to be influenced by the causal attribution offered by the individual.

In some cases, the situation itself provides the explanation made by the person, and the extensive social psychological literature on attributions documents many situational influences on the process (e.g., Harvey, Ickes, & Kidd, 1976, 1978, 1981). In other cases, the person relies on his or her habitual way of making sense of events that occur; here is where explanatory style enters the picture. All things being equal, people tend to offer similar sorts of explanations for disparate bad (or good) events. Accordingly, explanatory style is a distal influence on helplessness and the failures of adaptation that involve helplessness.

Explanatory style in and of itself therefore is not a cause of problems but rather a risk factor (Peterson & Seligman, 1984a). Given uncontrollable events and the lack of a clear situational demand on the preferred attribution for uncontrollability, explanatory style should influence how the person responds. Helplessness will be long-lasting or transient, widespread or circumscribed, damaging to self-esteem or not, all in accordance with the individual's explanatory style.

The Personal Control Tradition

The other ancestor of explanatory style is the tradition within psychology that looks at individual differences in beliefs with motivational and emotional significance. This tradition leads one to introduce notions like explanatory style in the first place. Why has this second ancestor been given less attention in our previous discussions than the first ancestor? We think the answer may be that it is a simpler and more glorious story to recount the progression:

> animal learning $\rightarrow$
> learned helplessness in animals $\rightarrow$
> learned helplessness in people $\rightarrow$
> research anomalies $\rightarrow$
> attributional resolution

This is an origin myth, showcasing us as true scientists who attend to our results and revise them as necessary. So far, so good, but it does not touch on why we resolved the anomalies in this literature as we did, by introducing an individual difference in the tendency to offer causal explanations. Certainly other resolutions might have been possible.

Our decision to add explanatory style to the helplessness model was not motivated by the given studies that produced anomalous results so much as by the intellectual air swirling about psychology in the 1970s. The "cognitive revolution" had been waged, successfully. Indeed, the learned helplessness tradition was one highly visible sign of this revolution within one of the last bastions of the noncognitivists: animal learning. At the time that learned helplessness researchers were encountering anomalous results, cognitive ideas were ubiquitous.

Attributional interpretations in particular were common, especially in the softer areas of psychology, to which learned helplessness researchers had been led by the practical implications of their model. One could not pick up a journal without seeing an "attributional reinterpretation" of this, that, or the other thing. The only thing lacking was an attributional interpretation of attributional interpretations, but because we are providing one now, the world has at last complete closure on life from an attributional perspective. Amen!

Just what was this tradition from which attributional theorizing arose? We have elsewhere identified it as a tradition of personal control, concerned with how people's thoughts and beliefs influence their attempts to control important outcomes in their lives (Peterson & Stunkard, 1989). This has been a long-playing tradition, and over the years, the specific role of causal beliefs has taken on ever-increasing importance.

In Cronbach's (1957) terms, the personal control tradition is different than that of animal learning, which emphasizes situational causes of behavior. The personal control tradition instead looks at individual differences and internal determinants. People differ in how they make sense of the world, and these differences channel their behavior in some directions rather than others. In this way, beliefs are accorded motivational and emotional significance.

One of the important figures here is Adler (1910/1964, 1927), who introduced the notion of striving for superiority to explain why people pursued the goals they did. To be sure, striving for superiority was a drive, but it was a drive that made sense only in light of the beliefs that one entertains about one's self and one's abilities. Adler was influenced by Vaihinger's (1911) "as-if" philosophy, which proposed that people act according to how they take the world to be. Said in the more modern language of attribution theory, people's goals and motives are shaped by their beliefs about the causal texture of the world—by their explanatory styles, as it were.

Adler inspired a whole generation of subsequent personality theorists of the psychodynamic ilk, individuals like Karen Horney, Erich Fromm, and Harry Stack Sullivan, who are called neo-Freudians but should probably be identified as neo-Adlerians (Peterson, 1992). These theorists de-emphasized biological drives and instincts and instead suggested that people's behavior is better ex-plained by attending to the social situations in which they find themselves (Brown, 1964). Further, people do more than respond blindly to their conflicts. They also seek active solutions. Their egos are creative, and defense mechanisms are seen not simply as responses but as coping strategies. Again, these ideas can be recast, quite easily, in the language of causal attributions. Indeed, most if not all of the classic defense mechanisms are explicitly attributional, so we have another precedent for looking at how individual differences in causal explanations affect subsequent behavior: mood, motivation, and thought.

At the time that the neo-Freudian approach was coalescing, social psychologist Lewin (1935, 1951) was proposing his highly influential topological psychology. His central construct was the *lifespace*, defined as all the forces acting upon an individual at a given time. The lifespace was defined by Lewin as a psychological reality, not a physical one, which drew the attention of psychologists to the ways in which people interpreted themselves, their worlds, and the relationships between the two. Modern attributional theorizing owes an obvious debt to Lewin (Weiner, 1990).

Another important figure in the personal control tradition was White (1959), who argued that people are driven to interact in a competent way with the environment. He called this drive *effectance motivation*, and the feeling that accompanied it he called *efficacy*. Importantly, effectance motivation could not be reduced to tissue needs. It legitimized, once again, a view of people as motivated to master their world and to control its outcomes.

Still other contributors to the personal control tradition were McClelland (1961) and Atkinson (1957), who studied achievement motivation. They were interested in individual differences: Why were people at times driven to achieve— to accomplish something difficult against a standard of excellence—and at other times not? Because a standard of excellence is part of the definition of achievement motivation, one's beliefs are put front-and-center. The person must believe that an outcome is worth pursuing, and he or she must constantly monitor progress toward that goal.

Atkinson was more analytic than McClelland, and subdivided achievement motivation into components: need for success, fear of failure, and so on. Thus, we see a statement that what people do is the result of a cognitive calculus: the weighting of different factors and their combination according to idiosyncratic rules.

At about the same time, attribution theory began in earnest with Heider's (1958) seminal discussion of naive psychology. He discussed how people made sense of their own actions and those of others, and he explicitly drew psychology's attention to how people answered "why" questions. Some of the contrasts he introduced—such as that between internal and external explanations—still dominate the field, as do such issues as whether attributions are accurate.

Heider's naive psychology was seized upon by several different theorists, notably Jones and Davis (1965), Kelley (1973), and Weiner (1986), who made it into what we now recognize as attribution theory. Because the cognitive revolution had now fired its first shots, the purely ideational aspects of attributions were increasingly emphasized. Motives and emotions were no longer seen as part of how the person makes sense of the world but rather as a consequence of given causal beliefs. Indeed, Kelley (1973) likened the everyday person to an experimental psychologist, "accounting for variance" via ANOVA-like designs, trying to decide what caused what.

As attributional theory evolved, it took two forms, one asking about the causes of attributions and the other about their consequences. The former line of work investigated such questions as whether people were "rational" or not in how they used information to arrive at their causal beliefs. The consensus that emerged was that people are somewhat sensitive to the actual events in the world, but that they are not normatively so, that is, they do not use information in a perfectly logical way (Nisbett & Ross, 1980).

The other line of work examined how people's attributional beliefs influenced their motives and emotions (Weiner, 1986). It was shown repeatedly that certain attributions undercut one's motivation, whereas others enhanced it. And certain attributions were linked to given feelings, whereas others were related to different feelings.

Both these lines of work were carried out largely within social psychology, which means attribution researchers usually did not look at individual differences in their own right. There is an irony here, of course, granted where the tradition started and the fact that many of those doing attribution research were personality psychologists. But in this case it was a personality psychology devoid of individual differences, as was common in the 1970s.

The yield of these lines of work was a rich vocabulary and set of research procedures waiting to be tapped by learned helplessness investigators. Interestingly, the notion of individual differences in causal attributions came not from attribution theorists per se, with their feet clearly in personality psychology, but rather from experimental psychologists, with their feet (paws?) in the animal learning laboratory.

Yet another important influence along the way was the theorizing of Rotter (1954), whose social learning theory did acknowledge the existence and importance of broad interpretive tendencies. Specifically, Rotter (1966) suggested that performance was under the sway of one's generalized expectancies. One did not do something unless it was expected that it would turn out in a given way. Several generalized expectancies exist, but perhaps most germane to explanatory style is the locus of control concept: whether someone generally expects rewards to emanate from his own actions (internal) or from outside, in chance, fate, or the machinations of powerful others (external).

Locus of control is obviously related to explanatory style, particularly to the internality dimension. Both concern themselves with the source of outcomes, inside or outside the person. Locus of control is an expectancy about the future, whereas internality refers to a cause in the past; however, this cause in turn sets the expectancy. In practice, because these are measured in different ways, they often diverge. Locus of control, at least as conceptualized by Rotter, collapses across good and bad events. In contrast, explanatory style assumes that one must look separately at responses to bad events and to good events. As it turns out, attributions for bad and good events often are independent, so this is a good decision.

Another version of social learning theory was proposed by Bandura (1969, 1973; Bandura & Walters, 1963). In recent years, it has become increasingly cognitive, stressing the importance of an individual's *self-efficacy*, defined as his or her belief that a given response leading to a specific outcome can be performed (Bandura, 1977a, 1986). Like locus of control, self-efficacy is obviously related to explanatory style. The chief difference is that self-efficacy is regarded as situationally specific and thus highly circumscribed, whereas explanatory style is more like a trait (see Peterson & Stunkard, 1992).

Throughout the 20th century, we see a continued interest in personal control. Various cognates have been proposed, with a gradual trend toward "cognizing" these cognates readily apparent. In the 1970s, these ideas reached a critical mass. In one direction, they were taken by learned helplessness researchers, who emphasized that causal explanations were traitlike, an individual difference.

EXPLANATORY STYLE:
MEASUREMENT AND APPLICATIONS

Explanatory style took off as its own line of research when measures of this individual difference began to be developed. The first measure was the Attributional Style Questionnaire (ASQ), used in a study by Seligman, Abramson, Semmel, and von Baeyer (1979) investigating one of the predictions of the attributional reformulation: Specifically, that people differed with respect to their habitual explanatory tendencies, and that those who favored internal, stable, and global explanations for bad events would be more likely to report symptoms of depression than those who favored external, unstable, and specific explanations.

Details of the ASQ and other measures of explanatory style are described in chapter 2 of this volume, but briefly, the ASQ presents subjects with hypothetical good and bad events involving themselves (e.g., "you go out on a date, and it goes badly"). Subjects are asked to imagine the event happening to themselves, and then to write down the event's "one major cause" if it happened to them. Then they use 7-point rating scales to indicate the degree to which the cause is internal, stable, and global.

These ratings are combined in various ways. Scores for the three dimensions of internality, stability, and globality may be formed, separately for bad events and for good events, by averaging the appropriate ratings. A composite explanatory style for bad events may be formed by averaging across the three dimensions for bad events. Similarly, a composite explanatory style for good events may be formed by averaging across the three dimensions for good events. Finally, an overall explanatory style score is sometimes created by substracting the composite score for bad events from the composite score for good events.

Because the earliest version of the ASQ had at best modest reliability, researchers fell into the practice of using composites as just described (Peterson et al., 1982). The effect was twofold. On the one hand, reliabilities were typically increased, because that many more items were used to estimate someone's explanatory style. But on the other hand, the roles assigned by the helplessness reformulation to the specific attributional dimensions were not able to be investigated.

Once available, the ASQ was used mainly in investigations of depression, following the lead of the attributional reformulation. Literally hundreds of studies were conducted that correlated ASQ responses with various indices of depression (see chapter 5, this volume). Several points can be made about this work.

First, because of the format of the ASQ, researchers stopped being interested in the uncontrollability of events, and contented themselves with studying attributions about bad events. Bad events and uncontrollable events overlap, perhaps considerably, but a moment's reflection shows that these are not identical. What was lost—at least in this research—was the concern of the original helplessness model with uncontrollability. This makes the helplessness literature less coherent than it should be. It also introduces possible error into research that uses the ASQ, because several recent studies suggest that it may be advantageous for someone to view controllable bad events as internally, stably, and globally caused (e.g., Brown & Siegel, 1988; Sellers & Peterson, 1993).

Second, researchers started to follow Peterson and Seligman's (1984a) lead in calling attributional style by a new name: *explanatory style*. The reason for this change in terminology was that *attribution* is an extremely broad term, referring to any property or characteristic linked to an event or outcome. We wanted to be clear that our interest was in causal explanations of events. Further, attribution has connotations of projection, as if the causal beliefs people entertain are somehow arbitrary. This also is a misleading implication, because often the reality of an event is of overriding importance in how it is explained. We similarly suspect that someone's explanatory style originates in reality. A depressive style may well arise from depressing experiences; in a sense, it is realistic.

Relatedly, we also took to calling explanatory style for bad events *pessimistic* when it was relatively internal, stable, and global, and *optimistic* when it was relatively external, unstable, and specific. The motive for this was largely to make the construct's meaning more accessible to the psychological community and the general public. Explanatory style does not necessarily mean anything to most people, but an optimistic view of the causes of events certainly does. The danger in this switch in terminology is that psychologists and everyday people alike are tempted to adopt a shorthand way of describing people as optimists or pessimists. However, people do not exist in two distinct clumps. By the way we measure them, most people are in the middle, neither optimistic nor pessimistic. It is only those at the extremes who can be accurately described as optimists or pessimists. We urge a cautious use of the terms optimistic and pessimistic, as adjectives to describe explanatory style, not as labels for a personality typology (Peterson, 1991).

Third, the majority of studies did not test the full helplessness reformulation but only aspects of it. The reformulation specifies a detailed account of the process by which people develop depression. Explanatory style, as we have already noted, is a risk factor, not an inevitable cause of problems. Presumably, explanatory style is catalyzed by actual bad events, and it is only when explanatory style induces someone to offer a given explanation that helplessness follows. Most studies have not investigated these subtleties, which would require at the very least a longitudinal design and an independent assessment of the occurrence of stressful life events.

Instead, studies have usually calculated the synchronous correlation between explanatory style and depressive symptoms, usually finding the predicted correlations (Sweeney, Anderson, & Bailey, 1986). But as Peterson and Seligman (1984a) noted, these are the least compelling studies vis-à-vis the helplessness reformulation because they are compatible with other possibilities (e.g., that depressive symptoms influence attributions and/or that some third variable is responsible for both depression and pessimistic attributional style).

Around this time, literature reviews began to appear summarizing the explanatory style/depression research, and for a while, it seemed that literature reviews were more popular than actual research. So, Coyne and Gotlib (1983) and Brewin (1985) presented skeptical reviews of the literature, whereas Peterson and Seligman (1984a); Sweeney et al. (1986); Peterson, Villanova, and Raps (1985); and Robins (1988) presented more enthusiastic views. Regardless, most of these reviews seemed to agree that studies simply correlating explanatory style with depressive symptoms were not going to resolve any issues; it was time to move to more sophisticated designs.

Also during this period, helplessness theory was used to generate numerous studies, but the results of these studies were not fed back to modify the theory. For about a decade, the attributional reformulation was not questioned by those in the helplessness tradition so much as tested, over and over. Then Abramson, Metalsky, and Alloy (1988, 1989) went back to the model and revised it in view of the research evidence that had accumulated. Their "hopelessness" theory of depression bears a strong family resemblance to the attributional reformulation, to be sure, but there are several critical differences that are highlighted in chapter 7.

Other researchers began to examine explanatory style in its own right, extending it to questions and topics not explicitly part of the original helplessness model or reformulation. Some of this work was of the dust-bowl approach, made possible by the existence of a questionnaire that—despite problems with reliability—seemed paradoxically to possess spectacular validity. Researchers correlated explanatory style with a variety of outcomes, from binge eating to compulsive gambling (see Peterson et al., 1993). The conclusion suggested by these far-flung studies is that explanatory style indeed is a basic individual difference. It taps something very important about people.

Sometimes we wax philosophical and speculate that explanatory style reflects one's strength of will, reviving a long-dormant psychology of connation. Some people are passive and listless in the face of challenge, whereas other people are vigorous and active. Explanatory style captures this contrast.

Other extensions were more deliberate, we think, and reflected a conscious decision to see if explanatory style applied to topics to which—by the logic of its meaning—it should apply. Achievement—by students, workers, and/or athletes—has been one profitable extension (see chapters 9–12). Another important extension was to physical health (see chapters 13 and 14). Still other intriguing extensions have been to developmental issues (see chapters 3 and 4), psychopathology (see chapters 5, 7, and 8), and psychotherapy (see chapter 6).

A number of these extensions followed the development of a new way to measure explanatory style, using a flexible content analysis method. This technique, called Content Analysis of Verbatim Explanations (CAVE), stemmed from our observation that causal explanations, identical to those given by respondents to the ASQ, were abundant in spontaneous writing or speaking. Was it possible to identify these explanations in verbatim material, extract them, and then to rate them along the dimensions of internality, stability, and globality, having researchers do what subjects do on the ASQ? The answer proved to be yes, and explanatory style so assessed proves reliable, consistent, and valid (Peterson, Schulman, Castellon, & Seligman, 1992).

A new chapter in explanatory style research was thus made possible, what Peterson and Seligman (1984a) facetiously dubbed Seldonics, after the psycho-historian of science fiction fame. Subjects not able to or willing to participate in typical research could be studied with the CAVE technique, as long as they had left behind suitable material containing causal explanations about themseles. To date, we have studied psychotherapy transcripts, interviews, open-ended questionnaires, political speeches, sports stories, and responses to projective techniques. Chapter 2 provides more detail on the CAVE.

CURRENT QUESTIONS AND CONCERNS[1]

Despite the great interest generated by the explanatory style construct, questions can be raised and concerns can be specified about state-of-the-art research. Peterson (1991) articulated current conceptual and methodological issues, and the following presentation draws on his discussion. In some cases, answers to apparent puzzles are already at hand; in others, further work is needed.

Why Form a Composite?

One of the cogent criticisms of explanatory style is Carver's (1989) query into why explanatory style researchers often create a composite of internality, stability, and globality ratings, and then treat this composite as "the" index of explanatory style. He correctly observed that this makes it impossible to ascertain the roles played by the individual dimensions. He further argued that there may be little

---

[1]Material in this section was adapted from Peterson (1991), and is reprinted with the permission of Lawrence Erlbaum Associates.

theoretical justification for forming such a composite, and thus he recommended against doing so.

On the one hand, individual dimensions of explanatory style have been examined and reported in any of a number of published studies. For instance, see Peterson and Seligman (1984a, Studies 1–5). On the other hand, there indeed has been a trend to report only the composite, and so Carver's (1989) question must be addressed. We agree that a composite makes it impossible to examine the specific roles assigned by the helplessness reformulation to particular dimensions (see Peterson & Villanova, 1988). Is there any justification for using a composite besides economy of presentation?

There are several possible answers that come to mind. First, many of the outcomes to which explanatory style has been related are not theoretically specific to the three dimensions. Consider depression as a whole, the glut of emotional, physical, motivational, and cognitive symptoms that make up this problem. If we lump these symptoms together, as is done in diagnosing and/or assessing the severity of depression, we have no reason to think that internality should be more or less related to depression than stability or globality.

Perhaps the use of composites is justified when the outcomes are not specific to individual dimensions. However, this answer undercuts the point that a researcher's theoretical purpose should dictate which dimensions of explanatory style are examined in a given study. If outcomes are not specific to the three dimensions, then why use these dimensions at all, either separately or in a composite?

Studies that do focus on differential correlates with the three dimensions of explanatory style share in common the use of outcome measures that are theoretically specific to a given dimension. Eaves and Rush (1984) showed that the stability of explanatory style for bad events predicted the chronicity of a depressive reaction. Alloy, Peterson, Abramson, and Seligman (1984) showed that the globality of explanatory style for bad events influenced the generality of helplessness deficits across different laboratory tasks. Several studies have looked at the relationship between the internality of explanatory style for bad events and self-esteem (e.g., Ickes & Layden, 1978; Tennen & Herzberger, 1987). In terms of the specific claims of the reformulated helplessness model of depression, these studies are much more informative than those that merely show a correlation between a composite explanatory style score and a measure of depression.

A second answer to the question of why one might form a composite is suggested by Carver (1989) himself. If the various dimensions capture a higher order notion, a so-called latent variable, this would justify their combination. Such a case can be made for explanatory style. As already emphasized, internality, stability, and globality all have something to do with the extent and nature of helplessness deficits. The more of each that is present, the greater should be the deficit in which we are interested. So, a composite mixes together apples and oranges, but the result can be construed as fruit salad.

Similarly, the composite of explanatory style captures something about the essence of helplessness, with each dimension making its contribution. Someone who scores highly on all three dimensions of explanatory style is more likely to be passive and demoralized than someone who scores low on all three (Peterson & Seligman, 1984a).

Internality, stability, and globality ratings are rarely orthogonal to each other. They were proposed on an a priori basis, with no claim that the actual universe of attributions would fall at right angles along these dimensions. Invariably, stability and globality correlate highly with one another, so much so that we suggest that they be regarded as a common factor of hopelessness (Peterson & Seligman, 1985; see also Abramson et al., 1988, 1989). It may be that a global cause is necessarily a stable one, because it must last long enough to influence outcomes in different domains. Sometimes internality is correlated with stability and globality (e.g., Peterson et al., 1982), and sometimes it is independent (e.g., Peterson & Villanova, 1988), so here the latent variable argument starts to fall apart.

One should always look at the ingredients that are combined into these entities. It may well be that in a given case the assumption of a latent variable will be violated. Or perhaps one dimension will prove more critical than the others in predicting some criterion. The automatic creation of a composite cannot be justified.

What About Explanatory Style for Good Events?

The discussion so far has focused mainly on explanatory style for bad events. However, some research has looked at explanatory style for good events. Two generalizations can be offered about this research (Peterson & Seligman, 1984a). First, explanatory style for good events is often independent of explanatory style for bad events. Second, the correlates of explanatory style for good events tend to be the opposite of the correlates of explanatory style for bad events and usually less robust. For example, internal, stable, and global attributions for good events correlate weakly with the absence of depressive symptoms, as opposed to the stronger correlations between internal, stable, and global attributions for bad events and the presence of depressive symptoms.

What is the theoretical significance of explanatory style for good events? The reformulated learned helplessness model is silent because it concerns itself only with how people respond to bad events. But we are still left with the empirical relationships between explanatory style for good events and outcomes like depression. One possible explanation is that explanatory style for good events influences the degree to which we savor our triumphs in life (cf. Weiner, 1986). The positive expectations and good feelings engendered by an upbeat explanatory style for good events may buffer us against the depressing effects of loss and disappointment (Taylor & Brown, 1988).

An adequate investigation of explanatory style for good events should measure both positive and negative life events, as well as the good and the bad moods that may follow in their wake (see Needles & Abramson, 1990). We have elsewhere speculated that explanatory style for good events directly influences one's reaction to those events, while affecting negative outcomes like depression only indirectly (Peterson & Seligman, 1985; see also Abramson et al., 1989). But it remains a possibility that explanatory style for good events directly affects how we respond to bad events (e.g., "there must be a pony here—look at all the manure").

Research into explanatory style for good events may not yield as rich data as has research into explanatory style for bad events, simply because people are less "mindful" when thinking about good events (Langer, 1989). Their responses are more likely to be off the tops of their heads (Taylor & Fiske, 1978), and people's cliches are not as psychologically revealing as the results of their active search for the causes of bad events (Wong & Weiner, 1981). Still, an interesting direction of inquiry might be to understand why explanatory style for good events is independent of that for bad events. Perhaps the answer lies somewhere in differential socialization of the two.

Are There Historical or Cultural Limitations on Explanatory Style?

The possibility must be acknowledged that people's tendencies to offer causal attributions show historical or cultural boundaries. We doubt that a time or place has ever existed in which individuals do not engage in making sense of what they see, particularly their own behaviors and the behaviors of others. But causal explanations—those pointing to antecedent events that co-vary with phenomena of interest—are obviously but one way to make sense of the world (cf. Pepper, 1942).

Causal attributions may be a special concern of residents in Western societies during the late 20th century. In other words, causal attributions for behavior may be offered only by people who possess a highly articulated sense of self as distinct from the world, who exalt individuality, and who try to "predict and control" the events that befall them (Baumeister, 1986; van den Berg, 1983; Weisz, Rothbaum, & Blackburn, 1984). Perhaps the popularity of explanatory style as a research topic reflects its good fit with the collective psychology of the United States in the late 20th century.

We can observe cultural and historical differences with respect to the given causal attributions that people offer. For instance, Miller (1984) compared the causal attributions for behaviors made by Indians and Americans, and found that the former group favored contextual explanations (e.g., roles, norms), whereas the latter group favored dispositional explanations (e.g., traits, attitudes). Her subjects were of different ages, and she found that this cultural difference became more pronounced with increasing age. Socialization into a particular culture apparently entails learning characteristic explanations for behavior (see chapter 12, this volume).

If people in a given time or place do not offer causal explanations, then explanatory style is a meaningless construct with which to characterize these people. If people offer causal explanations that differ from those usually made by research subjects in the here and now, then we have several interesting empirical questions in need of answers. Can these explanations be sensibly described along dimensions of internality, stability, and globality? Do these individuals show a characteristic style? Does this style relate to outcomes as predicted by the reformulated helplessness theory? And so on.

Do People Have a Consistent Explanatory Style?

The original version of the ASQ had low internal consistencies for the individual dimensions (Peterson et al., 1982). They were certainly above zero, showing that subjects did evidence a degree of consistency across the different events they explained. But some critics have argued that this means that people do not have an explanatory style, that they are inconsistent with respect to how they explain different events (e.g., Arntz, Gerlsma, & Albersnagel, 1985).

At this point, the issue has been resolved. Peterson and Seligman (1984a) noted that the reality of the events that people explain has something to do with the causes chosen. What this means is that when we try to assess "style" from just a few events, we run the risk of measuring not a personality characteristic but simply reality. Low reliability should ensue. If we increase the number of events for which attributions are made, then we should come ever closer to measuring a psychological style—presumably by cancelling out extraneous determinants of given attributions.

This is exactly what happens. Peterson and Villanova (1988) described an Expanded Attributional Style Questionnaire, for instance, which increases the number of bad events in the original ASQ from 6 to 24, with an impressive increase in the internal consistency of the individual dimensions. These consistencies, in the .7 to .9 range, are thoroughly acceptable as measures of individual differences.

The CAVE technique also yields more satisfactory reliabilities of explanatory style to the degree that more events as opposed to fewer are used. For instance, Peterson, Seligman, and Vaillant (1988) found much more satisfactory consistency of explanatory style when measures were based on 10 events with attributions than did Peterson, Bettes, and Seligman (1985) who used but 2 events.

This is not supposed to be a dizzying insight. As Peterson and Villanova (1988) observed, the point is really a statistical truism long followed by those concerned with scale development. As long as items show a somewhat positive correlation with each other, the reliability of any scale can be increased simply by adding more items. For some reason, this truism has not filtered into the explanatory style literature, and with some frequency we see the failure of given measures of explanatory style confused with the nonexistence of the construct they purport to measure.

Another view on individual consistency concerns itself with the stability of explanatory style over time. Presumably, if subjects do not have a consistent explanatory style, test–retest reliability should be nil. But in the original description of the psychometric properties of the ASQ, an adequate degree of test–retest reliability over a 5-week period was shown (Peterson et al., 1982). Similar consistency has been reported in children, this time over periods of months (Nolen-Hoeksema, Girgus, & Seligman, 1986). Finally, using the CAVE technique to measure explanatory style from material provided by research subjects, Burns and Seligman (1989) found consistency of explanatory style over more than five decades. Such stability across time is good evidence for consistency at any given point in time.

So, people's explanations are consistent across different events and stable across time, as shown by statistically significant correlations. The magnitude of these correlations is invariably modest, but no lower than those involving most other personality characteristics. The magnitude of correlations should not be evaluated out of context. Explanatory style is as coherent an individual difference as most personality constructs.

Does Explanatory Style Predispose "Spontaneous" Attributions?

Here is another question about explanatory style that has been affirmatively answered in the literature, although perhaps there has not been enough attention to the confirming studies. This question takes on various forms. When the helplessness reformulation was first proposed, the question was raised whether people do in fact make "spontaneous" causal attributions (e.g., Wortman & Dintzer, 1978).

The success of the CAVE technique in finding causal explanations in a variety of verbal material shows that people indeed offer attributions. Causal attributions abound in psychotherapy sessions, press conferences, political speeches, letters, diaries, sports stories, open-ended questionnaires and interviews, and essays (e.g., Peterson, Bettes, & Seligman, 1985; Peterson, Luborsky, & Seligman, 1983; Peterson, Seligman, & Vaillant, 1988; Zullow, Oettingen, Peterson, & Seligman, 1988).

Weiner (1986) reviewed several altogether different research literatures and again found ample evidence that people display spontaneous causal thinking, without prompts from a researcher. Thus, the first doubt about the relationship of explanatory style to actual attributions is laid to rest by observing that people indeed offer attributions in the course of thinking about the events that befall them.

The second form this question takes is to acknowledge that people offer attributions but then doubt that explanatory style as assessed with the ASQ pertains to them (e.g., Cutrona, Russell, & Jones, 1984). In other words, attributions about hypothetical events (like those on the ASQ) are said to be unrelated to attributions about actual events. We have already explained that there will be instances when we should expect these relationships to be attenuated: any time the "reality" of the event and/or social consensus suggests a causal explanation. If one looks only at these sorts of events, then explanatory style will not show a relationship.

The trick is to look elsewhere. Then there is good evidence that explanatory style (as assessed from attributions about hypothetical events) relates to particular attributions about actual events. Peterson and Villanova (1988) described just such a study. Explanatory style as measured with the Expanded ASQ correlated with attributions aggregated across a variety of bad events in someone's life. This procedure presumably reduced any systematic influence of reality on actual attributions. In this study, some specificity of prediction was shown. Internality of explanatory style correlated with internality of actual attributions to a greater degree than did stability of explanatory style. Stability and globality proved to be more entwined, as our previous discussion would imply.

Metalsky, Halberstadt, and Abramson (1987) showed that explanatory style as measured with the ASQ at the beginning of a school term predicted the actual attributions made by college students for their exam performance some weeks later. Similarly, Atlas and Peterson (1990) demonstrated that explanatory style measured with the ASQ predicts the attributions made by patrons at a harness racing track for the outcomes of races on which they lost money.

More generally, several studies have examined the relationship between the ASQ and the CAVE, finding modest convergence between explanatory style assessed in these two ways (see Peterson & Seligman, 1984a). Stated another way, attributions about hypothetical events relate to attributions about actual events, so long as one gives the personality variable a fair chance to operate. This criticism is reminiscent of the overly stringent view of "traits" used some years ago by those who wished to argue against their existence. No trait theorist ever expressed the opinion that a trait was evident in every possible situation (Hogan, deSoto, & Solano, 1977). The more constrained a situation, the less likely an individual difference is to manifest itself. With respect to explanatory style, constraints are provided by the actual event that is being explained. Keeping this in mind should help explanatory style researchers find topics where attention to individual differences in the use of attributions should prove fruitful.

Why Are the Correlations Involving Explanatory Style Ostensibly So Low?

The typical correlation with explanatory style is in the ubiquitous .20 to .30 range, and some critics dismiss these as disappointingly low (e.g., Cutrona, 1983). This criticism is not fair because given variables, whether experimental or correlational, rarely account for more than about 10% of the variance in other variables (e.g., Funder & Ozer, 1983). Let us mention an important article by Rosenthal and Rubin (1982) concerning the interpretation of the magnitude of correlation coefficients. This point is not sufficiently well made within personality psychology, where it is so apt.

Rosenthal and Rubin (1982) began with the observation that correlation coefficients are not readily grasped by most people who hear about them. One knows they range from −1.00 through 0.00 to 1.00, of course, but then when we hear that a correlation is "only" .20 or .30, this certainly does not seem very high. When we square the correlation and find that it accounts for "only" 5%–10% of the variance, this seems even more unsatisfactory. Rosenthal and Rubin (1982) proposed that we cast these measures of association in a different form.

Suppose we have a medical treatment that reduces one's risk of dying from a disease from a higher probability to a lower one. Reduction in risk certainly has an intuitive meaning, and it is possible to express correlation coefficients in terms of this metric. So, if we consider one variable to be the medical intervention, and the other the reduction in risk, how would we translate a correlation of .30? Simply the reduction of risk from about .65 to .35: a virtual cutting in two of the likelihood of dying. This correlation seems worth taking seriously.

Let us illustrate how recasting the same data can change the impressiveness of a relationship's magnitude (see also Rosenthal, 1990). In a recent study, we showed that explanatory style for bad events correlates with the number of days ill that one reports in a month (Peterson, 1988). The correlation coefficient itself appears modest, only .27. But then we divided the sample into the top and bottom half with respect to composite explanatory style. The top half of the sample (subjects with a more pessimistic explanatory style) showed a twofold difference in number of days ill when compared to the bottom half (subjects with a more optimistic explanatory style): 7.89 versus 3.94.

We suggest that many of the criticisms about the way in which explanatory style research has been conducted take investigators to task for problems that no longer exist. There is good evidence that explanatory style is a consistent individual difference, that it pertains to the actual attributions that people offer in everyday life, and that its relations with external variables are as robust as the correlates to be expected of any personality dimensions.

SUMMARY

Explanatory style is a cognitive personality variable that reflects how people habitually explain the causes of events. The explanatory style construct emerged from the learned helplessness tradition where it was introduced to explain variation in people's response to uncontrollable events. More generally, explanatory style is part of a tradition within psychology that focuses on individual differences in people's thoughts and beliefs and how these influence motivation, emotion, and behavior. Explanatory style has been popular for several reasons, including the availability of straightforward measures and the persuasiveness of its applications to failures of human adaptation. Questions and concerns still exist with regard to the meaning and measurement of explanatory style, which should keep psychologists busy into the foreseeable future.

2
▼▼▼▼▼▼▼

The Measurement of Explanatory Style

Karen Reivich
University of Pennsylvania

This chapter chronicles the current state of the measurement of explanatory style. The three most commonly used methods for assessing explanatory style are described and critiqued. They are the Attributional Style Questionnaire (ASQ; Peterson, Semmel, von Baeyer, Abramson, Metalsky, & Seligman, 1982; Seligman, Abramson, Semmel, & von Baeyer, 1979), the Content Analysis of Verbatim Explanations technique (CAVE; Peterson, Luborsky, & Seligman, 1983), and the Children's Attributional Style Questionnaire (CASQ; Kaslow, Tannenbaum, & Seligman, 1978).

Several other methods for measuring explanatory style that are in various stages of development, or have been used less frequently, are also discussed. They are the Expanded ASQ (Peterson & Villanova, 1988), the Academic ASQ (Peterson & Barrett, 1987), and the Forced-Choice ASQ (Reivich & Seligman, 1991). For each of these measures I discuss the rationale behind their development, reliability and validity data, and research issues that need to be addressed.

THE ATTRIBUTIONAL STYLE QUESTIONNAIRE

The ASQ was developed in 1979 by Seligman et al. to investigate the central prediction of the attributional reformulation of the learned helplessness model: Those who tend to explain bad events with internal, stable, and global explanations will be more prone to depression than those who offer external, unstable, and specific explanations for bad events (Abramson, Seligman, & Teasdale, 1978). Chapter 1 discusses the reformulated learned helplessness model in greater detail.

Development of the Questionnaire

The ASQ is a self-report instrument containing 12 hypothetical situations: 6 negative events (e.g., "You can't get all the work done that others expect of you") and 6 positive events (e.g., "Your spouse [boyfriend/girlfriend] has been treating you more lovingly"). Of the 12 situations, 6 have an affiliation orientation and 6 have an achievement orientation. Affiliation items are those that present an event revolving around interpersonal relationships, whereas achievement items are those that present events regarding work, academic success, sports, and so forth. An example of an item used to assess explanatory style in the affiliation domain is: "You meet a friend who acts hostilely toward you." An example of an item used to assess explanatory style in the achievement domain is: "You do a project that is highly praised." Both affiliative and achievement-oriented items were included for two reasons. First, by including situations across a broad spectrum, a cross-situational "style" can be measured. Second, the inclusion of both types of items allows for the possibility that an individual may have an affiliative style that differs from his or her achievement style.

For each situation, subjects are asked to vividly imagine it happening to them and to decide what they believe would be the one major cause of the situation. This cause is recorded in the space provided. The subjects then indicate, on 7-point rating scales, the degree to which the cause is internal or external, stable or unstable, and global or specific with each dimension being rated separately. (1 = *completely external/completely unstable/completely specific*; 7 = *completely internal/completely stable/completely global*).

An early version of the ASQ also asked the subjects to rate how important the situation would be if it happened to them on a 7-point rating scale (1 = *not at all important*, 7 = *extremely important*). The importance ratings were included in light of the possibility that the proposed relationship of explanatory style and depression would occur only for events viewed as important by the individual, or more strongly for important events than for unimportant events (Peterson et al., 1982). Peterson et al., however, reported that the importance variable did not consistently mediate the attribution-depression correlation. This question was therefore deleted from subsequent versions of the questionnaire. The example in Table 2.1 illustrates the ASQ format.

Many issues influenced the instrument design. The reformulated theory required the measurement of the degree to which the individuals used the attributional dimensions of internality, stability, and globality as defined by Abramson et al. (1978). One approach could have been to follow the format of studies conducted by Rizley (1978); Klein, Fencil-Morse, and Seligman (1976); and Kuiper (1978) in which subjects were supplied with possible causes (e.g., ability, effort, task difficulty, luck, etc.) that were believed to correspond with the dimensions of concern.

There are problems, however, with this format. As Abramson et al. (1978) pointed out, these supplied causes do not correspond directly with the three

TABLE 2.1
Sample Question From the Attributional Style Questionnaire

Event: You meet a friend who acts hostilely toward you.

---

1. Write down one major cause of this event.

---

2. Is the cause of your friend acting hostile due to something about you or something about other people or circumstances?

Totally due to other people or   Totally due to me
circumstances   1   2   3   4   5   6   7
                                       (Circle one number)

3. In the future when interacting with friends, will this cause again be present?

Will never again be present   1   2   3   4   5   6   7   Will always be present
                                       (Circle one number)

4. Is the cause something that just influences interacting with friends or does it also influence other areas of your life?

Influences just this particular area   1   2   3   4   5   6   7   Influences all situations in my life
                                       (Circle one number)

Note.   From Peterson et al. (1982).

attributional dimensions. Furthermore, they are not an exhaustive list of possible attributions, nor can researchers be certain that the subject views the attribution in the same way as the theorist (Peterson et al., 1982). For example, some subjects may regard the degree of effort one extends as a stable characterological trait, whereas others may view it as an unstable behavioral trait.

Although the preceding concerns argue for an open-ended format, there are problems with that structure as well. For example, Elig and Frieze (1979) reported that open-ended attributional measures are less reliable than measures employing a forced-choice procedure.

Given these lines of research, Peterson et al. (1982) chose the ASQ structure previously described that combines both an open-ended format (the recording of the major cause) with a fixed format (the rating of the dimensions on a 1–7 continuum). This format allows for simple and objective quantification of responses without limiting the subject to certain attributions.

Another concern that guided the development of the ASQ was to maximize the degree to which the respondent projects his or her idiosyncratic belief system onto the stimuli. This concern rests on the assumption that causal explanations are based on both the objective determinants of an event and on one's explanatory style. In order to decrease the role of objective determinants, the ASQ contains simple, ambiguous, hypothetical events. These events require the respondent to construct the context surrounding the situations, which increases the likelihood that the subject will project his or her subjective interpretation onto the ambiguous situations.

Scoring

The ASQ yields six individual dimension scores and three composite scores. The six individual dimension scores are the following: the average of the internality ratings for the six negative events (IN: internal negative), the average of the stability ratings for the six negative events (SN: stable negative), the average of the six globality ratings for the six negative events (GN: global negative). Individual dimension scores are also formed in a similar manner based on the six positive events (IP, SP, and GP). There are also three composite scores formed. These are: composite negative explanatory style (CN), which is the composite score for the six negative events, summing across internal, stable, and global dimensions and dividing by the number of events; composite positive explanatory style (CP), the composite score for the six positive events; and a total score, composite positive minus composite negative (CPCN), the difference score between CP and CN.

Three other scores have been derived from the ASQ, although these are not used as frequently. They are a hopelessness (HN) and a hopefulness (HP) score. Hopelessness is determined by averaging the stability and globality dimensions for negative events, whereas hopefulness is the average of the stability and globality dimensions for positive events. That is, HN is taken to be the belief that the causes of negative events are permanent and pervasive (e.g., "My parents divorced because humans are simply not capable of maintaining honest, intimate bonds"). Hopefulness, in comparison, is the belief that when things go right, it is due to forces that will persist and affect many areas of our lives (e.g., "My misplaced wallet was returned because people, at heart, are caring and decent"). Just as CPCN is a composite measure formed by subtracting a subject's CN score from his or her CP score, some researchers also form the composite HPHN, which is the HN score subtracted from the HP score.

In summary, the ASQ can be scored by forming composite variables, which serve to bolster reliability by increasing the number of items used to assess explanatory style; or, through the individual attributional dimensions, which enable the researcher to examine the relationship between a particular dimension and a particular dependent variable.

Both scoring procedures have been used in explanatory style research. The question of when to form composite scores versus when to rely on the individual dimensions remains a critical issue. Composite scores boost reliability. Exploring the individual dimensions enables the researcher to more critically assess the relationship between specific attributional dimensions and an array of deficits.

The reformulated model makes specific predictions about the effects of each dimension on learned helplessness deficits. Internal explanations for negative events will lead to self-esteem loss. Stable explanations for negative events will lead to a greater chronicity of deficits. Global explanations for negative events will lead to the generality of deficits across situations. Therefore, studies designed to investigate outcomes that are theoretically relevant to a specific dimension should not rely solely on composite scores. Reporting that CPCN predicts pervasiveness of helplessness deficits does not speak to the claim that global attributions are predictive of the breadth of helplessness deficits.

It must be noted that although theoretically important, the individual dimensions do not have satisfactory reliabilities. Given the low reliabilities, validity statistics must be considered suggestive rather than conclusive. This is discussed in more detail later (see Peterson, 1991, and commentaries for a debate regarding the use of composite variables).

The use of composite scores may be justified in some studies. Not all research on explanatory style investigates the relationship of a particular dimension to a particular outcome. For example, research into achievement often relies on composite scores because there is no a priori reason to expect one particular dimension to have a unique role in an individual's ability to achieve.

Also, as is discussed later, the individual dimensions are rarely independent of each other. In order to test the hypotheses of the reformulated model, these dimensions need to be separated; however, it is likely that the three dimensions are conceptually related. For example, a specific attribution is often an unstable attribution. A fleeting occurrence such as a bad day, a sour mood, an unexpected spin on a ball, usually does not have the potency to affect many domains of our lives. This intercorrelation between the dimensions is another argument for the use of composite variables (see Table 2.2 for intercorrelations between dimensions from three studies).

It is not always obvious a priori whether or not there will be differential correlations between each dimension and the outcome variable, thus it may be prudent to examine the dimensions individually, as well as the composite scores (statistically correcting for the increased number of analyses). In terms of the reformulated theory, studies that elucidate the particular roles of the attributional dimensions are more informative than those that show a correlation between a composite explanatory style score and a given outcome.

Transparency

Is the ASQ transparent? That is, can respondents figure out how to answer the questionnaire in the most favorable manner? This is a critical question given the ASQ's potential for diagnostic and prognostic uses. Furthermore, because the ASQ has recently been used as a selection device in the hiring of life insurance agents—what better field in which to test if explanatory style can predict an individual's ability to thrive under adversity—Schulman and Seligman (1987) felt it was important to test the possibility of beating the questionnaire (i.e., faking responses to reflect the most desirable score).

In order to test the transparency of the ASQ, Schulman, Seligman, and Amsterdam (1987) designed a study in which subjects were given an incentive

TABLE 2.2

Measure	M	SD	Reliability	Stability^	r~
Attributional Style					
For good events					
Internality					
Time 1	4.61	1.48	.32	.53**	−.34**
Time 2	4.71	1.61	.43		−.31*
Stability					
Time 1	4.21	1.91	.55	.61**	−.47**
Time 2	3.91	1.89	.54		−.54**
Globality					
Time 1	4.67	1.58	.40	.54**	−.35**
Time 2	4.81	1.78	.55		−.39**
Composite					
Time 1	13.49	3.72	.66	.71**	−.53**
Time 2	13.43	4.10	.73		−.54**
For bad events					
Internality					
Time 1	2.30	1.57	.43	.63**	.45**
Time 2	2.47	1.73	.56		.28*
Stability					
Time 1	2.40	1.40	.42	.52**	.31*
Time 2	2.01	1.17	.13		.26*
Globality					
Time 1	1.88	1.27	.31	.64**	.21*
Time 2	1.61	1.26	.39		.26*
Composite					
Time 1	6.58	2.77	.50	.66**	.51**
Time 2	6.09	2.80	.54		.40**
Children's Depression Inventory					
Time 1	7.71	6.28	.86	.80**	
Time 2	7.16	5.92	.85		

Note. $N = 96$. Reliability is estimated by Cronbach's (1951) alpha. ^r with same measure in 6 months. ~With concurrent Children's Depression Inventory.

$*p < .05. **p < .001.$

to score well (i.e., optimistically: external/unstable/specific for negative events; internal/stable/global for positive events) on the questionnaire. Schulman et al. administered the ASQ to 61 college undergraduates who were randomized into three groups: controls, incentives, and incentives-plus-coached. The control group was given the ASQ only. The incentive group was given the ASQ and a cover page that stated the individual with the best score would be awarded $100. The incentive-plus-coached group was given the ASQ, the cover page, and also the following hint: "The ASQ measures how persistent an individual is under adversity. It does this by measuring one's expectations about positive and negative events. The best scores result in selecting the most optimistic causes for positive events and the least pessimistic causes for negative events."

These researchers found no significant differences among the three groups. Using an analysis of variance, they compared the mean ASQ scores among each of the groups. Comparisons of control and incentive group t tests revealed no significant differences for CPCN ($t = 0.6$, ns), CN ($t = 1.3$, ns), or CP ($t = 1.0$, ns). They also found no significant differences between the control group and the incentive-plus-coached group for CN ($t = 1.0$, ns) or CP ($t = 1.2$, ns), but a slight, nonsignificant difference on CPCN ($t = 1.7$, $p = .10$) with the incentive-plus-coached group having a slightly more optimistic style for positive and negative events combined.

The results of this study indicate that neither motivation to do well (the incentive group), nor motivation plus coaching, is sufficient to produce a more optimistic score. Even when subjects were encouraged (through the promise of $100—no small sum to a college student) to score as best they could and were told what type of answers would lead to the best score, they did not score significantly different from controls. Such a lack of transparency makes this test particularly robust against cheating, suggesting that short of being told explicitly what the desirable answers are, subjects may not be able to fake the desirable responses.

Internal Consistency

Internal consistency measures are used to determine the homogeneity of items, that is, whether the items measure the same property. Several studies have investigated the internal consistency of the ASQ. Seligman et al. (1979) examined the correlation between explanatory style and depression in college undergraduates and reported the following coefficient alphas (Cronbach, 1951) for subscales: negative event internality = .44, negative event stability = .63, negative event globality = .64, positive event internality = .39, positive event stability = .54, positive event globality = .58. Based on this study, the internal consistency of the individual dimensions range from poor to adequate.

Peterson et al. (1982) and Tennen and Herzberger (1987) also reported modest internal consistency for subscales, with Cronbach's (1951) alpha ranging from .21 to .69. Sweeney, Anderson, and Bailey (1986) conducted a meta-analytic review of explanatory style and depression. They calculated a reliability estimate by averaging the reported reliabilities from eight separate studies for which reliability data was available for all subscales. For negative outcomes, Sweeney et al. reported reliabilities of .52, .58, .52, and .73 for internality, stability globality, and composite measures. For positive outcomes, the reliabilities of the internality, stability, globality, and composite measures were .40, .67, .66, and .69, respectively.

Based on these findings, the ASQ subscales can be said to have unsatisfactory reliability. However, when composite scores are formed, substantially higher and satisfactory levels of internal consistency are found.

Consistency Across Valence

Peterson et al. (1982) found that the attributional composites for positive versus negative events are unrelated to each other. They reported a correlation of .02 in their sample of 130 undergraduate students. Schulman, Castellon, and Seligman (1989), on the other hand, found a small, significant correlation between CN and CP, −.24 ($p < .002$, $n = 160$). That is, in their sample, the more pessimistic an individual was regarding failures, the less optimistic he or she was regarding successes.

These data highlight the importance of analyzing explanatory style for positive events separately from explanatory style for negative events. What differentiates those who see doom and gloom across both successes and failures from those who compartmentalize hopelessness and pessimism to either successes or failures? One can speculate that the "consistent" pessimist is likely to have greater emotional and motivational difficulties than those of us who believe that we are potent, and the future is bright, for at least some of the events that occur in our lives.

Test–Retest Reliability

The reformulation of the learned helplessness model asserts that individuals have a fairly enduring explanatory style. Clearly, it would be inappropriate to use the term *style* if the explanations individuals offered for events were fickle. This is not to say that explanatory style cannot be changed. Indeed, the primary goal of cognitive therapy is to teach the client how to evaluate whether his or her thoughts are accurate, and if they are not accurate, how to change them (see chapter 11). However, theorists believe that without intervention, individuals have a characteristic way of explaining events that is stable over time (Abramson, Seligman, & Teasdale, 1978; Peterson et al., 1982; Peterson & Seligman, 1984a).

Studies by Golin, Sweeney, and Schaeffer (1981) and Peterson et al. (1982) have investigated the test–retest reliability of the ASQ. Golin et al. (1981) administered the ASQ to 206 undergraduate students and readministered the questionnaire to 180 of these students. For positive events, test–retest reliability coefficients were .66 for internality, .56 for stability, .51 for globality, and .67 for composite. For negative events, the test–retest correlations were .47 for internality, .61 for stability, .65 for globality, and .67 for composite (all $ps < .001$).

Although explanatory style may be stable, it is important to note that intervention can significantly change ASQ scores. Persons and Rao (1985) followed 32 depressed patients from hospital admission to discharge and found that ASQ scores changed significantly for negative events. Similarly, explanatory style has been found to change during cognitive therapy for unipolar depression (DeRubeis et al., 1989; Seligman et al., 1988). The temporal stability of explanatory style has also been investigated using the CAVE technique and the children's forced choice version of the ASQ (the details of these techniques are discussed later in this chapter). Using the content analysis technique, Burns and Seligman (1989) found that over a 52-year period, the test–retest correlation for CN was .54 ($p < .002$, $n = 30$) and for CP was .13 (ns). Seligman et al. (1984) found that in a sample of 8- to 13-year-old children test–retest correlations over a 6-month period were .71 for CP and .66 for CN ($ps < .001$, $n = 96$).

Based on these findings, explanatory style seems to be stable although not immutable. It can be changed through the course of cognitive therapy for unipolar depression and there may be individual differences in the extent to which someone has a true style. That is, some individuals may be more consistent in projecting their idiosyncratic explanations onto diverse situations, whereas others may be more situation and reality based. This implies a future direction for researchers. Analyses that only include individuals with a consistent style (i.e., have a small standard deviation across domains), may yield superior criterion validity.

Construct Validity

Studies of construct validity are conducted to validate the theory underlying the instrument. To test construct validity, the researcher determines certain relationships that should and should not exist between the construct and other measures, and determines whether these relationships are empirically supported. In one test of construct validity, Schulman, Castellon, and Seligman (1989) administered the ASQ to 169 undergraduates at the University of Pennsylvania. For this study, each hypothetical event and the cause the respondent wrote down was extracted from the ASQ and rated by three raters. The raters were naive to who the subject was and what other explanations they gave. (This technique is discussed in detail later in the chapter. Interrater reliabilities were satisfactory.)

The raters' ratings of the explanations correlated highly with the subjects' ratings on the ASQ. Correlations were .71 for CPCN, .48 for CN, and .52 for CP ($ps < .001$, $ns = 159$). Broken down by individual dimensions, the authors reported correlations of .61 ($p < .0001$) for internal negative, .24 ($p < .002$) for stable negative, .28 ($p < .0003$) for global negative, .67 ($p < .0001$) for internal positive, .30 ($p < .0001$) for stable positive, .07 (ns) for global positive. The authors pointed out that global positive is handicapped by a low interrater reliability (.48).

Criterion Validity

Criterion-related validity is established by comparing test scores with one or more criteria known to measure the attribute being examined. The predictive and concurrent validity of the ASQ has been confirmed in a variety of domains.

Peterson and Seligman (1984a) presented 12 studies (8 of which measured explanatory style with the ASQ) that lent support for the reformulated model in the domain of depression. Depressive deficits were associated with a negative style in students, depressed patients, prisoners, and children. Sweeney et al. (1986) and Robins (1988) did meta-analytic reviews of more than 100 explanatory style studies and found strong evidence for the predicted relationship between explanatory style and depression. Other, less complete reviews (e.g., Brewin, 1985; Coyne & Gotlib, 1983) were more mixed in their findings. Chapters 5, 8, 9, 10, and 11 cover these areas in detail.

Research also shows that the ASQ predicts achievement in several domains. In academia, explanatory style predicts grades among college undergraduates (Schulman, Keith, & Seligman, 1991) and predicts grades and attrition among West Point Military Academy cadets (Schulman et al., 1991). In sports, ASQ scores predict the performance of swimmers on major university swim teams, particularly following defeat (Seligman, Nolen-Hoeksema, Thornton, & Thornton, 1990). In the workplace, ASQ scores predict productivity in a 2-year longitudinal study of 766 life insurance agents (Schulman et al., 1991) and predicts productivity and retention in a 1-year longitudinal study of 104 sales agents (Seligman & Schulman, 1986). Chapters 12–15 discuss explanatory style and achievement in detail.

CONTENT ANALYSIS OF VERBATIM EXPLANATIONS

A second method for assessing explanatory style is the CAVE technique. One limitation of the ASQ is that it is a questionnaire. Thus, in order to assess an individual's explanatory style, he or she must consent to complete the questionnaire. This limits the number and the type of people for whom explanatory style can be measured. For example, as interesting as it would be to assess the styles of the world leaders, it seems unlikely that we could convince Sadam Hussein, Bill Clinton, and Mikhael Gorbachev to spend 15–20 minutes in a quiet room completing the ASQ. Nor could we assess the style of people like Vincent van Gogh, Madam Curie, or Helen Keller (at least, not without the aid of a medium).

Fortunately, Peterson et al. (1983) developed a technique to assess explanatory style such that expertise in the art of persuasion and time travel are not necessary. With the CAVE technique, famous, dead, or otherwise unavailable subjects can be studied as easily as undergraduate psychology students, providing that a personally written document is available. The only requirement of the document is that it contain causal attributions made by the person being studied. Happily, statements of causality are everywhere: Interviews, diaries, letters, essays, newspaper articles, therapy transcripts, and speeches are rife with causal explanations.

Before describing the CAVE technique in detail, there are a few conceptual issues that are pertinent to this method.

Concerns Surrounding the Use of Content Analytic Techniques

The content analysis of public records is not a novel research technique in the field of psychology (e.g., see reviews by Allport, 1942; Holsti, 1968; Krippendorf, 1980; Runyan, 1982; Simonton, 1981; Viney, 1983; Wrightsman, 1981). Some researchers, however, are critical of content-analytic techniques, claiming that this procedure is marred by bias and lack of precision. With regard to the CAVE technique, these criticisms have been addressed. As is later discussed, randomization and blind rating procedures are used to minimize bias and substantial training is implemented to increase the reliability of the technique.

The CAVE technique involves two independent steps: extraction of verbatim event and causal explanation couplets; and rating of the causal statements on the internality, stability, and globality dimensions of explanatory style. Both steps are completed by trained researchers who are naive to the identity of the subject as well as to the outcome measures. Both extracting and rating have proven highly reliable.

One benefit of this approach is that it may be more ecologically valid. The events described in the material are probably more relevant and meaningful to the individuals than are those events presented in the ASQ. Furthermore, these spontaneous causal explanations, not prompted by an investigator, are more likely to be honest because any demand characteristics associated with completing the questionnaire will be absent (Langer, 1978; Taylor & Fiske, 1978).

Reality Versus Style

Unlike the ASQ, the events used in the CAVE technique are usually not hypothetical; rather, they are occurrences from the subject's life. Therefore, reality can be a major determinant of the explanation offered. If the material from which the attributions are extracted is mainly reality driven, little will be learned about the idiosyncratic style of the individual. For example, suppose a woman loses her job because the company she works for has gone bankrupt. If when queried about why she lost her job, she explains, "The whole company folded! Can you believe it?!", we do not learn anything about this woman's habitual style.

Events, however, are often complex and the causes of the events are usually many and varied. For example, suppose a woman describes a fight that has recently occurred with her spouse after having dinner with a group of colleagues. Further, imagine that one of the guests at the dinner party was someone with whom she felt competitive, that her stomach was upset from the Cajun chicken, that her spouse had arrived late due to congestion on the freeway, and that she was vaguely worried about her daughter who was at home with a new babysitter. It is possible that all of these factors contributed to the interaction with her spouse, to say nothing of the factors that influenced his emotions and behavior.

But, when explaining to herself the cause of the fight, it is not likely that she will take into account (nor even be aware of) all of these factors. Most likely, she will explain the fight by only one or two of the many contributing variables. What then are the real causes of this situation? We need not digress into a philosophical discussion of reality in order to realize that the distinction between reality and subjective interpretation is a blurry one. Therefore, although the CAVE technique relies more on actual versus hypothetical events, these events are often as ambiguous as those found on the ASQ. ASQ items are ambiguous due to the dearth of information and context, real-life events are ambiguous due to the abundance of information that surrounds them.

Consistency in Explanations

Although explanatory style is regarded as a cognitive trait, it is not expected that people will maintain 100% consistency in their style at all times. Fluctuations occur across time and across situation. To use the CAVE technique effectively, several causal explanations must be found for an individual, and the events should span achievement and affiliation situations. The originators of the technique suggest that at least five negative events with explanations be analyzed in order for the assessment to be valid. Moreover, Peterson and Seligman (1984a) counciled that the term *style* should be reserved for individuals whose causal explanations show low variability across situations and time.

Positive Versus Negative Events

In much of the research with the CAVE technique, negative events with explanations are more abundant than positive events with explanations. People seem to think and speak more about their problems than their successes. Zautra and Reich (1983) found that individuals discuss negative events more than positive events and that negative events have a greater affect on one's life than do positive events. Moreover, Tversky and Kahneman (1981) found that the response to loss is more extreme than the response to gains. Researchers have also reported an asymmetry in the role that cognitions play in our behavior. Schwartz and Gottman (1976) reported that negative cognitions, or the reduction in them, have a greater effect on assertiveness than do positive cognitions. Similarly, the reduction in negative cognitions have been found to improve coping with medical stress and recovery from psychological illness with greater effect than do positive cognitions (Derry & Stone, 1979; Kendall et al., 1979; Mavissakalian, Michelson, Greenwald, Kornblith, & Greenwald, 1983). Furthermore, Peterson and Seligman (1984a) found that explanatory style for negative events is a more valid predictor of depressive deficits than the explanatory style is for positive events.

All this is to say that the dearth of positive events in verbatim materials should not deter the investigator. As Kendall and Hollon (1981) said, the "power of nonnegative thinking" may be more potent than the power of positive thinking. Sorry, Mr. Peale.

CAVE Training

Researchers interested in using the CAVE technique participate in an 8-hour workshop, led by an experienced CAVE trainer. Between workshop meetings, participants complete a number of assignments to practice extracting and rating. These assignments are then reviewed and discussed in detail during the workshop meetings. Although the workshop could be completed in 1 day, it is our experience that 2-hour meetings spread over the course of 4 days produce more competent and confident CAVErs.

Extracting Event-Explanation Units

An *event* is defined as any stimulus that occurs in an individual's environment or within the individual (e.g., thoughts or feelings) that has a positive or negative effect from that individual's point of view. Events can be mental (e.g., "I was embarrassed"), social (e.g., "I was invited to my employer's house for dinner"), or physical (e.g., "I hurt my elbow playing shuffleboard"). Events may occur in the past, present, or hypothetical future, but they must be unambiguously positive or negative from the subject's point of view. This latter point is often trickier than it seems. For example, "My wife and I started seeing a therapist" may be experienced as a negative event or a positive event depending on the individual. This should only be extracted if it is clear how this man views being in therapy. Events that have positive and negative elements ("I am seeing a doctor for my weight problem"), neutral events ("I took the letters to the post office"), or events that do not affect the subject ("There was a big fire at the train station in town"), should not be extracted.

Second, the subject must express his or her own explanation for the event. The subject cannot simply agree with or quote another person's explanation. For example, "Barry and I had a blowout of an argument yesterday. He says it's because I'm not a giving person" would not be an acceptable extraction because the causal explanation comes from Barry, not the subject. Although explanations must always be in the subject's own words, there are times when the event itself may be spoken by someone else. This occurs most frequently in therapy transcripts, in which the therapist states a problem from the patient's life. For example:

Therapist: Nicole, last week you mentioned that you and Monique were fighting a lot. Do you want to talk about that?

Patient: Yeah, it's her fault. She's so moralistic and pious all the time.

Events of this nature are fine, as long as the event is clearly good or bad in the subject's life.

Third, there must be a clear causal relationship between the explanation and the event, and not simply a sequence of events that describe without explaining. The explanation must answer the question "why" and it must be perceived by the subject as covarying with the event. Possible causes can include: (a) other events, (b) situational factors, (c) behaviors of the subject or others, (d) dispositions, (e) experiences, and so on. "I got a raise yesterday. My boss is so nice," is not an appropriate extraction because it is not clear that the subject is attributing the raise to the fact that the boss is nice. These might be two separate events that are not connected causally. Furthermore, the explanation of the event has to be more than proof or justification. "Her brother doesn't treat me well. He is always making derisive comments about my work," is not acceptable because the second sentence is an example of the event, not causal of the event. Nor, for that matter, is the first sentence causal of the second sentence. This example lacks a clear line of causality and therefore, should not be extracted. Explanations must clearly precede and bring about the events to be extracted.

The procedure begins by searching through any verbatim material, audiotaped, videotaped, or written, for event-explanation units. Even if the word "because" or its synonyms are missing, event-explanation units can be extracted if a clearly intended causal relationship can be inferred. Following are examples of acceptable event-explanation units (E = event, A = attribution):

E: I haven't missed a class this entire semester.

A: I'm determined to get the most out of school.

E: My father barely spoke to me during dinner.

A: He withdraws when he isn't doing well at work.

E: I'm in an awful mood today. You better keep your distance.

A: I blew a huge account today after working like crazy to make it come through.

Following are examples of unacceptable extractions:

E: I realized I was in a high-risk category for ovarian cancer

A: because I've been reading that a family history of cancer increases your chances of getting it. [This is not unambiguously positive or negative. Although it is good to be aware of being in a high-risk category so that precautionary measures can be taken, it will not be experienced as a positive event by the subject.]

E: I must be getting sick

A: because I feel lethargic and I have a bad cough. [The word "because" does not always mean a causal explanation will follow. In this case, the subject is giving proof or a definition of what she means by "getting sick" and is not giving the cause of her illness.]

Ideally, the event and the explanation should include enough information for the rater to be able to analyze all three causal dimensions. This may not always be feasible. If the explanation contains so little information on the causal dimensions that it would require raters to do guesswork on two of the three dimensions, it is best not to extract it.

Given the difficulty of rating extractions when they are taken out of context (details on the rating process follow), it is important to add relevant contextual information to the event and the explanation. The substance of the explanation, however, should be verbatim. Context is vital to the rater; the extraction is often unclear when isolated. Any added contextual information should be in parentheses, so that the rater understands that the material is context added by the extractor. For example:

E: I got it (prestigious accounting job)

A: because I did an internship with him (company vice president) for the last two summers.

E: He (husband) hasn't come in (to hospital) to visit me much.

A: He has the tendency to turn green and faint whenever he sees blood.

If one event has multiple explanations, then there should be as many event-explanation units as there are separate explanations. For instance, the sentence, "I didn't do well on my exam because I didn't sleep well last night and I didn't study as much as I should have," should be broken into two extractions:

E: I didn't do well on my exam

A: because I didn't sleep well last night.

E: I didn't do well on my exam

A: because I didn't study as much as I should have.

An explanation in one extraction may be an event for another extraction, or vice versa. For instance:

E: I haven't been sleeping well lately

A: because I've been worrying about getting into a good graduate program.

E: I've been worrying about getting into a good graduate program.

A: I didn't do as well on the GREs as I had hoped.

Extractions are randomized within and between subjects and are presented to three raters who are naive to their source. The randomization procedure is important because it ensures that the raters are not biased by previous ratings for the same subject and do not fall into entrenched rating patterns.

Finally, it has been found that independent judges agree more than 90% of the time whether or not an extraction should be included as a causal explanation (Peterson, Bettes, & Seligman, 1985). This level of agreement occurs when a stringent criterion for the identification of causal explanations is employed. Poor extractions degrade the data, thus a guiding principle for good extracting is "if in doubt, throw it out." As with most things, quality is preferable to quantity.

Rating of Extractions

As with the ASQ, ratings of explanations are assigned to each of the three dimensions—internal versus external, stable versus unstable, global versus specific—using a 7-point scale. Ratings range from 1 through 7 for each dimension, with a 7 representing the most internal, stable, and global explanations; and a 1 representing the most external, unstable, and specific explanations. For each dimension, the rater is attempting to rate the subject's perception of the internality, stability, and globality of the cause.

If there is insufficient information to assign a rating to any of the dimensions, then the rater is instructed to assign a 4, so as not to skew the rating.

The Internal Versus the External Scale

The 7-point scale for this dimension is divided into three regions: 1, if the individual attributes the cause to someone or something external to the self; 7, if the individual attributes the cause to any behavioral, physical, or mental characteristic about the self; and 2–6, if the individual attributes the cause of an event to some combination of self and other. Clearly, the difficulty in rating lies in narrowing down the 2–6 range and recording a single numerical rating. The internal versus external scale should not be confused with blame, credit, control, and so forth. Although these constructs are often expressed, the purpose of this scale is to distinguish between self-caused versus other-caused attributions only. It is not designed to further distinguish between subcategories of the internal dimension.

Examples of a 1 rating include explanations that invoke the actions of another person, the difficulty or ease of a task, or time and environmental factors (such as a natural disaster, the weather, or economics). Examples of a 7 rating include references to the individual's own personality or physical traits, behavior, decisions, ability or inability, motivation, knowledge, disability, illness, injury, age, and social or political classifications (such as widow, liberal, etc.). Ratings in the 2–6 range apply to explanations in which the cause shares both internal and external elements and is an interaction between self and another person or between self and the environment. Following are some examples:

E: I nailed the test

A: because it was ridiculously simple (Rating = 1).

E: They didn't give me the job

A: because they're prejudiced (Rating = 1).

E: My boyfriend and I keep fighting

A: because he can't accept my perfectionism (Rating = 2 or 3).

E: My daughter and I fight all the time.

A: We never seem to give each other the benefit of the doubt (Rating = 4).

E: I turn into a monster

A: when I get hungry (Rating = 4).

E: I need surgery on my knee.

A: It's in bad shape from all that skiing I do (Rating = 4 or 5).

E: I got the part in the play that everyone wanted

A: because I know how to turn on the tears (Rating = 7).

E: I didn't get the promotion

A: because I'm too old (Rating = 7).

The Stable Versus the Unstable Scale

This dimension refers to the persistence in time of the cause, whether the cause of the event is chronic (stable) versus temporary (unstable). It is crucial to distinguish between the stability of the cause and the stability of the events; we are concerned with the former. A useful framework from which to assess the stability of the cause is, "Given this event has occurred, how permanent is this cause?" We are not concerned with the stability of the event because many events are singular. Knowing the stability of an event tells us nothing about the individual's explanatory style. We are interested in how the event is explained and whether the individual believes that the cause of the event is permanent or temporary. Remember, the reformulated theory states that individuals who consistently offer stable causes will suffer chronic deficits. Therefore, to test this hypothesis we must rate only the stability of the attribution, regardless of the stability of the event.

There are four interacting criteria that help to determine the appropriate stability rating:

1. The tense of the cause. If the cause of an event is phrased in the past tense, then the rating would tend to be less stable than if the cause is in the present or progressive tense.

2. The probability of future reoccurrence of the cause. A cause that is unlikely to occur again would be less stable than a cause that is likely to occur again.

3. An intermittent versus a continuous cause. A cause that is intermittent, such as the weather, would be less stable than a continuous cause, such as a physical trait.

4. A characterological versus a behavioral cause. Explaining an event by a character trait (e.g., I am smart, greedy, indecisive, etc.) is more stable than attributing an event to a behavior (e.g., I did a smart thing. I made a bad decision. I prepared long and hard.).

These four criteria should be used as guidelines for determining a rating. They will not all be relevant in all cases, nor should they be weighted equally. For instance, the tense of the attribution should be used as a way to fine-tune the rating, knocking it up or down a point depending on the tense in which it is stated. Following are some examples:

E: I can't attend the conference
A: because I am going to a wedding (Rating = 1). [This cause is in the present tense but is unlikely to occur again.]
E: I was depressed
A: when my grandmother died (Rating = 2). [This cause occurred in the past, cannot occur again, but may have some ongoing influence.]
E: I always have trouble falling asleep
A: when it is hot (Rating = 3). [This cause is likely to occur again but only intermittently.]
E: My marriage is falling apart.
A: Getting married young showed bad judgment on my part (Rating = 3). [This cause is in the past tense, has a small probability of future occurrence, and is behavioral rather than characterological.]
E: I've been afraid to go out in the dark
A: since I was attacked (Rating = 4). [This cause occurred in the past, has a small probability of a future occurrence, but may exert an ongoing influence on behavior.]
E: I can't stop myself from eating
A: when I see someone else eating (Rating = 4). [This cause is in the present tense, will occur again, and is intermittent.]
E: It's difficult for me to express my anger.
A: That's just the way I was raised (Rating = 5). [This cause occurred continuously in the past and has an ongoing influence on behavior.]
E: I'm not doing well in school.
A: I am about as lazy as they come (Rating = 5 or 6). [This cause is in the present tense, will probably continue to occur, although it may change, and is characterological.]

E: I didn't get the job
A: because I'm a woman [or blind or stupid, etc.] (Rating = 7). [This cause is unalterable, characterological, and continuous.]

The Global Versus the Specific Scale

This dimension measures the extent to which a cause affects the entire life of an individual (global) or just a few areas (specific). This dimension is often the most difficult to rate. Typically, there is not enough information in the extraction to indicate the pervasiveness of the effects of the cause, nor do we always know which domains of the individual's life are particularly important. For example, poor batting ability would have a greater affect on a professional baseball player than on a home economics teacher; quality of friendships would tend to be more important to a gregarious person than to a recluse, and laryngitis would have a more global impact on an opera singer than a kick boxer. In the absence of such intimate knowledge, it is useful to consider the impact of a cause on the scope of an "average" individual's life in terms of two general categories—*achievement* and *affiliation*—each comprised of numerous subcategories. Clearly, this is an artificial distinction and is neither exclusive nor exhaustive, but as a heuristic it helps keep the rater from projecting his or her own biases onto the rating of globality.

Achievement, for instance, would include occupational or academic success, accumulation of knowledge or skills, sense of individuality or independence, and economic or social status. Affiliation includes intimate relationships, sense of belongingness, sex (although this may fall under the achievement domain for some people), play, and marital or familial health. An attribution may affect just one situation, part of one category, parts of both categories (such as mental or physical health), all of one category, or all of both categories.

It is crucial when rating globality that the stability dimension is held constant. That is, the rater is assessing at this point in time, not across time, how much of the individual's life is affected by the cause. Although the stable and global dimensions are significantly intercorrelated and probably often overlap in reality, it is important to rate each of these two dimensions independently of the other. Also, it is often helpful to consider the event when judging the globality of the cause, because the event is one effect in the universe of possible effects that may result from the causal explanation. The raters do not, however, rate only the effects mentioned in the event, because the cause may affect more than what has been stated. Rather, the event can be used to set the floor, below which the globality rating cannot pass. Consider the following examples:

E: I got a speeding ticket
A: I guess the cop had to fill her quota for the day (Rating = 1). [This attribution only affects this situation.]

E: Some of my relationships suffer a bit

A: because I'm not very spontaneous (Rating = 2 or 3). [This cause affects part of the affiliative category and possibly part of the achievement category.]

E: I feel less confident about myself

A: since I had my breast removed (Rating = 4 or 5). [This cause will probably affect some of affiliative and some achievement situations.]

E: I've had to cut back on my level of activity

A: since my heart attack (Rating 5 or 6). [This cause affects many aspects of a person's life.]

E: I've lost all zest. I've felt devastated

A: since my son died (Rating 6 or 7). [Most of both categories are affected by the death of a child. Notice if one of the possible outcomes of this attribution is that the person feels devastated, the floor for the globality rating must remain fairly high.]

E: I've been in a funk for weeks.

A: Nothing in life seems to matter anymore (Rating = 7).

The internal, stable, and global ratings for negative events are usually positively correlated. This is not believed to be an artifact of the procedure of content analysis because it occurs with other techniques of assessment as well (Peterson & Seligman, 1984a). Rather, it seems to reflect the way that people actually make causal explanations.

Interrater Reliability

Using Cronbach's analysis (1951), Schulman et al. (1989) found interrater reliability for the CAVE technique to be a satisfactory .89 for CN and .80 for CP. Broken down by individual dimensions, alphas for negative events were .93 for internal, .63 for stable, and .73 for global. For positive events, alphas were .95 for internal, .66 for stable, and .48 for global. Because reliabilities for the composite variables are better than for individual dimensions, as with the ASQ, researchers are encouraged to focus on the composite variables.

Intercorrelations Between Individual Dimensions

Table 2.1 contains the intercorrelations among dimensions. Similar to the ASQ, correlations between the dimensions are highly significant. Further, the same pattern was found in which the individual dimensions for positive events were more highly correlated than the individual dimensions for negative events.

CONSTRUCT VALIDITY: USES OF THE CAVE TECHNIQUE

In this section a variety of research projects in which explanatory style was assessed using the CAVE technique is discussed. Taken together, they provide considerable construct validity for the procedure.

The Course of Psychotherapy

Peterson and Seligman (1981) first used the CAVE technique to assess whether explanatory style plays a causal role in depression (for details on this study and other studies predicting depression, see chapter 5). Mardi Horowitz, a psychodynamic therapist and researcher, sent Peterson and Seligman brief excerpts from 12 therapy sessions with patients who suffered depression following a severe loss.

Members of Peterson and Seligman's research team extracted the transcripts and then distributed the randomized extractions to four naive raters. Composite measures were derived for each of the 12 patients, who were then rank-ordered in terms of optimistic versus pessimistic explanatory style. Peterson and Seligman mailed the ranks to Horowitz and waited to see if they accurately predicted his ranking of the patients in terms of level of depression.

Horowitz's response came as a surprise. Contrary to their assumption that the therapy sessions represented 12 different patients, Peterson and Seligman learned that the transcripts marked the beginning, middle, and end of the successful therapy of only four patients. And for each patient, the ranks identified where they had been in the course of therapy. In the beginning of therapy, explanations for negative events tended to be internal, stable, and global; at the end of therapy, explanations for negative events tended to be external, unstable, and specific.

This study supports similar research findings with the ASQ (Hamilton & Abramson, 1983; Persons & Rao, 1985) that indicate that explanatory style is an index of improvement in depression during the course of psychotherapy.

Depression Among College Students

To validate the CAVE technique further, Peterson, Bettes, and Seligman (1985) asked 66 undergraduates at the University of Pennsylvania to write essays about the two worst events that had occurred to them during the past year. After writing the essays, subjects completed the ASQ and the Beck Depression Inventory (BDI).

Two primary results from this study further support the validity of the CAVE technique. First, causal explanations were significantly correlated with the BDI scores as predicted by the helplessness reformulation. And second, scores derived by the CAVE technique significantly correlated with the corresponding scales on the ASQ (with the exception of stability): internality ($r = .41, p < .001$), stability ($r = .19$, ns), globality ($r = .23, p < .01$), and the composite ($r = .30, p < .01$).

Death in the Hall of Fame

Peterson and Seligman (1984b) wondered about the effects of a pessimistic style on global measures of functioning—morbidity and mortality (see chapter 1 for the reasoning that motivated this study). Peterson et al. stated that there are at least two mechanisms through which a pessimistic style could facilitate morbidity and mortality. First, a pessimistic explanatory style encourages passivity. If you believe life is a constant barrage of doom and gloom, there is little reason to change your diet, increase your exercise, or take your medicine. If this current illness does not get you, the next one certainly will. For those who firmly believe that bad things are permanent, any attempts at change are illogical.

Second, a pessimistic explanatory style may lead directly to lowered immune competence and increased susceptibility to illness (Jemmott & Locke, 1984; Kamen-Siegel, Rodin, Seligman, & Dwyer, 1991; Peterson, 1988). See chapter 14 for a discussion of explanatory style and health.

In order to investigate the effects of explanatory style on mortality, a very particular population was necessary. First, because a study of this nature using subjects who were currently young would take a prohibitively long time to yield results, most of the subjects should either be dead or very old. Second, the subjects must have made enough recorded statements while young so that their explanatory style could be evaluated. Third, because being physically ill might affect the types of explanations one makes, subjects should have been physically healthy when the statements were made. Fourth, to partially control for the effects of hardship on physical health, all of the subjects should have been successful. And finally, there must, of course, be enough individuals that meet the criteria so that the hypothesis can be tested statistically. Cohorts that fulfill all five requirements are not abundant. But, Peterson et al. did find one cohort that met their needs—members of the St. Louis Baseball Hall of Fame.

Focusing on members between 1900 and 1950, the investigators extracted and rated players' sports page interviews (for details of this study, see chapter 14). Of the 94 players, there were 30 for whom at least two causal explanations could be found for negative events and 26 for whom at least two causal explanations could be found for positive events. Peterson et al. correlated the players' composite style for both positive and negative events with age at death (or age in 1984, if still living).

The results of this study are encouraging. An optimistic style for positive events predicted longevity ($r = .45$, $p < .01$), whereas a pessimistic style for negative events showed the opposite relationship ($r = -.26$, $p < .08$). Although the results of this study are tentative, due to a small sample size, they do suggest that the CAVE technique might make predictive psychohistory possible (for other psychohistorical studies, see chapters 11 and 12).

The Health of Harvard Graduates

In a similar study, Peterson, Seligman, and Vaillant (1988) predicted morbidity from explanatory style for individuals who had participated in the Grant Study, a longitudinal investigation of the Harvard classes of 1939–1942 (Vaillant, 1977). The 99 subjects in this study gave interviews in 1946 about war experiences. Peterson et al. (1988) extracted and rated this material and found that explanatory style for negative events in 1946 predicted a global rating of physical health in 1970 (the rating of physical health was made by an internist who was naive to the other data. For details of this study, see chapter 14). That is, they found that explanatory style at age 25 predicts poor health at ages 45 through 60. Furthermore, these predictions held even when physical health and mental health at age 25 were controlled.

The four studies described here are only a sampling of the many studies that have used the CAVE technique to assess explanatory style. These studies, taken together, show the CAVE technique to be a valid and reliable tool. Investigators agree regarding the presence or absence of causal explanations in verbatim material. Raters agree in their blind ratings of these explanations. Subjects have a consistent style of causal explanations and, as predicted, it is related to depression, illness, and death.

The CAVE Technique Versus the ASQ: Is One Better?

Both techniques have advantages and disadvantages. The ASQ appears to have better validity in predicting depression (Schulman et al., 1989). Perhaps subjects can rate their own explanations more accurately than can an investigator. Also, the ambiguous events on the ASQ cut down on "reality" and encourage the subject to project his or her subjective interpretation of the event, enabling researchers to better tap into explanatory style.

The ASQ, however, has limitations. The most important of which is that only individuals who are willing to complete the questionnaire can be examined. There is no such problem with the CAVE technique. Although labor intensive, any verbatim material can be analyzed and the speaker of this material can become a subject of study. Furthermore, CAVEing turns the researcher into a time traveler. Longitudinal research that would otherwise take years and years to complete is reduced to weeks or months at a fraction of the cost.

THE CHILDREN'S ATTRIBUTIONAL STYLE QUESTIONNAIRE

The CASQ was developed for use with children approximately ages 8–14 (Kaslow et al., 1978). The format of the CASQ is less complicated than the ASQ, which was judged too difficult for children to reliably complete. The CASQ contains

48 items, each of which consists of a hypothetical positive or negative event involving the child and two possible causes of the event. Respondents are instructed to choose the cause that best describes why the event occurred. The two causes provided hold constant two of the attributional dimensions while varying the third. For example, the following sample item from the CASQ measures internality versus externality (while holding constant stability and globality): You go on a vacation with a group of people and you have a good time; (a) I was in a good mood (internal); (b) The people I was with were in good moods (external). Sixteen questions pertain to each of the three dimensions. Half of the questions provide positive events to be explained and half provide negative events.

Scoring

The CASQ is scored by assigning a value of 1 to each internal, stable, or global response and the value of 0 to each external, unstable, specific response. Subscales are formed by summing these scores across the appropriate questions for each of the three causal dimensions. Items are scored separately for positive events and negative events. Thus, the same scores can be derived from the CASQ as from the ASQ (CPCN, CN, CP, etc.).

Psychometric Properties of the CASQ

The CASQ was developed for use in a study investigating explanatory style and depressive symptoms among children (Seligman et al., 1984). This study was the first to test the predictions of the reformulation among 8- to 13-year-old children. Children were administered the CASQ and the Children's Depression Inventory (CDI; Kovacs & Beck, 1977) at two times, separated by a 6-month interval.

Table 2.2 presents the means, standard deviations, reliabilities, and stabilities of the CASQ at Time 1 and Time 2. CASQ subscale scores, like the ASQ, possessed only modest reliabilities. Although internal consistencies mostly exceeded scale intercorrelations, indicating that the scales were empirically distinguishable (Campbell & Fiske, 1959), they were not high. Higher reliabilities were obtained by combining the subscales (separately for positive events and for negative events) to form a composite, as is done with the ASQ (Peterson et al., 1982). The CASQ scores were fairly consistent over the 6-month interval (composite $rs = .71, .66, ps < .001$), showing explanatory style to be a stable individual difference among children, just as it is among adults (Peterson et al., 1982).

The results of this study indicate that the reformulation of helplessness theory applies to children as well as adults. As the authors predicted, children exhibiting depressive symptoms were more likely than nondepressed children to endorse internal, stable, global explanations for negative events. Furthermore, a pessimistic explanatory style predicted depressive symptoms in children at a 6-month follow-up, when initial levels of depression were controlled for. Since this study, several other studies using the CASQ have corroborated these findings (e.g., Kaslow, Rehm, Pollack, & Siegel, 1988; Kaslow, Rehm, & Siegel, 1984; Leon, Kendall, & Garber, 1980). Chapter 5 provides a complete review of empirical studies investigating explanatory style and depression in schoolchildren.

Summary

So far I have reviewed the ASQ, CAVE technique, and CASQ. These instruments are reliable and valid measures of explanatory style and have been used in hundreds of empirical studies investigating depression in adults and children, motivation, school achievement, sports achievement, political elections, and mortality. They are the tried and true measures of explanatory style. There are, however, several other instruments in various stages of development and validation that can also be used to measure explanatory style. I discuss some of these instruments next.

THE EXPANDED ASQ

Because of the previously mentioned problems with reliability, an expanded version of the ASQ was developed in order to boost reliabilities. This version contains 24 negative events, follows the same format as the ASQ, and is scored using the same procedures. Of course, only explanatory style for negative events can be derived from this instrument because there are no positive events included on the scale. Due to the increased sample of negative events, reliabilities are substantially improved: .66 for internality, .85 for stability, and .88 for globality, as compared to .44 for internality, .63 for stability, and .64 for globality from the ASQ (Peterson & Seligman, 1984a).

THE ACADEMIC ASQ

A 12-item academic version of the ASQ was developed to assess explanatory style, in relation to school achievement. This questionnaire was patterned exactly after the ASQ, except that it contained 12 negative events that referred to academic situations ("You cannot get all the reading done that your instructor assigns," "You cannot solve a single problem in a set of 20 assigned as homework," "You fail a final examination"). Again, the questionnaire uses the same scoring procedure as the ASQ, yet due to its specificity, it is most relevant in studies investigating academic achievement.

The Academic ASQ was designed to investigate the link between explanatory style for negative events and subsequent academic performance in university freshmen. Peterson and Barrett (1987) found that Academic ASQ is reliable (Cronbach's alpha = .84) and has criterion validity: The students who offered internal, stable, and global explanations for negative events did poorly in their college courses relative to students who invoked external, unstable, and specific explanations. This result held even when ability (as measured by SAT scores) and level of depression (as measured by the BDI) were controlled for.

THE FORCED-CHOICE ASQ

Reivich and Seligman (1991) developed a 48-item forced-choice version of the ASQ. Like the CASQ, the scale contains 24 positive events and 24 negative events. For each event, the subject is provided with two responses from which he or she must designate "the most likely cause" of the event. Each item is designed to test one of the three explanatory style dimensions. Thus, the response pair holds two of the dimensions constant, while altering the third dimension. For example, the item "A friend thanks you for helping him/her get through a bad time" is followed by the responses: (a) "I enjoy helping him/her through tough times," (b) "I care about people." Both responses are internal and stable, however, the first response is specific, whereas the second response is global.

There are 16 items, 8 positive events and 8 negative events, constructed to test each of the three dimensions. Furthermore, approximately one third of the items are achievement related, one third are affiliation related, and one third are health related. From this questionnaire, scores can be derived for all of the composite and individual dimensions by assigning a value of 1 to the internal, stable, and global responses and a value of 0 to the external, unstable, and specific responses, and then summing across the appropriate items.

The forced-choice format has both benefits and drawbacks. The forced-choice structure is clear and simple. Although some subjects have problems with the structure of the standard ASQ, virtually no subjects express difficulty with the forced-choice version. Also, the forced-choice version may be even more "cheat-proof" than the original because the dimensions are not designated as they are on the standard ASQ. These benefits, however, must be balanced against the drawbacks of this structure. Although the subjects did not express confusion regarding the completion of the questionnaire, some subjects did express frustration at the choices provided. This frustration is often expressed through the nonendorsement of items or by writing in a third response that the subject believes more accurately characterizes his or her interpretation of the event. Furthermore, by forcing the subject to choose between the responses provided, we are at best approximating his or her true explanatory style. The standard ASQ with its open-ended format and rating scales, and the CAVE technique with its verbatim material certainly capture more directly the idiosyncratic causal interpretations of the subjects.

In order to validate the Forced-Choice ASQ we approached passengers awaiting overseas flights at two international airports (they had lots of time to kill and rejoiced at the opportunity to pass the time in an interesting way) and asked them to complete the ASQ, the Forced-Choice ASQ, and the BDI. Correlations, as reported in the preceding section, between the ASQ and the Forced-Choice ASQ were .54 for CPCN ($p < .001$, $n = 82$), .39 for CN ($p < .001$, $n = 82$), .44 for CP ($p < .001$, $n = 82$), .41 for internal negative ($p < .001$, $n = 82$), .14 for stable negative (ns), .18 for global negative (ns), .40 for internal positive ($p < .001$, $n = 82$), .40 for stable positive ($p < .001$, $n = 82$), .17 for global positive (ns). Also, the Forced-Choice ASQ correlated .37 with the BDI ($p < .001$, $n = 82$). In the same study, the standard ASQ correlated .35 with the BDI ($p < .001$, $n = 79$).

The Forced-Choice ASQ should be considered a work in progress. Further refinement and validation are necessary before this instrument can be used reliably.

CONCLUSION

In this chapter, I have discussed the conceptual and methodological issues concerning the measurement of explanatory style. Three measures in particular—the ASQ, the CAVE technique, and the CASQ—have been proven reliable in the assessment of this construct. Several other measures are in various stages of development and validation and suggest arenas for future research.

This review mentions but a fraction of the research on explanatory style. The ASQ has been completed by hundreds of thousands of people. It has been translated into several foreign languages. The CAVE technique has been used to study world leaders, political movements, and cultural heros. The remainder of this book delves into this research and explores the domains of our lives that are changed by they way we interpret our successes and failures.

3

▼▼▼▼▼▼▼

The Origins of Explanatory Style: Trust as a Determinant of Optimism and Pessimism

Jane Penaz Eisner
University of California, San Francisco

Explanatory style affects a person's mental and physical health in important ways (see Peterson & Seligman, 1984a). Although these effects are well documented, we know little about the origins of individual differences in explanatory style. What makes one person optimistic and another person pessimistic? In this chapter, I explore answers to this question. I first review previous work examining the determinants of explanatory style. Next, I propose that trust of intimate others also affects the development of individual differences in explanatory style. Finally, I report a study that tests the impact of trust on explanatory style.

DETERMINANTS OF EXPLANATORY STYLE

Previous work in this area examines four different determinants of individual differences in explanatory style. I now consider this previous work and then introduce trust as another important determinant of explanatory style.

Teachers' Differential Performance Feedback. Teachers give boys and girls noticeably different performance feedback in the classroom (Dweck, Davidson, Nelson, & Enna, 1978). Dweck et al. examined teachers' performance feedback to fourth-grade children. Depending on a child's gender, teachers praised different aspects of the child's work. More than 90% of praise for boys' work related to intellectual competence. By contrast, significantly less (80.9%) of praise for girls focused on intellectual aspects of their work. Gender differences in teachers' negative evaluations were evident as well. Only 54.4% of teachers' criticisms of boys' work referred to intellectual incompetence. For girls, 88.9% of teachers' negative evaluations were directed at intellectual performance.

Does differential performance feedback, based on gender, affect children's explanatory styles? Researchers find a striking gender difference. Girls blame lack of ability—a stable characteristic—for poor performance. By contrast, boys ascribe their poor performance to an unstable cause: lack of effort (Dweck & Reppucci, 1973; Nicholls, 1975). In other words, girls make a pessimistic attribution about poor performance, whereas boys make an optimistic one.

Experimental work suggests that differential feedback patterns cause these gender differences in explanatory style. Dweck et al. (1978) conducted a laboratory study in which they reproduced the two feedback patterns found for teachers' criticism of children's work. When both boys and girls received the girls' feedback pattern, they ascribed their failure on a subsequent task to lack of ability. Children who received the boys' feedback pattern, however, attributed their failure to lack of effort. These results strongly suggest that differential performance feedback is one factor responsible for individual differences in explanatory style.

Modeling.   Children acquire a variety of behaviors and beliefs, both adaptive and maladaptive, by modeling significant others (Bandura, 1977b). Perhaps children learn a particular explanatory style by modeling the style of a primary caregiver, such as their parent. This hypothesis predicts a positive correlation between children's and parents' explanatory styles. Offering preliminary support, Seligman et al. (1984) found that a mother's explanatory style for bad events correlated with her child's style for bad events ($r = .39$, $p < .01$). Experimental work is necessary to demonstrate a causal link between mothers' explanatory styles and those of their children.

Differential Exposure to Noncontingency.   The reformulated theory of learned helplessness suggests a third account for individual differences in explanatory style (Abramson, Seligman, & Teasdale, 1978). According to the reformulated theory, a particular sequence of events leads to helplessness symptoms—the motivational, cognitive, and emotional deficits that parallel clinical depression. The sequence begins when an individual encounters an uncontrollable event and also perceives that his or her actions do not influence the event. The individual then posits an explanation for the cause of this failure to exert control. If the individual explains the failure with a stable cause, he or she will expect that future outcomes also will be uncontrollable. This expectancy produces helplessness deficits when the individual next encounters an uncontrollable event (see chapter 1).

As a direct extension of their theory, Abramson et al. (1978) proposed that repeated experience with uncontrollable events will lead a person to develop a pessimistic explanatory style, whereas exposure to controllable events will foster an optimistic explanatory style. Surprisingly, this hypothesis has received little research attention.[1] Recent work with children of divorce, however, provides some supporting evidence. Nolen-Hoeksema, Girgus, and Seligman (1991) reported that children who experience their parents' divorce or separation—both significant uncontrollable events—subsequently develop a more pessimistic explanatory style than do children whose parents remain together.

Genetic Influences. Other work provides evidence for the genetic transmission of explanatory style. Schulman, Keith, and Seligman (1991) found an intraclass correlation of .48 for explanatory style in monozygotic twins ($p < .0001$). By contrast, the explanatory styles of dizygotic twins were uncorrelated ($r = 0$, ns). The results suggest that the quality of one's explanatory style may have a genetic component.

Trust in Close Relationships. I suggest a fifth determinant of explanatory style: trust in close relationships. In brief, I argue that mistrust of intimate others spawns a pessimistic explanatory style, whereas trust of intimate others fosters an optimistic style. I now turn to trust and its causal role in the development of individual differences in explanatory style.

A DEFINITION OF TRUST

In my description (Eisner, 1992), trust in close relationships is an individual's belief that significant others can be relied on to safeguard that individual's welfare. Significant others are those people intimately involved in an individual's life. Examples of significant others include one's spouse, best friend, and parents. Further, welfare can be divided into three conceptually distinct categories: emotional, contractual, and physical. Intimate others safeguard an individual's emotional welfare when they avoid hurting his or her feelings unnecessarily; they ensure a person's contractual welfare when they adhere to simple rules of fair play between people; and they ensure a person's physical welfare by protecting his or her safety and health.

Previous investigations of trust in close relationships imply that trust is an attitude or state that changes depending on circumstances (e.g., Larzelere & Huston, 1980; Rempel, Holmes, & Zanna, 1985). By contrast, I argued and demonstrated that trust in close relationships can be an aspect of an individual's personality, or a trait (see Eisner, 1992).

---

[1]Instead, most researchers interested in the effects of differential exposure to noncontingency have examined the causal link between uncontrollable events—especially aversive ones—and helplessness deficits.

Another theoretically important characteristic of trust in close relationships is its basic nature. Erikson (1950) described trust as the starting point for subsequent healthy personality development. In this view, trust influences the quality of personality characteristics that follow it temporally in development. Drawing on Erikson, I suggest that trust in close relationships is fundamental in the following sense: Trust determines the quality of certain subsequently learned personality characteristics, and those personality characteristics do *not* affect how much one trusts intimate others.

TRUST AND EXPLANATORY STYLE

Explanatory style is one personality characteristic that trust in close relationships may affect over time. Specifically, I propose that trusting individuals will develop a more optimistic explanatory style over time, whereas mistrustful individuals will acquire a pessimistic explanatory style. But what is the link between trust and explanatory style?

My definition (Eisner, 1992) suggests that a child's mistrust will grow when significant others repeatedly fail to safeguard his or her emotional, contractual, and/or physical welfare. Empirical work indicates that the nature of these failures changes as a child ages (Rotenberg, 1980). Five-year-old children, for example, mistrust adults who fail to help another child, or fail to be "nice." Seven-year-old children mistrust an adult whose actions are inconsistent with his or her stated intentions; they mistrust an adult who breaks promises.

Repeatedly broken promises and unkind gestures foster mistrust because they harm a child's welfare. Such events are aversive, and the child is likely to experience them as such. Abramson et al. (1978) suggested that environmental situations in which desirable outcomes are likely, and undesirable outcomes are unlikely, prefigure an optimistic explanatory style. Trusting individuals, whose significant others safeguard their welfare, experience fewer aversive events than do mistrustful individuals. Consequently, we should expect that trust will help produce an optimistic explanatory style and mistrust will breed a pessimistic style. The following study was designed to test this expected relationship between trust in close relationships and explanatory style.

Method

Subjects

Subjects were undergraduate students enrolled in introductory psychology courses at the University of Pennsylvania. To encourage participation, we informed students that those who completed all three sets of questionnaires would be entered in a lottery for a cash prize. One hundred thirty-two subjects completed the first set of questionnaires. Of these original subjects, 103 completed the second set of questionnaires, and 95 completed the third set. More than half the subjects (54%) at each questionnaire administration were female. The median age at each questionnaire administration was 19, and the study sample was predominantly White.

Materials

Interpersonal Trust Questionnaire (ITQ; Eisner, 1992).   The ITQ is a 36-item scale designed to measure trust in close relationships. The questionnaire asks about respondents' trust of four significant others: mother, father, spouse (or boyfriend/girlfriend), and closest friend. Respondents are instructed to omit the items pertaining to a particular significant other if they currently do not have such a relationship. For example, a respondent whose mother is deceased would omit all questions pertaining to his or her mother. The average of an individual's responses yields his or her trust score. Scores can range from 1 to 5, with 5 indicating a high degree of trust in intimate others.

The development and validation of the ITQ are detailed elsewhere (see Eisner, 1992). In general, the ITQ is a valid, reliable instrument with good internal consistency. In this sample, test–retest reliability was .80 over a 5-week interval. The scale also demonstrated good internal consistency (Cronbach's alpha = .87).

Attributional Style Questionnaire (ASQ; Peterson et al., 1982).   The ASQ uses 12 hypothetical situations to assess explanatory style. Respondents are instructed to imagine vividly the situation presented in the ASQ. They then state one cause for the situation and answer three multiple-choice questions about the cause. These questions measure the three dimensions of explanatory style: internality, globality, and stability.

Six of the 12 hypothetical events presented in the ASQ are negative, and 6 are positive. Consequently, six subscales can be calculated from the ASQ: the internality, globality, and stability subscales for positive events, and the internality, globality, and stability subscales for negative events. Summing a respondent's scores on each of the positive events subscales yields a composite explanatory style score for positive events (CP). Similarly, summing a respondent's scores on each of the negative events subscales yields a composite explanatory style score for negative events (CN). Subtracting the composite negative score from the composite positive score results in an overall explanatory style score (CPCN).

The internal consistency and reliability of the ASQ were calculated for this sample. CPCN scores demonstrated adequate test–retest reliability over a 5-week interval ($r = .62$) and good internal consistency (Cronbach's alpha = .78).

Procedure

The ITQ and ASQ were administered to subjects three times, referred to as Times 1, 2, and 3. Although two administrations were adequate to test the study hypothesis, a third administration was planned to provide a replication of results.

Five weeks elapsed between each administration. Subjects received the question-naires in class, completed them at home, and returned them on the next day of class.

RESULTS

Two simultaneous findings were necessary to support the hypothesis that trust in close relationships may determine type of explanatory style. First, level of trust must predict subsequent quality of explanatory style. Second, type of ex-planatory style cannot predict later level of trust. Both findings were obtained in a series of regression analyses: (a) mistrust of intimate others predicted a pessimistic explanatory style over time, whereas trust of intimate others predicted an optimistic explanatory style over time, and (b) quality of explanatory style did not predict subsequent degree of trust in intimate others.

Trust As a Predictor of Explanatory Style.   Three regression analyses tested the ability of trust to predict changes in explanatory style over time. For each regression equation, CPCN at Time $n + 1$ was the dependent variable; ITQ at Time n and CPCN at Time n were independent variables. Thus, each regression analysis assessed whether ITQ scores predict subsequent CPCN above and beyond the influence of initial CPCN on subsequent CPCN.

The analyses revealed that, after controlling for initial CPCN, ITQ scores predict subsequent CPCN scores. With CPCN at Time 1 held constant, ITQ scores at Time 1 tended to predict CPCN at Time 2, $F(2, 96) = 1.49$, $p < .06$. With CPCN at Time 2 held constant, ITQ scores at Time 2 predicted CPCN at Time 3, $F(2, 87) = 4.06$, $p < .001$.[2] Finally, with CPCN at Time 1 and at Time 2 held constant, ITQ scores at Time 1 predicted CPCN at Time 3, $F(3, 86) = 2.80$, $p < .01$.

Partial F values, which were all positive, indicated as expected that trust predicts an optimistic explanatory style over time and mistrust predicts a pessimistic explanatory style over time. Three partial correlations were calculated to assess the magnitude of this longitudinal relationship between trust and explanatory style. In each correlation, initial explanatory style was held constant. Results indicated a significant, modest relationship between ITQ scores and subsequent CPCN. With initial CPCN partialed out, the correlations between ITQ at Time 1 and CPCN at Time 2, ITQ at Time 2 and CPCN at Time 3, and ITQ at Time 1 and CPCN at Time 3 were .20 ($p < .05$), .40 ($p < .01$), and .29 ($p < .01$), respectively.

Explanatory Style As a Predictor of Trust.   Regression analyses also dem-onstrated, as expected, that explanatory style does not predict subsequent trust level after controlling for initial trust level. For each of three regression equations,

---

[2] The number of subjects differed for each regression analysis because some subjects completed either the ASQ or the ITQ incorrectly in one or more of the questionnaire administrations.

ITQ at Time $n + 1$ was the dependent variable; CPCN at Time n and ITQ at Time n were independent variables. CPCN at Time 1 did not predict ITQ scores at Time 2 when ITQ scores at Time 1 were held constant, $F(2, 100) = .001$, $p > .88$. Similarly, when ITQ scores at Time 2 were held constant, CPCN at Time 2 did not predict ITQ scores at Time 3, $F(2, 88) = 1.10$, $p > .27$. Finally, CPCN at Time 1 did not predict ITQ scores at Time 3 when ITQ scores at Times 1 and 2 were held constant, $F(3, 91) = .586$, $p > .56$.

Discussion

The results support the hypothesis that trust in close relationships may help determine the quality of one's explanatory style. As expected, degree of trust predicted quality of explanatory style over time, whereas quality of explanatory style did not predict subsequent levels of trust. These results were obtained over two separate 5-week periods and over the total 10-week period. In addition, the longitudinal relationship between trust and explanatory style moved in the expected direction: Mistrust predicted a pessimistic explanatory style, whereas trust predicted an optimistic style.

CONCLUSION

Explanatory style, a complex cognitive phenomenon, is likely to have multiple determinants. Previous work, reviewed in this chapter, suggests at least four different determinants. This chapter proposes that trust in close relationships also plays an important causal role in the development of individual differences in explanatory style. The results reported here suggest that, over time, mistrust may lead to pessimism and trust may foster optimism.

Many avenues for future research exist in this area. Experimental work is necessary to provide direct evidence for a causal link between explanatory style and proposed determinants such as trust in close relationships. Other work might focus on the relative importance of various determinants. Trust and initial explanatory style, for example, account for only half the variance in subsequent explanatory style (rs squared ranged from .41 to .66). Developmental research in this area also may prove fruitful: Quite likely, some determinants wield a greater influence than others at different stages of cognitive and emotional development. In conclusion, research on the origins of explanatory style promises a wealth of intellectual challenges for the future.

ACKNOWLEDGMENT

This material is based on work supported under a National Science Foundation Graduate Fellowship to the author while at the University of Pennsylvania.

4

▼▼▼▼▼▼▼

Explanatory Style and Achievement, Depression, and Gender Differences in Childhood and Early Adolescence

Susan Nolen-Hoeksema
Stanford University

Joan S. Girgus
Princeton University

Although we would like to think of childhood as a time of joy and freedom from stress, some children's lives are not happy. They often are faced with difficult life events, such as their parents' divorce or a serious illness or death in the family. Their work at school may deteriorate. They may become sad, unmotivated, and depressed.

Not all children who face negative life events, however, become depressed or show deterioration in their functioning. Over the last few years, there is increasing evidence that one mediator of children's emotional and behavioral reactions to events is explanatory style. That is, children with a more optimistic, efficacious explanatory style are less likely than children with a more pessimistic style to become frustrated and helpless or to show symptoms of depression.

In this chapter, we review the evidence that children's explanatory styles influence their reactions to events. We also evaluate the evidence for the popular belief that girls are more likely than boys to have a pessimistic explanatory style, which leads them to become helpless in many achievement situations and to be more prone to depression.

Much of the data for this chapter comes from three studies that we have conducted with children ranging in age from 8 to 15. Of these studies, two were longitudinal in design: The first followed 168 third, fourth, and fifth graders for five testing sessions over 15 months; the second began with several hundred third and fourth graders, who were then tested every 6 months for 5 years. The third study was cross-sectional in design; in it, we tested 400 children, approximately evenly divided among Grades 4, 6, 8, and 10, and between boys and girls.

DEVELOPMENT OF EXPLANATORY STYLE
IN CHILDHOOD AND EARLY ADOLESCENCE

In adults, a pessimistic explanatory style, particularly for negative life events, is a risk factor for depression (Peterson & Seligman, 1984a) and affects functioning in such areas as academic achievement (Metalsky, Abramson, Seligman, Semel, & Peterson, 1982), employment (Seligman & Schulman, 1986), and athletics (Seligman, Nolen-Hoeksema, Thornton, & Thornton, 1990). Before asking whether these relationships, or similar ones, hold for children and adolescents as well, we need to know more about the development of explanatory style itself. When and how do explanatory styles emerge during the life course? Do children exhibit optimistic and pessimistic explanatory styles as adults do?

In our studies, we used the Children's Attributional Style Questionnaire (CASQ; Kaslow, Tannenbaum, & Seligman, 1978) to assess the children's explanatory style (see chapter 2). The CASQ has 48 items in which a positive or a negative event is described (e.g., "You get an A on a test.") and then two possible causes of that event are described (e.g., "Because you are good at that subject." and "Because you were lucky."). Children are asked to imagine each event happening to them, then to choose which of the two causes best describes why that event would happen to them. Answers to the 48 items can be scored separately for positive and negative events to indicate the child's tendency to choose internal, stable, and global causes. A pessimistic explanatory style is defined as one in which the causes of bad events are seen as internal, stable, and global and the causes of good events are seen as external, unstable, and specific (Abramson, Seligman, & Teasdale, 1978).

Do children have consistent explanatory styles as adults do (Burns & Seligman, 1989)? In our second longitudinal study, we asked children to fill out the CASQ every 6 months for 5 years. The children were in the third and fourth grades when the study began and in the seventh and eighth grades when the study ended.

TABLE 4.1
Stability Correlations: Fall × Spring Explanatory Style Scores

	Grade			
	4	5	6	7
Positive events	.56	.61	.54	.59
Negative events	.56	.56	.66	.51
Composite scores	.57	.60	.63	.56

$p < .01$.

TABLE 4.2
Stability Correlations: Explanatory Style Over 5 Years

	4th Grade × 5th Grade	4th Grade × 6th Grade	4th Grade × 7th Grade	4th Grade × 8th Grade
Positive events	.54	.45	.27	.35
Negative events	.50	.36	.35	.47
Composite scores	.57	.40	.33	.40

$p < .01.$

Table 4.1 shows the stability correlations for explanatory style scores over the 6-month period from fall to spring for each year of the study; Table 4.2 shows the stability correlations for explanatory style from the first year to the fifth. Overall, explanatory style seems to be fairly stable over middle to late childhood. The fact that the correlations over 5 years are almost as strong as the correlations over 6 months suggests that, for most children, an explanatory style is reasonably well in place by the age of 9, and is then sustained at least until early adolescence. (Later in this chapter, we discuss mechanisms by which explanatory styles might be altered during childhood.)

Table 4.3 shows mean scores on the CASQ for the 5 years of the study. A more pessimistic style is indicated by lower scores for positive events and higher scores for negative events. Between the ages of 9 and 13, explanatory style for positive events becomes somewhat more optimistic, whereas explanatory style for negative events does not change.

Sex Differences in Explanatory Style

Do boys and girls have similar explanatory styles? Table 4.4 shows the means for composite explanatory style (positive events score minus negative events score) for the boys and girls in our 5-year longitudinal study. The boys consistently have more pessimistic explanatory styles than the girls. When the composite scores are broken down into negative events scores and positive events scores, boys are much more pessimistic than girls in their explanations for negative events, but there is no

TABLE 4.3
Mean Explanatory Style Scores

	Grade				
	4	5	6	7	8
Positive events*	13.4	13.2	14.0	14.2	13.7
Negative events	7.5	7.6	7.5	7.6	7.9

*$p < .05.$

TABLE 4.4
Mean Composite Explanatory Style Scores

	Grade				
	4	5	6	7	8
Boys	4.5	4.7	6.1	6.4	5.0
Girls	7.3	6.6	6.9	6.8	6.7

Sex difference: $p < .05$.

difference between the boys and the girls for positive events. In our cross-sectional study, for the same age range of Grades 4–8, a similar picture emerged: The boys were more pessimistic than the girls, although for this sample the difference was stronger for positive events than for negative events.

EXPLANATORY STYLE AND ACADEMIC ACHIEVEMENT

Children's explanations for their performance on school tasks have been a focus in the achievement motivation literature for years (cf. Dweck & Elliott, 1983). Prior to the introduction of the construct of explanatory style in 1978 (Abramson et al., 1978), attribution researchers were concerned primarily with whether children attributed outcomes to stable or unstable factors. Weiner (1974) argued that attributing failures at tasks to stable factors, such as low ability, would lead children to expect that the failure would recur, and thus they would show lowered motivation and persistence. In contrast, attributing failures to unstable factors, such as insufficient effort, would lead children to expect that future failures can be prevented, resulting in no decreases in motivation and persistence. Studies employing a variety of measurement techniques have generally supported these predictions (see reviews by Dweck & Elliott, 1983; Weiner, 1974).

In our 5-year longitudinal study of elementary school children, we have directly assessed the relationships between explanatory style, as defined in the reformulated learned helplessness theory (Abramson et al., 1978), children's achievement-related behaviors (Nolen-Hoeksema, Girgus, & Seligman, 1992), and school achievement (Paul, Girgus, Nolen-Hoeksema, & Seligman, 1989). In addition to the child's self-report of explanatory style on the CASQ every 6 months, the children's teachers rated each child's tendency to show learned helplessness deficits (low motivation, giving up easily, saying "I can't do this") in frustrating achievement-related settings. Finally, we obtained standardized achievement test scores for the children once a year.

There was a slight tendency for children who reported pessimistic explanatory styles to exhibit helplessness behaviors in school achievement settings at the same point in time, according to their teachers (see Table 4.5). This relationship

TABLE 4.5
Concurrent Correlations Between Explanatory Style
and Achievement-Related Helplessness Behaviors

	Grade			
	4	5	6	7,
Boys	−.13	−.23*	−.31*	−.30*
Girls	.02	−.23*	−.11	.14
Total sample	−.06	−.23*	−.24*	−.24*

*p < .05.

seems to increase somewhat for boys as they move from middle to late childhood, whereas for girls, the relationship is more mixed.

If we now ask whether children's pessimistic explanatory style and achievement-related helplessness behaviors in the fall predict their performance on a standardized achievement test in the spring, we find the following (see Table 4.6). There seems to be a weak relationship between explanatory style and academic achievement 6 months later; children with a pessimistic explanatory style do somewhat worse on standardized achievement tests than children with an optimistic explanatory style. There is, however, a strong relationship between teacher reports of helpless behaviors in academic settings and academic achievement 6 months later; the more helpless the child according to the teacher, the less well the child will do on a subsequent achievement test. Thus, teachers clearly are able to identify children prone to helpless behaviors, who may also have problems on standardized achievement tests.

Sex Differences in Explanations for Academic Success and Failure

Several studies on sex differences in explanations for academic success and failure have been conducted with children (e.g., Eccles, Adler, & Meece, 1984;

TABLE 4.6
Correlations Between Fall Explanatory Style and
Achievement-Related Helplessness and Spring Academic Achievement

	Grade			
	4	5	6	7
Fall Expl. Style × Spring Academic Ach.	.11*	.14**	.01	.12
Fall Ach. Helplessness × Spring Academic Ach.	.64***	.25***	.43***	.53***

*p < .10. **p < .05. ***p < .01.

Gitelson, Petersen, & Tobin-Richards, 1982; Nicholls, 1975). Although, on the basis of these studies, it is often claimed that girls make less adaptive explanations for success and failure than boys, the actual results are frequently more complicated. For example, Nicholls (1975) asked children to work on a series of difficult tasks, first in a practice session, then in a test session. Some problems were solvable, others unsolvable. After the practice session, Nicholls asked the children whether they thought their success or failure resulted from luck, ability, effort, or task difficulty; girls were significantly more likely than boys to attribute failures in the practice session to lack of ability, whereas boys were significantly more likely than girls to attribute failures in the practice session to bad luck. No significant sex differences were found, however, in attributions to effort or task difficulty for the practice session or in attributions to effort, ability, luck, or task difficulty for the test sessions. (There also were no sex differences in the children's persistence at test tasks: That is, despite the differences in boys' and girls' attributions about their performance on practice tasks, boys did not persist more at actual test tasks than girls did.) These results clearly are in opposition to the results we reported earlier from the CASQ scores, in which boys were more likely than girls to make attributions that were more internal, stable, and global for negative events and more external, unstable, and specific for positive events.

Many other studies of sex differences in children's explanations for success and failure have found no evidence that girls offer more maladaptive explanations than boys (e.g., Parsons, Meece, Adler, & Kaczala, 1982). Indeed, as we noted earlier, in both our 5-year longitudinal study and our cross-sectional study, we found that, before the age of 13, boys showed a more maladaptive explanatory style than girls (Nolen-Hoeksema et al., 1992).

Why have some previous studies found that girls make more maladaptive explanations for success and failure than boys, when our studies and other studies have found either no sex differences in children's explanations or that boys are more maladaptive than girls in their attributional biases? There are at least three possible explanations for the differences between the results of our studies and other studies of sex differences in children's attributions. First, the methods of assessing explanatory tendencies in our studies and methods in previous achievement motivation studies were very different. In the achievement motivation studies, children were asked for their explanations of their performance on cognitive tasks (e.g., anagrams). In our studies, children were asked for explanations of events in a number of different domains, including schoolwork, peer relationships, family relationships, and extracurricular activities. Perhaps girls do give more maladaptive explanations for academic successes and failures than boys, but boys' explanations for bad events in most other domains are often more maladaptive than girls'. Parsons and her colleagues (1982) found that, even within the realm of academic success and failure, how broadly the questions range across academic subjects can affect the resulting sex differences. When children are asked for their explanations of their performance in feminine-stereotyped subjects (e.g., English), as well as in masculine-stereotyped subjects (e.g., math), no sex differences in explanatory tendencies are found. Thus, the tendency for girls to give more maladaptive explanations found in the achievement motivation literature may be confined to a narrow range of cognitive tasks.

Another difference between previous studies and our studies is that, in previous studies, children usually were asked to voice their explanations of their performance to an experimenter, whereas in our studies, we used a questionnaire to assess explanatory tendencies. Perhaps girls are more modest and boys are more self-aggrandizing in the attributions they voice to an adult but, on a more anonymous questionnaire, boys reveal that they harbor more pessimistic explanatory tendencies than girls. That is, girls may be more self-confident and boys may be less self-confident than they put forward in a public disclosure setting such as a laboratory study.

Finally, in most previous achievement motivation studies, children were asked whether their success or failure at a task was due to task difficulty/ease, effort, luck, or ability. Frieze and Snyder (1980) found that when children are given the opportunity to express spontaneous explanations of their performance, they almost never use luck, and often give explanations other than the typical four, such as "wanting to do well." This suggests that forcing children to choose from among the traditional four attributions leads to a distorted picture of children's true explanatory tendencies. In our studies, children were asked to consider a wide variety of explanations for different events, with the goal of assessing children's tendencies to choose internal versus external, stable versus unstable, and global versus specific explanations. Our results indicate that, when given more opportunity to exercise their explanatory biases, boys reveal a more pessimistic bias than girls.

When we consider the fact that, during childhood, boys tend to perform less well in achievement settings than girls, it is not so surprising that we find boys somewhat more pessimistic in their explanatory styles than girls. That is, previous claims that girls tend to make more pessimistic attributions in achievement settings, and to give up and become helpless more easily, never really fit the data showing that girls are better achievers in elementary school than boys (Maccoby & Jacklin, 1974). The question is, therefore, do girls become more pessimistic than boys later in life and, if so, why? We take up this question later in the chapter.

EXPLANATORY STYLE AND DEPRESSION IN CHILDHOOD AND EARLY ADOLESCENCE

Traditional psychoanalytic theory held that children were too immature psychologically to engage in the processes that lead to depression (Rie, 1966). Since the 1970s, however, it has become clear that children, particularly after age 6, can experience and report adultlike symptoms of depression (cf. Kovacs & Beck, 1977; Puig-Antich, 1986). Studies of depressive symptoms in school-aged children show that approximately 10%–23% of children report mild-to-moderate levels of depression at any given time (Nolen-Hoeksema et al., 1986; Smucker, Craighead, Craighead, & Green, 1986). Depressions that meet psychiatric criteria for disorders are less common in children; only 2%–5% of school-aged children met the criteria for a unipolar depression in one large study in which children in the general population participated in psychiatric interviews (Anderson, Williams, McGee, & Silva, 1987).

Some theorists have argued that, although children may experience depressive symptoms, these symptoms usually remit quickly and should not be taken too seriously (cf. Lefkowitz & Burton, 1978). Yet, in our longitudinal study of school-aged children, we found that children's levels of depression, as assessed by the Children's Depression Inventory (CDI; Kovacs, 1985), remained remarkably stable over 5 years ($r = .53$; Nolen-Hoeksema et al., 1992). In addition, the children with high levels of depressive symptoms showed chronic deficits in social skills and achievement-oriented behaviors. Similarly, in a study of 65 school-aged children with diagnosed unipolar depressive disorders, Kovacs and colleagues found that the mean duration of Major Depressive Episodes was 32 weeks (Kovacs, Feinberg, Crouse-Novak, Paulauskas, & Finkelstein, 1984). Of the children with the diagnosis of Dysthymic disorder, 21% had been experiencing this level of depression for over 5 years. Thus, a substantial minority of children experience moderate-to-severe depression, and these depressions are likely to persist for long periods of childhood.

Explanatory Style as a Risk Factor for Depression

Several studies indicate that children with more pessimistic explanatory styles, according to their CASQ scores, give more depressed responses on self-report depression scales (Kaslow, Rehm, & Siegel, 1984; Nolen-Hoeksema et al., 1986, 1992; Seligman et al., 1984). In addition, children with diagnosed depressive disorders show more pessimistic explanatory styles than nondepressed children (Asarnow, Carlson, & Guthrie, 1987; Kaslow et al., 1984; McCauley, Mitchell, Burke, & Moss, 1988). The strength of the relationship between explanatory style and depression may increase with age. Nolen-Hoeksema et al. (1992) found that the correlation between CASQ scores and self-report depression scores was .24 in a sample of third graders, but when the same children were in the seventh grade, the correlation was .48. As children develop cognitively, they become more likely to think of themselves and their actions in terms of stable traits and talents (Harter, 1983). Some children have a negative perspective on their traits and talents, and this perspective appears to be more closely linked with their emotional well-being as they grow older.

Correlations do not establish causation, however. What is the evidence that a pessimistic explanatory style leads to depression in children? Our longitudinal studies were designed to address this question. In both our longitudinal studies, we found that children with pessimistic explanatory styles at one point in time were more likely to be depressed at a later point, even after we controlled for the children's initial levels of depression (Nolen-Hoeksema et al., 1986, 1992). This suggests that children with pessimistic explanatory styles are more likely to become depressed or to remain depressed over time.

What leads some children to develop a pessimistic explanatory style? In our 5-year longitudinal study, one experience that appeared to lead to changes in explanatory style was an episode of depression (Nolen-Hoeksema et al., 1992). Children who had a period of depression developed more pessimistic explanatory styles while they were depressed. Moreover, after the children's depression levels subsided, their explanatory styles remained just as pessimistic as they had been at the peak of their depression. There was no evidence, even 2 years after the children first developed high levels of depressive symptoms, that their explanatory styles were improving, even though their levels of depressive symptoms had declined significantly by that time. Thus, depression seemed to lead children to develop a more pessimistic explanatory style, which they retained even after their depression had passed.

How would depression lead to a pessimistic explanatory style in a child? Depression is often accompanied by achievement problems and low peer status (Nolen-Hoeksema et al., 1986, 1992). Repeated failures in school and interactions with peers could convince a child that bad events are stable, global, and internally caused. Also, negative life events may lead to both a depressed mood in a child and a conviction that bad things continually happen and there is nothing he or she can do to prevent them. Yet, regression analyses in our 5-year longitudinal study suggested that the children's explanatory styles for negative events worsened if they experienced elevated depressive symptoms, whether or not they were also experiencing negative life events, problems in achievement-related behaviors or social skills, or low peer popularity. This suggests that depression may affect children's explanatory styles through other mechanisms. Depressed affect tends to bias information processing so that negative thoughts and interpretations of events are more accessible (Blaney, 1986; Bower, 1981). Perhaps a child who is depressed for a substantial period during the development of his or her explanatory style develops a pessimistic style because pessimistic cognitions are highly accessible and salient.

These results suggest that interventions should be considered for children with moderate-to-high levels of depression, both so that their depression subsides and so that they do not develop pessimistic explanatory styles. Cognitive-behavioral interventions designed to change pessimistic cognitive styles have only recently been adapted for children (cf. Gillham, Reivich, Jaycox, & Seligman, 1993; Jaycox, Reivich, Gillham, & Seligman, 1993; Meyers & Craighead, 1984; Stark, 1990). The few available studies of the efficacy of cognitive-restructuring treatments for depressed children suggest that such treatments can be successful in reducing negative cognitions and depression (Butler, Miezitis, Friedman, & Cole, 1980; Reynolds & Coats, 1986; Stark, 1990; Stark, Reynolds, & Kaslow, 1987). Additional studies are needed to determine whether these improvements persist over time.

Sex Differences in Depression and Explanatory Style

One of the most reliable findings in the epidemiology of depression is that adult women are about twice as likely to be depressed as men (Nolen-Hoeksema, 1987, 1990; Weissman & Klerman, 1977). This result has been obtained for both subclinical levels of depressive symptoms and for diagnosable depressive disorders. This difference in rates of depression is not apparent among children, however. Most studies of preadolescent children find either that there are no sex differences in rates of depression, or that boys are somewhat more likely to be depressed than girls (Anderson et al., 1987; Kashani, Cantwell, Shekim, & Reid, 1982; Nolen-Hoeksema et al., 1992). But, sometime between the ages of 12 and 15, girls begin to show higher rates of depression than boys (Allgood-Merten, Lewinsohn, & Hops, 1990; Girgus, Nolen-Hoeksema, & Seligman, 1989; A. Petersen, Sarigiani, & Kennedy, 1991). This greater rate of depression in females has been obtained for every adult age group except the elderly (Nolen-Hoeksema, 1990).

How is explanatory style related to the pattern of sex differences in childhood and adolescence? As discussed earlier, although prepubescent girls may make more pessimistic attributions than boys in laboratory achievement tasks (e.g., Dweck & Gilliard, 1975), girls show more optimistic explanatory styles than boys on questionnaires that ask about a variety of situations (Nolen-Hoeksema et al., 1992). Of course, this fits with the pattern of sex differences in depression before puberty: Boys are somewhat more likely than girls to be depressed.

In our cross-sectional study of 4th, 6th, 8th, and 10th graders, we explored changes with age in sex differences in depressive symptoms. As shown in Table 4.7, depressive symptoms declined with age for boys and increased with age (particularly between Grades 6 and 8) for girls. As a result of these age trends, there was a significant interaction between age and gender; the 4th- and 6th-grade boys had higher levels of depressive symptoms than the girls, whereas the 8th- and 10th-grade girls had higher levels of depressive symptoms than the boys. This pattern is consonant with other data in the literature that suggests that, before puberty, there are either no sex differences in depression or boys are more likely to be depressed than girls, whereas after puberty, girls and women have substan-

TABLE 4.7
Mean Depressive Symptoms Scores

	Grade			
	4	*6*	*8*	*10*
Boys	8.0	7.3	7.8	6.8
Girls	6.7	6.7	9.8	9.2

tially higher levels of depressive symptoms than boys and men, a sex difference that continues until old age (Nolen-Hoeksema, 1990).

Are there changes in explanatory style scores that presage, parallel, or follow these changes in depression scores? As Table 4.8 shows, in the explanatory style data from this cross-sectional study, the 4th-, 6th-, and 8th-grade boys were somewhat more pessimistic than the girls, whereas the 10th-grade girls were slightly more pessimistic than the boys. The data for the girls in this study paralleled the depression data; the girls became both more depressed and more pessimistic between 6th and 8th grade. Conversely, the boys had fewer depressive symptoms as they grew older but became steadily more pessimistic until 8th grade, and then rebounded to their 4th-grade level of pessimism in 10th grade.

Thus, the data from this study suggest a switch in the direction of sex differences in depression between ages 11 and 13: Before this age period, boys are more likely to be depressed than girls but, after this age period, girls are more likely to be depressed than boys. There is also a suggestion in the data that both girls and boys become more pessimistic between ages 11 and 13, but, whereas boys rebound and become more optimistic between ages 13 and 15, girls continue to be as pessimistic at 15 as they were at 13.

How might we explain a pattern in which girls and boys both become more pessimistic with the onset of adolescence but boys then become more optimistic as they move through adolescence, whereas girls continue to be quite pessimistic? We outline three explanations here, although there may be others.

First, other people's expectations for and evaluations of girls and boys, and their attributions for girls' and boys' successes and failures, may become increasingly sex-biased as children grow older. Several studies of adults have shown that the qualifications and performances of women are evaluated more negatively than those of men, even when those qualifications and performances are identical (see Wallston & O'Leary, 1981). For example, Firth (1982) found that, when a job application with a male name on it was sent to an accounting firm, the applicant was more likely to pass an initial screening than when the same application was submitted with a female name on it. Sex-linked biases in evaluations appear to be stronger when the criteria for evaluation are relatively subjective and ambiguous (Basow, 1986). As children enter high school, college, and the world of work, evaluations of them probably become more and more subjective, thus making the opportunities for sex biases in evaluations more

TABLE 4.8
Mean Composite Explanatory Style Scores

	Grade			
	4	*6*	*8*	*10*
Boys	4.4	3.6	2.4	4.2
Girls	4.9	5.2	3.1	3.7

likely. This may undermine their self-esteem at a time when they are struggling with identity issues.

Similarly, other people's attributions for girls' and boys' successes and failures may become increasingly sex-biased as children grow older. For adults, there seem to be reliable biases in the attributions people make for men's and women's performances. In general, when a man does well at a task, evaluators tend to attribute his success to ability but, when a woman succeeds, they tend to attribute her success to luck. Conversely, when a man fails, his failure is often attributed to bad luck but, when a woman fails, her failure is often attributed to lack of ability (see Basow, 1986; Feather & Simon, 1975; Taynor & Deaux, 1973). These attributional biases are stronger for competitive, masculine-stereotyped tasks than for tasks that are traditionally seen as "women's work." But, competitive, masculine-stereotyped tasks are more highly valued than feminine-stereotyped tasks (Deaux & Taynor, 1973), and thus, the negative attributional biases that women face appear to operate most strongly in tasks that are highly valued.

As girls grow older and attempt to compete in highly valued areas (e.g., science, medicine, higher paid working-class jobs), they may increasingly face messages that their accomplishments are due to external, unstable, specific factors (e.g., luck, affirmative action programs) and failures are due to internal, stable, and global factors (e.g., lack of ability, "women's weak personality"). If they internalize these messages, girls could develop more and more pessimistic explanatory styles. In turn, boys may increasingly receive messages that their accomplishments are due to internal, stable, and global factors (e.g., ability) and their failures are due to external, unstable, and specific factors (e.g., affirmative action programs). Thus, boys may develop an increasingly optimistic explanatory style, or at least maintain the optimism they have as children.

Second, the actual amount of control and number of opportunities girls have in their lives may decrease as they grow older. The evaluative and attributional biases just described appear to contribute to women getting fewer rewards for their accomplishments and fewer opportunities to compete (Firth, 1982; Heilman & Guzzo, 1978). As girls and boys reach adolescence, adults, especially parents, may, for safety and other reasons, restrict the opportunities that girls have to try new activities, while encouraging boys to do more things on their own (Simmons & Blyth, 1987). Outright job discrimination and sexual harassment of women on the job and in schools exist, and may impact on women's advancements and their well-being (Crosby, 1982; Hamilton, Alagna, King, & Lloyd, 1987; Nolen-Hoeksema, 1990). Furthermore, sexual abuse of females increases in adolescence and clearly contributes to helplessness and depression in some women (Cutler & Nolen-Hoeksema, 1991; Nolen-Hoeksema, 1990). All of these types of experiences may lead adolescent girls or young women to believe that the causes of negative events in their lives are stable and global. Indeed, one of the most stable and global attributions they may make for these events is that they are female. Because adolescent boys and young men face such experiences much less often, they can develop their talents and exploit opportunities as they grow older.

Third, there is evidence that, in early adolescence, some girls become very concerned about one characteristic of themselves that is frustratingly stable and seems to affect many areas of their lives: their physical appearance. Girls appear to dislike the physical changes they undergo in puberty, especially the weight and fat they gain and the loss of the long, lithe, prepubescent look that is idealized in modern fashions; in contrast, boys like the increase in muscle mass and other pubertal changes their bodies undergo (Dornbusch et al., 1984; A. Petersen, 1979; Simmons, Blyth, Van Cleave, & Bush, 1979). In turn, body satisfaction appears to be more closely related to self-esteem and depression in girls than in boys (Allgood-Merten, Lewinsohn, & Hops, 1990; Lerner & Karabenick, 1974). Thus, girls' attitudes toward their physical changes at puberty are more negative than boys' and, at the same time, girls' self-esteem is more tied to their body image than boys'. Further, girls are pressured by society to achieve an ideal body shape that, for most of them, is impossible to achieve. Thus, many girls may experience frustration and helplessness trying to control their body shape. This frustration and helplessness of girls who try unsuccessfully to control their body shape (and the social status in which it plays a role) may lead some girls to develop a pessimistic way of explaining other events in their lives (cf. McCarthy, 1990).

Clearly, much more research is needed before we know what changes girls' and boys' explanatory styles undergo from childhood into early adolescence and adulthood, and the link between these changes and the increase in depression in females relative to males that occurs at the same time. This seems an important area for research. The more we understand about the emergence of sex differences in depression and explanatory style in adolescence, the better able we may be to prevent the abundance of depression in adult women.

SUMMARY

Children apparently develop quite consistent explanatory styles by the age of 9; that is, by middle childhood, they have developed characteristic ways of explaining the good and bad things that happen in their lives. As a result, individual children are more or less pessimistic or optimistic (i.e., believe that the causes of negative events are internal, stable, and global or, alternatively, believe that the causes of negative events are external, unstable, and specific). During middle and late childhood, there is either no sex difference in explanatory style, or boys are more pessimistic than girls. Among adolescents and adults, there is either no sex difference in explanatory style, or girls and women are more pessimistic than boys and men.

Attributing failure at academic tasks to stable factors apparently results in the expectation of continued failure and lowered motivation and persistence. Children who are more pessimistic are more likely to exhibit helplessness behaviors in academic-achievement settings; children who exhibit helplessness behaviors have lower achievement test scores. Some studies have found that girls make less adaptive explanations for academic success and failure, whereas other studies have found no sex difference, and still others have found that boys make less adaptive explanations. There are at least three possible reasons for these disparate results: Some of the studies asked children for explanations of their performance on cognitive tasks, whereas others asked children for explanations of events in a number of different domains, including schoolwork, peer relationships, family relationships, and extracurricular activities; some of the studies asked children to voice their explanations to an adult experimenter whereas others used an anonymous questionnaire; and some of the studies asked children to choose among explanations that they rarely use spontaneously.

Children with more pessimistic explanatory styles are more depressed on self-report depression scales, and the correlation between explanatory style and depression increases with age. Children with pessimistic explanatory styles at one point in time are more likely to be depressed at a later point, even after controlling for their initial levels of depression. Children with pessimistic explanatory styles are more likely to become or to remain depressed over time. An episode of depression seems to lead to the development of a more pessimistic explanatory style, that then remains even after the levels of depressive symptoms have subsided. Prior to adolescence, either boys are more likely to be depressed than girls, or boys and girls are equally likely to be depressed; by the middle of adolescence, girls are much more likely to be depressed, and this sex difference continues until old age. Although explanatory style is clearly correlated with depression in adults, we do not know yet whether a switch in sex differences in explanatory style contributes to the increase in depression in girls in adolescence.

5

▼▼▼▼▼▼▼

The Role of Causal Attributions in the Prediction of Depression

Clive J. Robins
Adele M. Hayes
Duke University Medical Center

Although the concept of *explanatory* or *attributional style* has been extended to a broad range of human behavior, as evidenced by this volume, its roots are in the reformulated learned helplessness theory of depression (Abramson, Seligman, & Teasdale, 1978). The development of that theory is described in chapter 1 of this volume; it is important here only to note that there are several links in the chain of the theory, from uncontrollable or negative outcomes, to the types of casual explanations that a person makes for such outcomes, to expectations of future controllability or lack of control over outcomes, to the symptoms of depression. The theory also proposes that individuals differ systematically in their propensity to make internal, stable, and global causal attributions for negative outcomes, referred to as a pessimistic or depressogenic *explanatory style*. This theory has generated a vast body of research but, unfortunately, much of it has concerned simply whether there is a link between the types of attributions that an individual makes and their depressive symptoms. Research has often ignored the other variables in the model and, therefore, has not tested it adequately. Over the past decade, however, these studies have become increasingly sophisticated, generally moving from concurrent to prospective designs, and from examining only the bivariate relations between attributions and depression to more complex, diathesis-stress designs that also incorporate the occurrence of negative outcomes and their interaction with explanatory style.

In this chapter, we begin with a review of the empirical evidence regarding the association between causal attributions and depression. Then we address some possible reasons why some of these studies may have failed to obtain positive findings, specifically, the roles of inadequate sample sizes and the psychometric limitations of the measures used. Following this, we take up several theoretical issues that remain unresolved, including: (a) whether explanatory style plays a causal role in the development of depression, or is simply a concomitant feature; (b) whether a maladaptive explanatory style is specific to depression or only some subtypes of depression, or is found also in other psychiatric disorders; (c) whether the attributions of depressed persons reflect a negative bias, or are actually more accurate than those of nondepressed persons; and (d) the possible need to expand or refine the model by incorporating other important psychological variables, including the interactions of attributions and events in specific content domains.

RELATIONS BETWEEN CAUSAL ATTRIBUTIONS AND DEPRESSION

In this section, we discuss first the findings from concurrent design studies of depression and attributions for negative events, then prospective studies, followed by diathesis-stress studies. Finally, we discuss the relation of depression to attributions for positive events. Studies of different populations are reviewed separately, because there remains much controversy over whether clinical depression lies on a continuum with the mildly dysphoric mood states commonly studied in undergraduate samples, or whether it represents a different entity that may have a different etiology. We distinguish also between subjects' causal attributions for hypothetical events and those for their own naturally occurring events. As we do not believe that attributions for experimental tasks accurately reflect the attributions that individuals make for actual events in their lives they are not included in this review.

Concurrent Design Studies

College Students.   Most studies of this population of convenience have assessed causal attributions only for hypothetical situations, typically using the Attributional Style Questionnaire (ASQ; Peterson et al., 1982). Although these studies are too numerous to describe individually here, the composite of all three dimensions (internal, stable, and global) of attributions for negative events, that we henceforth refer to as *composite negative* (CN), almost always has been found to be significantly related to depression (Robins, 1988). However, in most studies in which the three dimensions have been examined separately, some dimensions are significant and others not, with little consistency across studies (Robins, 1988).

Relatively few studies have examined the causal attributions that college students make for their own naturally occurring negative events. In most of these studies, only the globality dimension was significantly related to depression (Cochran & Hammen, 1985; Hammen & Cochran, 1981; Hammen, Krantz, & Cochran, 1981; Robins & Block, 1989).

Depressed Adult Patients. There is strong support for the prediction that depressed patients and nondepressed controls differ significantly on the CN composite as well as each of the separate dimensions (e.g., Eaves & Rush, 1984; Hamilton & Abramson, 1983; Raps, Peterson, Reinhard, Abramson, & Seligman, 1982). As in the studies with college students, however, these attributional differences are less consistent for naturally occurring events. Miller, Klee, and Norman (1982) found depressed patients scored higher than nondepressed controls on the attributional composite concerning their own stressful events. Cochran and Hammen (1985) found both internal and global attributions for stressful events to be related to level of depression, but Gong-Guy and Hammen (1980) reported group differences only on the internal dimension.

Postpartum Women. In the relatively few studies of postpartum women, there is little support for a concurrent relation between attributions and depression. No such relations were found for any of the ASQ attribution dimensions or composite (Manly, McMahon, Bradley, & Davidson, 1982), nor for postpartum womens' attributions for child-care stress nor daily events (Cutrona, 1983). However, depressive symptoms were related to their causal attributions for "maternity blues" (Cutrona, 1983).

Children and Adolescents. Several studies with essentially unselected children found their level of depression to be related to CN on the Childrens Attributional Style Questionnaire (CASQ; Blumberg & Izard, 1985; Kaslow, Rehm, & Siegel 1984; Robins & Hinkley, 1989; Seligman et al., 1984). Of these studies, two reported on the separate dimensions. Seligman et al. (1984) reported significant relations for all three, whereas Robins and Hinkley (1989) found support only for the stability dimension.

Asarnow and Bates (1988) found that inpatient depressed children scored significantly higher than nondepressed psychiatric inpatient children on the CN, although only a subgroup (55%) of their depressed children showed elevated scores. Studies of clinically disturbed adolescents have not found concurrent relations between attributions for negative events and depression (Benfield, Palmer, Pfefferbaum, & Stowe, 1988; Curry & Craighead, 1990). However, in both of these studies the more depressed adolescents did report more external, unstable, and specific attributions for positive events. These convergent findings of a relation of depression with attributions for positive, but not for negative events, is intriguing and warrants attempts at replication.

As far as we can determine, no studies have examined how depression in children or adolescents is related to their attributions for events that actually occur to them.

Other Populations. Feather (1983) found level of depression among combined samples of 69 unemployed, 78 employed, and 101 student subjects to be related to the internality, stability, and globality of their attributions for hypothetical events, though these relations were all small and most were significant only with a one-tailed test. With regard to actual events, Feather and Barber (1983) reported an unusual finding; although scores on the Beck Depression Inventory (BDI) were significantly related to the internality of mens' attributions for their own unemployment, a measure of depressive affect alone was related to more external attributions for unemployment. This finding is difficult to interpret. In a study of school teachers, Hammen and deMayo (1982) found that levels of depression were not significantly related to either the internality nor stability (they did not assess globality) of attributions for real stressful events.

In summary, there is fairly strong evidence for a concurrent relation between depression and causal attributions for hypothetical negative events among college students, adult clinical samples, and both normal and clinical samples of children. The evidence regarding attributions for actual events in these populations is much weaker. There is little or no support for such a relation among postpartum women, adolescent clinical samples, unemployed men, or school teachers, for either hypothetical or actually occurring events.

Prospective Studies

In general, the relatively few studies that have looked prospectively at the relations of either explanatory style or attributions for particular events to later depression have been far less supportive than investigations of their concurrent relations.

College Students. Although an early study by Golin, Sweeney, and Schaeffer (1981) found support for a prospective relation of ASQ stable, global, and composite measures to later depression, other prospective studies with undergraduates have failed to find any significant relation of negative ASQ or actual event attributions to later depression (Cochran & Hammen, 1985; Needles & Abramson, 1990; Peterson, Schwartz, & Seligman, 1981).

Depressed Adult Patients. Surprisingly, there are almost no prospective studies of attributions for negative events among currently depressed patients. Firth and Brewin (1982) reported that among depressed patients, stable attributions for, and perceived lack of control over, their own naturally occurring stressful events were both related to later levels of depression, whereas internal and global attributions were not. Cochran and Hammen (1985) found none of the attribution dimensions for stressful events to be related to later depression levels among older depressed patients.

Postpartum Women. Results of several studies that have followed women prospectively from pregnancy into the postpartum period have been mixed. O'Hara, Rehm, and Campbell (1982) found that depression level postpartum was significantly predicted by the difference between the ASQ negative and positive event composite scores (CN and CP) during pregnancy. Cutrona (1983) obtained a similar finding for CN alone. Similar studies, however, have found no prospective relations between women's postpartum depression levels and their ASQ scores during pregnancy (Manly et al., 1982; O'Hara, Neunaber, & Zekoski 1984) nor their attributions for their most upsetting recent naturally occurring event (Whiffen, 1988).

Children and Adolescents. We located only one prospective study of the relations between attributions and depression in children and none in adolescents. Seligman et al. (1984) reported that the CN scores of 96 third- to sixth-grade children on the CASQ were related to their depressive symptoms 6 months later, after controlling for depression level at the initial assessment.

Community Subjects. One prospective study has received much attention because of its large sample. Lewinsohn, Steimmetz, Larson, and Franklin (1981) followed a large community sample over several months, and compared subjects who developed an episode of depression ("onset cases") with those who were not depressed at any time during the study ("noncases"). These two groups did not differ on any of the cognitive measures administered, including a measure of internal versus external attributions. It should be noted, however, that this study did not use the ASQ, but rather a locus of control measure that has not been used widely in attribution research.

In summary, studies with college students, adult clinical samples, and a community sample provide little or no support for a prospective relation between causal attributions for hypothetical or actual negative events and later depression. The studies of postpartum depression provide very mixed evidence, and the positive findings for children are based on only one study.

Diathesis-Stress Studies

It is clear from the preceding review that many studies did not find significant relations between attributions and depressive symptoms. Even in those that did, the size of the relations was typically modest. Although this might at first seem to call into question the reformulated learned helplessness theory, the logic of that theory actually does not require a strong bivariate relation between attributions and depression, either concurrently or prospectively. The theory states that it is only when individuals are faced with negative, and particularly uncontrollable negative, events that the particular attributions they make for the events will, in turn, influence their levels of depressive symptoms. If differing levels of stressful events among subjects are not considered in the analysis, then subjects with very low levels of stressful life events would dilute the relations found between attributions and depressive symptoms. Relatively few studies so far have included measures of both attributions (the proposed diathesis) and life events (the proposed stress) and examined the interactions between these two sets of variables in predicting depression.

Concurrent Design Diathesis-Stress Studies. Robins and Block (1989) found that levels of depressive symptoms among 83 undergraduates were related to the interaction of CN scores on the ASQ and frequency of recent negative life events. Consistent with the model, the relation between negative life events and depressive symptoms was greater among subjects who had a more dysfunctional explanatory style. This interaction, however, was not significant for any of the individual attribution dimensions, nor were attributions for actual events related to the corresponding ASQ measure, nor to the interaction of the ASQ and event frequency. Rothwell and Williams (1983) examined the interaction of attributions and events by comparing men who recently had become unemployed with those who remained employed. Depressive symptom levels were associated with ASQ negative internal scores for the unemployed men, but not for the employed subjects, consistent with the idea that a tendency toward self-blame would accentuate the effect of unemployment on depression. Depression level was not significantly related to ASQ stability nor globality scores for either subject group. In the only concurrent diathesis-stress analysis with a clinical sample (psychiatric inpatients), no significant relation between level of depressive symptoms and the interaction of ASQ negative scores with frequency of recent life events was found (Persons & Rao, 1985).

Prospective-Design Diathesis-Stress Studies. An adequate test of the reformulated learned helpless model requires, at least, a prospective study that examines the interaction of explanatory style and stressful events that occur between the baseline and later assessments. Only three such studies have been published to date and all used college students as subjects. The relevance of these studies to clinical depression remains to be determined.

Metalsky, Abramson, Seligman, Semmel, and Peterson (1982) reported that ASQ internal and global attributions were related to depressed mood following an examination among students who failed to achieve a grade with which they would be satisfied, but not among students who succeeded in meeting their goals, thus demonstrating the hypothesized diathesis-stress interaction. However, a post hoc analysis of these data demonstrated that the differences between the correlations for the two groups did not differ significantly (Williams, 1985). Partly in response to this critique, Metalsky, Halberstadt, and Abramson (1987) replicated and expanded upon the earlier study. They extended the ASQ to contain 12 negative outcomes rather than 6, which increased its reliability, and examined subjects' attributions for hypothetical achievement and interpersonal events separately. Attributional style was assessed by a "generality" measure (the sum of stability and globality), because more recent theoretical statements (e.g., Abramson, Metalsky, & Alloy, 1989) propose that only these dimensions are related to depressive symptoms in general, and the internal dimension to self-esteem. Immediately after the examination, students' moods were related to their examination results, but not to their explanatory style nor to the interaction of explanatory style and examination performance. However, 2 days later, mood levels were significantly related to the interaction of examination performance and generality scores for achievement events. Failure students who rated negative achievement outcomes on the extended ASQ as due to relatively unstable and specific causes showed an increase in depressed mood immediately after obtaining their examination results, but their mood had improved by 2 days later. Failure students who tended to make stable and global attributions for negative achievement outcomes showed a similar decrement in mood following their poor examination performance, but had not rebounded by 2 days later. This study also demonstrated that subjects' moods were related to the particular attributions that they made for their examination performance and that, in turn, these attributions were related to their scores on the extended ASQ. This finding is consistent with the model's proposition that the effects of explanatory style on mood are mediated by attributions for actual events. This was the first study to examine mood reactions to a negative event in a fine-grained manner over a period of days, and the difference between the immediate postevent results and those obtained several days later is very interesting and merits replication. Metalsky et al. suggested that immediate mood responses may not result from causal attributions, but rather from other cognitions about events, whereas causal attributions are processes that occur later.

Follette and Jacobson (1987) also attempted to replicate Metalsky et al. (1982), using an expanded ASQ (Peterson & Villanova, 1988) that contains 24 hypothetical negative events. They did not replicate the finding of an interaction between explanatory style and performance, but did find that students' attributions for their examination performance predicted depressed mood on the same day they received the examination results. Follette and Jacobson (1987) did not assess mood several days after students received their grades and so may have missed the delayed interaction effect reported by Metalsky et al. (1987). They also did not examine explanatory style for achievement events separately from interpersonal events.

In summary, analyses of the concurrent relation between depression and the interaction of explanatory style with the occurrence of negative events have provided weak or no support for such a relation in college students, unemployed men, and psychiatric patients, whereas prospective studies have been somewhat more supportive, but few in number.

Attributions For Positive Events

Although the reformulated learned helplessness theory does not make any strong predictions about attributions for positive events, Abramson, Garber, Edwards, and Seligman (1978) did speculate that depression also might be related to external, unstable, and specific attributions for positive events—opposite to the pattern for negative events. The proportion of significant findings regarding depression and attributions for positive events is approximately the same as for negative events.

Concurrent-Design Studies. Most concurrent-design studies of college students that examined attributions for positive events have reported some significant relation with depression (an exception is Nezu, Kalmar, Ronan, & Clarijo, 1986). Sweeney, Schaeffer, and Golin (1982) and Nezu, Nezu, and Nezu (1986) reported that the ASQ composite (internal, stable, and global) for positive events (CP) was significantly inversely related to depressive symptoms. Several other studies have found such relations for the composite and also for the internal and stable dimensions (Blaney, Behar, & Head 1980; Carver, Ganellen, & Behar-Mitrani, 1985; Golin et al., 1981). These latter three studies found no significant relation between global attributions for positive events and depressive symptoms, in marked contrast to most findings regarding attributions for negative events, in which the global dimension has received the strongest support (Hammen, 1985; Robins, 1988).

In contrast to the studies with college students, the few studies that have examined attributions for positive events among adult psychiatric patients have generally not found relations with depression (Miller et al., 1982; Heimberg, Vermilyea, Dodge, Becker, & Barlow, 1987). However, Persons and Rao (1985) reported that depression level among psychiatric inpatients was related to more unstable attributions for ASQ positive events and to the interaction of life event frequency with external attributions for positive events.

Studies of children generally have supported a relationship between depression and attributions for positive events as assessed by the CASQ. Among unselected school children, Seligman et al. (1984) found level of depression to be related to all three attribution dimensions, whereas Robins and Hinkley (1989) obtained significant results for the stability dimension only. Blumberg and Izard (1985) reported only the CP scores, which were significantly related to depressive symptoms among girls, but not boys. Significant relations between attributions for CASQ positive events and depression level or diagnosis have been reported in two studies of children seen in an outpatient psychiatric or child guidance clinic (Friedlander, Traylor, & Weiss, 1987; Kaslow et al., 1984), and in two studies of child psychiatric inpatients (Benfield et al., 1988; Curry & Craighead, 1990). No negative results have been reported for clinical child samples.

Prospective-Design Studies. Very few studies have reported on relations between depression and attributions for positive events prospectively. In an early study, Golin et al. (1981) found that only stability was inversely related to later levels of depression among college students. Seligman et al. (1984) reported that CP was not related to depression levels in unselected children 6 months later, when initial depression levels were controlled. It may be that attributions for positive events play a less important role in the development of depression than they do in determining whether the depression is maintained or remits. Needles and Abramson (1990) studied a group of 42 undergraduates who initially scored at least 16 on the BDI, indicating a moderate level of depression. Recovery, defined as a BDI score of 9 or less at a 6-week follow-up, was associated with the interaction of a CP and the frequency of positive events during the follow-up period.

In summary, there is strong support for a concurrent relation between attributions for hypothetical positive events and depression among college students (except for global attributions) and among normal and clinical samples of children, but little support in clinically disturbed adults. There is little evidence regarding a prospective relation with onset or exacerbation of symptoms, but some evidence that attributions for positive events may influence the course of depression.

To summarize this review of the relations between attributions and depression, although a large number of studies have reported findings consistent with the reformulated learned helplessness theory, many other studies, particularly those with a prospective design, have reported less supportive findings, and there is much inconsistency in the literature regarding which particular dimensions are related to depression. Possible explanations for this inconsistent support include: (a) the frequently insufficient power of statistical analyses to detect the relatively modest relations that might exist in the population, (b) insufficiently reliable measurement instruments for the assessment of attributions, (c) the fact that the vast majority of the studies' designs have not adequately instantiated the theoretical model that they purport to test, and (d) the possibility that the theory itself may be in need of further clarification and expansion. The remaining sections of this chapter take up each of these issues in turn.

STATISTICAL POWER CONCERNS

Perhaps because of the inconsistent findings on the relations between attributions and depression, reviewers of this literature have arrived at remarkably different conclusions. Some have suggested that there is little evidence of such relations (Coyne & Gotlib, 1983), or that only global attributions have received fairly consistent support (Hammen, 1985), whereas others have claimed that there is substantial support for all three dimensions (Peterson & Seligman, 1984a; Sweeney, Anderson, & Bailey, 1986). In an attempt to make sense of this inconsistent literature, Peterson, Villanova, and Raps (1985) related the significance status of published analyses to various methodological parameters of the studies. They found that stable and global attributions for negative events and the composite measure, but not internal attributions, were more likely to be significantly related to depression when they were assessed in studies with larger samples, for hypothetical rather than actual events, and for a greater number of events. These factors frequently covaried, however, and it is not possible to determine from the data reported which of these three methodological parameters primarily accounts for the variability in significant findings.

A larger sample size will always, other things being equal, provide greater power for statistical tests to detect true effects that exist in the population and, therefore, would be expected to be one of the most important determinants of whether studies yielded significant findings. Other factors also contribute to statistical power, including design and data analytic considerations, such as reliability of measures and the choice of continuous or categorical scaling of data. Robins (1988) reviewed the published literature on attributions for negative events and depression, and computed the statistical power of the tests conducted in those studies. Of the 87 analyses reported, only 8 (from six studies) had an a priori probability of .80 or better of detecting a small-to-medium size effect (e.g., $r = .20$) if it existed in the population sampled from, and the mean probability for all analyses was only .44. Only 35 of the 87 analyses had .80 power or better to detect even a medium-sized effect (e.g., $r = .30$), and the mean power to detect such an effect was .67. In general, this body of research has been investigated with grossly insufficient statistical power to reject the null hypothesis. Furthermore, level of statistical power strongly affected whether or not studies found a significant relation. For example, considering all studies, only the negative attribution composite was quite consistently related to depression (the individual dimensions being very inconsistent), whereas in the five studies that had high levels of statistical power and reported on all individual dimensions, the stable and global dimensions were also significant. Sweeney et al. (1986) concluded from a meta-analysis that depression was related to all three dimensions. This discrepancy between reviews may have arisen because the meta-analysis procedure cumulates both significant effects and effects that are not significant but are in the predicted direction. It may be, therefore, that there is a small, but relatively elusive, relation of depression to internal attributions.

It is clear that investigators in this area need to be more concerned about the statistical power of their analyses. Three steps in particular would be helpful in enhancing power: (a) the use of more reliable measures of attributional processes in order to increase the effect sizes found; (b) the use of samples of sufficient size, determined prior to the study by computing power for the tests to be conducted, using an estimate of expected effect size; and (c) the use of continuous measures in analyses wherever possible, rather than categorical treatment of data, in order to retain maximally sensitive information.

PSYCHOMETRIC CONCERNS

A number of issues concerning the measurement of explanatory style are the focus of chapter 2 of this volume. Nevertheless, we discuss here how findings on the relations of depression to causal attributions may be influenced by the type and adequacy of attribution measures.

Does the ASQ Measure Explanatory "Style"?

The reformulated learned helplessness model proposes that individuals are relatively consistent in their attributions for the causes of events of a particular valence. This conceptualization underlies the use of the ASQ, in which scores are summed across diverse hypothetical situations. The consistency assumption can be tested by examining the reliability of the ASQ or similar measures. The common practice of summing the scores on the internal, stable, and global dimensions to form a composite score rests on a second assumption that these three dimensions tend to covary. The use of the ASQ as an index of explanatory style also assumes that scores are a good proxy for the attributions that subjects make for their own naturally occurring events. We now examine the empirical evidence regarding each of these three assumptions.

Reliability of the ASQ. Chapter 2 reviews in detail the reliability and validity of various instruments for assessing explanatory style. Many studies have reported internal consistency estimates for the ASQ dimension scores that are at best low to moderate. In perhaps the most compelling (because of its large sample of 1,133 undergraduates) of these studies, Cutrona, Russell, and Jones (1984), reported fairly typical internal consistency estimates of .33, .59, .62, and .66 for the internal, stable, global, and composite scores for negative events, respectively. With regard to stability of scores over time, several studies have reported moderate test retest reliability coefficients, that typically ranged between about .5 and .6 over a period up to 2 months (Cutrona et al., 1984; Johnson & Miller, 1990; Zautra, Guenther, & Chartier, 1985). Reliability coefficients of this magnitude for such a brief interval are less than ideal for personality trait measures, but demonstrate some degree of stability.

Relations Among the Internal, Stable, and Global Dimensions. Only the composite ASQ scores have demonstrated anything approaching acceptable levels of internal consistency. Yet one might question the conceptual legitimacy of forming such a composite unless there is evidence that the three individual dimensions of which it consists covary at least moderately. However, the evidence for this is poor. For example, Zautra et al. (1985) reported that the internal and stable dimensions correlated .01, the internal and global dimensions .27, and the stable and global dimensions .42 in a sample of college students. Robins and Block (1989) reported correlations of .14, .25, and .28, respectively. Although the correlations of the global dimension with the other two dimensions were significant in both studies, even they are relatively low in magnitude. We would argue that these data and the reliability data necessitate that future research will require more reliable measures of each of the individual attribution dimensions than those provided by the ASQ.

Attributions for Hypothetical and Naturally Occurring Events. A number of studies have examined whether purported measures of explanatory style from the ASQ are indeed related to subjects' causal attributions for their own naturally occurring events. In general, these relations have not been strong. Miller et al. (1982) found no significant correlations between psychiatric inpatients' ASQ scores and their attributions for their own most stressful recent life event. Robins and Block (1989) found that students' attributions for their three most upsetting recent events correlated with the corresponding ASQ negative measures only .09, −.06, .20, and .27 for the internal, stable, global, and composite scores, respectively. Cutrona et al. (1984) reported that the internal, stable, global, and composite attributions of 85 postpartum women for child-care stress, maternity blues symptoms, and daily stressors, when averaged, correlated .13, .18, .25, and .19 with the corresponding ASQ negative scores. The results were similar for a group of selected subjects who were highly consistent on the ASQ. One study reported somewhat more positive findings. Zautra et al. (1985) had students complete a 14-day log of their single most positive and negative daily events and their causal attributions for them. The investigators did not report the relations for the individual dimension scores, but did report a correlation of .55 between the log for negative events and CN scores and a correlation of .38 between log positive events and CP scores. With the exception of this one study, there is little evidence that the ASQ is a reasonable proxy for actual event attributions. Some investigators have even suggested that, because the types of situations described on the ASQ are so dissimilar to the severe events and chronic difficulties often associated with clinical depression (Brown & Harris, 1978), the ASQ or other measures involving hypothetical situations are unlikely to be useful in studying clinical depression (Brewin, 1985; Hammen, 1985). However, recent studies that have employed extended or expanded versions of the ASQ have reported somewhat more encouraging results regarding their relations with attributions for actual events (Follette & Jacobson 1987; Metalsky et al., 1987; Peterson & Villanova, 1988). We now discuss these new measures further.

Newer Measures

In the past several years, at least two new questionnaires for assessing explanatory style have been developed in response to perceived psychometric limitations of the ASQ (see chapter 2 this volume). Peterson and Villanova (1988) retained the 6 negative events of the ASQ and added 18 more for a total of 24 negative events in their Expanded ASQ (EASQ). Internal consistencies in a sample of 139 students were .66, .85, and .88 for the internal, stable, and global dimensions, respectively, figures that are considerable higher than those typically reported for the original ASQ, and that were replicated almost exactly by Follette and Jacobson (1987). Peterson and Villanova (1988) reported correlations of the EASQ dimensions with depression similar in magnitude to those usually found with the original ASQ. Correlations with the corresponding scores for subjects' naturally occurring events of .32, .18, and .36 for internal, stable, and global attributions, respectively (Peterson & Villanova, 1988) and .38 for the composite scores (Follette & Jacobson, 1987) have been reported. Together, these findings provide strong support for the reliability, and moderate support for the construct validity, of the EASQ. Peterson and Villanova (1988) noted that the internal versus external dimension on their measure still is not adequately reliable and suggested that it may represent a multidimensional construct.

Metalsky et al. (1987) also developed an "extended ASQ," which consists of 12 negative outcomes—6 achievement-related and 6 interpersonal. They did not report on the three individual dimensions, but only on a generality measure. Coefficient alpha for generality in a sample of 94 undergraduates was .79 for negative achievement outcomes and .77 for negative interpersonal outcomes. These figures are close to, although somewhat lower than, the figures reported by Peterson and Villanova (1988) for the stable and global dimensions, possibly because the Metalsky et al. (1987) measure consists of half the number of items, that were then subdivided for analysis into achievement and interpersonal items, leaving only 6 items per scale rather than 24. Nonetheless, the reliabilities obtained by Metalsky et al. (1987) are strong enough for research purposes. Generality for achievement outcomes also quite strongly predicted subjects' attributions for their examination performance ($r = .59$) and their mood responses to achievement failure, as we described earlier. Both the Metalsky et al. (1987) and the Peterson and Villanova (1988) measures show encouraging signs of being improvements over the original ASQ. We look forward to the results of further validation studies of these instruments. One potentially serious limitation of these measures, however, is the high proportion of items that seem relevant primarily to students and young adults (e.g., regarding school and dating situations). There remains a need for reliable measures of explanatory style that are more relevant to other adult populations.

To date, there is relatively little evidence that individuals typically spontaneously make causal attributions when thinking about stressful events (a key assumption of the reformulated learned helplessness model), nor whether such spontaneous attributions are related to those given when solicited by a questionnaire like the ASQ (see chapter 2). Such evidence may now be more readily obtained. Seligman, Peterson, and colleagues (1984) developed a coding system for extracting causal attributions or explanations for events from naturally occurring speech or text—the Content Analysis of Verbatim Explanations (CAVE). In an initial study of this procedure, Peterson, Bettes, and Seligman (1985) demonstrated that adequate interjudge agreement on the causes and attributions extracted using the CAVE procedures can be obtained; they reported correlations with depressive symptom levels that ranged between .29 and .36 across the internal, stable, global, and composite measures. However, only the internal dimension correlated significantly with its corresponding ASQ measure, and the internal consistencies of the CAVE dimensions were very modest and indeed poorer even than those of the ASQ. Of note, attributions were assessed for only two events; the procedure may need to be used across a greater number of situations in order to derive an internally consistent measure of explanatory style. Riskind, Castellon, and Beck (1989) used the CAVE procedure to analyze daily thought records of psychiatric outpatients in the early stages of cognitive therapy. They found that patients with major depression scored significantly higher on stable and global, but not internal, explanations for bad events than patients with generalized anxiety disorder. Depressed patients also scored higher than the norms for students from a different study, whereas generalized anxiety subjects did not. This study therefore demonstrated that the CAVE procedure can provide useful data with psychiatric patients. However, it did not test the utility of this measure against the ASQ. In a study somewhat relevant to this comparison, Schulman, Castellon, and Seligman (1989) extracted the causes that undergraduates wrote for the hypothetical events of the ASQ and rated them using the CAVE procedure. Attribution dimensions scored by the CAVE procedure showed good internal consistency and correlated quite strongly with subjects' own dimension ratings ($r = .48$ for the CN score). Both measures correlated significantly with level of depressive symptoms. It should be noted that this study does not address the issue of whether subjects make spontaneous causal attributions that are related to depression, but rather is a study of whether judges and subjects agree on the dimension ratings of subjects' casual attributions. The results do suggest that the CAVE is a viable option for assessing attributions when subjects can not fill out a questionnaire measure.

EXPERIMENTAL DESIGN CONCERNS

As our earlier review indicated, the great majority of studies of causal attributions and depression have used a design inadequate for testing the reformulated learned helplessness model. A number of design issues need to be addressed in future work in order to test the model more specifically, several of which we discuss later (see Alloy, Hartlage, & Abramson, 1988 for a more elaborated discussion of these and other design issues).

A major design consideration is that in order to test the diathesis-stress aspect of the model adequately, it is necessary to manipulate or measure actual negative events that occur to subjects, and to determine both how the interactions between events and explanatory style are related to later depression and also whether this relation is mediated by the particular attributions that subjects make for the events. Most studies to date have ignored subjects' recent histories of stressful events when depression was assessed. Without knowledge of this, the theory would not predict strong relations between explanatory style and depression.

A second major design consideration is how to demonstrate the causal direction of the attribution–depression relationship. According to the reformulated learned helplessness theory, the tendency to make internal, stable, and global attributions for negative outcomes plays a contributory role in the etiological chain leading to the development of depression, rather than simply being itself an effect of depression. Because the great majority of relevant studies have used a concurrent design, their results are equally consistent with either direction of causality (Brewin, 1985). One way to attempt to distinguish between these two rival hypotheses is to compare currently depressed subjects with those whose depression has remitted, or to compare remitted subjects with those who have never been depressed, in order to determine whether remitted subjects still show the depressogenic explanatory style. Results of several such studies suggest that attributions indeed are affected by the depressed state. Lewinsohn et al. (1981) found no difference between recovered and never depressed subjects on a measure of internal versus external causal attributions. Hamilton and Abramson (1983) found that ASQ composite difference scores (CP–CN) of depressed inpatients no longer differed from normal at discharge from the hospital. Similarly, Asarnow and Bates (1988) reported that remitted depressed children's CASQ scores did not differ from those of children who never had been depressed and differed significantly from those who currently were depressed. The only study that has found elevated scores on an attribution measure among remitted depressed patients (Eaves & Rush, 1984) has been criticized for using too liberal criteria for remission.

So the evidence suggests that dysfunctional attributions do not persist beyond the depressed state, which has led some critics to conclude that they can not play a causal role in the onset of depression. But do these findings necessarily mean that explanatory style plays no causal role in the development of depression and that dysfunctional attributions are simply an epiphenomenon? Beck (1967) and others have long argued that dysfunctional cognitive schemata typically remain dormant until activated by relevant stressors; therefore, outside of a depressive episode, and in the absence of a relevant stressor, the diathesis would not be revealed readily. Miranda and Persons (1988) recently reported findings that are consistent with the idea that dysfunctional attitudes may reflect an enduring trait, but that their manifestation and assessment will be influenced by the current depressive state. Specifically, they found that individuals who currently had some depressive symptoms and histories of diagnosable depressive episodes showed elevated dysfunctional attitudes, whereas individuals who were not currently experiencing depressive symptoms, but had histories of depressive episodes did not, which demonstrates a state effect. However, individuals who were currently experiencing some depressive symptoms but had no history of actual depressive episodes did not show elevated dysfunctional attitudes, which suggests that not only the depressive state, but also vulnerability to actual episodes, is necessary for elevated dysfunctional attitudes. This finding has been replicated since by Miranda, Persons, and Byers (1990). Therefore, it may be that, as with other dysfunctional cognitive schemata, a dysfunctional explanatory style characterizes many individuals who are vulnerable to depression, but that it remains latent outside of depressive episodes. If so, then it may be possible to prime or activate subjects' attributional tendencies by using mood induction procedures or other means (Riskind & Rholes, 1984). No studies yet have examined the effects of such mood induction procedures on assessment of attributions.

In light of the demonstrations that depressed mood affects attributions, prospective designs of initially nondepressed persons are essential in order to examine the temporal relations among variables in the model. Although prospective designs can not demonstrate causality, they can help investigators to distinguish between rival causal models. Many of the more recent investigations have adopted a prospective design. One of the questions that remains to be answered is the best time lag to employ between measurements (Cochran & Hammen, 1985). The finding of Metalsky et al. (1987) that the predictors of mood reactions immediately following a negative event were different than the predictors several days later underscores the importance of the timing of assessments. For the present, it seems prudent to take repeated measures of mood and relevant events or other possible etiological factors as frequently as logistic considerations permit.

We have noted the importance of prospective designs that follow initially nondepressed subjects in an attempt to predict who later becomes depressed. If the outcome to be studied is diagnosable depression, which does not have a high incidence in the general population (Weissman et al., 1988), then either an extremely large initial sample is needed, as in the community study by Lewinsohn et al. (1981), or subjects have to be selected on the basis of their risk for developing depression. One version of a high-risk design has been to follow subjects who have recently recovered from a clinical depression in order to predict later symptom recurrence or relapse. To date, three such studies have been reported. Rush, Weissenburger, and Eaves (1986) found that the ASQ negative scores of depressed patients at the end of treatment did not significantly predict their levels of depressive symptoms at a 6-month follow-up, after controlling for symptoms at the end of treatment. Seligman et al. (1988) reported a similar finding for a 1-year follow-up. However, both of these studies demonstrated trends in the predicted direction and had very low statistical power to detect such effects because of samples of only 15 and 29, respectively. Evans et al. (1992) reported that, among 50 treatment responders, several personality and social cognition measures assessed at the end of treatment predicted relapse during a 2-year follow-up. However, when they controlled for level of depressive symptoms at the end of treatment, the only variable that still predicted relapse was the difference between CN and CP scores on the ASQ. This is some of the strongest evidence to date that explanatory style may play a causal role in the development of later depression. Future studies will need to determine whether this finding can be replicated and, if so, whether the mechanism of the effect operates through an interaction between explanatory style and the occurrence of stressful events.

Another promising high-risk design involves the study of children who have a depressed parent. Such children show elevated rates of depression as well as a broad range of behavior problems, but the mechanisms through which this risk factor operates are as yet poorly understood. One possible mechanism is the development of dysfunctional cognitive processing styles, possibly through modeling or other aspects of the parent–child relationship (see chapter 4). Jaenicke et al. (1987) found that 8- to 16-year-old children of mothers with major mood disorder (unipolar or bipolar) had higher CN scores on the CASQ than children of normal or medically ill mothers, and that these scores were related to observed maternal criticism of the child. However, CASQ scores did not predict the development of a depressive disorder during a 6-month follow-up, after controlling for initial diagnosis or depressive symptom level but did predict later nondepressive diagnosis (Hammen, Adrian, & Hiroto, 1988). A follow-up period of only 6 months may be too brief for sufficient incidence of depressive disorders to occur.

In the previous sections, we dealt with the lack of uniform support for the reformulated learned helplessness model by pointing to several methodological and conceptual concerns that need to be addressed in future research, including greater statistical power, more adequate measures of attributions, and several experimental design issues. We turn now to ways in which the model itself may require some clarification and expansion, some of which recently have been addressed in another revision of the model by Abramson et al. (1989). These issues include: (a) whether the model is specific to depression, or also applies to other psychopathologies, and to what types of depression it applies; (b) whether the attributions that depressed individuals make for events are distorted, or are more accurate representations of reality than those of nondepressed individuals; (c) whether causal attributions are the most important psychological factors in depression or whether other types of attributions or processes play roles of equal or greater importance; (d) whether the possible etiologic role of causal attributions is moderated by other psychological factors; and (e) whether explanatory style is relatively domain specific, creating vulnerabilities for particular individuals to particular classes of stressful events.

SPECIFICITY OF THE MODEL

Although internal, stable, and global attributions have been proposed to be vulnerability factors for depression, the possibility that they are related to psychopathology in general has been examined in several studies.

Depression Versus Other Psychiatric Disorders

The causal attributions of depressed and schizophrenic subjects have been compared in two studies. Both found more maladaptive internal, stable, and composite ASQ attributions for negative events in depressed inpatients than in schizophrenics (Raps et al., 1982; Zimmerman, Coryell, Corenthal, & Wilson, 1986). However, these differences were not significant in the Zimmerman et al. study, perhaps because their depressed group included psychotically depressed and bipolar patients. In both studies, depressed and schizophrenic patients did not differ on the global dimension.

Mineka (chapter 8, this volume) reviews the role of explanatory style in anxiety, so here we only briefly review the literature comparing the attributions of depressed and anxiety-disordered patients. As in the studies comparing depressed and schizophrenic patients, investigators have typically reported similarities between depressed and anxiety-disordered groups on the globality dimension. Dysthymics did not report more global attributions than a heterogeneous group of anxiety-disordered patients (Heimberg et al., 1987) nor more than specific groups of agoraphobics, social phobics, and panic-disordered patients (Heimberg et al., 1989). Dysphoric college students did not differ on the global dimension from students with test anxiety (Ingram, Kendall, Smith, Donnell, & Ronan, 1987). In one study, which used the CAVE procedure, patients with major depression did report more global attributions than generalized anxiety patients (Riskind et al., 1989). Similarities between mood and anxiety disorders also have been found on the internality dimension. Neither patients with major depression (Riskind et al., 1989) nor dysthymics (Heimberg et al., 1987, 1989) reported more internal attributions for negative events than did anxiety-disordered patients. However, Ingram et al. (1987) found that dysphoric college students attributed negative events to more internal causes than test-anxious students.

Depressed subjects made more stable attributions for negative events than individuals with various types of anxiety disorders in all four of the noted studies, and had more maladaptive CN scores in the three studies that reported them. Although these findings suggest that at least attributions to stable causes may be specific to depression, some evidence also calls this conclusion into question.

Ganellen (1988) found that ASQ global, stable, and composite scores for negative events covaried with both depression and anxiety levels among a group of mood and anxiety-disordered patients. Seligman et al. (1988) found that depressed patients who were also anxious had more pessimistic explanatory styles than those who were not anxious, which suggests that anxiety-disordered individuals may also make maladaptive attributions for undesirable events and that when a person has both disorders, their pessimism is exacerbated.

In summary, studies that compare depressed with schizophrenic or anxiety-disordered patients have not provided compelling evidence for an explanatory style that is specific to depression. However, it is difficult to draw firm conclusions because of the small number of studies. Also, the vastly different levels of depression across these studies may account for inconsistencies in some of the results. The casual attributions of those with major depression may differ from those with dysthymia or milder dysphoric states.

Depression Versus General Emotional Distress

Several studies have examined the possibility that a dysfunctional explanatory style is associated with general emotional distress, rather than with a diagnosis of depression. Miller et al. (1982) found no differences between depressed inpatients and nondepressed, nonschizophrenic inpatients on CN (although this conclusion is weakened by their use of only half of the ASQ events). However, the depressed patients did make more maladaptive attributions for their own most stressful events. Hammen et al. (1988) reported that, although neither attributions nor the interaction of attributions and event stress predicted development of a diagnosis of depression among children of mood disordered or medically ill patients, they did predict development of nondepressive psychiatric diagnoses, as well as increases in depressive symptom levels.

One type of general distress that may cut across psychiatric disorders is neuroticism. This may even be the construct examined in the many studies that tested the attributional model using college students with self-reported dysphoria. In one study with such a sample, Hill and Kemp-Wheeler (1986) found that only the part of the variance in depression associated with neuroticism was related to internal and stable attributions. These results suggest that explanatory style may be related more to neuroticism than to depression specifically, but the study only included mildly depressed students and may not generalize to clinical depression. Johnson, Petzel, and Munic (1986) compared groups of patients differing in both level of general psychopathology and level of depression. Only the more severely depressed patients made more internal, stable and global attributions than the nondepressed patients, whereas mildly to moderately depressed individuals did not differ from the nondepressed groups. Level of general psychopathology was not related to subjects' attribution ratings. This study then provides rather more support for specificity of explanatory style to more severe depression.

Another form of general distress that is associated with a variety of emotional disorders is low self-esteem. It may be that a pessimistic explanatory style is more a function of low self-esteem than of depression. The reformulated helplessness theory proposes that only internal attributions are specifically associated with low self-esteem. In dysphoric college students, self-esteem has been found to be a better predictor of explanatory style than current level of depression (Tennen & Hertzberger, 1987). In a replication with an inpatient sample, Tennen, Herzberger, and Nelson (1987) found that when self-esteem level was statistically controlled, the relationship between depression and explanatory style was eliminated. However, when level of depression was controlled, self-esteem still predicted explanatory style. Because most studies of attributions and depression have not assessed subjects' levels of self-esteem, variations on this construct may be another source of inconsistent results. In future studies, it may be useful to consider levels of both depression and self-esteem.

Subtypes of Depression

Another line of research relevant to the specificity question concerns whether a maladaptive explanatory style is associated with only certain subtypes of depression. Some of the confusion in the attributional literature may arise from the heterogeneity of depression itself. Both the original and reformulated versions of learned helplessness theory were proposed to be specific to reactive depression, but this specificity has also been called into question. The traditional reactive versus endogenous distinction in the psychiatric literature, based on presumed etiology, has been replaced largely by the melancholic versus nonmelancholic distinction, based primarily on clinical signs and symptoms. Many of the behavioral changes seen in the dogs of the early learned helplessness experiments closely resemble features of endogenous or melancholic, rather than reactive depression. Most studies comparing melancholic and nonmelancholic unipolar depressives have found no significant differences, although the attributions of both groups differed significantly from nondepressed controls (Eaves & Rush, 1984; Seligman et al., 1988, Zimmerman, Coryell, & Corenthal, 1984). One study (Willner, Wilkes, & Orwin, 1990) even found that melancholics made more internal, stable, and global attributions for ASQ negative events than nonmelancholics, even though the two groups did not differ in the severity of their depression. Seligman et al. (1988) also reported no significant difference between the explanatory styles of unipolar and bipolar depressed patients.

Hopelessness depression has recently been proposed as a subtype of depression to which the attributional model specifically applies (Abramson et al., 1989). The details of this subtype are presented in chapter 10 of this volume. Much work remains to be done to verify the existence of hopelessness depression as a subtype, to assess it independently of the construct of hopelessness, and to determine whether hopelessness precedes and is specific to depression.

DEPRESSIVE REALISM?

Considerable evidence has accumulated that demonstrates that nondepressed persons also engage in schema-driven information processing that can result in distortions. In a series of four experiments, Alloy and Abramson (1979) found that nondepressed students saw themselves as having more control over an experimental task than they actually had, whereas mildly depressed students judged the contingencies more accurately. This began a flurry of research on "depressive realism"—the notion that it is the nondepressed people who distort information and the depressed who see the world more accurately. In research on attributions, nondepressed individuals exhibit a systematic tendency to make more internal, stable, and global attributions for positive events than for negative events, often referred to as a "self-serving" bias (Miller & Ross, 1975), which is hypothesized to help maintain their self-esteem. In contrast, depressed individuals are more evenhanded (similar) in their attributions for positive and negative events (see Alloy & Abramson, 1988, for a review). This has been interpreted to mean that the depressed persons' judgments are more accurate, even though less self-enhancing, and that these individuals are "sadder but wiser" (Alloy & Abramson, 1979). However, most of the studies cited in support of the notion of depressive realism do not include measures of objective reality, so we do not know whether bias can be inferred from asymmetry in attributions for positive and negative outcomes and accuracy from evenhandedness (Miller & Moretti, 1988). Moreover, Sackeim and Wegner (1986) found that nondepressed students exhibited the self-serving bias, mildly depressed students appeared more evenhanded, and clinically depressed subjects displayed a "self-punitive" bias. In line with these and other findings, some authors have suggested a tripartite distinction: Mental health seems to be associated with positive distortions, mild depression, or dysphoria with few distortions, and severe depression with negative distortions (Ackermann & DeRubeis, 1991; Ruehlman, West, & Pasahow, 1985). It may be that nondepressed, dysphoric, and depressed individuals all engage in schematic (and hence biased) processing, but that the content of their schemata differ. Because there are usually no normative models to evaluate the accuracy of causal attributions, it may be more fruitful to look at whether a given individual's attributions are rational, given their past experiences (Miller & Morretti, 1988).

There is a substantial body of literature indicating that the actual life circumstances of depressed individuals are more negative than those of nondepressed people, whether as a cause or consequence of depression, or both. They are often characterized by impoverished interpersonal relationships, more than the usual number of stressful life events, and feedback on the negative interpersonal impact of their depressive symptoms (e.g., social withdrawal, hopelessness, crying). It may, therefore, be quite accurate for such individuals to attribute many of these events to relatively internal, stable, and global factors, and thereby develop a generalized tendency to attribute events, including hypothetical ones, to such factors. In line with this, Robins and Block (1989) found that causal attributions for stressful events could be significantly predicted by the number of such events that subjects recently had experienced. Indeed, this was a stronger predictor even than ASQ scores. Additionally, there is some evidence that experimenters agree with the attributions that depressed patients make for the negative events that they experience (Miller et al., 1982). As Krantz (1985) aptly concluded: "While it is undoubtedly true that depressives fail to see that 'every cloud has a silver lining,' it also appears that depressives have more clouds on the horizon than do nondepressives" (p. 607). Studies testing cognitive theories of depression need to assess the actual social context of those that they study and its influence on their cognitive processing.

ARE CAUSAL ATTRIBUTIONS THE MOST IMPORTANT PSYCHOLOGICAL FACTORS IN DEPRESSION?

Preattributional Variables

Preattributional variables are those variables hypothesized to be involved in the formation of attributions. Consensus and consistency judgments are two such preattributional variables. Consensus judgments refer to an individual's evaluation of whether he or she is more or less likely than others to experience a given outcome. Consistency judgments concern the person's perception of how often an outcome has occurred to him or her in the past. Brewin and Furnham (1986) found that a preattributional composite that combined consensus and consistency judgments had a direct relation to depression among college students that was not mediated by explanatory style. They suggested that these preattributional variables may be important determinants of depression in their own right, perhaps even more important than causal attributions. However, their finding is called into question by a study by Crocker, Alloy, and Kayne (1988) who separated the perceptions of the self and the perceptions of others that go into making consensus judgments. Whereas perceptions of the self relative to others had only a direct effect on depression, perceptions of the self alone had both a direct effect on depression and an effect mediated by explanatory style. Crocker et al. argued that Brewin and Furnham did not find evidence of attributional mediation because their composite consensus score confounded perceptions of self with perceptions of others, and it is only perceptions of the likelihood of events happening to the self that influence attributions. In future research on preattributional variables, it will be important to include clinically depressed samples and to consider the reality of negative events in their lives. Judgments of consensus may reflect an accurate summary of a social history where bad things do happen to the depressed person more than to others. Similarly, judgments of consistency may simply reflect the finding that more negative events do occur in the lives of depressed persons. Consensus and consistency judgments both play a role in the recent hopelessness theory of Abramson et al. (1989).

Selection of Causes

In most studies of attributions and depression, subjects were asked to nominate one major cause of an event and then rate that cause on the internal, stable, and global dimensions. Typically, only the dimensional ratings have been used in analyses and nothing has been done with the actual causes selected. It is possible that the choice of causes themselves, or other dimensions of them, may play a role in the development of depression. Krantz and Rude (1984) found that subjects' selections of the cause of a negative event (ability, effort, task difficulty, or luck) did not map as predicted onto their ratings of those causes on the internal, stable, and global dimensions. For example, although experimenters may view luck as an external and unstable factor, some depressed persons might view it as external but stable, or even as internal and stable, depending on their histories. These investigators also found that subjects' selections of causes and their dimensional ratings each contributed uniquely to the prediction of depression level, which suggests that perceptions of causes other than the three dimensions focused on by helplessness theory may be important in depression.

Another constraint of the research paradigms in the attributional literature is the implicit assumption that people attribute life events to only one cause. Dimensional ratings are assessed on the basis of one cause per event. However, Flett, Pliner, and Blankstein (1989) found that dysphoric students attributed hypothetical and real events to a greater number of causes than nondepressed subjects. In addition, more depressed students reported deriving more enjoyment from analyzing reasons for behavior (attributional motivation) and made more complex contemporary external explanations (e.g., the influence of society on people) than their nondepressed counterparts. These studies suggest that depressed individuals may be more attributionally complex than the nondepressed, in that they may entertain a greater number of ideas about the causes of events. This factor is not captured by most current research designs.

Characterological Self-Blame

Other attributional constructs that have shown promise in predicting depressive symptoms are perceived responsibility for the occurrence of negative events and the closely related concept of self-blame. Studies have found that depressed patients feel that they deserve more blame for negative events than praise for positive events (e.g., Sackheim & Wegner, 1986). Janoff-Bulman (1979) introduced the more specific distinction between characterological and behavioral self-blame. Both types of self-blame refer to internal causes, but blaming one's character implies a cause that is relatively stable and uncontrollable, whereas blaming one's behavior implies a cause that is more changeable or controllable. A number of studies have found characterological self-blame to be positively associated with depressed mood, and behavioral self-blame to be negatively associated with depressed mood (Peterson et al., 1981; Stoltz & Galassi, 1989;). Other investigations have reported comparable results with constructs that seem conceptually very similar. For example, depression has been found to be positively related to internal, stable attributions for negative events, but inversely related to internal, unstable attributions (Zautra et al., 1985); positively related to internal, stable, and global attributions for uncontrollable causes of negative events, but inversely related to such attributions for controllable causes (Brown & Siegel, 1988); and positively related to ability and trait attributions for negative events, but inversely related to strategy and effort attributions (Anderson, Horowitz, & French, 1983). Additionally, Stoltz and Galassi (1989) reported that the tendency to make more characterological attributions accounted for more of the variance in depression than the internal or composite measures of the ASQ. In chapter 2 of this volume, Reivich discusses controllability as a dimension on the ASQ.

Other Event Perceptions

A number of event perceptions other than causal attributions may be important factors in depression. Robins and Block (1989) found that the composite of internal, stable, and global attributions for students' own most upsetting recent events predicted only 12% of the variance in their depression scores, of which only global attributions (14% of depression score variance) were a significant predictor. In contrast, 36% of depression variance was accounted for by a broader set of perceptions of those same events, the most influential of which included global attributions, but also perceived amount of life change resulting from the event, and perceived social support available to deal with the event. Hammen and her colleagues (e.g., Gong-Guy & Hammen, 1980; Hammen & Cochran, 1981; Hammen & deMayo, 1982) have argued that assessments of the impact of negative events (inferred consequences) may strongly influence a person's emotional reactions to them, independently of causal attributions. Another type of event perception that has been shown to be related to depression is the perceived importance of the event (Tennen et al., 1987, Study 2). The hopelessness model of Abramson et al. (1989) includes perceived importance and perceived consequences of the event as contributors to hopelessness and depression.

Coping Expectancies

Coping expectancies have not been directly compared with explanatory style in the prediction of depression, but there is some evidence to suggest that these secondary appraisals of events (Lazarus & Launier, 1978) are important variables.

In testing his self-efficacy model, Bandura (1986) showed that those who view themselves as inefficacious are at risk for high levels of emotional distress, poor coping, and maladaptive behavior. Individuals who view themselves as ineffective problem solvers have been found to be more depressed than those who view themselves as effective problem solvers (Heppner, Baumgardner, & Jackson, 1985). It is likely that individuals with low coping expectancies will develop "hopelessness expectancies" when encountering negative life events. In support of this, Bonner and Rich (1988) found that problem-solving appraisal and its interaction with life stress are independent predictors of hopelessness beyond depressed mood.

It will also be important to assess actual problem-solving or coping skills to examine the extent to which coping expectancies reflect reality and whether these expectancies add anything to the prediction of depression beyond an assessment of actual coping skills. There is some evidence to suggest that actual problem-solving abilities moderate the association between explanatory style and depression (Nezu, Kalmar, Ronan, & Clarijo, 1986). The ASQ composite for negative events, problem solving, and the interaction of the two variables accounted for more than 50% of the variance in depression scores, whereas the ASQ composite alone accounted for only 37% of the variance. It seems that having better problem-solving skills may serve as a buffer against the effects of negative events, even when the individual attributes the cause to internal, stable, or global factors.

DOMAIN-SPECIFIC INTERACTIONS OF ATTRIBUTIONS AND EVENTS

It may be fruitful to examine subjects' attributions for affiliation and achievement situations separately because they may be more consistent within each of these domains than across domains. Furthermore, several theorists have suggested that individuals who are prone to become depressed tend to have personality characteristics that make them especially vulnerable to events in one or both of these areas, such characteristics being referred to as anxious attachment and compulsive self-reliance (Bowlby, 1977), dependency and self-criticism (Blatt, Quinlan, Chevron, McDonald, & Zuroff, 1982), sociotropy and autonomy (Beck, 1983), or needs for a dominant other or a dominant goal (Arieti & Bemporad, 1980). There is a rapidly growing body of empirical support for a distinction between the affiliation and achievement domains (Robins, 1994) but to date, only a handful of studies have looked at the relation of depression to causal attributions in each of these specific domains. Berndt, Berndt, and Kaiser (1982) found that, among female undergraduates, depression level was related to internal attributions for the ASQ negative affiliation situations only. Anderson et al. (1983) found that the positive relation of depression level among students to characterological attributions for failure, and its negative relation to behavioral attributions, were significant both for interpersonal and noninterpersonal situations, but were considerably stronger for the interpersonal situations. In a study described earlier, Metalsky et al. (1987) found, as predicted, that sustained increases in depressed mood were related to the interaction of poor examination performance and a depressogenic explanatory style for the negative achievement situations, but not for the negative interpersonal situations on their Extended ASQ. There have been no prospective studies to date looking at the interaction of actual interpersonal events with specific attributions for such events. However, Robins (1994) found that concurrent depression level among female students (but not male students) was significantly predicted by the interaction of negative achievement events with the ASQ negative achievement composite and also by the interaction of negative interpersonal events with the ASQ negative interpersonal composite. As predicted by the model, the noncongruent interactions were not significant.

Another approach to the question of attributions and specific content vulnerabilities has been to examine whether dependency and self-criticism, or sociotropy and autonomy, are related to different patterns of causal attributions. Brewin and Furnham (1987) and Brown and Silberschatz (1989), in studies of college students and psychiatric outpatients, respectively, found self-criticism to be related, as predicted, to internal attributions for ASQ negative events, and also to stable and global attributions. They had predicted that dependency would be related to more external attributions for negative events, but both groups of researchers found that dependency was also related to internal and global attributions (and also to stable attributions in the Brown and Silberschatz study). However, these researchers did not examine whether attributional patterns might differ for the interpersonal and achievement situations on the ASQ. Robins (1994) addressed this question and also examined the data separately for men and women. For men, sociotropy was not correlated with any of the ASQ measures, but autonomy was correlated with the generality and composite scales for negative achievement events, and with the composite score for negative interpersonal events. For women, autonomy was not correlated with any of the ASQ measures, but sociotropy was significantly related to composite attribution scores for negative achievement situations, but not to attributions for interpersonal situations. In summary, dysfunctional attributional patterns were associated with sociotropy in women and with need for autonomy in men, but the types of events about which dysfunctional attributions were made did not specifically match the predominant personality mode.

To summarize the preceding studies on specific domains of attribution, there are some promising leads, but all these studies, with the exception of Metalsky et al. (1987), have used the original ASQ, which includes too few of each type of item to form adequately reliable scales for each content area. Nevertheless, the results of these studies encourage further investigation of these issues using more reliable scales such as those developed by Metalsky et al. (1987) and Peterson and Villanova (1988).

CONCLUSION

The reformulated helplessness theory of depression has generated a vast literature on the relations between depression and causal attributions that has yielded very inconsistent results. However, most investigations have been seriously hampered, frequently by insufficient sample sizes, and almost always by insufficiently reliable attribution measures. Furthermore, most empirical studies have grossly oversimplified the predictions made by the theory by testing only concurrent bivariate relations between attributions and depression, rather than the prospective interactions between explanatory style and negative events actually proposed by the theory. The theory itself is challenged by findings suggesting that maladaptive attributions may be simply effects of the depressed state and that other psychological variables show important associations with depression. Despite over a decade of research, the verdict is not yet in. Recent developments encourage us to believe that more adequate tests of the model can and will be conducted. These developments include: (a) the increasing use of prospective and diathesis-stress interaction designs; (b) the development of more reliable measures of explanatory style; (c) demonstrations that cognitive diatheses can be latent outside of depressive episodes; and (d) the continuing maturation of the model itself by incorporating additional cognitive and environmental variables, and by differentiating between reactions to interpersonal and achievement situations.

Explanatory Style in the Treatment of Depression

Robert J. DeRubeis
University of Pennsylvania

Steven D. Hollon
Vanderbilt University

EXPLANATORY STYLE: STABLE TRAIT OR CHANGEABLE CHARACTERISTIC?

The study of explanatory style in treatment research poses a special dilemma. Is explanatory style a stable trait, and thus a potential predictor of treatment response or relapse? This predictive role would be a familiar one for explanatory style, as evidenced in the other chapters in this book. Or is explanatory style a changeable characteristic, a statelike feature of a person, so that its change during therapy would be of interest? This latter formulation would seem to go against the assumptions made in most research on explanatory style. In this chapter we see that perhaps explanatory style can have it both ways, at least within the context of cognitive therapy for depression.

COGNITIVE THERAPY

The effects of cognitive therapy have been investigated in a number of studies with depressed patients. In these studies, cognitive therapy has most frequently been compared to antidepressant medications, the acknowledged treatment standard for depression, and it has fared at least as well as the medication regimes against which it has been compared. It should be noted, however, that most studies of cognitive therapy for depression have been conducted without a minimal treatment or pill–placebo control group, so that more definitive conclusions about its efficacy await data from studies that do include such controls (see Hollon, Shelton, & Loosen, 1991).

Before we discuss the role of explanatory style in cognitive therapy, we describe the essential features of the therapy and the theories that attempt to explain its effects. All cognitive theories of depression suggest that depression is, in part, the consequence of negative beliefs and maladaptive information processing, with the different theories focusing on different aspects of cognition. Beck and colleagues have emphasized the role of depressive schemata—organized knowledge structures with associated biases in information processing (Beck, 1967; Kovacs & Beck, 1978a, 1978b), whereas Seligman and colleagues have ascribed causal priority to causal attributions (Abramson, Seligman, & Teasdale, 1978; Abramson, Metalsky, & Alloy, 1989; Peterson & Seligman, 1984a). In both instances, cognitive structures or processes are seen as representing the individual difference component in a diathesis-stress model. Individuals with a propensity for dysfunctional thinking are not expected to become depressed until they encounter negative life events, but, in such instances, they should be more likely to become symptomatic than individuals with no such proclivity.

Cognitive therapy is predicated on the notion that correcting negative beliefs and modifying maladaptive information processing can reduce the symptoms of depression (Beck, 1970). Patients are encouraged to treat their beliefs as hypotheses that can be subjected to empirical disconfirmation, and they are trained to recognize and compensate for the operation of distortions in information processing (Beck, Rush, Shaw, & Emery, 1979).

In the first few sessions of a 3-month course of cognitive therapy, therapists typically focus on presenting a general cognitive model. They train patients in systematic self-monitoring procedures, and try to get them to increase their engagement in activities and to test the accuracy of their beliefs through a variety of behavioral activation strategies. After a few sessions, the focus shifts toward efforts to identify specific beliefs associated with emotional upset, or beliefs that interfere with coping in specific situations. In the middle weeks of treatment, most of the sessions (and the majority of the between-session assignments) are devoted to exploring the validity of those beliefs and identifying the operation of general information-processing biases. By the final third of treatment, the focus shifts once again, this time to more general underlying assumptions and information-processing propensities. These more general attitudes and processes have usually been identified during the earlier phase when specific beliefs were tested. By the final weeks of treatment, most patients are relatively symptom free.

According to Hollon and Garber (1980) and Abramson et al. (1989), causal attributions play a larger role in the onset of depression, whereas negative expectations are more closely associated with its maintenance once it begins. Although the propensity for making certain types of causal attributions in the face of negative life events may play a role in triggering a given episode of depression, once begun, it is the sense of hopelessness and negative expectations that continue the process. Such a formulation suggests that efforts at prevention are best targeted at attributional change, whereas the treatment of an existing episode is expected to proceed most powerfully if it focuses on the disconfirmation of negative expectations.

THE COGNITIVE PHARMACOTHERAPY PROJECT

We attempted to test hypotheses about the mediation of change and relapse prevention in a comparative treatment project—the Cognitive Pharmacotherapy Treatment (CPT) project (Hollon et al., 1992). In this study, 107 nonpsychotic, unipolar depressed outpatients were randomly assigned to 12 weeks of treatment with cognitive therapy, imipramine pharmacotherapy (drugs alone), or combined cognitive-pharmacotherapy. (There were two drug-alone cells—one in which patients were tapered from imipramine after 12 weeks. In the other cell, patients were continued on imipramine during the first year of the 2-year follow-up.) All patients were drawn from individuals requesting treatment for depression at a community hospital and clinic in metropolitan St. Paul, Minnesota, and all treatment personnel were drawn from the professional therapists and pharmacologists in those settings.

Improvement in Depressive Symptoms. Of the patients, 64 completed all 12 weeks of treatment (16 in cognitive therapy, 32 in imipramine pharmacotherapy, and 16 in the combined condition). With regard to change in symptom severity, there was a nonsignificant advantage evidenced by the combined treatment condition. Some portion of that advantage resulted from a tendency for less responsive patients to drop out of treatment in the combined condition. Differences in symptom reduction were negligible between the two single modalities. Both cognitive therapy and pharmacotherapy showed about as much change as would be expected for clinically effective interventions (75% of the patients showed at least partial response sufficient to allow the discontinuation of treatment at the end of 12 weeks; over 50% in each modality were fully recovered by the end of treatment). Further, in contrast to findings reported by Elkin et al. (1989), there was no indication of a differential advantage of pharmacotherapy over cognitive therapy among the more severely depressed or endogenous patients.

Mediation of Improvement. In addition to questions about symptom outcome, we were also interested in investigating the mediation of change in these very different treatment modalities. We were especially interested in possible specific effects of cognitive therapy or pharmacotherapy on cognition or biology—domains that might be expected to change more in the respective relevant treatments.

In this chapter, we summarize our findings with the cognitive measures, including those obtained with our measure of explanatory style.

In this study, four measures of cognition were taken at pre-, mid-, and posttreatment: the Automatic Thoughts Questionnaire (ATQ; Hollon & Kendall, 1980), the Hopelessness Scale (HS; Beck, Weissman, Lester, & Trexler, 1974), the Dysfunctional Attitudes Scale, Form A (DAS; Weissman & Beck, 1978), and the original Attributional Style Questionnaire (ASQ; Seligman, Abramson, Semmel, & von Baeyer, 1979).

The ATQ is a 30-item self-report questionnaire that assesses the frequency with which patients experience 30 depressotypic self-statements (e.g., "I'm no good," "I'll never make it"). In this study, the primary use of the ATQ was as a measure of "surface" cognitive phenomena (Beck et al., 1979), including expectations.

The HS is a 20-item true/false self-report measure intended to tap the tone of the respondent's expectations about the future. High scorers on this scale endorse such items as "Things just won't work out the way I want them to."

The DAS (Form A) is a series of 40 attitudinal statements that were written to represent depressotypic "underlying assumptions" (Beck et al., 1979). Examples are "I cannot be happy unless most people I know admire me," "If I fail at my work, then I am a failure as a person." Patients check the degree to which they endorse these statements on a 7-point Likert scale. Changes in attitudes represented on the DAS are seen as important to the process of cognitive therapy by some theorists (see Beck, 1984; Kovacs & Beck, 1979).

On the ASQ, respondents are asked to imagine 12 life events (6 positive, 6 negative), and to assign causes for those life events. Respondents then rate the degree to which each cause is internal, stable, and global. The ASQ yields several indices that are highly correlated with each other. We report on only one of these indices—the composite of internality, stability, and globality for positive events minus negative events (CPCN; see chapter 2 on measurement of explanatory styles). Its psychometric properties are the most consistent in the literature on the ASQ (Peterson & Seligman, 1984a). Seligman et al. (1988) reported a high correlation of change in explanatory style with change in depression in a sample of patients treated with cognitive therapy.

All four cognitive measures evidenced significant and substantial improvement from pre- to mid-treatment in both groups. Moreover, there were no group differences in the amount of change on any of these measures during this period. Change on these measures was not specific to cognitive therapy at mid-treatment.

Early ASQ, DAS, and HS change each significantly predicted subsequent depression change in cognitive therapy. Such a predictive relation was not found for any of these measures in the drug-only group. The ATQ did not predict subsequent change in either group.

We then analyzed between-group differences in the relation of early cognitive change to late symptom change. Was change on any of these measures more related to subsequent change in the cognitive therapy group than in the drug-alone group? Both the ASQ and the DAS showed this pattern. The between-group difference on neither the HS nor the ATQ was significant. Thus, early ASQ improvement and early DAS improvement differentially predicted subsequent symptom change, depending on treatment group.

These findings suggest that a set of cognitive constructs, as measured by the ASQ and DAS, play a mediational role in the reduction of symptoms during cognitive therapy. However, the mediational role they play appears to be neither necessary nor sufficient, as the relationship between change on these variables and subsequent symptom change was not found in the drug-alone group.

Elsewhere we have proposed an explanation for this pattern of results (see DeRubeis et al., 1990). Concerning the ASQ finding, it may be that early change in explanatory style facilitates the working through of problems in cognitive therapy. As patients' explanatory styles change, they may become more optimistic about their efforts to help themselves in therapy. As they become less rigid in assigning internal, stable, and global causal explanations for bad events in their lives, they may then become more willing to examine evidence, to test alternatives, and to question the implications of their beliefs. In this way, patients become more likely to bring the techniques of the therapy into their everyday lives. The strategies they have learned in therapy can then have a continuing ameliorative effect on depressive symptoms.

Specificity of Explanatory Style Change in Cognitive Therapy. At posttreatment we did find a significant difference between the cognitive therapy and drug-treated groups on the ASQ. Most of our depressed patients had exhibited a pessimistic explanatory style prior to treatment. We found that patients treated with drugs alone—even those whose symptoms had remitted—continued to exhibit this negative style at the end of treatment. The mean CPCN score of imipramine-treated patients who had remitted was similar to that of patients who had not remitted. In contrast, the explanatory styles of remitted cognitive therapy-treated patients improved substantially. Thus, we found a specific effect of cognitive therapy on explanatory style, relative to medication treatment alone, but this difference did not appear until the end of treatment. We point this out because although most symptom change occurred by the sixth week of treatment, it was not until the posttreatment assessment that the ASQ differentiated those who responded to cognitive therapy from those who responded to drugs alone. These results are noteworthy, if for no other reason than that it has been difficult for researchers to find specific effects of cognitive therapy relative to pharmacotherapy (e.g., Blackburn & Bishop, 1983; Simons, Garfield, & Murphy, 1984; but see Imber et al., 1990, for an exception).

Prevention of Relapse. All patients were followed for 2 years posttreatment follow-up. Among treatment completers who evidenced at least a partial response, patients treated with either cognitive therapy alone or combined cognitive-pharmacotherapy were withdrawn from all treatment at the beginning of the follow-up phase. Those patients who showed at least a partial response to pharmacotherapy alone were randomly assigned to either medication continuation or medication withdrawal. Those who were assigned to medication continuation stayed on imipramine for only the first year of the 2-year follow-up.

Survival analyses, treating "time-to-first-relapse" as the event of interest, indicated that patients previously treated with cognitive therapy (either alone or in combination with medication) were significantly less likely to relapse (18%) than were patients withdrawn from medication (50%; see Evans et al., 1992) in the follow-up period. Of patients who were continued on study medication, 32% relapsed during the 2-year period; this rate did not differ significantly from either of the other two groups. However, at the end of the first year, before the medication was discontinued in the medication continuation group, the relapse rate was (nonsignificantly) lower in the medication continuation group relative to the group that had not been maintained on medication (20% vs. 50%).

These follow-up findings suggest that treatment with cognitive therapy confers protection against subsequent symptomatic relapse even after treatment termination. They further suggest that the prophylactic effect of short-term cognitive therapy is at least as great as the protection afforded by continued pharmacotherapy. It is unlikely that the relapses in the medication withdrawal condition were the consequence of withdrawal per se, because neither patients who received the combined treatment nor patients whose medications were continued for the first year of the 2-year follow-up showed any particular increase in risk following medication withdrawal. Further, prior cognitive therapy has been associated with comparable rates of relapse prevention in other similar studies (Blackburn, Eunson, & Bishop, 1986; Kovacs, Rush, Beck, & Hollon, 1981; Simons, Murphy, Levine, & Wetzel, 1986). Across the four studies (the three just cited plus the CPT project), rates of relapse following successful pharmacotherapy have averaged 65%, whereas rates of relapse following cognitive therapy have averaged only 25% (Hollon, 1990).

Definitive conclusions cannot be drawn from these findings. The samples followed in any given study have been quite small and, in some instances, the observed differences were as much a consequence of differential return to treatment as any actual renewal of symptoms (Hollon, Shelton, & Loosen, 1991). And if these findings indicate a true prevention effect, it is still not clear whether what is being prevented is the onset of wholly new episodes, or the return of symptoms associated with the treated episode—*recurrence* and *relapse*, respectively (Hollon, Evans, & DeRubeis, 1990). Nonetheless, these data do suggest a prophylactic effect for cognitive therapy following treatment termination that has not been found for other existing treatments of depression.

Change in Explanatory Style as a Mediator of the Relapse Prevention Effect. Is there evidence that altering explanatory style actually confers protection against the subsequent onset of depression? We think there is. Although no completed studies have attempted to reduce risk by altering explanatory style in a currently nondepressed sample, data from the CPT project suggest that such efforts may, at least in part, account for cognitive therapy's apparent prophylactic effect. As already described, patients treated with cognitive therapy evidenced a significantly lower rate of relapse following treatment termination than did patients treated with medications only (Evans et al., 1992). Further, cognitive therapy produced greater change in explanatory style, particularly among treatment responders, than did pharmacotherapy, despite the fact that the two treatments produced comparable change in depression. Finally, the bulk of the change in explanatory style in cognitive therapy came during the last 6 weeks of treatment, well after the bulk of the change in depressive symptoms. This is when the greatest change in explanatory style might have been expected, given the early emphasis in cognitive therapy on specific behaviors and beliefs, and the later emphasis on more general tendencies such as negative explanatory styles.

Did explanatory style predict relapse following treatment termination? Pretreatment scores on the ASQ did not, but scores at termination did. (Relations were tested using proportional hazards linear models to regress "time-to-first-relapse" on the potential predictor variables; Cox, 1972.) Scores on a variety of cognitive indices at posttreatment also predicted subsequent relapse, but largely because they covaried with residual levels of depression following treatment. When posttreatment depression was controlled for statistically, only explanatory style remained a significant predictor of subsequent relapse.

Did quality of cognitive therapy predict change in explanatory style? This also appeared to be the case. Independent raters listened to audiotapes and rated sessions from all patients in the study. An index of the adherence of the sessions to cognitive therapy was constructed from the cognitive therapy scale of the Minnesota Therapy Rating Scale (DeRubeis, Hollon, Evans, & Bemis, 1982), and the Cognitive Therapy Scale (Young & Beck, 1980). These ratings significantly predicted change in explanatory style from pretreatment to posttreatment, suggesting that better adherence to cognitive therapy procedures leads to greater change in explanatory style. Moreover, the ratings provided a more powerful prediction of subsequent prevention than did simply knowing which treatment condition the patient had received.

Could changes in explanatory style be said to mediate cognitive therapy's apparent preventive effect? That is, could cognitive therapy be said to exert its protective influence by virtue of modifying depressotypic explanatory style? In order to explore this issue, we used regression analyses to contrast a model positing a causal mediational role for explanatory style versus one in which the relation between explanatory style and the subsequent prevention of relapse was purely spurious. In the spurious model, cognitive therapy would change explanatory style and prevent relapse through separate mechanisms, with no direct causal link between explanatory style and relapse prevention.

According to Baron and Kenny (1986), at least three conditions need to be met for a construct to be said to mediate the causal relation between treatment and outcome. First, the purported mediator should itself be predicted by the treatment variable. As previously described, cognitive therapy produced greater change in explanatory style than did pharmacotherapy among the treatment responders, and the magnitude of that relation was even larger when variation in the quality of execution of cognitive therapy was taken into account. Second, the treatment variable should predict outcome (in this instance relapse), when the purported mediator is not considered. Cognitive therapy should be associated with a significant reduction in subsequent relapse, which it was. Finally, the relation between the purported mediator must remain significant when the dependent variable (relapse) is regressed simultaneously on both that mediator and the independent variable (treatment). Once again, this was the case. (There is a fourth index, that controlling for the mediator should reduce the magnitude of the relation between the treatment variable and the outcome. This criterion was also met in the CPT data set.)

Thus, the pattern of relations observed in the CPT data set is consistent with the formulation that cognitive therapy reduces risk for subsequent relapse, at least in part, by virtue of changing maladaptive explanatory style (Abramson et al., 1989; Hollon & Garber, 1980; Seligman, 1981). Given the size of the sample involved and the resultant instability of relations observed, we consider this finding to be suggestive, and we emphasize the need for replication. Nonetheless, this is the first study to examine the role of explanatory style as a potential mediator of risk reduction, and given that the findings observed conformed so closely to what had been predicted from existing theory, we think they are noteworthy.

Given the design of the CPT project, we were unable to conduct the optimal tests of the mediation of acute treatment effects (cf. Baron & Kenny, 1986). In order to test these hypotheses more specifically, studies are needed that compare cognitive therapy against a minimal treatment condition (see DeRubeis et al., 1990).

There are no other studies in which the mediational role of explanatory style in risk reduction been examined. Although several other studies have examined whether cognitive therapy reduces subsequent risk (which it appears to do), none have assessed changes in explanatory style across treatment. Eaves and Rush (1984) found that variation in explanatory style at posttreatment predicted subsequent symptom status in a sample of inpatients and outpatients. But this finding was not replicated in a sample of remitted outpatients (Rush, Weissenburger, & Eaves, 1986). It should be noted that most of the patients in those two studies were treated with medications, and not with cognitive therapy. Clearly, what is needed are more studies that compare interventions designed to produce change in explanatory style versus those that do not. Ongoing assessments of change in explanatory style need to be made, so that these changes can be related to subsequent prevention of relapse. Whether the apparent mediation of relapse prevention we observed will be replicated remains an open empirical question.

Even more critically, whether this apparent mediational status will extend to the prevention of wholly new episodes, either in people with no prior history or in people treated for existing depressions, remains to be determined. We currently have work underway examining both questions, but we hope that other investigators will also explore these issues.

It appears, then, that explanatory style, a trait that remains relatively stable across the life span (Burns & Seligman, 1989), can be changed through cognitive therapy. Moreover, such change may be critical in cognitive therapy, at least for the long-term effects of the treatment.

THE MEANING OF THERAPY-PRODUCED CHANGE IN EXPLANATORY STYLE

The findings concerning the role of explanatory style change in cognitive therapy are encouraging, because they point to a mediator of the relapse prevention effect. But what do they mean? How can change in explanatory style be conceptualized? One way to address this question is to consider two very different kinds of psychological change. Either or both might: (a) occur in cognitive therapy, (b) be relatively specific to cognitive therapy, and (c) account for its short-term or long-term effects on symptoms. These two kinds of change can be labeled *schema change* and *the acquisition of compensatory skills* (see Barber & DeRubeis, 1989; Hollon & Kriss, 1984).

The schema-change hypothesis suggests that, during cognitive therapy, fundamental, deep changes occur in the way the patient sees the world, especially his or her role in the world. Patients whose schemas have changed after cognitive therapy would experience and exhibit changes in basic assumptions, or presumptions, about the reasons bad events happen to them when they do. They would also exhibit a tendency to draw more benign conclusions about the implications of untoward events. For example, whereas prior to treatment patients might have believed themselves to be unlovable, they now believe themselves to be lovable. Or, patients who believed themselves to be worthless now believe themselves to be virtuous. An observer would see such a change in the form of less dire reactions (attributions and expectations) following rejection or failure. Patients would experience this kind of change by noticing that their immediate interpretations of instances of rejection or failure are simply not as volatile, not as "hot."

We would expect patients who have changed in this way to be relieved of their depressive symptoms, and they should be less vulnerable to future episodes of depression as well. In traditional terms, what we have described is akin to personality restructuring or personality change. This is a plausible kind of change, and perhaps the most desirable kind of change that could be produced by a psychotherapy.

However, as clinicians and researchers we have some difficulty with the hypothesis that cognitive therapy produces substantial schema change. As clinicians, we question the plausibility of such a hypothesis. The kinds of schemas that are said to change are also those that are the deepest ones. Their development is assumed to derive from some combination of constitutional factors and early learning (Beck, 1967; Kovacs & Beck, 1978a, 1978b). As such, these schemata have been used, habitually, for a very long time by the time therapy begins. But, cognitive therapy is a short-term treatment—3–4 months in duration, involving 10–20 sessions. Although it is not impossible for such deep change to occur in this period of time, we have not seen such changes in the clinic. We submit that such change, even if it does occur in some cases, is not a common outcome of cognitive therapy.

As researchers, we see that it has been difficult for investigators to obtain specific effects on purported measures of schema. That is, on self-report schema measures such as the DAS, patients do change in cognitive therapy, but they also change in other therapies, such as medication treatments, that are not expected to produce such schema change (e.g., Simons, Garfield, & Murphy, 1984). We should mention that in one study, a specific effect of cognitive therapy on one aspect of the DAS was found (Imber et al., 1990). In general, however, changes on such measures appear not to be specific to cognitive therapy. If they are not specific, it is still possible that they mediate short-term change, because it may be that in medication treatment these measures change as a consequence of change in mood (Hollon, DeRubeis, & Evans, 1987). But unless a measure distinguishes cognitive-therapy-treated from medication-treated patients at the end of treatment, it cannot account for any protection against relapse that a course of cognitive therapy might confer.

We now describe the compensatory skills hypothesis. This hypothesis states that the mediator of outcome in cognitive therapy is the acquisition and application of a set of thinking and planning skills; skills patients can apply whenever they become aware of negative emotional reactions—sadness, fear, anger, and so forth. Indeed, strictly speaking, compensatory skills encompass the ability to recognize and label negative emotional reactions in their nascent stages. The idea is that depressed patients have for a long time employed their maladaptive response patterns, or schemata, so that their schematic responses are automatic in that they require no effort or attention. Rather, they just leap to mind. On this view, the leverage that the therapist has is to help the patient see that (a) there is a thought or belief behind the emotional reaction, without which the patient would have a different emotional reaction, or a much attenuated reaction; (b) the thought is not necessarily the "Truth"; and (c) there are many ways to question or challenge the thought or belief. The ways to question or challenge beliefs, such as gathering evidence, seeking alternative explanations, and so on, constitute the details, or techniques, of cognitive therapy (Beck et al., 1979). According to the compensatory skills hypothesis, very little in the psychology or personality of the patient changes in cognitive therapy. Instead, new abilities are added or learned; abilities that help the patient to chip away at and master current concerns and problems. These same abilities can then be used in an incipient episode of depression after treatment has ceased. The patient can call on these skills to blunt what otherwise would spiral into a full-fledged depressive episode.

A casual, or even keen observer might not be able to tell whether a patient's reaction to a potentially upsetting event is benign because of change in schemata or because the patient has acquired new skills. But the patient should experience these two phenomena differently. For patients who are compensating, the old schemata should still be operating. Thus, their initial, automatic reactions to rejection or failure should contain familiar elements described well by the pessimistic explanatory style—self-blame, dire predictions, and overgeneralizations. But they will, perhaps very quickly, recognize that these reactions are not necessarily the only ones to have. They will then curtail their natural reaction, using the methods of cognitive therapy, so that the reaction does not persist, or snowball. This entire sequence could take place in a brief moment, but the compensatory skills hypothesis says that such a sequence does take place, and that it is the ability of patients to use these methods that makes them well and keeps them well.

This sequence of reactions can be contrasted to that of patients whose schemas have changed. For such patients, negative interpretations of potentially upsetting events should no longer occur to them any more frequently than they do to people who never had a tendency toward depressive thinking. In psychodynamic terms, achieving schema change can be likened to changing wishes and expectations at a basic level, whereas acquiring compensatory skills is similar to building defenses (cf. Luborsky, 1984).

Does cognitive-therapy-produced change in explanatory style reflect schema change or the use of compensatory skills? If we assume that respondents reply to the ASQ prompts with the first thing that comes to mind, then their answers should reflect their deep beliefs, or schemas. If, on the other hand, after cognitive therapy responses to the prompts provided by the ASQ reflect an active challenging of automatic, or schema-driven, responses, we would say that positive responses reflect the development of compensatory skills. Because respondents are allowed as much time as they like to answer questions on the ASQ, there is no way to know whether our cognitive-therapy-treated patients were exhibiting a change in their schemas or, rather, an increase in their ability to use the skills they learned in therapy.

FUTURE DIRECTIONS

Testing Explanatory Style as a Mediator of Change in Cognitive Therapy. Findings regarding the role of explanatory style in risk reduction in cognitive therapy need to be replicated. In addition, studies must be conducted that test explanatory style as a mediator of the acute effect of cognitive therapy. To do so, investigators will need to include a less powerful treatment, so that the tests of mediation can be performed (see DeRubeis et al., 1990). In addition, other measures should be included to allow for a better understanding of the meaning of change in explanatory style. Convergent and discriminant validity studies are needed here, as they are in explanatory style research in general. Are measures of explanatory style related statistically to measures of other, possibly similar, constructs, such as neuroticism (Eysenck & Eysenck, 1968), optimism (Scheier & Carver, 1985), or self-esteem (Coopersmith, 1987; see Kamen, 1989)? If explanatory style is related statistically to any of these constructs, this could inform our understanding of the meaning of change in it.

In addition, there needs to be more work on convergent methods of measuring explanatory style. One promising method is the Content Analysis of Verbatim Explanations (CAVE) technique, a technique that is thoroughly described in chapter 2 of this volume (see also Peterson, Luborsky, & Seligman, 1983). Briefly, explanations in respondents' naturally occurring speech are coded along the explanatory dimensions (internality, specificity, globality). The advantage of this method for treatment research over the use of the ASQ is that it can catch subjects off guard. That is, on the ASQ, subjects have the time and opportunity to be "careful" about the kinds of explanations they give, and they are allowed to characterize their own answers on the explanatory dimensions. As noted earlier, patients who have been through cognitive therapy may have learned what the "bad" answers are on the ASQ. As such, their answers might reflect an understanding of what they are supposed to say, and may not reflect a change in the way they naturally explain good and bad events. But with the CAVE technique, the raw material can be obtained in a setting in which respondents may not be overly careful about their answers. Their natural way of explaining events is therefore allowed to come through.

One drawback of the CAVE technique, however, is that is has the potential to confound individual differences in respondents' explanatory styles with the realities of their lives. With the CAVE technique, as it has been used to date, respondents talk about their own lives and the events that have occurred in them. Thus, the actual internality, stability, and globality of the causes of the events they discuss is allowed to vary between respondents, because the realities of the events constrain the subjects' verbatim explanations. So, two patients whose styles of explaining events may be similar could look very different on the CAVE if, for example, one patient talked about temporary difficulties while the other talked about long-standing difficulties that are likely to persist well into the future. One way around this problem would be to construct an oral version of the ASQ, in which patients would be given standard prompts to react to. They would talk about the cause(s) of these events, as they do for the CAVE procedure, and their responses could be rated by raters, as they are on the CAVE.

Is Primary Prevention Possible?   In our discussion of prevention, we focused on those who have already experienced an episode of depression, an important goal in its own right. But perhaps more important are efforts, currently underway, to forestall the onset of initial episodes (Lewinsohn, 1987; Munoz, Ying, Armas, Chan, & Gurza, 1987; Vega, Valle, Kolody, & Hough, 1987). The question in these studies is whether programs that combine cognitive and behavioral elements can be delivered to people at risk before they experience their first episodes of depression in such a way as to prevent it. The present authors are also involved in such an effort, along with Martin Seligman.

Over the past several years Seligman and his colleagues have adapted cognitive therapy for use with euthymic individuals. They have applied these methods to individuals at risk for occupational failure, athletes who wished to improve their performance, and school children identified as at risk for disturbance.

In the project currently underway, college students at high risk for affective disturbance are being identified. Those scoring in the upper quartile on the ASQ will serve as the high-risk sample. A random half of the subjects will be assigned to an assessment-only control group. The other half will participate in a series of workshops modeled after cognitive therapy. The workshop series consists of eight 2-hour group sessions. Of central interest are three questions. First, does participation in such workshops confer risk reduction? Second, is there an effect of the workshops on explanatory style? And, finally, if the answer to the first two questions is "yes," does change in explanatory style mediate risk reduction?

SUMMARY AND CONCLUSIONS

Although explanatory style is considered to be a stable trait, it appears that at least one form of therapy, cognitive therapy, produces substantial change in it. Moreover, the change in explanatory style that cognitive therapy produces may play a critical role in the reduction of distress, the prevention of future distress, or both. The existing evidence for these propositions is scant, but promising. Whether change in explanatory style is accomplished by means of altering existing predispositions or by providing compensatory skills to counteract these predispositions, is a question that has yet to be resolved.

7

▼▼▼▼▼▼▼

Hopelessness Depression

Lyn Y. Abramson
University of Wisconsin

Lauren B. Alloy
Temple University

Gerald I. Metalsky
Lawrence University

This chapter presents the hopelessness theory of depression (Abramson, Metalsky, & Alloy, 1989), a revision of the 1978 reformulated theory of helplessness and depression (Abramson, Seligman, & Teasdale, 1978). Complementing clinical and taxonometric approaches, this theory represents a theory-based approach to the classification of a subset of depressive disorders that is process-oriented rather than symptom-oriented (see also Seligman, 1978). In essence, the hopelessness theory postulates the existence in nature of an as yet unidentified subtype of depression, hopelessness depression, that may be lurking among the various disorders currently called *depression*. We describe the hypothesized cause, symptoms, course, therapy, and prevention of hopelessness depression as well as its relation to other types of depression and nondepression. In addition, we discuss how to search for hopelessness depression to see if it exists in nature and conforms to its theoretical description.

STATEMENT OF THE HOPELESSNESS THEORY OF DEPRESSION

Cause

In contrast to symptom-based approaches to the classification of the depressive disorders (see Kendell, 1968), cause figures prominently in the definition of hopelessness depression. Although most current classification systems are largely symptom-based, few would disagree that, when possible, classification of psychopathologies by etiology in addition to other factors is more desirable than classification by symptoms alone insofar as the former generally has more direct implications for cure and prevention than the latter (McLemore & Benjamin, 1979; Skinner, 1981). Overall, the hopelessness theory specifies a chain of distal and proximal contributory causes hypothesized to culminate in a proximal sufficient cause of the symptoms of hopelessness depression.

A Proximal Sufficient Cause of the Symptoms of Hopelessness Depression: Hopelessness. According to the hopelessness theory, a proximal sufficient cause of the symptoms of hopelessness depression is an expectation that highly desired outcomes will not occur (e.g., rewards will not occur) and/or that highly aversive outcomes will occur (e.g., punishment will occur) and that no response in one's repertoire will change the likelihood of occurrence of these outcomes. Abramson et al. (1989) viewed this theory as a hopelessness theory because the common language term *hopelessness* captures the core elements of the proximal sufficient cause featured in the theory: negative expectations about the occurrence of highly valued outcomes (a negative outcome expectancy) and expectations of helplessness about changing the likelihood of occurrence of these outcomes (a helplessness expectancy). Throughout the chapter, we use the term *hopelessness* to refer to this proximal sufficient cause. Abramson et al. used the phrase "generalized hopelessness" when people exhibited the negative outcome/helplessness expectancy about many areas of life. In contrast, "circumscribed pessimism" occurs when people exhibit the negative outcome/helplessness expectancy about only a limited domain. They suggested that cases of generalized hopelessness should produce severe symptoms of hopelessness depression, whereas circumscribed pessimism is likely to be associated with fewer and/or less severe symptoms.

According to the theory, hopelessness is a proximal sufficient, but not a necessary, cause of depressive symptoms. The theory therefore explicitly recognizes that depression may be a heterogeneous disorder and allows for the possibility that other factors such as genetic vulnerability, neurotransmitter aberrations, loss of interest in reinforcers, and so forth, may also be sufficient to cause depressive symptoms. Thus, the hopelessness theory presents an etiological account of one hypothesized subtype of depression, hopelessness depression.

One Hypothesized Causal Pathway to the Symptoms of Hopelessness Depression. How does a person become hopeless and, in turn, develop the symptoms of hopelessness depression? As can be seen in Fig. 7.1, the hypothesized causal chain begins with the perceived occurrence of negative life events (or nonoccurrence of positive life events).[1] Negative events serve as "occasion setters" for people to become hopeless. At least three types of inferences people may make

---

[1]For the sake of brevity, we use the phrase *negative life events* to refer to both the occurrence of negative life events and the nonoccurrence of positive life events.

Hopelessness Theory of Depression

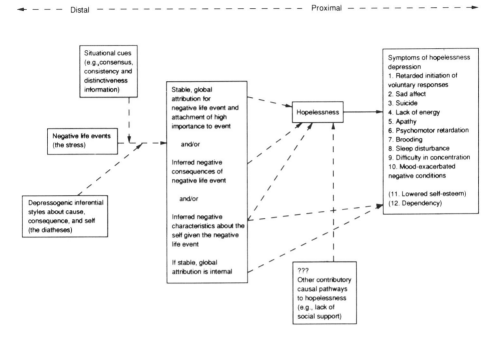

FIG. 7.1. Causal chain specified in the hopelessness theory of depression (arrows with solid lines indicate sufficient causes; arrows with broken lines indicate contributory causes).

modulate whether or not they become hopeless and, in turn, develop the symptoms of hopelessness depression in the face of negative life events: (a) inferences about why the event occurred (i.e., inferred cause or causal attribution), (b) inferences about consequences that might result from the occurrence of the event (i.e., inferred consequences), and (c) inferences about the self given that the event happened to the person (i.e., inferred characteristics about the self).

Proximal Contributory Causes: Inferred Stable, Global Causes of Particular Negative Life Events and a High Degree of Importance Attached to These Events. Relatively generalized hopelessness and the symptoms of hopelessness depression are more likely to occur when negative life events are attributed to stable (i.e., enduring) and global (i.e., pervasive) causes and viewed as important than when they are attributed to unstable, specific causes and viewed as unimportant.

What influences the kinds of causal inferences people make? People's causal attributions for events are, in part, a function of the situational information they confront (Kelley, 1967; McArthur, 1972). People tend to attribute an event to the factor or factors with which it covaries. According to this view, people would be predicted to make internal, stable, and global attributions for an event (e.g., being battered by a husband) when they are confronted with situational information suggesting that the event is low in consensus (e.g., other women are not battered by this man), high in consistency (e.g., frequently being battered by this man), and low in distinctiveness (e.g., being put down by many other people; Kelley, 1967; Metalsky & Abramson, 1981). Thus, informational cues make some causal inferences for particular life events more plausible than others and some not plausible at all (see also Hammen & Mayol, 1982). Social psychologists have suggested a number of additional factors that also may guide the causal attribution process, including expectations for success and failure, motivation to protect or enhance one's self-esteem, focus of attention, salience of a potential causal factor, and self-presentational concerns, to name a few. In a later section, we discuss a more distal cause, cognitive style, that is also hypothesized to influence the causal inferences that people make.

Proximal Contributory Causes: Inferred Negative Consequences of Particular Negative Life Events.   Hammen and her colleagues (e.g., Gong-Guy & Hammen, 1980; Hammen & Cochran, 1981; Hammen & deMayo, 1982) argued that the inferred consequences of negative events, independent of causal inferences for these events, may modulate the likelihood that people will become depressed when confronted with a negative life event. For example, a student may attribute his or her low scores on the Graduate Record Examination (GRE) to distracting noises in the testing room (an unstable, specific attribution) but infer that a consequence of his or her poor performance on the GRE is that he or she never will be admitted to a graduate program in mathematics, his or her preferred career choice. Abramson et al. (1989) suggested that inferred negative consequences moderate the relationship between negative life events and the symptoms of hopelessness depression by affecting the likelihood of becoming hopeless. Following the same logic as for causal attributions, inferred negative consequences should be particularly likely to lead to hopelessness when the negative consequence is viewed as important, not remediable, unlikely to change, and as affecting many areas of life. When the negative consequence is seen as affecting only a very limited sphere of life, relatively circumscribed pessimism rather than generalized hopelessness should result.

Proximal Contributory Causes: Inferred Negative Characteristics About the Self Given Negative Life Events.   In addition to inferred consequences of negative events, Abramson et al. (1989) suggested that inferred characteristics about the self given these events also may modulate the likelihood of formation of hopelessness and, subsequently, the symptoms of hopelessness depression. Inferred characteristics about the self refer to the inferences a person draws about his or her own worth, abilities, personality, desirability, and so forth, from the fact that a particular negative life event occurred. Such a concept appears central in Beck's (1967) description of cognitive processes and depression. For example,

Beck (1976) reported the case of a depressed suicidal woman who previously had had a breach in her relationship with her lover Raymond and said, "I am worthless." When the therapist asked why she believed she was worthless, she replied, "If I don't have love, I am worthless" (pp. 99–100). Again, following the same logic as for causal attributions, inferred negative characteristics about the self should be particularly likely to lead to hopelessness when the person believes that the negative characteristic is not remediable or likely to change and that possession of it will preclude the attainment of important outcomes in many areas of life. When the negative characteristic is seen as precluding the attaiment of outcomes in only a very limited sphere of life, relatively circumscribed pessimism rather than generalized hopelessness should result. Inferred characteristics about the self given negative events may not be independent of causal attributions for these events, but it is useful to conceptualize and operationalize them as distinct.

For the occurrence of a given negative life event, the three kinds of inferences (cause, consequence, and self-characteristics) may not be equally important in contributing to whether or not the person becomes hopeless and, in turn, develops the symptoms of hopelessness depression. For example, a young girl's inferences about the negative consequences of her mother's death, rather than about its cause or immediate implications for her view of herself, may be most important in contributing to whether or not she becomes hopeless.

Distal Contributory Causes: Cognitive Styles. Individual differences may exist in people's characteristic tendencies to make depressogenic inferences when confronted with a negative life event. We refer to these patterns of inference as *cognitive styles*. For example, as a complement to social psychologists' work on the situational determinants of causal attributions, Abramson et al. (1978) suggested a more distal factor that also may influence the content of people's causal inferences for a particular event: individual differences in attributional style (see also Ickes & Layden, 1978). Some individuals may exhibit a general tendency to attribute negative events to stable, global factors and to view these events as very important, whereas other individuals may not. We use the phrase *hypothesized depressogenic attributional style* to refer to this tendency.

Individuals who exhibit the hypothesized depressogenic attributional style should be more likely than individuals who do not to attribute any particular negative event to a stable, global cause and view the event as very important, thereby incrementing the likelihood of becoming hopeless and, in turn, developing the symptoms of hopelessness depression. However, in the presence of positive life events or in the absence of negative life events, people exhibiting the hypothesized depressogenic attributional style should be no more likely to develop hopelessness, and therefore the symptoms of hopelessness depression, than people not exhibiting this attributional style. This aspect of the theory is conceptualized usefully as a *diathesis-stress component* (Metalsky, Abramson, Seligman, Semmel, & Peterson, 1982). That is, the hypothesized depressogenic attributional style (the diathesis) is a distal contributory cause of the symptoms of hopelessness depression that operates in the presence, but not in the absence, of negative life events (the stress).

The logic of the diathesis-stress component implies that a depressogenic attributional style in a particular content domain (e.g., for interpersonal-related events) provides "specific vulnerability" (cf. Beck, 1967) to the symptoms of hopelessness depression when an individual is confronted with negative life events in that same content domain (e.g., social rejection). This specific vulnerability hypothesis requires that there be a match between the content areas of an individual's depressogenic attributional style and the negative life events he or she encounters for the attributional diathesis-stress interaction to predict future symptoms of hopelessness depression (cf. Alloy, Hartlage, & Abramson, 1988; Anderson & Arnoult, 1985; Anderson, Horowitz, & French, 1983; Hammen, Marks, Mayol, & deMayo, 1985; Alloy, Kayne, Romer, & Crocker, 1992; Metalsky, Halberstadt, & Abramson, 1987).

As with causal inferences, individual differences may exist in the general tendency to infer negative consequences and negative characteristics about the self given the occurrence of negative life events. It is not known whether or not such cognitive styles are independent of the hypothesized depressogenic attributional style. Abramson et al. (1989) suggested these two additional cognitive styles also are diatheses that operate in the presence, but not in the absence, of negative life events according to the specific vulnerability hypothesis. Abramson et al. referred to these three negative styles as *cognitive diatheses*. Beck's (Weissman & Beck, 1979) concept of dysfunctional attitudes and Ellis' (1977) concept of irrational beliefs appear to overlap, in part, with these cognitive diatheses.

Cognitive styles probably are best conceptualized as continua with some people exhibiting more negative styles than others. Similarly, it may be more appropriate to speak of a continuum of negativity of life events. The continuum view suggests a titration model (cf. Zubin & Spring, 1977) of the diathesis-stress component. The less negative a person's cognitive style, the more negative an event needs to be in order to interact with that style and contribute to the formation of symptoms. Thus, although many cases of hopelessness depression will occur among cognitively vulnerable people when they are confronted with negative events, people who do not exhibit the cognitive diatheses also may develop hopelessness depression when they are confronted with events sufficient to engender hopelessness in many or most people (e.g., a person who is put in a concentration camp and repeatedly told by the guards that the only way to leave the camp is as a corpse). In a related vein, it is likely that major negative life events are not required to initiate the series of inferences hypothesized to culminate in the symptoms of hopelessness depression. Instead, the occurrence of more minor events, chronic stressors or even daily hassles also may trigger the hypothesized depressogenic inferences among cognitively vulnerable people.

In addition to the cognitive factors described previously, interpersonal (e.g., lack of social support; Brown & Harris, 1978; Lipman & Alloy, 1992; Panzarella-Tse, Alloy, & Lipman, 1992), developmental (e.g., sexual, physical, and psychological abuse; Rose & Abramson, 1992; Rose, Leff, Halberstadt, Hodulik, & Abramson, 1992) and even genetic factors also may modulate the likelihood that a person will develop hopelessness and, in turn, the symptoms of hopelessness depression (see Tiger, 1979, for an intriguing discussion of genetic and biological factors in the development of hope and hopelessness).

Symptoms

Hopelessness depression should be characterized by a number of symptoms. The 1978 reformulation contains descriptions of two of these symptoms, and Abramson et al. (1989) retained them in the hopelessness theory: (a) retarded initiation of voluntary responses (motivational symptom), and (b) sad affect (emotional symptom). The motivational symptom derives from the helplessness expectancy component of hopelessness. If a person expects that nothing he or she does matters, why try? The incentive for emitting active instrumental responses decreases (Alloy, 1982; Bolles, 1972). Sadness derives from the negative outcome expectancy component of hopelessness and is a likely consequence of the expectation that the future is bleak. Abramson et al. no longer included the third symptom described in the 1978 reformulation, the cognitive symptom (associative deficit), because work on depressive realism (e.g., Alloy & Abramson, 1979, 1988; Alloy, Albright, Abramson, & Dykman, 1990; Dykman, Abramson, Alloy, & Hartlage, 1989) has not supported it.

Hopelessness depression should be characterized by other symptoms as well. Insofar as hopelessness is a key factor in suicide attempts and suicidal ideation, suicide attempts and suicidal ideation are likely symptoms of hopelessness depression (Beck, Kovacs, & Weissman, 1975; Kazdin, French, Unis, Esveldt-Dawson, & Sherick, 1983; Minkoff, Bergman, Beck, & Beck, 1973; Petrie & Chamberlain, 1983). If lack of energy, apathy, and psychomotor retardation are, in part, concomitants of a severe decrease in the motivation to initiate voluntary responses (see Beck, 1967), then they should be symptoms of hopelessness depression. Abramson et al. (1989) hypothesized that to the extent that people brood about the highly desired outcomes they feel hopeless to attain, sleep disturbance (e.g., initial insomnia) and difficulty in concentration will be important symptoms of hopelessness depression. Based on work showing that mood affects cognition (e.g., Bower, 1981), Abramson et al. predicted that as individuals suffering from hopelessness depression become increasingly sad, their cognitions will become even more negative.

Although not necessarily symptoms of hopelessness depression, low self-esteem and/or dependency sometimes will accompany the other hypothesized symptoms. Lowered self-esteem will be a symptom of hopelessness depression when the event that triggered the episode was attributed to an internal, stable, global cause as opposed to any type of external cause or to an internal, unstable, specific cause. In addition, lowered self-esteem should occur in cases of hopelessness depression when people have inferred negative characteristics about themselves which they view as important to their general self-concept and not remediable or likely to change. Finally, dependency frequently may co-occur with lowered self-esteem because the conditions that give rise to lowered self-esteem will leave the person feeling inferior to others and thereby increase the likelihood that he or she may become excessively dependent on them (Brewin & Furnham, 1987).

In general, circumscribed pessimism (i.e., when people are hopeless about only a limited domain) may not be associated with the full syndrome of the symptoms of hopelessness depression. Circumscribed pessimism is likely to produce fewer and/or less severe symptoms than generalized hopelessness. Whereas the motivational deficit should occur in cases of circumscribed pessimism, sadness may be less intense or even absent. Similarly, people with circumscribed pessimism should be less likely to commit suicide or exhibit the other hypothesized symptoms of hopelessness depression. Thus, circumscribed pessimism should lead to an identifiable behavioral syndrome, but this syndrome should be characterized primarily by a motivational deficit in the relevant domain.

Course

In considering the course of a disorder, the concepts of *maintenance, recovery, relapse,* and *recurrence* need to be distinguished (Klerman, 1978). Maintenance refers to the duration of a given episode of a disorder and recovery refers to its remission. Relapse is a return of clinically significant symptoms within a relatively short period following remission, whereas recurrence is the onset of a new episode following a prolonged interval of remission.

Insofar as hopelessness is viewed as a proximal sufficient cause of the symptoms of hopelessness depression, the maintenance or duration of an episode of hopelessness depression should be influenced by how long this expectation is present. The more stable a person's attribution for a negative life event, the longer the person will be hopeless and, consequently, symptomatic. As a corollary, the maintenance of hopelessness should be influenced by the stability of the attribution for the event that triggered the given episode and by the stability of attributions for newly occurring negative life events (see Brown & Harris, 1978; Lloyd, Zisook, Click, & Jaffe, 1981). Maintenance also may be influenced by the consequences the individual infers from the fact that he or she is depressed, as well as by the attribution he or she makes for the depression itself (Nolen-Hoeksema, 1991). Similarly, maintenance may be influenced by the characteristics the individual infers about him or herself given that he or she is depressed. More generally, any factor that influences the duration of hopelessness should, in turn, influence the maintenance or chronicity of the symptoms of hopelessness depression. These predictors of the duration of a given episode of hopelessness depression follow directly from the logic of the hopelessness theory. In addition, the possibility exists that once an individual becomes hopeless, some biological or psychological processes are triggered that need to run their course and do not dissipate as quickly as hopelessness. Such factors might maintain a hopelessness depression after hopelessness remits. Similarly, other factors such as lack of social support also may influence the duration of an episode of hopelessness depression after hopelessness remits.

Needles and Abramson (1990) proposed a model of recovery from hopelessness depression that highlights positive events. They suggested that the occurrence of positive events provides the occasion for people suffering from hopelessness depression to become "hopeful" and, in turn, nondepressed. Analogously to the logic of the diathesis-stress component, they suggested that people with a style to attribute positive events to stable, global causes should be particularly likely to become hopeful and, in turn, nondepressed when confronted with a positive event (or a reduction in negative events). Thus, positive events and inferences about them (cause, consequence, self-characteristics) may be particuarly important in recovery from hopelessness depression.

Given the logic of the hopelessness theory, relapse or recurrence of hopelessness depression should be predicted by the reappearance of hopelessness because, by definition, a *relapse* or *recurrence* is a new onset of hopelessness depression. Thus, the etiological chain hypothesized to culminate in the onset of the symptoms of hopelessness depression also applies directly to the relapse or recurrence of these symptoms. Hence, people with cognitive diatheses will be more likely to have relapses or recurrences of hopelessness depression when confronted with negative life events than people who do not exhibit these diatheses. The stronger the diathesis, the lower the threshold of stress needed to result in a relapse.

Therapy and Prevention

The hopelessness theory specifies an etiological chain, thus each link suggests a point for clinical intervention. A major advantage of using the proximal–distal continuum to order the events that cause hopelessness depression is that it not only suggests points of intervention for reversing current episodes but also suggests points for decreasing vulnerability.

Treating Current Episodes of Hopelessness Depression.   Any therapeutic strategy that undermines hopelessness and restores hopefulness should be effective in remediating current symptoms of hopelessness depression (see also Hollon & Garber, 1980). Hopelessness could be attacked directly. Alternatively, the proximal causes (e.g., stable, global attributions for particular negative life events) that contribute to a person's current hopelessness could be attacked. Insofar as negative events and situational information supporting depressogenic inferences contribute to the maintenance of hopelessness, therapeutic interventions aimed at modifying the hopelessness-inducing environment should be helpful. Finally, if the person's own behavior is, to some degree, contributing to the depressogenic events and situational information he or she encounters, then personal behavior change would be an important therapeutic goal.

Preventing Onset, Relapse, and Recurrence of Hopelessness Depression. According to the hopelessness theory, the three hypothesized cognitive diatheses put people at risk for initial onset, relapse, and recurrence of hopelessness depression. Therefore, modifying cognitive diatheses is an important goal for prevention. Insofar as the cognitive diatheses require negative life events to exert their depressogenic effects, prevention efforts also might be directed toward lessening the stressfulness of events in the environments of cognitively vulnerable people. Finally, primary prevention efforts could be aimed at building nondepressive cognitive styles and environments.

Relation of Hopelessness Depression to Other Types of Depression and Psychopathology

Does the concept of *hopelessness depression* map onto any nosological category of mood disorders currently diagnosed (e.g., dysthymia) or does this concept cut across the various nosological categories of mood or even nonmood disorders currently diagnosed (cf. Rose, Leff, Halberstadt, Hodulik, & Abramson, 1992; Seligman, 1978)? Hopelessness depression most likely includes subsets of individuals from various currently diagnosed categories of depression (e.g., major depression, dysthymia, etc.) and may even include some depressed individuals who a priori would not be expected to be hopelessness depressives (e.g., some endogenous depressives). Moreover, based on empirical and clinical studies of the comorbidity of anxiety and depression, Alloy, Kelly, Mineka, and Clements (1990) suggested that hopelessness depressives may be more likely to suffer from anxiety than are people with other subtypes of depression. These authors suggested that anxiety is caused by the helplessness expectancy component of hopelessness.

A second nosological question is which diagnostic categories of depression, if any, involve fundamentally different etiological processes, and perhaps symptoms and therapy, than those involved in hopelessness depression. Klein's (1974) concept of endogenomorphic depression (see also Costello's, 1972, concept of "reinforcer ineffectiveness depression") which maps closely on to the *DSM-III-R* category of major depressive episode with melancholia, may be fundamentally distinct from the concept of hopelessness depression. The hypothesized core process in endogenomorphic depressions is impairment in the capacity to experience pleasure rather than hopelessness.

A core question concerns the relationship between the concept of hopelessness depression and depression as a whole. Abramson et al. (1989) suggested that the relationship of hopelessness depression to depression as a whole is analogous to the relationship between a subtype of mental retardation (e.g., PKU syndrome, cretinism, etc.) and mental retardation in general. Just as some symptoms of a particular subtype of retardation may be associated with retardation in general (e.g., low IQ), particular hypothesized symptoms of hopelessness depression (e.g., sadness) are considered symptoms of all or most subtypes of depression. Other hypothesized symptoms of hopelessness depression (e.g., motivational deficit) may only partially overlap with the symptoms of other forms of depression. Finally, still other symptoms of hopelessness depression (e.g., suicide and suicidal ideation) may not be associated with other forms of depression. Thus, just as physicians do not define a particular subtype of retardation on the basis of symptoms alone because of potential overlap in some symptoms across subtypes, hopelessness depression is not defined on the basis of symptoms alone. Instead, following the logic of workers in medicine more generally, Abramson et al. defined hopelessness depression in terms of cause, symptoms, course, therapy, and prevention.

Nondepression

The hopelessness theory offers some predictions about how people maintain a positive emotional state. According to the theory, the occurrence of a negative event provides a challenge to a positive emotional state. Making any of the three depressogenic inferences for negative events about cause, consequence, or self should increase the likelihood that hope will be lost and, as a result, the positive emotional state will break down. In contrast, refraining from making these inferences should allow hope to endure and, as a result, the challenge to be withstood and a positive state maintained.

The logic of the hopelessness theory also suggests that the occurrence of a positive event provides an opportunity to enhance one's emotional state. Making any of the following inferences when a positive event occurs should serve to facilitate a positive emotional state by restoring or increasing hope: (a) attributing the positive event to stable, global factors; (b) inferring positive consequences; and/or (c) inferring positive characteristics about the self.

SEARCH FOR HOPELESSNESS DEPRESSION: TOWARD AN EVALUATION OF THE HOPELESSNESS THEORY

How might we search for hopelessness depression to see if it exists in nature and conforms to theoretical description? Some of our colleagues expressed puzzlement and even mystification about how to determine whether or not a theory-based subtype of depression exists in nature or have suggested that a search for hopelessness depression involves circular reasoning. In contrast, we suggest that at a conceptual level, the search for hopelessness depression is straightforward and does not involve anything spooky. To assert that hopelessness depressions exist in nature is simply to say that the hopelessness theory is true (cf. Clark, 1983). We search for the hopelessness depression subtype by testing the hopelessness theory.

A variety of possible methodological approaches exist for searching for hopelessness depressions and distinguishing them from other types of depression. For example, a symptom-based approach would involve determining if a subgroup of depressives exhibits the symptoms hypothesized to be associated with hopelessness depression (e.g., retarded initiation of voluntary responses, etc.). A symptom-based approach commonly has been utilized by workers in descriptive psychiatry, where categories of depression traditionally have been formed on the basis of symptom similarity. However, we believe a symptom-based approach alone would be unsatisfactory in the context of work on the hopelessness theory. The basic problem is that some or all of the symptoms hypothesized to be characteristic of hopelessness depressions conceivably may be present in other types of depression as well (e.g., endogenomorphic depression; Klein, 1974). Moreover, hopelessness depression is defined as a subtype on the basis of other dimensions as well (e.g., cause). In contrast to a purely symptom-based approach, the hopelessness theory of depression points to a process-oriented approach for searching for hopelessness depressions.

Search for Hopelessness Depression: A Research Strategy

A search for hopelessness depression involves at least five components: (a) a test of the etiological chain hypothesized to culminate in the manifest symptoms of hopelessness depression; (b) an examination of the hypothesized manifest symptoms of hopelessness depression; (c) a test of theoretical predictions about the course, remission, relapse, and recurrence of hopelessness depression; (d) a test of theoretical predictions about the cure and prevention of hopelessness depression; and (e) delineation of the relationship among hopelessness depression, other subtypes of depression, and other types of psychopathology.

A test of the etiological chain featured in the hopelessness theory involves an examination of the diathesis-stress and causal mediation components of the theory. An adequate test of the diathesis-stress component involves at least two parts: (a) a demonstration that the interaction between the hypothesized cognitive diatheses and negative life events predicts future depressive symptoms, specifically the symptoms of hopelessness depression; and (b) a demonstration that this interaction predicts the complete constellation of symptoms hypothesized to constitute the hopelessness subtype of depression as opposed to only a subset of these symptoms or symptoms that constitute other subtypes of depression. "Specific vulnerability" predictions also should be tested.

An adequate test of the causal mediation component of the hopelessness theory involves testing these hypothesized probability linkages:

1. Individuals who exhibit the hypothesized cognitive diatheses should be more likely than individuals who do not to make one of the three hypothesized depressogenic inferences (cause, consequence, self). Because depressogenic cognitive styles contribute to, but are neither necessary nor sufficient for, the particular inferences a person makes, this probability linkage should be greater than 0 but less than 1.0.

2. The three hypothesized depressogenic inferences (cause, consequence, self) should increase the likelihood of becoming hopeless. Again, because these inferences are hypothesized to contribute to, but not be necessary or sufficient for, the formation of hopelessness, this probability linkage also should be greater than 0 but less than 1.0.

3. The occurrence of hopelessness should increase the liklihood of the development of the symptoms of hopelessness depression. Because hopelessness is hypothesized to be a sufficient cause of the symptoms of hopelessness depression, this probability linkage should equal 1.0 in the ideal case of error-free measurements.

A necessary condition for the validity of the hopelessness theory is that the hypothesized manifest symptoms of hopelessness depression should be intercorrelated with one another and not as highly correlated with other symptoms found both in depression and other psychopathologies. Moreover, this hypothesized constellation of symptoms must be correlated with hopelessness. Finally, hopelessness must temporally precede the formation of this symptom constellation.

A basic prediction from the hopelessness theory is that the duration of hopelessness should predict the course or chronicity of the symptoms of hopelessness depression. The etiological chain hypothesized to culminate in the onset of the symptoms of hopelessness depression also should predict relapse and recurrence of these symptoms.

Specific predictions follow from the hopelessness theory about the cure and prevention of hopelessness depression. Reversing hopelessness should result in a remission of a current episode of hopelessness depression. Modifying the three hypothesized cognitive diatheses should decrease vulnerability to future hopelessness depression.

No explicit predictions about the relationship of hopelessness depression to other subtypes of depression and other forms of psychopathology can be drawn from the hopelessness theory. However, from a descriptive psychiatric standpoint, it is important to determine if hopelessness depression maps onto any currently diagnosed nosological category of mood disorders (e.g., dysthymia, unipolar major depression, etc.) or, alternatively, cuts across currently diagnosed mood and even nonmood disorders.

In discussing how to search for hopelessness depression, we note the possibility that future work may not corroborate the existence of hopelessness depression as a bona fide subtype with characteristic cause, symptoms, course, treatment, and prevention. Instead, the etiological chain featured in the hopelessness theory may be one of many pathways to a final common outcome of depression. In this case, it would be more compelling to speak of a hopelessness cause, as opposed to a hopelessness subtype, of depression.

EMPIRICAL VALIDITY OF THE HOPELESSNESS THEORY

Because the theory is relatively new, the evidence about its validity is still being collected. However, we and others have conducted a number of studies that test it.

Etiological Chain: Proximal Sufficient Cause Component

A key prediction of the hopelessness theory is that hopelessness temporally precedes and is a proximal sufficient cause of the symptoms of hopelessness depression. An alternative hypothesis is that hopelessness has no causal status and, instead, is simply another symptom of depression. Relevant to distinguishing between these two views, Rholes, Riskind, and Neville (1985) conducted a longitudinal study and reported that college students' levels of hopelessness at Time 1 predicted their levels of depression 5 weeks later at Time 2 over and above the predictive capacity of depression at Time 1. Similarly, in their prospective study, Carver and Gaines (1987) demonstrated that, after controlling statistically for earlier levels of depressive symptoms, dispositional pessimists were more likely to develop postpartum depression than were optimists. Although these results do not establish that hopelessness actually caused depressive symptoms at a later time, they do support the temporal precedence of hopelessness in predicting change in depressive symptoms (see also Riskind, Rholes, Brannon, & Burdick, 1987, for a demonstration that the interaction of attributional style and negative expectations predict future depression).

In addition to the above longitudinal studies, a number of cross-sectional studies and one longitudinal study have tested whether hopelessness is specific to depression or is a more general feature of psychopathology. Abramson, Garber, Edwards, and Seligman (1978) reported that hospitalized unipolar depressives were more hopeless than both hospitalized nondepressed control subjects and nondepressed schizophrenics. Interestingly, the unipolar depressives were also more hopeless than the depressed schizophrenics. Hamilton and Abramson (1983) found that hospitalized unipolar depressives were more hopeless than a hospitalized nondepressed psychiatric group with mixed diagnoses (e.g., schizophrenia, anxiety disorders, and personality disorders) as well as a nondepressed community control group. Beck, Riskind, Brown, and Steer (1988) found that psychiatric patients suffering from major depression were more hopeless than patients suffering from generalized anxiety disorder and a group of "mixed" psychiatric patients (diagnoses other than depression or anxiety). Finally, in a longitudinal study of college undergraduates, Alloy and Clements (1991) found that hopelessness predicted levels of depression a month later, even when state anxiety was partialled, whereas hopelessness did not predict state anxiety a month later once depression was partialled. Taken together, these studies suggest that hopelessness is specific to depression and not a general feature of psychopathology. However, individuals suffering from other disorders (e.g., schizophrenia) may develop hopelessness depression if they come to believe that there will be no relief from their disorder.

To what degree must people's cognitions of hopelessness be active to exert an influence on their moods? In this regard, Needles and Abramson (1992) stressed the importance of distinguishing between the content and the activation of a belief (see also Kim & Alloy, 1992). They showed that among depressed people, changes in depressive mood can be produced by merely changing the level of activation of cognitions of hopelessness without altering the content of these cognitions. These results suggest that future revisions of the hopelessness theory incorporate the distinction between content and activation of beliefs.

Etiological Chain: Diathesis-Stress and Causal Mediation Components

Relevant to these components, a multitude of cross-sectional and longitudinal studies have examined the relationship between attributional style and depression (see Barnett & Gotlib, 1988; Brewin, 1985; Coyne & Gotlib, 1983; Peterson & Seligman, 1984a; Sweeney, Anderson, & Bailey, 1986, for reviews). Overall, these studies have shown that the tendency to make internal, stable, and global attributions for negative events is associated with severity of concurrent and future depressive symptoms in college students, patients, and other samples. However, the corroborative findings have not always been strong.

We argued elsewhere that this research strategy is inappropriate to test the diathesis-stress component (Abramson et al., 1988, 1989; Alloy et al., 1988). Recently, a number of studies have been conducted that do provide a more powerful test of the diathesis-stress component (and in some cases the causal mediation component) of the hopelessness theory. In a prospective field study, Metalsky et al. (1987) found that college students who showed a style to attribute negative achievement events to stable, global causes experienced a more enduring depressive mood reaction to a low midterm grade than did students who did not exhibit this style. Consistent with the diathesis-stress component, attributional style for negative achievement events was not associated with students' mood reactions in the absence of the low grade. Interestingly, whereas students' more enduring depressive mood reactions were predicted by the interaction between attributional style and midterm grade (consistent with the diathesis-stress component), their immediate depressive mood reactions were predicted solely by the outcome on the exam (see also Follette & Jacobson, 1987). The results also provided support for the specific vulnerability hypothesis in that attributional style for negative achievement events, but not for negative interpersonal events, interacted with students' outcomes on the exam (an achievement event) to predict their enduring depressive mood reactions. Finally, consistent with the mediation component of the theory, failure students' attributional styles predicted their particular attributions for their midterm grades that, in turn, completely mediated the relation between attributional style and their enduring depressive mood responses.

Recently, Metalsky, Joiner, Hardin, and Abramson (1993) replicated the Metalsky et al. (1987) findings and further showed that, consistent with the mediation component, students who showed a style to attribute negative achievement events to stable, global causes became more hopeless upon receipt of a low grade than did students who did not exhibit this style. This increase in hopelessness, in turn, mediated the enduring depressive reaction to the low grade exhibited by the former group of students. In addition to examining predictions from the hopelessness theory itself, Metalsky et al. also integrated this theory with the self-esteem theories of depression. Qualifying the diathesis-stress predictions of the hopelessness theory, they found that among students who exhibited a style to attribute negative achievement events to stable, global causes, only those who also exhibited low self-esteem developed the hopelessness-mediated enduring depressive mood response to a low grade.

With a design similar to Metalsky et al. (1987), Alloy, Kayne, Romer, and Crocker (1992) used causal modeling techniques to test the diathesis-stress and causal mediation components of the hopelessness theory and obtained support for both components. Alloy et al. additionally reported that the interaction between attributional style and midterm grade predicted change in depressive symptoms as well as in transient depressive mood responses. Recently, Alloy, Albright, Fresco, and Whitehouse (1992a, 1992b) conducted a longitudinal study of individuals exhibiting *DSM-III-R* cyclothymia, dysthymia, hypomania, or no diagnosis. Alloy et al. (1992a, 1992b) brought these subjects into the laboratory on three occasions over a 9-month period; once during a normal mood state (Time 1) and on two other occasions (Times 2 and 3) during one of these subjects' naturally occurring dysfunctional mood states (e.g., cyclothymics were studied during one normal, one depressive, and one hypomanic mood state). Consistent with the diathesis-stress component of the theory, Alloy et al. (1992b) found that subjects' attributional styles for negative events measured at Time 1 during the normal mood state interacted with negative life events to predict changes in subjects' depressive and hypomanic symptoms at Times 2 and 3, even after initial levels of depression and hypomania were controlled. In addition, attributional styles for negative events were stable across changes in subjects' depressive and hypomanic symptoms from Times 1 to 3 (Alloy et al., 1992a). In another longitudinal study, Nolen-Hoeksema, Girgus, and Seligman (1986) asked whether life events and attributional styles interacted to predict school children's future depression. They obtained partial support for the diathesis-stress component of the theory with negative life events interacting with attributional style in some analyses but not in others. Finally, relevant to the causal mediation component, Brown and Siegel (1988) conducted a prospective study of stress and well-being in adolescence and reported that judgments of control over negative events interacted with attributions for them to predict future depression.

The diathesis-stress component of the theory was examined in two laboratory studies. Using a prospective design, Alloy, Peterson, Abramson, and Seligman (1984) found that students who typically attribute negative life events to global causes showed a wider generalization of learned helplessness deficits to new situations when they were exposed to uncontrollable events than did individuals who typically attribute negative life events to more specific causes. Sacks and Bugental (1987) tested the diathesis-stress component in a laboratory study involving social failure or success (interaction with an unresponsive or responsive confederate). Supporting the diathesis-stress component, attributional style predicted short-term depressive reactions to the stressful social experience as well as the behaviors accompanying such a reaction.

Recently, Alloy, Lipman, and Abramson (1992) tested the attributional vulnerability component of the hopelessness theory with a retrospective behavioral high risk paradigm. Consistent with prediction, currently nondepressed, but attributionally vulnerable subjects exhibited more frequent and more severe episodes of past major depressive disorder and hopelessness depression than did currently nondepressed attributionally invulnerable subjects. Using a prospective version of the behavioral high-risk paradigm, Alloy and Just (1992) found that currently nondepressed, attributionally vulnerable subjects exhibited higher levels and greater within-day and across-day variability of depressive symptoms, and of hopelessness depression symptoms in particular, than did nondepressed, attributionally invulnerable subjects.

Related to the diathesis-stress component, Clements and Alloy (1990) tested the theory's prediction that frequently depressed students should be particularly likely to exhibit the hypothesized depressogenic attributional style. Consistent with prediction, they found that depression-prone students had more negative attributional styles than students who were not depression-prone, regardless of current depression level.

Another issue relevant to the diathesis-stress component that has been examined empirically concerns the relationship between attributional style and self-esteem. According to the hopelessness theory, self-esteem will be lowered when a negative event is attributed to an internal, stable, global cause as opposed to any type of external cause or to an internal, unstable, specific cause. In contrast to the 1978 reformulation, the hopelessness theory postulates that attributing a negative life event to an internal cause does not, by itself, contribute to lowering self-esteem. Our revision requiring internal, stable, global attributions for negative events to lower self-esteem is based on a number of studies (e.g., Crocker, Alloy, & Kayne, 1988; Dweck & Licht, 1980; Janoff-Bulman, 1979) showing that internal attributions per se are not maladaptive and, in some cases, may be very adaptive (e.g., attributing failure to lack of effort leads to increased trying). Consistent with the hopelessness theory, and at odds with the 1978 reformulation, Crocker et al. (1988) found that self-esteem was a function of all three attributional dimensions (internality, stability, and globality) as opposed to just internality. Subjects who made internal, stable, global, as opposed to simply any internal attribution (e.g., internal, unstable, specific) for negative life events exhibited low self-esteem.

Insofar as dysfunctional attitudes overlap, in part, with the cognitive diatheses, studies examining dysfunctional attitudes and negative life events in predicting depression are relevant to evaluating the diathesis-stress component. In this regard, Olinger, Kuiper, and Shaw (1987) administered the Dysfunctional Attitudes Scale (DAS; Weissman & Beck, 1979) and DAS–Contractual Contingencies Scale (DAS–CC; Olinger et al., 1987) to subjects. The DAS–CC was designed to measure the presence or absence of life events that impinge on a person's dysfunctional attitudes. Consistent with the diathesis-stress component, subjects who were cognitively vulnerable (high DAS) and experienced negative events impinging on their vulnerability (high DAS–CC) were more depressed than both cognitively vulnerable subjects who did not experience the relevant negative life events (high DAS, low DAS–CC) and subjects who were not cognitively vulnerable (low DAS with either high or low DAS–CC scores). Similarly, Wise and Barnes (1986) reported that a normal sample of college students who were cognitively vulnerable (high DAS scores) and exposed to negative life events during the past year were more depressed than students who also were cognitively vulnerable but not exposed to a high rate of negative life events as well as students who were not cognitively vulnerable regardless of life events. In a clinical sample, DAS scores and negative life events scores exerted main effects in predicting depression. A limitation of these two studies is that they employed cross-sectional designs.

Related to the mediation component, some investigators (e.g., Brewin, 1985) questioned whether people's attributional styles predict their causal attributions for particular negative life events. As we previously indicated, in their tests of the causal mediation component of the theory, Metalsky et al. (1987) and Alloy et al. (1992b) found that attributional styles did, in fact, predict particular causal attributions (see also Follette & Jacobson, 1987, for similar results). Moreover, support for the mediation component of the hopelessness theory challenges the alternative hypothesis that some antecedent or correlate of the cognitive diathesis is actually mediating depressive reactions.

A further aspect of the mediation component of the hopelessness theory involves whether people's attributions or attributional styles predict the formation of hopelessness. Consistent with this component, as we pointed out earlier, in their naturalistic field study in the classroom, Metalsky et al. (1993) found that a depressogenic attributional style for achievement events predicted increases in hopelessness upon receipt of a low midterm grade. Similarly, in a laboratory study, Alloy and Ahrens (1987) demonstrated that a depressogenic attributional style contributed to depressives' pessimism in predicting future events. More generally, Weiner's (1985a) work has demonstrated that people's causal attributions affect their expectancies about future events.

The hopelessness theory predicts that attributions for particular life events should be predicted by situational information as well as attributional style. Consistent with this prediction, Haack, Metalsky, Dykman, and Abramson (1992) found that both depressed and nondepressed students' causal attributions were influenced by consensus, consistency, and distinctiveness information. Similarly, Crocker, Alloy, and Kayne (1988) found that people's perceptions of consensus information mediated their attributional styles (see also Alloy & Ahrens, 1987).

Symptoms

Although the studies examining the association between hopelessness and depression are promising, they do not provide a wholly adequate test of the proximal sufficient cause component of the theory. As we have argued elsewhere (Abramson et al., 1988, 1989; Halberstadt, Mukherji, Metalsky, Dykman, & Abramson, 1984), insofar as hopelessness theory postulates a subtype of depression, it is inappropriate to simply lump all depressives together and examine their levels of hopelessness to test the theory. Fortunately, some investigators have begun to examine the relationship between hopelessness and the hypothesized individual symptoms of hopelessness depression and have reported a strong association between hopelessness and suicide attempts and ideation (Beck et al., 1975; Kazdin et al., 1983; Minkoff et al., 1973; Petrie & Chamberlain, 1983).

More recently, Alloy and Clements (1991) used a prospective design to test whether hopelessness predicted the particular symptoms hypothesized to be part of the hopelessness depression syndrome but not other symptoms of depression not considered to be part of the hopelessness depression syndrome nor symptoms of other psychopathologies. They found that hopelessness significantly predicted six of the symptoms hypothesized to be part of the hopelessness depression syndrome. Hopelessness did not predict significantly any of the depression symptoms not hypothesized to be part of hopelessness depression (e.g., anhedonia, irritability, appetite/weight disturbance, somatic disturbance) and it did not predict any anxiety symptoms (somatic anxiety, phobias, or obsessive-compulsive symptoms). Surprisingly, hopelessness did predict hostility, paranoia, and psychoticism. Moreover, Alloy and Clements (1991) also found that the attributional diathesis-stress interaction featured in the theory predicted both hopelessness and the symptoms hypothesized to comprise the hopelessness depression subtype over time.

Course

The course component was tested directly in four studies. Consistent with prediction, Needles and Abramson (1990) reported that attributional style for positive outcomes interacted with positive life events to predict recovery from hopelessness. When positive events occurred in their lives, depressed students with a style to attribute positive events to stable, global causes showed a dramatic reduction in hopelessness relative to depressed students who did not exhibit this style. This change in hopelessness was accompanied by a reduction of depressive symptoms. Students who did not experience an increase in positive events, regardless of style, also did not show such dramatic reduction of hopelessness.

In a 2-year follow-up, Evans et al. (1992) reported that patients treated cognitively (cognitive therapy alone or in combination with drugs) showed half the relapse rate of patients treated with drugs alone who were then withdrawn from medication. Patients kept on medication also showed reduced relapse. Posttreatment attributional styles evidenced greater change in cognitively treated patients than in patients treated purely pharmacologically and, consistent with prediction, was the only cognitive variable that predicted subsequent relapse when residual depression was partialled out (the other two cognitive diatheses—consequences and self were not assessed). Further analyses suggested that change in attributional styles mediated the relapse preventive effect of cognitive therapy.

In a follow-up of psychiatric patients, Rush, Weissenburger, and Eaves (1986) reported that the presence of dysfunctional attitudes (high DAS scores) at remission from depression predicted the presence of depression 6 months later. Although not statistically significant, a similar pattern was found for attributional style. A limitation of this study was its small sample size ($n = 15$).

Finally, Lewinsohn, Steinmetz, Larson, and Franklin (1981) found that unipolar depressed community volunteers who held negative expectations about the future and perceptions of low control (in our terminology, the two features of hopelessness) at Time 1 were less likely to recover over an 8-month period compared with unipolar depressives who did not exhibit these cognitions, controlling for initial level of depression (see also Eaves & Rush, 1984).

Cure and Prevention

A number of studies have documented the efficacy of cognitive therapy for unipolar depression. The goals of cognitive therapy as currently practiced (cf. Beck, Rush, Shaw, & Emery, 1979) overlap with the goals for treatment and prevention of hopelessness depression. Therefore, empirical work demonstrating the efficacy of cognitive therapy for unipolar depresion provides some support for the validity of the hopelessness theory's therapeutic predictions. Future work is needed to examine predictions about treatment of hopelessness depression in particular. In addition, predictions about the prevention of hopelessness depression need to be tested. Finally, the hopelessness theory's novel clinical predictions (e.g., amelioration of current hopelessness will lessen current depressive symptoms but will not, by itself, decrease the likelihood of future relapse of depression) need to be tested.

Relation of Hopelessness Depression to Other Types of Depression and Psychopathology

Recently, Rose, Abramson, Hodulik, Leff, and Halberstadt (in press) asked which depressed people exhibit the depressogenic cognitive styles featured in the hopelessness theory and which do not. They used three approaches with a psychiatric inpatient sample to identify subgroups of depressives whose extremely negative cognitive styles distinguished them from other depressives: (a) they examined the cognitive styles of depressives representing all currently diagnosed depression subtypes in their sample; (b) they examined the cognitive styles of depressed patients who spontaneously verbalized cognitions consistent with a negative cognitive style and described characteristics identifying these depressives; and (c) they asked whether non-nosological variables such as sex, developmental events, depression history, and severity of depression predicted cognitive styles among depressed inpatients. The three approaches converged on a consistent finding: borderline personality disorder, developmental maltreatment, and severe depression characterize depressed patients who exhibit extremely negative cognitive styles. These results suggest that hopelessness depression probably does not map on to any currently diagnosed category of depression and instead may cut across currently diagnosed categories of depression and other psychopathology.

Rose et al. pointed out that the relationship they found between developmental trauma and adult negative cognitive style integrates current work on the hopelessness theory with its precursor, Seligman's (1975) work on learned helplessness in animals. Techniques used to induce helplessness in laboratory animals now seem similar to the traumatic abuse histories of Rose et al.'s depressed research subjects who exhibited markedly negative cognitive styles. Thus, Rose et al. underscored the importance of incorporating the element of trauma into the hopelessness theory.

Recently, Davidson, Abramson, Tomarken, and Wheeler (1992) began to provide an empirical integration of the hopelessness theory with biological approaches to vulnerability to depression. Previously, Davidson and his colleagues showed that depressed individuals show greater relative right-sided anterior activation of their cerebral hemispheres than do nondepressed individuals. Furthermore, these cerebral activation differences appear to be, at least in part, state-independent. Asymptomatic remitted depressives exhibited greater relative right-sided anterior activation than never depressed control subjects. Based on these and other data, Davidson and his colleagues have suggested that relative right anterior hemispheric activation may mark vulnerability to depression. In their integrative study, Davidson et al. showed that nondepressed individuals with relative right anterior hemispheric activation also exhibited a style to attribute negative life events to internal, stable, global causes. Thus, individuals identified as at risk for depression according to the hopelessness theory, because they exhibit the hypothesized depressogenic attributional style, also exhibit the cerebral hemispheric activation pattern currently hypothesized to produce biological risk for depression. Davidson et al. speculated that a depressogenic attributional style in conjunction with right anterior temporal asymmetry may reflect a common biocognitive process which increases risk for depression.

CONCLUSION

Does hopelessness depression exist? Work testing the hopelessness theory provides promise that hopelessness depression, or something similar to its theoretical description, indeed may exist in nature. We look forward to future research that further reveals the nature of this hypothesized disorder.

ACKNOWLEDGMENTS

Preparation of this chapter was supported by NIMH Grant R01MH43866, a Vilas Associate Award, and a Romnes Fellowship to Lyn Y. Abramson and NIMH Grant R01MH48216 to Lauren B. Alloy.

8

▼▼▼▼▼▼▼

Explanatory Style
in Anxiety and Depression

Susan Mineka
Cynthia L. Pury
Alice G. Luten
Northwestern University

Much research over the past decade has addressed the hypothesis of the refor-mulated learned helplessness theory of depression (Abramson, Seligman, & Teas-dale, 1978) that depressed individuals tend to have a particular explanatory style, and that individuals who have this explanatory style when nondepressed are at risk for depression if negative life events occur. The hypothesized depressive explanatory style is characterized by internal, stable, and global attributions for negative events, and external, unstable and specific attributions for positive events.[1] Although not every study examining the question of whether depressed individuals have this explanatory style has corroborated this hypothesis, there have been a large number of supportive studies. Indeed, Sweeney, Anderson, and Bailey (1986) conducted a meta-analysis of 104 studies and concluded that there was strong support for the link between the pessimistic explanatory style for negative events and depression, and weak to moderate support for the link between the pessimistic style for positive events and depression. As discussed later, evidence supporting the idea that a pessimistic explanatory style in nonde-pressed individuals serves as a diathesis for depression is somewhat more mixed

---

[1]For the sake of simplicity, we will hence forth refer to this hypothesized depressive explanatory style as a pessimistic explanatory style. Furthermore, we will generally refer to "explanatory style" rather than to the original term "attributional style" to be consistent with the title of this book. However, we tend to agree with others (e.g., Abramson, Dykman, & Needles, 1991) that there are good reasons to prefer the original term.

(for reviews see Abramson, Metalsky, & Alloy, 1989; Barnett & Gotlib, 1988; Peterson & Seligman, 1984a).

In striking contrast to the amount of attention that has been devoted to the relationship of the pessimistic explanatory style to depression is the dearth of attention devoted to the question of whether this explanatory style also occurs in other related forms of psychopathology such as the anxiety disorders. Indeed, the vast majority of studies included in the Sweeney et al. (1986) meta-analysis included only depressed and nondepressed (normal) subjects. Thus, this meta-analysis supports the idea that the measures of explanatory style which have been used are *sensitive* to detect potentially important cognitive processes in depression. Unfortunately, however, this meta-analysis tells us nothing about whether this explanatory style is *specific* to depression (see Heimberg et al., 1989; Heimberg, Vermilyea, Dodge, Becker, & Barlow, 1987). The importance of examining the specificity of this particular explanatory style to depression was recognized soon after the reformulated helplessness model was proposed (e.g., Raps, Peterson, Reinhard, Abramson, & Seligman, 1982). Several of the early studies examining this issue were strongly supportive of what Garber and Hollon (1991) have labeled *broad* specificity of the pessimistic explanatory style to depression versus other forms of general psychopathology. Only recently, however, have researchers begun to address the other interesting issue of what Garber and Hollon (1991) term *narrow* specificity. That is, is the pessimistic explanatory style specific to depression versus other more closely related disorders such as the anxiety disorders? (See Maser & Cloninger, 1990; Kendall & Watson, 1989, for two edited volumes on the topic of the overlap between anxiety and depressive disorders.)

RESEARCH ON SENSITIVITY AND SPECIFICITY OF THE DEPRESSIVE OR PESSIMISTIC EXPLANATORY STYLE

In the first study on the broad specificity issue, Raps et al. (1982) compared the explanatory style of unipolar depressed inpatients with that of nondepressed schizophrenic inpatients and with that of hospitalized nondepressed medical/surgical patients. The results of this study provided reasonably strong support for the idea that the particular explanatory style postulated to be specific to depression is not associated with schizophrenia or with being hospitalized for medical/surgical reasons. For negative events, the depressed patients made more internal, stable, and global attributions than both of the other groups, with only the depressed–schizophrenic comparison for globality failing to reach significance. As is often found, external, specific, and unstable attributions for positive events were less specific to depression. In particular, on a composite measure of explanatory style for positive events (formed by summing the scores for the three attributional dimensions) depressed patients did differ from the medical/surgical patients, but not from the schizophrenics. Although Raps et al. acknowledged that "a schizophrenic comparison group is not an exhaustive control for psychopathology," they further maintained that these results did at least provide "a step toward assessing the specificity of the learned helplessness reformulation to depression" by showing that it is not a general feature of all psychopathology (p. 103). Similar conclusions about specificity were reached by Johnson, Petzel, and Munic (1986), who compared the explanatory style of depressed patients with that of a general psychopathology (heterogeneous) control group.

In spite of these initial positive findings for broad specificity, not all studies have provided strong support for the specificity of the pessimistic explanatory style. For example, Miller, Klee, and Norman (1982), using half of the items from the original Attributional Style Questionnaire (ASQ), did not find significant differences between depressed inpatients and a mixed group of nondepressed inpatients on attributional composite scores. The groups differed in the expected direction only on attributions for their recent most stressful life event. One possible explanation for these negative findings is that Miller et al. used only half of the items of the original ASQ to assess explanatory style; this is known to reduce the reliability and validity of the ASQ (cf. Peterson & Seligman, 1984a). However, another study by Hamilton and Abramson (1983) that used the original full-length ASQ also found only a marginally significant difference between depressed inpatients and a mixed group of nondepressed inpatients on a composite difference score that measures self-serving versus self-derogating attributional patterns. As expected, the depressed patients did differ significantly from a normal control group of community volunteers. Thus, although the results of Raps et al.'s and Johnson et al.'s studies do suggest that the hypothesized depressive explanatory style does not occur in all forms of psychopathology, the Miller et al. (1982) and Hamilton and Abramson (1983) findings suggest that this pattern of results may not always be found.

IMPORTANCE OF EXAMINING EXPLANATORY STYLE AND ANXIETY DISORDERS

All of the studies reviewed earlier focused on the issue of broad specificity and did not address the potentially more interesting and important narrow specificity question, that is, whether this explanatory style occurs in more closely related disorders such as the anxiety disorders. As noted by Heimberg et al. (1987, 1989), the possible relationship of this explanatory style to anxiety disorders is of particular interest because maladaptive cognitions are also now thought to play an important role in the etiology and maintenance of anxiety disorders (e.g., Beck & Emery, 1985). At first glance one might predict different explanatory styles given that a number of investigators have noted that the themes of depressed and anxious patients' automatic thoughts may differ in content. For example, it has been observed that the thoughts and images of depressed patients tend to focus on themes of failure and loss whereas the thoughts and images of anxious patients tend to focus on themes of anticipated harm, threat, or danger (Beck, 1967, 1976; Beck & Clark, 1988). Finding differences in the content themes of the thoughts of depressed and anxious patients does not, however, bear directly on the issue of whether depressed and anxious patients may have similar explanatory styles. In other words, depressed and anxious patients' thoughts could focus on different types of negative events and have different themes, but both could be characterized by a tendency to attribute negative events to internal, stable, and global causes. For example, an agoraphobic who has a panic attack might make the following pessimistic attribution for the occurrence of the panic attack: "When I feel dizzy and disoriented like this, I feel convinced that I must have a brain tumor that the doctor has not yet detected and that I'll die from it."

Another reason why this possibility needs to be carefully examined is that according to the reformulated learned helplessness theory (Abramson et al., 1978), causal attributions about uncontrollable events are hypothesized to play a crucial role in the etiology and maintenance of one form of depression; however, their possible role in the etiology and maintenance of anxiety disorders is not addressed. Similarly, the hopelessness theory of depression (Abramson, Metalsky, & Alloy, 1989) proposes that explanatory style may be a vulnerability factor for one type of depression, but implicitly not a vulnerability factor for anxiety. Yet there is increasing evidence that uncontrollability over internal and external events undoubtedly plays a strong role in the etiology and maintenance of anxiety disorders as well as depressive disorders (see Barlow, 1988, 1991; Mineka & Kelly, 1989, for reviews of the role of uncontrollability in anxiety). Thus, although Seligman (1974, 1975) emphasized the parallels between learned helplessness in animals and human reactive depression, it is now known that there are also many important parallels between learned helplessness phenomena and certain anxiety disorders. For example, much higher levels of fear are conditioned to neutral stimuli paired with inescapable as opposed to escapable shock (e.g., Mineka, Cook, & Miller, 1984; Mowrer & Viek, 1948). In addition, infant monkeys reared in controllable environments where their operant responses produced food, water, and treats showed less fear and anxiety in several different stressful situations than did infant monkeys reared in uncontrollable environments where these same reinforcers were delivered noncontingently (Mineka, Gunnar, & Champoux, 1986). Therefore, given the role of uncontrollability in anxiety, it would seem to be an important question to determine whether explanatory style also plays a role in moderating the effects of uncontrollable events in patients with anxiety disorders.

Questions about the possible relationship of a pessimistic explanatory style to anxiety disorders are not only of interest because of the related theoretical perspectives on the role of uncontrollability that have been proposed for depression and anxiety. Further interest in this issue arises from the growing literature on comorbidity between anxiety and depressive disorders. Although a full review of this literature is well beyond the scope of this chapter, some highlights of the major features of comorbidity are reviewed to underscore the importance of the specificity question as it relates to explanatory style in depression versus anxiety.

EMPIRICAL DIFFERENTIATION
OF ANXIETY AND DEPRESSION

The question of whether depression and anxiety can be differentiated in a reliable and valid way has received a great deal of attention over the years, but only recently have significant advances been made in understanding the real scope of the problem. Clark and Watson (1991a, 1991b), for example, have shown that the overlap between various measures of depression and anxiety occurs at many levels, including measures of self-report, clinician ratings, diagnoses, and family/genetic factors. For example, two recent reviews (Dobson, 1985; Gotlib & Cane, 1989) concluded that the correlation between various self-report measures of anxiety and depression was nearly as high as the correlation between separate measures of each construct. As noted by Clark and Watson, this pattern of findings of poor discriminant validity for all self-report measures of anxiety and depression does not occur because respondents simply fail to adequately discriminate between their own mood states. Indeed, a very similar pattern of poor discriminant validity is obtained between self-report measures and clinician ratings of depression and anxiety, and between separate clinician ratings of the two constructs (see Clark, 1989; Clark & Watson, 1991a, 1991b, for reviews). Thus, examining the pattern of discriminant validity, this picture emerges: "the correlation found between measures of depression and anxiety is not a superficial one (e.g., due to unreliable scales or the inherent limitations of self-reports) that can be eliminated through simple methodological improvements. Rather, the overlap is pervasive and deeply rooted" (Clark & Watson, 1991a, p. 47).

Furthermore, the overlap occurs not only at the symptom level, but also at the diagnostic level. The hierarchical rules of the *DSM-III* generally precluded a diagnosis of an anxiety disorder if there was a coexisting depressive disorder (American Psychiatric Association, 1980). Once investigators began to drop the hierarchical rules, the full extent of comorbidity between anxiety and depressive disorders at the diagnostic level began to emerge (e.g., Barlow, 1985, 1988; Barlow, DiNardo, Vermilyea, Vermilyea, & Blanchard, 1986; DiNardo & Barlow, 1990). In their recent review, Clark and Watson (1991a) noted that approximately half of patients receiving a depressive disorder diagnosis also receive an anxiety disorder diagnosis, and vice versa. However, as discussed later, the extent of comorbidity varies considerably from one anxiety disorder to another. Finally, there is also considerable evidence from family and genetic studies of the relationship between anxiety and depressive disorders (Barlow, 1988, 1991; Clark & Watson, 1991a,

1991b; Merikangas, 1990; Weissman, 1990), although it is possible that a genetic link with depression is stronger for some anxiety disorders than for others.

Currently the dominant theoretical approach to understanding the overlap between anxiety and depressive symptoms is that of Watson, Clark, and Tellegen (Clark & Watson, 1991a, 1991b; Tellegen, 1985; Watson, Clark, & Carey, 1988). According to these investigators, the strong overlap between various measures of depression and anxiety reflects the fact that most measures of both of these constructs are tapping the broad personality dimension of Negative Affectivity/Neuroticism (trait NA), or a state measure of Negative Affect (state NA). State and trait NA are defined to be "broad and general mood and personality dimension[s] characterized by the experience of various negative affective states" (Clark & Watson, 1991a, p. 47). These negative affective states include distress, anger, guilt, fear, disgust, and worry. However, these investigators also hypothesize that anxiety and depression can be distinguished on the basis of a second orthogonal mood known as positive affect (state PA) and a second broad personality dimension known as positive affectivity (trait PA). PA reflects a sense of energy and enthusiasm about life, and includes mood descriptors such as excited, delighted, interested, enthusiastic, and proud. A variety of lines of evidence reviewed by these investigators (e.g., Clark & Watson, 1991a, 1991b; Watson et al., 1988) converges on the conclusion that, whereas anxiety and depression share a high loading on NA, they are distinguished by levels of PA. In particular, depressed, but not anxious individuals, are consistently found to be low on PA, reflecting fatigue and a lack of energy or enthusiasm. More recently, Clark and Watson (1991b) expanded their model to include a third component. In their tripartite model the third component consists of physiological tension and autonomic hyperarousal, which tends to be specific to anxiety disorders (see also Clark, Watson, & Mineka, 1994).

OTHER IMPORTANT FEATURES OF COMORBIDITY BETWEEN ANXIETY DISORDERS AND DEPRESSION

In a recent review of the literature on comorbidity of anxiety and depression, Alloy, Kelly, Mineka, and Clements (1990) suggested that there appear to be four important phenomena of comorbidity that need to be accounted for by any theory attempting to explain this comorbidity. We believe that all four of these phenomena appear to have some bearing on the possibility that the pessimistic explanatory style may not be specific to depression. Although space does not permit a detailed review of the evidence supporting the existence of these phenomena, they are briefly described so that their relevance to the question of specificity can be discussed.

One of the four phenomena of comorbidity identified by Alloy, Kelly et al. (1990) concerns *the sequential relationship between anxiety and depression.*

Evidence on both intraepisode and lifetime comorbidity suggests that anxiety more often precedes depression than the reverse. With intraepisode comorbidity, one most typically sees a biphasic pattern of response to a stressful event (such as a loss), in which agitation and anxiety occur first, to be followed by depression, disorganization, and despair. This biphasic response pattern to the loss of an attachment object has been carefully described by Bowlby (1973, 1980), based on his observations of childrens' and adults' responses to separation and loss. A similar biphasic response pattern probably also follows a variety of other stressors. With studies examining lifetime comorbidity, a majority have reported that among people who experience both anxiety and depressive disorders within a lifetime, the anxiety disorder is more likely to precede the depressive disorder than the reverse (e.g., Angst, Vollrath, Merikangas, & Ernst, 1990; Freud, 1926/1959; Kendell, 1974; Merikangas, 1990). One possible explanation for this is that prolonged feelings of helplessness engendered by the inability to control anxiety-related symptoms (e.g., panic attacks, obsessive thoughts and/or compulsive rituals, nightmares and flashbacks) may lead eventually to the person giving up and becoming hopeless and depressed. (See Alloy, Kelly et al., 1990; Garber, Miller, & Abramson, 1980, for a detailed discussion.)

The sequential relationship between anxiety and depression is important in the present context because it suggests that if a pessimistic explanatory style represents a diathesis for certain forms of depression (e.g., Abramson et al., 1978, 1989; Peterson & Seligman, 1984a), then it may also represent a diathesis for certain forms of anxiety that are sometimes followed by depression. Unfortunately, the vast majority of the prospective studies that have examined the diathesis-stress component of the reformulated helplessness and hopelessness theories of depression have never carefully examined anxious symptomatology (e.g., Metalsky, Abramson, Seligman, Semmel, & Peterson, 1982; Metalsky, Halberstadt, & Abramson, 1987; Metalsky, Joiner, Hardin, & Abramson, 1993). Certainly the high degree of overlap between anxious and depressed symptoms in most of the self-report instruments used in these studies (and consequent lack of discriminant validity) makes it very difficult to determine if these studies have actually examined whether a pessimistic explanatory style specifically predicts depression as opposed to anxiety, or their combination (see further discussion of this issue later).

A second phenomenon of comorbidity identified by Alloy, Kelly et al. (1990) concerns the *differential comorbidity between depression and the anxiety disorders*. In particular, at least preliminary evidence suggests that certain anxiety disorders such as panic disorder (with or without agoraphobia), obsessive–compulsive disorder, and posttraumatic stress disorder, are more likely to be accompanied by depression, than are other anxiety disorders such as simple and social phobia, and possibly generalized anxiety disorder. These findings suggest that one might be more likely to find the pessimistic explanatory style associated with those anxiety disorders that are most commonly comorbid with depression. If this were true, then it would also be important to determine whether any association between a pessimistic explanatory style and those anxiety disorders is due just to the presence of a concurrent depressive disorder, or whether it might occur independent of depressive symptomatology. In the latter case, the presence of a pessimistic explanatory style simply may represent a possible diathesis for later depression, or alternatively may suggest that this explanatory style is not specific to depression.

The third phenomenon of comorbidity suggested by Alloy, Kelly et al. (1990) is what they termed the *relative infrequency of pure depression*. They reviewed numerous studies suggesting that within episodes of illness, it is much more common to find individuals with pure symptoms of anxiety than with pure symptoms of depression (e.g., see Dobson, 1985, for a review). In addition, a good number of studies reviewed by Alloy et al. suggested that individuals with a primary depressive diagnosis are also more likely to meet criteria for an anxiety disorder diagnosis than vice versa. If pure depression (without anxious symptomatology or an anxiety disorder diagnosis) is relatively rare, then it again becomes important to examine whether the hypothesized depressive explanatory style is specific to depression versus anxiety. Given the high level of comorbidity between anxious and depressive symptoms, and the relative infrequency of pure depression, it would be reasonable to hypothesize that many of the studies contributing to Sweeney et al.'s (1986) meta-analysis on explanatory style and depression included a majority of individuals with both anxious and depressive symptoms. Indeed, we are not aware of any studies that have examined explanatory style in patients with pure depression.

Finally, the fourth phenomenon of comorbidity discussed by Alloy, Kelly et al. (1990) concerns the *common and unique symptoms of anxiety and depression*. As suggested earlier in the review of the Watson-Clark-Tellegen approach to differentiating anxiety and depression, the two categories of disorder share many common features (negative affect and affectivity), but can also be distinguished by certain features as well. For example, Clark and Watson (1991a, 1991b) have suggested that low positive affect is a distinguishing characteristic that only occurs in depression, and that heightened autonomic arousal is a distinguishing characteristic for anxiety disorders. Alloy et al. (see also Abramson et al., 1989; Garber et al., 1980) suggested that hopelessness is also a distinguishing characteristic between depression versus anxiety. For the present purposes it would be important to know whether the pessimistic explanatory style is more closely associated with depressive symptoms that are unique to depression (e.g., low positive affect and hopelessness) or to depressive symptoms that overlap heavily with those of anxiety (e.g., negative affect).

Summary

We reviewed various aspects of the comorbidity between anxiety and depression in some detail in an attempt to provide a rationale for the importance of studying the pessimistic explanatory style in various anxiety disorders. In the next section we review the current status of knowledge about this topic and follow this with a discussion of the methodological limitations and shortcomings of studies in this area, along with suggestions for future research.

REVIEW OF EMPIRICAL FINDINGS CONCERNING THE RELATIONSHIP OF EXPLANATORY STYLE AND ANXIETY

Overview

As is seen in the following review, the majority of the studies on this topic unfortunately have compared only two of the three or more relevant groups of subjects that should be included in a study examining specificity of explanatory style. Some studies have compared an anxiety disordered group with normals; if group differences occur, the question is still open as to how similar the anxiety disordered group would be to a depressed group. Other studies have compared an anxiety disordered group with a depressed group; if group differences occur, the question remains as to how similar the anxiety disordered group would be to a normal group (e.g., they might be intermediate). The ideal design is obviously one in which multiple anxiety disordered and depressed groups are compared with each other and with a normal control group, all within one study.

Although a few investigators have developed their own measures, the majority of studies in this area have used the ASQ (Peterson et al., 1982; Seligman, Abramson, Semmel, & vonBaeyer, 1979) or the Expanded ASQ (Peterson & Villanova, 1988) as their measure of explanatory style. The ASQ is a self-report measure asking subjects to "vividly imagine" a series of successes and failures in both achievement and social realms. For each event, the subject writes down the one main cause, then rates that cause on internality, stability, and globality. In an attempt to examine naturally occurring attributions for real events, Peterson and Seligman (1984b) developed a technique called the Content Analysis of Verbatim Explanations (CAVE), which uses a coding system to analyze the internality, stability, and globality of causal explanations found in diaries, speeches, and other sources of written or spoken language. Only one study reviewed here has used the CAVE technique for scoring explanatory style. (See chapter 2, this volume, for a discussion of measurement issues.)

As previously discussed, anxiety is not a unitary phenomenon, and undoubtedly different etiological factors are likely to be associated with the different anxiety disorders. Therefore, it is quite possible that the role of explanatory style may differ across clinical categories of anxiety disorders (such as agoraphobia, generalized anxiety disorder, and social phobia) as well as for the various categories of subclinical anxiety (such as trait anxiety, test anxiety, and social anxiety). It is also quite possible that certain anxiety disorders have a distinct explanatory style that is different from the pessimistic explanatory style. The following discussion focuses on what is known about explanatory style in each of the separate categories of anxiety disorders. Some studies find one or two features of the pessimistic explanatory style to be associated with certain anxiety disorders (e.g., stable and/or global attributions for negative events but not internal), whereas others find the full three component pessimistic explanatory style.

Subclinical Anxiety

At the level of subclinical anxiety, it is unclear whether there is a distinctive explanatory style. For example, using an unselected undergraduate sample, Dowd, Claiborn, and Milne (1985) conducted a series of multiple regression analyses to investigate the relationships among depression, anxiety, and attributional style. Using the ASQ, they found that global attributions for bad events (but not stable and internal) explained a small but significant portion (3%) of the variance in trait anxiety scores. When depression was added in as an additional predictor variable, however, none of the ASQ measures contributed significantly to the explained variance in trait anxiety. Dowd et al. pointed out that, although depression and anxiety were significantly correlated in this study, depression explained only about 5% of the variance in trait anxiety scores. Therefore, they suggested that anxiety may have some specific association with global attributions for negative events that is not accounted for by its relationship to depression. Nevertheless, given the finding that globality did not significantly predict trait anxiety when depression was also used as a predictor, this suggestion seems highly speculative.

Dowd et al. did not find any relationship between state anxiety scores and explanatory style. Furthermore, they did not find consistent evidence for the pessimistic explanatory style in depression, finding only that stable attributions for bad events were related to depression. In summary, this study suggested, in a highly preliminary manner, that there may be a specific explanatory style associated with high trait anxiety, but evidence was lacking for an explanatory style in either depression or anxiety that involves more than one of the hypothesized attributional dimensions.

In another study using an unselected college student sample, Nezu, Nezu, and Nezu (1986) investigated the relationship between pessimistic attributional style, measured using the ASQ, and several measures of distress. Using canonical correlation, they found that trait anxiety (relatively stable dispositions to experience anxiety in a wide range of situations), state anxiety, and depression were significantly correlated with pessimistic explanatory style for both positive and negative events. Not surprisingly, depression and anxiety were also significantly correlated in this study, making it impossible to interpret the specific relationship of explanatory style to anxiety. This study's emphasis on the potential relationship of both anxiety and depression to explanatory style is interesting, but it is unfortunate that they did not attempt to disentangle the effects of depression and anxiety. Looking cross-sectionally in what was actually a prospective study, Ralph and Mineka (1993) also found anxiety (as measured by the Beck Anxiety Inventory), as well as depression (as measured by the Beck Depression Inventory; BDI), to be significantly correlated with pessimistic explanatory style for negative events using Peterson and Villanova's Expanded ASQ (1988). Thus, at least two studies have found the pessimistic explanatory style to be associated with anxiety in nonclinical populations, although for reasons discussed earlier, it is difficult to disentangle the effects of depression versus anxiety given the strong common denominator between the two—namely, negative affect (see further discussion of this issue later).

Clinical Anxiety

Heimberg et al. (1987) used the ASQ to examine the attributions of two clinically diagnosed groups and a group of normal controls.[2] One of the clinical groups was dysthymic and the other was a heterogeneous group of anxiety disordered patients. The dysthymic group was subdivided into those that showed moderate levels of depression (BDI between 12 and 25) and those that showed high levels of depression (BDI > 25). Similarly, the anxious group was further subdivided into those that showed low levels of depression (BDI < 12) and those that showed moderate levels of depression (BDI between 12 and 25). They found evidence for the pessimistic explanatory style in both groups of dysthymic subjects, who, according to a composite attributional measure, made more internal, stable, and global attributions for negative events than did normal subjects. When the individual attributional dimensions were analyzed separately, they found that both dysthymic groups made significantly more stable and global attributions for negative events while their tendency toward greater internality did not reach statistical significance. Moreover, the attributions of moderately depressed anxious subjects were similar to the attributions of both dysthymic groups along the dimensions of internality, stability, and globality. They also found that even nondepressed, clinically anxious subjects tended to make more global attributions for negative events compared to normals which is, of course, consistent with Dowd et al.'s (1985) finding that trait anxiety was associated with more global attributions for negative events.

For positive events, Heimberg et al. (1987) found that the dysthymic patients with BDI scores greater than 25 made more external and unstable attributions than did the nondepressed anxious group. Although the difference was in the expected direction, the explanatory style for positive events of these highly

---

[2]Heimberg et al. (1987, 1989) modified the ASQ to investigate the degree to which subjects felt that the causes of events resulted from their own actions and how much control they might expect to exert over these causes in the future. The potential importance of the perceived controllability of causes will be discussed later in this chapter.

depressed dysthymics was not significantly different from that of the normals. Moderately depressed anxious subjects also made more unstable attributions for positive outcomes than did nondepressed anxious subjects.

A major limitation of the Heimberg et al. (1987) study was that their anxious group was heterogeneous in composition, consisting of individuals diagnosed with panic disorder (with and without agoraphobia), social phobia, simple phobia, and generalized anxiety disorder. Therefore, as they acknowledged, their findings do not permit an analysis of the potential differences in the relationship of explanatory style to the different anxiety disorders, thereby also weakening any general conclusions that can be drawn from this study. Keeping this in mind, Heimberg et al. (1989) added new subjects to their 1987 data set, nearly doubling the sample sizes, permitting analysis by specific anxiety disorder. They found a relationship between anxiety and depressive attributional style for some anxiety disordered groups but not for others. As noted earlier, this finding is not surprising given that clinical anxiety covers a heterogeneous collection of disorders with presumable differences in etiology and symptomatology. Thus, explanatory style, as well as other cognitive processes, may not show the same relationship to all anxiety disorders. The remainder of this review is organized according to what is known about the relationship of explanatory style to each of the major categories of anxiety disorders.

Agoraphobia and Panic Disorder

Although evidence of the relationship between explanatory style and agoraphobia is somewhat mixed, there are indications that agoraphobics may show the pessimistic explanatory style for negative events. Heimberg et al. (1989) compared the explanatory styles (as measured by the ASQ) of carefully diagnosed normals, dysthymics, social phobics, and panic patients with and without agoraphobia. They found that agoraphobics, social phobics, and dysthymics all scored higher on the ASQ composite measure for negative events than did panic patients without agoraphobia, who scored higher than normal controls. For positive events, however, dysthymics had a significantly lower composite score (i.e., more external, unstable, and specific) than social phobics and normals, who had significantly lower composite scores than did agoraphobics and panickers.

Fisher and Wilson (1985) found that agoraphobics made more internal attributions for negative events (both general negative events on the Helplessness Questionnaire, which appears to be an early version of the ASQ, and specific negative events relevant to agoraphobia) than did normals. The two groups did not differ in internality for causes of positive events. Unfortunately, this study did not include a depressed control group.

Broadbeck and Michelson (1987) also found that agoraphobics made significantly more global attributions for bad outcomes (on the ASQ) than for good outcomes. This pattern was reversed for matched, nonpsychiatric controls. Examining between group differences, they found that agoraphobics attributed negative events to more global causes than controls, and positive events to less global causes than controls. However, unlike Heimberg et al.'s (1989) study, there was no difference between agoraphobics and controls in internality or stability of attributions as measured by the ASQ. Broadbeck and Michelson also examined attributions of success or failure on an experimental task and found that agoraphobics made more global attributions for performance on a difficult anagram task than did normals, again with no differences between groups in internality or stability. Although agoraphobics were more depressed than controls, these patterns of effects did not change when level of depression was used as a covariate. However, a major limitation of this study is that they did not use a depressed control group.

In a study comparing panic patients (with or without agoraphobia) and patients with other anxiety disorders who had all experienced at least one panic attack, Kenardy, Evans, and Oei (1990) found no differences in explanatory style for good or for bad outcomes between the two groups. Unfortunately, no normal control group or depressed group was included for comparison purposes. Nevertheless, although it is risky to compare results across studies, it should be noted that the results for Kenardy's two groups were quite similar to those reported by Heimberg et al. (1989) for agoraphobics (who did differ significantly from normal controls in their explanatory style).

In a study of panic patients both with and without agoraphobia, Ganellen (1988) found that the stability and globality dimensions of explanatory style (but not internality) on the ASQ were correlated with both level of depression and level of anxiety, but were not uniquely related to either. Although data were collected for ASQ positive events as well as for negative events, only the results for the negative events were presented. Unfortunately, Ganellen also did not include either a healthy control group or a nonpanicking depressed group. In addition, neither Ganellen nor Broadbeck and Michelson provided the reader with mean ASQ scores, so it is not possible to compare their results with those of other studies. Thus, these four studies (Broadbeck & Michelson, 1987; Fisher & Wilson, 1985; Ganellen, 1988; Kenardy et al., 1990) that each compared only one or two of the three or more relevant groups necessary for drawing conclusions about specificity produced a somewhat less clear-cut pattern of results than the Heimberg et al. (1989) study, which had all of the relevant groups.

In one final study, Hoffart and Martinsen (1990) measured attributional style (using a Norwegian translation of the ASQ) in three diagnostic groups. They examined inpatients who were agoraphobics and did not qualify for any depression diagnosis (agoraphobics), unipolar depressed patients who did not qualify for any anxiety diagnosis (depressives), and agoraphobics who also qualified for a diagnosis of unipolar depression (comorbid patients); unfortunately, they did not also include a normal control group. They found that their comorbid patients exhibited a more global explanatory style for negative events than did agoraphobics, with depressed patients exhibiting an intermediate amount of globality.

Examining attributions for the causes of positive events, they found that agoraphobics made more stable attributions for positive events than did the depressives. Depressed patients had a more external, unstable, and specific attributional style for good events than either comorbid or agoraphobic patients. At first glance these results of Hoffart and Martinsen seem different than those reported by Heimberg et al. (1989). However, it is worth noting that Hoffart and Martinsen's mean ASQ stability and globality scores for their agoraphobic and depressed groups were almost identical to the agoraphobic and depressed means obtained by Heimberg et al., who did find that agoraphobics' explanatory styles were more internal, stable, and global for negative outcomes in comparison to a nonpsychiatric control group (which Hoffart and Martinsen did not have). BDI levels were also similar for the depressed and agoraphobic groups between the two studies. This apparent similarity of average explanatory style in these two very different samples is at least as striking as the apparent discrepancy in the reported patterns of significant differences in the two studies.

Thus, although the evidence is far from conclusive, it appears that agoraphobics may have an explanatory style that is similar to depressives', at least for negative events. All of the six studies reviewed show at least some tendency for agoraphobics to show an explanatory style that is similar to the pessimistic style for negative events. At least one study (Heimberg et al., 1989) suggests that these attributional patterns are not due entirely to depressive symptomatology. However, five of the six studies reviewed lacked at least one of the proper control groups (i.e., either depressed and/or normal control groups). Thus, although some comparisons can be made between studies, results must be interpreted with caution. By contrast, the evidence regarding explanatory style for positive events is much more mixed. Of the four studies that examined attributions for positive events, three found that agoraphobics' explanatory style was more like that of normals than like that of depressives for positive events. It is interesting to speculate that having a more internal, stable, and global explanatory style for positive events may help serve to protect many agoraphobics from severe levels of depression given Needles and Abramson's (1990) findings that this kind of explanatory style predicts recovery from depression when good events happen.

Social Phobia and Social Anxiety

Individuals with social phobia may exhibit a similar explanatory style to that seen in depressives. In the only study that used a clinical sample, Heimberg et al. (1989) found that, after controlling for level of depression, social phobics' explanatory style (as measured by the ASQ) appeared to be very similar to the pessimistic explanatory style. Even though these social phobics were only mildly depressed, they tended to attribute bad events to more internal, stable, and global causes (and to attribute good events to more external, unstable, and specific causes) than did agoraphobics and dysthymics when level of depression was controlled for. Given that about one half of the situations on the ASQ are social or affiliation-oriented situations, this finding for social phobics may not be too surprising as the ASQ asks them about their feared situations. The potential importance of the content of the situations used in the ASQ is discussed later.

In another study with a nonclinical sample, Alden (1987) manipulated the pattern of social feedback given to socially anxious and nonsocially anxious undergraduates where social anxiety was assessed by the Social Avoidance and Distress Inventory (SAD; Watson & Friend, 1969). Subjects were told that their task was to become acquainted with another student (a confederate), but that before the actual experiment, they were to practice by becoming acquainted with the experimenter. Subjects were told that they performed at either an above or below average level by both the experimenter and the confederate. Thus, in this $2 \times 2 \times 2$ design, both high and low socially anxious subjects received feedback of consistent failure, improving performance, declining performance, or consistent success. Subjects' attributions were then measured by ratings of the importance of ability, effort, task difficulty, and luck in their performance in the experiment. Alden found that within socially anxious subjects, feedback of improvement led to the most internal attributions. However, these attributions were made to the unstable factor of effort rather than to the stable factor of ability. Within nonanxious subjects, the most internal and stable attributions—to ability—were made to consistently positive feedback. Across all success and failure conditions, socially anxious subjects made more external attributions to luck and task difficulty than nonanxious subjects did.

In another study of nonclinical social anxiety, Johnson, Petzel, and Johnson (1991) demonstrated that shy subjects showed the pessimistic explanatory style. Specifically, subjects who scored high on the SAD, which measures general discomfort in social situations, showed the pessimistic explanatory style for the Affiliation subscale of the ASQ measuring attributions in social situations, even when controlling for level of depression. Subjects who scored high on the Fear of Negative Evaluation scale (Watson & Friend, 1969), which measures fear of disapproval and negative evaluations, tended to show the pessimistic explanatory style in both affiliation and achievement situations, even when controlling for level of depression.

Thus, one study using a clinical sample suggests that socially phobic individuals may also have an internal, stable, and global explanatory style for negative events. Moreover, Alden's study of nonclinical social anxiety, although not as strongly supportive of the pessimistic explanatory style for social anxiety, nonetheless suggests that socially anxious individuals make unstable attributions for social success. And Johnson et al.'s study of shy subjects, where shyness was measured by two of the most widely used scales in the study of social anxiety, found that such subjects tended to show a pessimistic explanatory style.

Generalized Anxiety Disorder (GAD)

In what is apparently the only study examining explanatory style in generalized anxiety disorder and unipolar depression, Riskind, Castellon, and Beck (1989) found evidence suggestive of specificity of a pessimistic explanatory style to unipolar depression. They used the CAVE technique (Peterson & Seligman, 1984b; see chapter 2, this volume) to examine the attributions made for negative events in the thought diaries of patients receiving therapy. They found that unipolar depressives had a higher attributional composite for negative events than did GAD patients. Furthermore, when analyzing the individual dimensions, they found that unipolar depressives made significantly more stable and global attributions for negative events than did GAD patients. These findings suggest that, relative to GAD, stable and global attributions for negative events are specific to depression. Unfortunately, the absence of a normal control group in this study means that we do not know whether the GAD patients may show an intermediate explanatory style.

Posttraumatic Stress Disorder (PTSD)

Mikulincer and Solomon (1988) found preliminary evidence for a specific explanatory style in PTSD; however, this style did not appear to be equivalent to the pessimistic explanatory style seen in depressives. Using a sample of 262 Israeli soldiers who had suffered from combat stress reaction (CSR) during battle, they examined the relationship between PTSD symptomatology and attributions 2 and 3 years postcombat. Explanatory style was measured at both points in time using a self-report inventory similar to one used by Arkin and Maruyama (1979); subjects were asked to recall one good and one bad event from the past 3 months and to rate each event on a 7-point scale on the attributional factors of ability, effort, luck, and difficulty of the situation. In order to translate these factors into the attributional dimensions of locus, stability, and controllability of the cause (Weiner, 1979, 1985a), Mikulincer and Solomon asked a group of 60 undergraduate psychology students to rate the attributional factors of ability, luck, effort, and difficulty along the previously mentioned attributional dimensions. More than 70% of these students rated ability as internal, stable, and uncontrollable; effort as internal, unstable, and controllable; luck as external, unstable, and uncontrollable; and situational difficulty as external, stable, and uncontrollable. Accordingly, attributions made for these factors by the combat veterans were combined to form six new scores, reflecting the dimensions of locus, stability, and controllability for good and bad events separately. It should be pointed out that these attributional dimensions do not completely map onto the dimensions assessed by the ASQ, which has been used to measure explanatory style in most of the studies discussed. The locus dimension in this study seems equivalent to the internal–external dimension assessed by the ASQ. The stability dimension seems equivalent to that measured by the ASQ; unfortunately, the globality dimension was not assessed in this study. The assessment of the controllability dimension in this study represents an improvement over the standard ASQ, because the latter does not even address the issue of controllability (a point discussed later).

Partial correlations were calculated between PTSD symptomatology and attributions at Time 2 (3 years postcombat) which controlled for all Time 1 measures, including Time 1 attributions (2 years postcombat). This longitudinal analysis revealed that intensified PTSD symptomatology at Time 2 was associated with the following pattern of attributions: more external, stable, and uncontrollable attributions for the causes of bad events and more external attributions for the causes of good events. It should be noted that although these data cannot be interpreted to suggest a causal role between attributions and PTSD symptomatology, they do show preliminary evidence of a potentially important relationship between the two constructs.

Mikulincer and Solomon suggested that external attributions for both good and bad events may relate to the failure of PTSD victims to accept responsibility for events in their lives. This overall tendency contrasts with that of depressed patients, who tend to make internal attributions for bad events and external attributions for good events. Thus, this study suggests that conceptually distinct explanatory styles may occur in different forms of psychopathology. However, this study has a number of significant limitations that preclude drawing strong conclusions at this time. First, because they did not assess depression levels, it is difficult to interpret the unique contribution of PTSD symptomatology to explanatory style; this issue is especially important given that depression is a common symptom of PTSD. Second, because explanatory style was not measured using the ASQ, it is difficult to compare directly the findings of this study with most of the other studies reviewed. Relatedly, because explanatory style was assessed using only two events, the measure used in this study may not be very reliable (cf. Peterson & Seligman, 1984a). Moreover, the two events recalled may have been the most dramatic or salient events experienced and this may have constrained the subjects' style of explanation. Finally, one can question the validity of the students' ratings that led to ability being rated as uncontrollable, and situational difficulty as being stable.

McCormick, Taber, and Kruedelbach (1989) also examined the relationship between PTSD symptoms and attributional style, as measured by the ASQ (Peterson et al., 1982). Using a sample of patients in treatment for alcohol dependence and/or pathological gambling, McCormick et al. (1989) found that PTSD symptoms were significantly related to more pessimistic attributions (using composite measures) for both negative and positive events. Although they did find a relationship between depression level and PTSD symptoms, they did not explore whether the relationship between pessimistic attributions and PTSD symptoms was independent of depression level. In summary, although both

Mikulincer and Solomon (1988) and McCormick et al. (1989) found preliminary evidence for a relationship between pessimistic attributions and PTSD, neither study directly addresses whether or not pessimistic attributions are related to PTSD solely through the presence of concomitant depressive symptomatology.

METHODOLOGICAL CONSIDERATIONS

The Heterogeneous Nature of Anxiety Disorders

As noted earlier, the anxiety disorders comprise a broad spectrum of psychological problems, from simple phobias to PTSD. Given this broad range, the results of Heimberg et al. (1989) are not surprising: Patients with different anxiety diagnoses have different explanatory styles. Of all the studies we reviewed, however, only Heimberg et al. (1989) compared different anxiety diagnoses within the same study. Many of the studies reviewed also lack within-study comparisons of depressed and/or normal controls with the anxiety disordered group. The relationship of depression to the pessimistic explanatory style is well documented, and what some have called the "self-serving" explanatory style of normals (compared to depressives) has also been heavily researched (e.g., Peterson & Seligman, 1984a; Sweeney et al., 1986). Although one can obtain some useful information by comparing the results (e.g., ASQ scores) of different studies with each other, this approach does not provide the same sort of rigorous comparison that can be made when all subjects are from the same study. Therefore, an ideal investigation of explanatory style and anxiety disorders should compare different anxiety groups to both depressives and nondepressed, nonanxious controls. So far, it appears that Heimberg et al. (1989) has been the only study to attempt this sort of comparison.

The Importance of Longitudinal Designs

It is impossible to delineate fully the relationship between explanatory style, anxiety, and depression until prospective studies are conducted in which explanatory style is measured in a subclinical population and used to predict, in interaction with other causal factors, who will become clinically anxious and depressed. In addition to the failure of many of the studies reviewed to measure depression, none of the studies reviewed employed such a prospective design. With the exception of Mikulincer and Solomon (1988), each investigated the co-occurrence of pessimistic explanatory style and anxiety in a cross-sectional fashion. And, as previously discussed, causal conclusions cannot be drawn from the Mikulincer and Solomon study because they investigated the strength of the relationship between explanatory style and PTSD at two points in time after the onset of PTSD.

To our knowledge, there are only a few studies published in which both depression and anxiety have been used as outcome variables. In discussing longitudinal studies, it is important to note that such studies which fail to assess the experience of negative life events do not provide strong tests of the reformulated learned helplessness model (Abramson et al., 1978) or of the hopelessness model (Abramson et al., 1989). According to these theories, explanatory style is hypothesized to serve as a diathesis, which may predict the onset of depression if negative life events are encountered. As such, Peterson and Seligman (1984a) and Abramson et al. (1978, 1989) pointed out the value of experiments of nature, in which the occurrence of negative life events is measured within a longitudinal design. Peterson and Seligman discussed evidence (e.g., Bukstel & Kilmann, 1980; Metalsky et al., 1982) that supported the hypothesis that the combination of a depressive explanatory style (the diathesis) and negative life events (the stress) significantly predicts depressive symptoms. Similarly, Abramson et al. (1989) reviewed additional research supporting this hypothesized diathesis-stress component (e.g., Metalsky et al., 1987). Metalsky et al. (1993) recently reported another such study. Again, however, anxiety levels were not assessed in these studies, making it impossible to draw conclusions about the specificity of this diathesis-stress model to depression.

The results of the few prospective studies that have used measures of anxiety as well as depression are mixed and therefore inconclusive regarding whether a pessimistic explanatory style in combination with negative life events predisposes to anxiety as well as depression. For example, Johnson and Miller (1990) did not find explanatory style in combination with self-reported life events to predict levels of anxious mood 1 month later, but they also did not find the predicted significant relationship for depressed mood either. Similarly, using a related design but better measures of anxiety and depression (as well as measures of negative and positive affect), Ralph and Mineka (1993) also did not find pessimistic explanatory style in combination with self-reported negative life events to predict levels of depression, anxiety, negative or positive affect 1 month later. By contrast, DeVellis and Blalock (1992) did find partial support for the hopelessness theory of depression in a prospective study of rheumatoid arthritis patients, but their study found similar results using separate depression and anxiety subscales, suggesting nonspecificity. Rounding out the mixed pattern of results is a study by Metalsky and Joiner (1992) who used a design quite similar to that of Johnson and Miller (1990) and to that of Ralph and Mineka (1993), although they also included a measure of hopelessness. In their study they did find that pessimistic explanatory style in interaction with negative life events (mediated through the effects of hopelessness) predicted future levels of depression but not anxiety. This appears to be the only prospective study which has found the depression-specific diathesis-stress interaction predicted by both the reformulated helplessness theory (Abramson et al., 1978) and the hopelessness theory (Abramson et al., 1989).

Ideally, such longitudinal designs should assess depression and anxiety levels at several points in time in order to investigate the possibility that explanatory style in anxiety is a predisposing factor to depression, given the evidence that anxiety often precedes depression. It is not only of interest to determine whether or not explanatory style preferentially predisposes individuals to depression versus anxiety, but also to determine whether or not a particular explanatory style provides an important link in the sequential relationship between anxiety and depression. Perhaps anxious individuals who also have a maladaptive explanatory style are more likely to develop depression than anxious individuals who lack such an explanatory style. Using the diathesis-stress model, another possibility is that explanatory style predisposes individuals to anxiety, and that the experience of negative life events by these individuals may make the onset of depression even more likely.

Limitations of Current Measures of Explanatory Style

As discussed earlier, Heimberg et al. (1989) found that social phobics showed an internal, stable, and global composite explanatory style for negative events, as measured by the ASQ. This result should not be surprising given the nature of the instrument most often used to measure explanatory style. The ASQ asks subjects to imagine an event happening to them, to list the cause of that event, and then to rate that cause on several dimensions. Half of these target events involve social situations (social failure and loss on the negative items and social success on the positive items) that are prominent sources of concern to social phobics. Suppose that half of the negative items on the ASQ asked subjects to vividly imagine failures to properly handle snakes instead of failures in the social realm. If this were the case, it would not seem unreasonable to hypothesize that snake phobics might appear to have an internal, stable, and global explanatory style for negative events, because 50% of the failure items on the ASQ would be based on events that are the focus of their fears. We believe that further investigations of explanatory style and social anxiety should examine explanatory style for social events separately from explanatory style for other types of events.

In addition, one should keep in mind that the specific events of the ASQ are all loss or failure events. Theoretically, loss and failure events have been more closely linked with depression, whereas threat events have been more closely linked with anxiety (e.g., Bowlby, 1980; Finlay-Jones & Brown, 1981). If the ASQ assessed attributions for threatening events that are anticipatory in nature, we might see a greater tendency for anxious subjects to attribute such events to internal, stable, and global causes. Our laboratory has recently developed such a modification that includes items such as "The doctor says that the results of your recent physical exam may be cause for concern" or "Your romantic partner may be losing interest in you" (as opposed to "your steady romantic relationship ends" as on the original ASQ). The anticipated threatening events are rated on the same dimensions of internality, stability, and globality as on the original ASQ. Preliminary results suggest that the composite scores on the Threat ASQ are correlated quite highly (approximately .70) with scores on the original expanded ASQ (Peterson & Villanova, 1988) and are also significantly correlated with anxiety in a nonclinical population as measured by the Beck Anxiety Inventory (Luten, Ralph, & Mineka, 1994; Ralph & Mineka, 1993). Whether or not the Threat ASQ correlates more highly with clinical anxiety disorders than does the original ASQ remains to be determined.

Important Questions for Further Research

In addition to the suggestions for future research that stem from the design limitations of current research, there are several other important questions that stem from our earlier review of the prominent features of anxiety and depression comorbidity. One such question for future research arises from observations of the importance of uncontrollability in the etiology and maintenance of both anxiety and depression. Although controllability and locus of control are related constructs, it is important to clarify further the distinction between the two. In the present context, *controllability* refers to the individual's perceived ability to control the causes of events about which he or she is making causal attributions (e.g., Heimberg et al., 1987, 1989; Mikulincer & Solomon, 1988). Locus of control, on the other hand, refers to a more pervasive, traitlike characteristic that is less situation specific. Thus, if an individual has an external locus of control, it is reasonable to assume that he or she perceives the causes of many specific situations as uncontrollable. Given the growing evidence previously discussed for the importance of uncontrollability in both depression and anxiety, it is reasonable to hypothesize that, relative to normals, both depressed and anxious individuals more frequently perceive the causes of specific situations as uncontrollable. On a more general trait level, one would also predict that such individuals have a greater external locus of control. In fact, evidence reviewed by Emmelkamp (1982) and Brewin (1988) supports this hypothesized relationship between anxiety (and depression) and external locus of control.

It is worth noting that the reformulated learned helplessness model deals explicitly only with the pessimistic explanatory style of making attributions for uncontrollable events (although there was much less emphasis on the importance of uncontrollability in the reformulated model than in the original learned helplessness model). However, many of the bad events that may contribute to an individual's depression or anxiety may in fact be controllable, or at least perceived as controllable. The hopelessness theory of depression (Abramson et al., 1989), which represents a reformulation of the 1978 model, does in fact discuss the importance of the perceived occurrence of negative life events, rather than of uncontrollable events per se. Because perceived uncontrollability appears to be an important factor for understanding both depression and anxiety, further research is warranted on both locus of control and the tendency to perceive the causes of events as controllable versus uncontrollable (in an attributional context). Specifically, both locus of control and the perceived controllability of causes may represent important dimensions that partially determine which particular explanatory style may occur in various anxiety disorders.

A second important question stems from consideration of the common and distinct features of depressive and anxious symptomatology. As discussed earlier, anxious and depressive symptoms, whether assessed by self-report or by clinician ratings, tend to co-occur, and most of the instruments used to assess the two constructs have poor discriminant validity. Furthermore, there is a high degree of comorbidity between the anxiety and depressive disorders, and there may be some common underlying genetic diatheses. Given these interrelationships between anxiety and depression at so many different levels of analysis, it is perhaps not too surprising that the pattern of findings for the relationship of the hypothesized depressive explanatory style to the anxiety disorders is not yet entirely clear. One useful way to pursue this relationship is to examine the relationship between explanatory style and positive and negative affectivity. Clark and Watson (1991a, 1991b) argued that anxiety and depression share high negative affectivity, but can be distinguished by positive affectivity (on which only depressives are low). An important question, therefore, is to determine whether the pessimistic explanatory style is more related to high levels of negative affect or to low levels of positive affect (see also Clark et al., 1994). A recent study conducted in our laboratory on a large sample of college students has indeed shown that all three components of the pessimistic explanatory style for negative events are as highly correlated with standard measures of NA as with the BDI. By contrast, there was no significant correlation between explanatory style and a standard measure of PA (Luten et al., 1994; Ralph & Mineka, 1993). Unfortunately, this study only examined explanatory style for negative events (using Peterson & Villanova's, 1988, expanded ASQ). Thus, the possibility remains that an internal, stable, and global explanatory style for negative events may be nonspecific for depression and anxiety, but that an external, unstable, and specific explanatory style for positive events may be specific for depression. This possibility is suggested by the earlier review of explanatory style in the various anxiety disorders; it was much more common for the explanatory style for negative events to be similar in depression and anxiety than for the style for positive events to be similar.

Other important questions arise when considering the often observed sequential relationship between anxiety and depressive disorders. If the pessimistic explanatory style occurs with certain anxiety disorders, this could simply reflect the fact that these individuals may be vulnerable to depression. If, during an anxiety episode, this explanatory style is serving as a vulnerability factor for later depression, the occurrence of negative life events might not always be necessary in order for the anxiety to lapse into depression. This is because many of the prominent negative uncontrollable events in anxiety disorders are the anxiety symptoms themselves (e.g., obsessive thoughts in OCD, flashbacks and nightmares in PTSD, and panic attacks in panic disorder, cf. Barlow, 1988, 1991; Mineka & Kelly, 1989). Thus, it is possible that a pessimistic explanatory style occurring during an anxiety disorder might predict that the patient would eventually respond to the occurrence of these uncontrollable anxiety symptoms with depression. Negative life events could also be expected to play a similar mediating role.

These considerations also lead to interesting possibilities for predicting patterns of intraepisode and interepisode comorbidity of anxiety and depressive disorders. If important features of the pessimistic explanatory style occur in certain anxiety disorders, are these the same disorders that are most commonly associated with depression? Some suggestions that this may be the case are hinted at in the literature reviewed earlier. Specifically, both panic disorder (with and without agoraphobia) and PTSD are often comorbid with depression, and there is also some suggestion that these disorders may be associated with at least certain features of the pessimistic explanatory style, even when levels of depression are controlled for in the statistical analyses. Unfortunately, there are as yet no studies examining explanatory style in obsessive–compulsive disorder, another disorder that is often comorbid with depression. There is, however, one exception to this pattern in Heimberg et al.'s study (1989) that also found the pessimistic explanatory style to be associated with social phobia, even though levels of depression were very low. Nevertheless, the literature on comorbidity of social phobia and depression is quite mixed (see Alloy, Kelly et al., 1990, for a review). Furthermore, as noted earlier, what role the high number of social failure events in the ASQ plays in this finding is unclear at present. Thus, much more needs to be understood about the interrelationships of social phobia, depression, and explanatory style before it can be determined if the findings of Heimberg et al. (1989) do or do not fit with the predicted patterns of comorbidity. Finally, it is also possible that pessimistic explanatory style in some anxiety disorders may be a vulnerability factor for later depression. So for example, even if intraepisode comorbidity of social phobia and depression were low, it might be that prolonged experience with social phobia in someone with a pessimistic explanatory style may lead to depression.

CONCLUSIONS

It is obvious from the present review that far too little is presently known about the specificity of the hypothesized depressive or pessimistic explanatory style to depression versus anxiety. This is perhaps not too surprising given that the importance of these questions about specificity has only come under careful scrutiny in the past 5 years as interest in the theoretical and empirical relationships between depression and anxiety has increased dramatically. It is our hope that this chapter has documented why this issue is interesting and important, and what seem to be some of the most important questions to explore in the future.

9

▼▼▼▼▼▼▼

Explanatory Style and Achievement in School and Work

Peter Schulman
University of Pennsylvania

Research since 1980 has supported the theory that explanatory style predicts achievement in various domains, such as in school, work, sports, and politics. In this chapter, I first discuss the attributional reformulation of the learned helplessness theory and how it relates to achievement. Second, I review related theories of achievement. Third, I review four studies relating explanatory style to school achievement and four studies relating explanatory style to work achievement. Finally, I discuss the implications of this research for school intervention programs and corporate selection, placement, and training programs. Later chapters in this section discuss the role of explanatory style in sports and politics, and cross-cultural differences in explanatory style.

THE ATTRIBUTIONAL REFORMULATION
OF LEARNED HELPLESSNESS THEORY

The original learned helplessness theory stated that experience with uncontrollable events can lead to the expectation that desired outcomes are independent of one's actions (Maier & Seligman, 1976; Seligman, 1975). This expectation of helplessness leads to three types of deficits that closely resemble human depression: motivational (lowered response initiation and persistence), cognitive (inability to perceive contingencies between actions and outcomes), and emotional (sadness and lowered self-esteem).

Everyone experiences uncontrollable aversive events, yet not everyone develops the expectation of helplessness and these helplessness deficits. The attributional reformulation addresses this issue of individual differences and predicts who is more vulnerable or resistant to learned helplessness (Abramson, Seligman, & Teasdale, 1978; Seligman, Abramson, Semmel, & von Baeyer, 1979). According to the reformulation, individuals who habitually attribute negative events to internal, stable, and global causes and positive events to external, unstable, and specific causes (the pessimistic style) are at greater risk for helplessness deficits than those with the opposite, optimistic style.

The process by which explanatory style impacts on achievement in this diathesis-stress model is as follows. The explanations individuals habitually make for their successes and failures lead to expectations that affect their reactions to future successes and failures. These expectations create self-fulfilling prophecies that either enhance or undermine performance. Expectations can affect performance through a variety of behaviors. Individuals with an optimistic explanatory style may be more likely, for example, to take initiative, persist under adversity, take risks, be decisive, engage in quality problem-solving strategies, and be more assertive than individuals with a pessimistic style.

Any complete theory of achievement must discuss the issues of intelligence, motivation and task demands, as well as expectations. It is not just the ability to succeed and the desire to succeed that are critical to performance, but also the belief that one will succeed. All three factors interact to determine performance. This chapter focuses on how an individual's explanations and expectations impinge on achievement.

RELATED THEORIES OF ACHIEVEMENT

There are several theories of achievement that overlap with the attributional reformulation of the learned helplessness theory and they should be noted. These theories discuss the relevance of the perception of control, expectation of control, or explanations of negative events to achievement.

In the field of social learning, Rotter's locus of control theory states that the extent to which an individual has a generalized expectancy that rewards are contingent on behavior will be a determining factor in performance, skill acquisition, and achievement motivation. Numerous studies demonstrate the validity of this construct. See Rotter (1966); Lefcourt (1976); and Phares (1976) for a review of this literature. The research of McClelland, Atkinson, Clark, and Lowell (1953); Atkinson (1958); and Crandall (1963) indicates that individuals who are high on the need for achievement also tend to believe that outcomes are related to their efforts.

Bandura's (1982) theory of self-efficacy also relates to performance and achievement motivation. Bandura defines self-efficacy as the assessment of whether one possesses the necessary abilities to achieve a desired outcome. Judgments of self-efficacy, he stated, "determine how much effort people will expend and how long they will persist in the face of obstacles or aversive experiences" (p. 123).

Vroom (1964) introduced expectancy theory into industrial-organizational psychology. Vroom asserted that performance is a multiplicative function of valence (the perceived value of an outcome), instrumentality (the belief that there exists a given performance that will achieve a desired outcome), and expectancy (the belief that one's efforts will lead to the necessary performance). The theory predicts that when valence and instrumentality are held constant, expectancy will be positively correlated with performance. There is some evidence to support this prediction (Garland, 1984; Locke, Motowidlo, & Bobko, 1986).

Dweck and her associates conducted some pioneering research showing a link between childrens' explanations for failure and subsequent performance. In a series of studies, they found that children who attributed their academic failure to stable and global factors, such as lack of ability or stupidity, were more likely to give up following failure than children who attribute failure to unstable and specific factors, such as luck or a lack of effort. Stable and global explanations for failure correlated with lower initiative, persistence, quality of problem-solving strategies, and lower expectations for future success (Diener & Dweck, 1978, 1980; Dweck, 1975; Dweck & Goetz, 1978; Dweck & Licht, 1980; Dweck & Reppucci, 1973; Dweck & Wortman 1982). Dweck's research differs from explanatory style research in that the subjects offered verbal explanations of failure (that were analyzed by the researchers) as opposed to performing an analysis of each of the attributional dimensions (internality, stability, and globality). Research by Eccles (1983) and Weiner (1974, 1978, 1979, 1985a) also showed that particular explanations for academic success and failure correlate with subsequent motivation and performance.

The previously mentioned research supports the notion that perceptions, expectations, and explanations of negative events all bear a relationship to achievement. The following explanatory style research substantially adds to this evidence.

EXPLANATORY STYLE RESEARCH

Following is a review of four studies on the relationship between explanatory style and school achievement and four studies on explanatory style and work achievement.

Explanatory style in these studies was measured by the Attributional Style Questionnaire (ASQ), the primary instrument for measuring explanatory style (Seligman et al., 1979; Peterson et al., 1982). On this questionnaire, subjects generate a cause for six hypothetical positive events and six negative events and then rate the cause on a 1-to-7 scale for three causal dimensions: internal versus external, stable versus unstable, and global versus specific causes.

The ASQ yields scores for three main measures: the composite positive explanatory style (CP), the composite negative explanatory style (CN), and the combination of these two scores (CPCN). Higher scores are more optimistic scores for CPCN and CP and lower scores are more optimistic scores for CN. Past research indicates that CPCN and CN are the most valid empirical predictors of helplessness deficits (Peterson & Seligman, 1984a; see chapter 2, this volume, for details).

EVIDENCE: EXPLANATORY STYLE AS A PREDICTOR OF SCHOOL ACHIEVEMENT

Study 1: First-Year Grades of College Freshmen (Peterson & Barrett, 1987)

This study addressed whether the ASQ could predict first-year college grade point averages (GPA) controlling for SAT scores and a measure of depression, the Beck Depression Inventory (BDI; Beck, 1967). In short, explanatory style correlated significantly with first-year GPA and significantly predicted first-year GPA when SAT scores and depression were partialled out.

In the beginning of their freshman year, 87 students from the Virginia Polytechnic Institute and State University took the BDI and the academic version of the ASQ. This modified ASQ was patterned exactly after the original ASQ except that it presented subjects with 12 hypothetical negative academic events. The original ASQ is different in that there are 6 positive events and 6 negative events, 6 achievement-oriented and 6 affiliation-oriented events. As discussed earlier, explanations for negative events are often better predictors of various outcomes than explanations for positive events, but it is not clear whether there are advantages in making the content of the event relevant to the sample being tested.

Also measured were several factors that may intervene between explanatory style and academic performance. Subjects took questionnaires measuring specificity of academic goals (Locke, Shaw, Saari, & Latham, 1981), their self-efficacy with respect to achieving these goals (Bandura, 1986), and information was obtained on the number of visits made to academic advising.

The explanatory style for these 12 negative events correlated significantly with cumulative first-year GPA in the expected direction ($r = -.36$, $p < .001$). When SAT score and BDI were partialled out, the CN partial correlation with first-year GPA was $-.28$ ($p < .01$).

After partialling out SAT and BDI, CN correlated $-.30$ ($p < .005$) with goal specificity, $-.29$ ($p < .002$, $n = 65$) with number of advising visits, and $-.16$ (ns) with self-efficacy. Goal specificity ($r = .25$, $p < .02$) and advising visits ($r = .25$, $p < .05$, $n = 65$), in turn, had significant partial correlations with first-year GPA.

These results support the reformulated learned helplessness theory. Students with an optimistic explanatory style for negative events received better grades in their first year of college than those with a pessimistic style, even when measures of ability and depression were controlled for. Further, those with an optimistic style had more specific goals and actively sought out more academic advising. Goal specificity and number of advising visits in turn predicted GPA.

Study 2: First Semester Grades of College Freshmen
(Schulman et al., 1990)

This study asked two questions: (a) Does explanatory style predict first semester college GPA above and beyond traditional measures of ability, such as SAT scores, achievement test scores, and high school rank? (At the University of Pennsylvania, a weighted average of these three measures form the predictive index [PI], a measure the Admissions Committee uses to predict college GPA.); and (b) do those who exceed their predicted grades have a better explanatory style than those who do not?

The interaction of CP and PI significantly predicted GPA, but ASQ scores alone did not correlate with GPA. Further, those who had better grades than the PI prediction were significantly more optimistic than those who had worse grades than the PI prediction.

At the beginning of their first fall semester, 289 freshmen at the University of Pennsylvania completed the ASQ. The PI correlated .54 ($p < .0001$) with first semester GPA, but the ASQ did not correlate significantly with GPA. The ASQ correlated inversely and significantly with the PI (CPCN: $r = -.20$, $p < .002$; CN: $r = .11$, $p < .05$; CP: $r = -.18$, $p < .002$).

In a regression analysis, there was a significant interaction effect for CP × PI ($F = 5.4$, $p < .02$) and a marginal interaction effect for CPCN × PI ($F = 3.2$, $p < .07$) in the prediction of GPA when PI and the respective ASQ measure was partialled out. The CN × PI interaction was not significant. None of the ASQ measures alone predicted GPA when PI was partialled out.

In a t-test analysis, those who exceeded the PI prediction of their grades had a significantly better CPCN ($t = 2.3$, $p < .02$) and CP ($t = 2.8$, $p < .006$) than those who did worse than the PI prediction. There was no difference in CN scores.

These results lend mixed support to the reformulated learned helplessness theory. The CP score and PI combined predicted first semester GPA better than either measure alone. Also, CPCN and CP discriminated those who exceeded their predicted grades from those who underachieved.

It is not clear, however, why the ASQ did not correlate with GPA and why CN did not predict GPA above and beyond the PI. The authors assert that not enough time may have elapsed for these college freshmen to accumulate the bad academic events necessary for this diathesis-stress model to be predictive. The

next study examines the influence of explanatory style on the academic performance of students with more college experience.

Study 3: Grades of College Upperclassmen
(Schulman et al., 1990)

The ASQ was completed by 175 University of Pennsylvania upperclassmen in
an abnormal psychology course at the beginning of the semester. The ASQ and
PI were used to predict GPA in that semester. Unlike the freshmen in Study 2,
the subjects in this study were a mix of sophomores, juniors, and seniors, and
therefore were more likely to have experience with negative academic events.

The prediction was that those with a pessimistic explanatory style are at greater
risk for helplessness deficits and reduced performance following negative events
than those with an optimistic explanatory style. Both the ASQ and PI correlated
significantly with GPA and the ASQ significantly predicted GPA when PI was
partialled out.

The PI correlated .29 ($p < .0001$) with GPA for that semester. The ASQ also
correlated significantly with GPA in the expected direction (CPCN: $r = .23$, $p
< .01$; CN: $r = -.19, p < .01$; CP: $r = .15, p < .05$). CP correlated positively with
the PI ($r = .22, p < .01$) and CPCN and CN did not correlate with the PI.

In a regression analysis, there was a significant interaction effect for CP × PI
($F = 4.4, p < .04$) in the prediction of GPA when PI and CP were partialled out,
but not for CN × PI or for CPCN × PI. CN ($F = 8.1, p < .005$) and CPCN ($F
= 8.3, p < .005$), however, significantly predicted GPA when PI was partialled
out, but CP did not.

In a t-test analysis, students in the best quartile of GPA had a significantly
better CN ($t = 2.1, p < .04$) and CPCN ($t = 2.5, p < .02$) than those in the worst
quartile of GPA. There was no significant difference in CP scores.

Compared to the results of the freshman sample in Study 2, explanatory style
was a stronger predictor of GPA for upperclassman while the PI became a weaker
predictor of GPA. Unlike Study 2, CN was a significant predictor of GPA in
Study 3. One possible explanation for this is that as negative events accumulate,
one's explanatory style for negative events and expectations of future academic
performance have a growing impact on academic achievement, whereas ability
has a declining impact. Once again, however, it is not clear why some ASQ
measures were significant predictors in some analyses, whereas other ASQ
measures were not.

There are two factors that may have handicapped the effects of explanatory
style on GPA in Studies 2 and 3. First, one of the purposes of these studies was
to measure the effect of explanatory style above and beyond ability. The PI,
however, is not a pure measure of ability because one of its components, high
school rank, derives from a performance that may in part reflect the effects of
explanatory style.

Second, the University of Pennsylvania is a highly selective institution with a restricted range of academic talent. It is therefore plausible that explanatory style would bear a stronger relationship with GPA in a population with a broader distribution of talent.

Study 1 possibly overcomes these two handicaps somewhat. Study 1 only used SAT scores as a measure of ability and, because the students came from a less selective state school, there may have been a less restricted range of talent. Furthermore, grades were measured over the first year rather than just the first semester, which may have allowed for more negative events to accumulate. This may explain the stronger relationship between explanatory style and GPA in Study 1 than in Study 2. It is also important to note that Study 1 used a modified, academic negative events-only version of the ASQ that may have better tapped students' interpretations of academic performance.

Study 4: First-Year Grades and Dropping Out from West Point (Schulman et al., 1990)

This study investigated whether the ASQ could predict first-year academic grades and drop-outs at the United States Military Academy at West Point, New York.

The ASQ was completed by 1,184 individuals at this officer training school in the beginning of the summer, before the first year of classes. ASQ and SAT scores were used to predict two outcomes: cumulative first-year grades and dropping out (dropping out of a highly stressful boot-camp–type introduction to military life in the summer before classes or dropping out during the first year of classes).

CPCN and CN significantly predicted first year GPA when SAT scores were partialled out (CPCN: $F = 3.7, p < .03$; CN: $F = 5.3, p < .01$). The ASQ, however, did not correlate with first-year GPA but SAT scores correlated .58 with GPA ($p < .0001$). CPCN correlated inversely with SAT ($r = -.09, p < .002$), but CP and CN did not correlate significantly with SAT.

In a t-test analysis, those who dropped out of boot camp or the first year of classes had a significantly more pessimistic CPCN score than those who did not drop out ($t = 2.1, p < .02$). CP and CN did not significantly predict dropping out.

This study adds mixed support to the reformulated learned helplessness theory. CPCN predicted first year GPA when SAT scores were partialled out but did not correlate with GPA. It is important to note that this is a highly selective academy, with average SAT scores for this sample at about 1,200. So, as in Studies 2 and 3, restriction of range may diminish explanatory style effects. This study does make an important contribution to the helplessness literature: CPCN predicted quitting, a central helplessness deficit.

Predicting dropping out at West Point has theoretical and practical importance. Theoretically, the rigors of military training and education are a good test of this diathesis-stress model. Practically, identifying individuals at risk for dropping out has implications for selection, placement, and training. By the end of the first year, about 20% of the subjects in this sample dropped out. This represents wasted time, money, and needless human distress. Helplessness prone individuals may best be steered away from the rigors of this kind of program or go through special training to fortify them against such challenges. It may also be useful to place individuals who are particularly helplessness resistant in the high pressure positions.

These first four studies suggest that explanatory style is related to school performance and quitting. Following is a review of four studies on the relationship between explanatory style and work achievement.

EVIDENCE: EXPLANATORY STYLE AS A PREDICTOR OF WORK ACHIEVEMENT

Study 5: A Cross-Sectional Study of Sales Productivity (Seligman & Schulman, 1986)

This study investigated the relationship between explanatory style and the productivity of 94 life insurance salespeople who had experience ranging from several months to several decades. Productivity was defined as commissions earned on the sale of life insurance policies in their first or second year of experience. Agents with less than 1 or 2 years of data were excluded from the analysis.

Like the West Point study (Study 4), this is a good test of the diathesis-stress model. Sales agents repeatedly encounter rejection and indifference from prospective clients. It is inevitable that agents will fail to sell insurance more often than they succeed. Consequently, the turnover rate among life insurance agents is very high, as are the training costs. About 78% of the life insurance agents hired in the United States quit within 3 years (Life Insurance Marketing Research Association [LIMRA], 1983). Do agents with an optimistic explanatory style perform better than those with a pessimistic style? (Because this is a cross-sectional study, all subjects were by definition employed when the data was collected, so there is no measure of dropping out in this study.)

The explanatory style for negative events significantly correlated with sales productivity. Optimists sold significantly more insurance than the pessimists did. CN correlated $-.19$ ($p < .07$) with first-year sales and $-.39$ ($p < .01$) with second-year sales. Sales agents who scored above the CN median (optimists) sold 29% more insurance in their first year than agents who scored below the CN median ($t = 1.4$, $p < .01$). Differences were more pronounced in the second year. Agents who scored above the CN median sold 130% more insurance in their first year than agents who scored below the CN median ($t = 2.0$, $p < .03$). Sample sizes in the second year are only about half as large, however, because many agents had not completed their second year. CPCN results were not significant at the median division but were significant at the quartile and decile splits. CP was not significant.

Sales agents with an optimistic explanatory style sold more insurance than those with a pessimistic explanatory style. Further, explanatory style better discriminated between the high and low producers in the second year than in the first year. This speaks to the theory discussed in Studies 2 and 3, that explanatory style becomes a better predictor of performance as time goes on and negative events accumulate.

Because explanatory style was measured after production was collected, the question of causal direction is unanswered. There are several possibilities. Explanatory style could precede and predict productivity, productivity could affect explanatory style, there could be a bidirectional influence, or there may be an underlying third variable. Study 6 is a longitudinal study that better addresses the issue of causality.

Study 6: A Longitudinal Study of Sales Productivity and Turnover (Seligman & Schulman, 1986)

This study asked whether explanatory style could predict sales productivity and turnover. After being hired, but before training and any sales experience, 103 life insurance sales agents took the ASQ. Productivity and turnover data was collected for 1 year. (I use the term *survivor* to refer to those who had not quit at the end of 1 year.) Results are presented only for the CPCN measure. CP and CN were marginally significant predictors but better predictors when combined to form CPCN.

Explanatory style significantly predicted sales productivity in the agents' second 6 months of sales experience but not in the first 6 months. Further, explanatory style significantly predicted whether or not the agent would survive the first year. CPCN correlated .27 ($p < .03$) with the second 6 months of sales but did not correlate significantly with the first 6 months of sales. Agents who scored above the CPCN median sold 9% more insurance in their first 6 months ($t = .7$, ns) and 25% more insurance in their second 6 months ($t = 1.6$, $p < .06$) than those who scored below the CPCN median. Agents who scored in the top quartile of CPCN sold 40% more insurance in their first year ($t = 1.9$, $p < .03$) than those in the bottom quartile.

Agents who scored above the CPCN median survived at twice the rate of agents who scored below the CPCN median (above median survivors = 67%, below median survivors = 33%; $X^2 = 6.6$, $p < .005$). (59 of the 101 agents for whom there was survival information dropped out by the end of the first year.) Agents who scored in the top quartile of CPCN survived at almost three times the rate of agents who scored in the bottom quartile of CPCN (top quartile survivors = 74%, bottom quartile survivors = 26%; $X^2 = 8.4$, $p < .002$).

In summary, agents with an optimistic explanatory style were more likely to survive their first year and sell more insurance than agents with a pessimistic style. The authors present several possible reasons why explanatory style did not predict productivity in the first 6 months. In the first few months agents are still in training, learning the necessary skills and product knowledge and work closely with their manager in making sales. As time goes on and they begin to work more independently and experience more negative events, explanatory style may play a larger role in sales success.

The findings of Studies 5 and 6 indicate that explanatory style predicts sales performance, but this does not rule out the possibility that there may be a bidirectional influence between explanatory style and performance. Like the West Point Study (Study 4), these findings have practical implications. Identifying individuals at risk for dropping out and poor performance has implications for selection, placement, and training, especially given the very high turnover rates and training costs. Training costs are estimated conservatively at $30,000 per life insurance agent. These implications are discussed in more detail later in the chapter.

Study 7: A Second Longitudinal Study of Sales Productivity and Turnover (Seligman & Schulman, 1986)

Based on the results in Studies 5 and 6, Metropolitan Life decided to administer the ASQ to about 15,000 sales applicants to replicate these studies, track their productivity and survival for 2 years, and also use the ASQ to hire a small group of agents.

Because applicants are motivated to score well on the ASQ in order to be hired, this raises the question of whether validity will hold up under such conditions. In a study on the transparency of the ASQ, Schulman, Seligman, and Amsterdam (1987) found that college students given a monetary incentive to score well scored no differently from those not given a monetary incentive (see chapter 2).

One of Metropolitan Life's goals was to increase their sales manpower without a loss in productivity per agent or survival rates. To do this, they used the ASQ to hire a small number of agents who scored just slightly below their currently used selection test but scored well on the ASQ. Their currently used selection test is the Career Profile (CP: LIMRA, 1984), a widely used personality profile that yields a score by matching the profile of the applicant to the profiles of past successful insurance agents. Scores range from 1 to 19 and managers were allowed to hire those who scored 12 or more.

Of the 14,000 applicants who completed the ASQ, 543 were hired on the basis of scoring 12 or more on the Career Profile and doing well in interviews. I call them the *regular agents*. In addition, 138 agents who failed the Career Profile in the 9 to 11 range but scored above the CPCN median were hired. I call them the *special agents*. Also, there were 85 agents who failed the Career Profile and scored below the CPCN median who were hired. I call them the *special agent control group*.

It is important to note that none of these groups were randomly selected. As long as applicants passed the selection criteria, managers had wide latitude in hiring decisions. This introduced a serious selection bias, especially among the special agent control group, that failed both tests and were not technically allowed to be hired. Those who were hired in spite of this probably had qualities compelling enough for the manager to hire them in violation of company policy. This selection bias eliminates the possibility of a random control group and should handicap ASQ effects.

There were four major findings from this study. First, special agents sold more insurance and survived at a higher rate than the special agent controls. Special agents sold 44% more in the first year ($t = 2.5$, $p < .01$) and 70% more in the second year ($t = 2.6$, $p < .01$) than the special agent controls. Second-year sample sizes are smaller due to dropping out. The special agents' survival rate was marginally better than the special agent controls' survival rate at the end of 2 years (36% vs. 26%: $X^2 = 2.6$, $p < .07$).

Second, special agents produced and survived as well as the regular agents. There were no significant differences between the special and the regular agents. The most important implication of these first two findings is that the ASQ could be successfully used to identify applicants who failed the Career Profile and normally would not be hired but, if they had an optimistic explanatory style, would produce and survive as well as agents who passed the Career Profile.

Third, regular agents with an optimistic explanatory style sold more insurance in their second year than regular agents with a pessimistic explanatory style. (There was no production difference using the median CPCN split. The following production statistics are based on the top three quartiles CPCN versus the bottom quartile CPCN.) There was no difference in survival rates. Regular agents with an optimistic style sold 8% more in their first year ($t = .6$, ns) and 31% more in their second year ($t = 1.8$, $p < .04$).

Fourth, combining all three groups for a survival analysis, the ASQ significantly predicted survival among the low producers, but not the high producers. As reported previously, the ASQ marginally predicted survival among agents who scored 9 to 11 on the Career Profile and did not predict survival among regular agents. Because high producers may quit for different reasons than low producers, such as better job opportunities, analyses were done separately on these two groups. Among the low producers, those with an optimistic explanatory style had a higher survival rate ($X^2 = 3.4$, $p < .05$) than those with a pessimistic explanatory style.

Study 8: Using the ASQ for Sales Selection
(Seligman & Schulman, 1986)

Based on the results in Study 7, Metropolitan Life decided to use the ASQ to hire agents who scored just below the currently used selection test cutoff (9–11 on the Career Profile) but scored well on the ASQ (above the CPCN median).

Because they instituted this hiring policy, about 875 of these special agents have been hired. These special agents have produced and survived as well as the regularly hired agents in their first year and a half. This replicates some of the findings of Study 7. (There are no true control groups for purposes of comparison, because the ASQ was used in the selection process and those who failed the ASQ were not hired.) This has helped Metropolitan Life achieve its goal of increasing sales manpower and revenue without a decline in productivity per agent or survival rates.

DISCUSSION AND IMPLICATIONS

These eight field studies support the notion that the attributional reformulation of the learned helplessness theory is related to achievement at school and at work. Individuals who habitually explain their successes and failures with optimistic explanations are more likely to be high achievers and not quit than those who make pessimistic explanations.

Further, these findings suggest that explanatory style precedes, predicts, and is one of the causes of achievement, although these field studies are not fine-grained enough to illuminate the precise mechanism. Explanatory style (especially for negative events) seems to predict performance above and beyond ability and has greater predictive power over time as adverse experiences accumulate.

Questions, however, still remain. Why are different ASQ measures predictive in different studies? How does each attributional dimension relate to the various outcomes? In Studies 2 and 4, why is it that explanatory style predicts grades above and beyond ability but does not correlate with grades? In Study 7, why does explanatory style predict quitting among low producers but not among high producers? What is the mechanism by which explanatory style influences performance? These are important questions to consider, yet the weight of the evidence converges in favor of the model.

The results of these studies have important implications for individuals in academic and work settings. Intervention with students at risk for poor grades and dropping out could help bring performance closer to potential and reduce drop out rates. Intervention could take place through academic advising or existing university counseling services.

Prevention programs, however, may be especially effective among children, to immunize them against the inevitable setbacks and effect change before cognitive styles become entrenched. A children's depression prevention program is currently being developed and piloted by Seligman, Hollon, Freeman, and their associates. This program adapts cognitive therapy methods for elementary school children and includes such techniques as identifying automatic negative thoughts, reality testing the accuracy of these thoughts, and searching for alternative interpretations and explanations for adverse experiences.

In the workplace, these findings have implications for selection, placement, and training, especially for positions fraught with adversity. In insurance sales, for example, the high turnover rates (78% within 3 years) indicate that an agent who can bounce back from the frequent rejection and failure is the exception rather than the rule. Such high rates of quitting represent not only large financial costs in training and management, but needless suffering as well.

Identifying individuals who are particularly helplessness resistant or prone may be advantageous to both the individual and the organization. Hiring those who have a more optimistic explanatory style for the most challenging and stressful positions may improve the person–environment fit and have financial benefits. Preventive or remedial explanatory style training for all, or for selected high-risk individuals, could help immunize them against the difficulties inherent in that position. Such a training program has also been developed by Seligman and his associates.

10

▼▼▼▼▼▼▼

Sports and Explanatory Style

David Rettew
Karen Reivich
University of Pennsylvania

The belief that psychological factors play a profound role in athletic performance is not new. "The mental part of the game" is commonly invoked with terms such as *momentum, confidence,* and *homefield advantage* to explain both the expected and surprising outcomes of athletic competition. There are few who would dispute the tremendous drive and determination required to mold raw talent into a successful athlete. Yet despite the obvious importance and pervasiveness of this aspect of sports, there is much to learn about the nature of these mental components and their effect on performance.

The development of explanatory style (ES) theory provides an excellent opportunity to look at athletic performance within the framework of an extensively studied model. Instruments such as the Attributional Style Questionnaire (ASQ) and the Content Analysis of Verbatim Explanations (CAVE) technique are reliable and valid (Peterson et al., 1982; Schulman, Castellon, & Seligman, 1989) and allow for a quantitative description of ES.

Also, athletic performance provides an almost prototypical model of human achievement. There are few other domains where the difference between success and failures is better defined than in the context of winning and losing in sports. Sports provide researchers of ES with a domain that is well documented quantitatively. From points to times to batting averages, the world of sports is saturated with statistics. This makes the measurement of achievement specific and precise.

The domain of sports also lends itself to the exploration of group explanatory style. The majority of ES research has involved the assessment of individuals (see chapter 12 for an exception). The prediction of achievement from a team's

ES suggests that this approach may be valuable in investigating the performance of other organizations (e.g., sales teams).

Cognitive Variables in Sports Research

There have been a number of studies that address sports performance and attribution. Using instruments such as Russell's (1982) Causal Dimension Scale, which measures attributions along the dimensions of locus of control, stability, and controllability, athletes have been found to invoke internal, stable, and controllable attributions following athletic success (Gill, Ruder, & Gross, 1982; McCauley & Gross, 1983). Other investigators have found that attributions become more external as the event and its causes become more ambiguous (Spink & Roberts, 1980). Similarly, more external attributions such as luck or bad officiating are more common when the outcome is unexpected as judged by past performance (Iso-Ahola, 1977; Roberts, 1977; Spink, 1978).

Although these studies provide a better understanding of the interaction between events and attributions, the causative role of attributions in determining future outcome in sports has not been addressed prior to the investigations reported here.

Predictions of Performance

The present chapter describes three studies which investigated the relationship between ES and athletic performance. The first study tested the predictive validity of ES in the Atlantic Division of the National Basketball Association for both the 1982–1983 and the 1983–1984 seasons. It was hypothesized that the ES of a team could be assessed in one season and used to predict the ability of a team to come back from a defeat, after controlling for the team's ability. In the second study, the predictive validity of ES in Major League Baseball was tested. We hypothesized that the ES in one season would predict the number of games won in the following season, again, after controlling for the team's ability. This study also investigated possible mechanisms through which ES has its effect. The third study predicted performance of top-ranked collegiate swimmers from the University of California at Berkeley (Seligman, Nolen-Hoeksema, Thornton, & Thornton, 1990). In addition to predicting future performance from ES, an experimental manipulation was introduced so that the mechanism of the effect could be studied. In this study, it was hypothesized that after a "rigged" defeat, swimmers with a pessimistic ES, would swim significantly worse in the following trial, whereas swimmers with an optimistic style would not.

BASKETBALL

In this study, team ES was assessed for five teams of the Atlantic Division of the National Basketball Association. ES was assessed using the CAVE technique. Briefly, this procedure uses written or spoken material to derive ES. Good and bad events and their causes are extracted and rated along the dimensions of internality, stability, and globality. When many extractions are rated and averaged, composite scores for individuals or teams can be obtained (see chapter 2).

To obtain verbatim quotations three sources were used. The primary source of quotations in both seasons was the weekly journal *The Sporting News*. We also used two computer information services. These services provided the text of the hometown newspapers of the teams studied.

A subject was included in the study if he met two conditions: (a) at least one direct quotation containing either a good or bad event and its explanation was found, and (b) the player was on the same team during the subsequent season. For each extraction, three naive raters (naive to the hypotheses of the study and the identity of the player) quantified the explanation along the three causal dimensions. To reduce bias, the final score was an average of the three ratings. Sample extractions and ratings are presented in Table 10.1 (see also Seligman, 1991).

The ES of the team was calculated by pooling and averaging all extractions made by the team's players. Thus, the entire team was the subject, rather than the individual player. This technique provided for a natural weighting effect. Those players who made the strongest contributions to a team's performance were likely to have greater media attention, thus more extractions analyzed. Data calculated with other weightings, such as averaging the ES of each player first, produced similar results.

For the 1982–1983 season, there were 185 extractions for bad events (37 per team) and 640 extractions for the 1983–1984 season (128 per team).

The principal dependent variable was performance after a defeat measured in the target season (the season following the season in which ES was assessed). To control for ability, the Las Vegas point spread was used as a measure of the team's talent. This system takes into account the team's overall ability as well

TABLE 10.1
Sample Events and Explanations

Event	Explanation	Ratings
Player is in a slump. (bad event)	"I've been putting too much pressure on myself. Now I'm relaxed."	S/U = 3 G/S = 6 I/E = 7
"I'm not frustrated." (good event)	"Because I have confidence that I have what it takes."	S/U = 7 G/S = 7 I/E = 7
Subject missed an easy shot. (bad event)	"My timing was off for a second."	S/U = 1 G/S = 1 I/E = 7
Player hadn't scored for two quarters. (bad event)	"They were playing great defense for a change."	S/U = 1 G/S = 1 I/E = 1

Note. S/U = Stable/unstable dimension (higher score more stable). G/S = Global/specific dimension (higher score more global). I/E = Internal/external dimension (higher score more internal).

as other factors such as whether the game is being played at home or away, recent performance, injuries, and so forth. We hypothesized that teams with a more optimistic ES would beat the point spread in a game following a loss more often than teams with a more pessimistic ES.

Coming Back From Defeat and ES

Teams with a more optimistic ES for bad events performed significantly better in games following a loss than teams with a pessimistic ES. Means, standard deviations, and reliabilities of the measures are presented in Table 10.2. The percentages of games won after a loss and the ES scores for each team are presented in Table 10.3.

Stepwise regressions were performed to test ES as a predictor of performance, over and above a measure of the team's skill or ability. That is, if good teams have optimistic explanatory styles and bad teams have pessimistic explanatory styles (not an unreasonable proposition), then the relationship between ES in one season and performance in the next, may simply indicate that, in general, good teams stay good and bad teams stay bad. To control for ability, a team's win percentage in the season ES was assessed was used as a covariate. Given previous

TABLE 10.2
Means and Reliabilities of Measures: Basketball Study

Measure	Mean	SD	Reliability
1982–1983 Season			
Explanatory Style			
CN	10.39	2.32	.69
CP	12.94	2.24	—
CPCN	2.70	1.38	—
Performance			
Postloss	.497	0.13	—
Win% (1982–1983)	.585	0.12	—
Win% (1983–1984)	.570	0.16	—
1983–1984 Season			
Explanatory Style			
CN	12.07	0.41	.70
CP	12.08	3.14	—
CPCN	0.01	3.20	—
Performance			
Postloss	.606	0.14	—
Win% (1983–1984)	.570	0.16	—
Win% (1984–1985)	.564	0.17	—

Note. CN = composite negative explanatory style. CP = composite positive explanatory style. CPCN = CP minus CN. Postloss = the percentage of games following a loss in which the team beat the Las Vegas point spread. For all measures $n = 5$ except for CP and CPCN ($n = 4$).

TABLE 10.3
Explanatory Style and Winning After a Defeat

Team	Postloss	CN of Previous Season (Rank)
	1982–1983 Season	
Celtics	0.684 (1)	7.81 (1)
Knicks	0.567 (2)	8.90 (2)
Bullets	0.463 (3)	10.98 (4)
Sixers	0.392 (4)	10.34 (3)
Nets	0.378 (5)	13.90 (5)
	1983–1984 Season	
Celtics	0.813 (1)	11.47 (1)
Bullets	0.631 (2)	11.94 (2)
Nets	0.622 (3)	12.18 (3)
Sixers	0.522 (4)	12.59 (5)
Knicks	0.440 (5)	12.19 (4)

Note. CN = composite negative explanatory style. Postloss = the percentage of games following a loss in which the team beat the Las Vegas point spread.

positive findings linking performance and ES in other domains, one-tailed p values are reported (Kamen & Seligman, 1986; Schulman & Seligman, 1986).

In this model, composite explanatory style score for negative events (CN) significantly predicted wins following a loss [$F(3,9) = 4.69$, $p < .05$] and the model accounted for nearly 55% of the variance. In separate analyses, composite explanatory style score for positive events (CP) and the overall composite of explanatory style, CP minus CN (CPCN) were not significant predictors. It should be noted that the explanatory style score most relevant for this analysis is CN. It is how one views failures or bad events (i.e., the loss of a basketball game) that should predict how one does following a failure or bad event.

Win Percentage and Explanatory Style

ES did not predict overall win percentage in the target year after controlling for win percentage from the year ES was assessed. It should be noted, however, that the correlation between win percentage from Year 1 to Year 2 was extremely high ($r = .72$, $p < .02$). Thus, overall performance across the years is quite stable, leaving little room for ES to have an impact.

BASEBALL

We measured the ES of the 12 teams of the National League using the CAVE technique. This procedure was used during the 1985 season to predict performance in the 1986 season. We replicated our results using ES during the 1986 season to predict performance in 1987. When appropriate, data was also analyzed with or without the ES of the team's pitchers.

As a result of analyzing approximately 15,000 pages of sports reporting for the 1985 season, we were able to include 168 players who had at least one extraction and 72 players for whom we could find at least three extractions. This yielded an average of 39 extractions for bad events per team. For the 1986 season, there were 137 subjects for whom we had at least one extraction and 46 for whom we had at least three extractions, yielding an average of 23 extractions for bad events per team.

The primary measure of team performance used in this study was the percentage of games a team won in the target season (win percentage). Also of interest was a team's batting average under pressure in the target season. "Pressure" statistics were derived from Siwoff, Hirdt, and Hirdt (1985, 1986, 1987) and were defined as a batting performance in the seventh, eighth, and ninth innings when the difference in score between the teams was three runs or less. Means and standard deviations for both dependent and independent variables are presented in Table 10.4.

Win Percentage and Explanatory Style

In general, we found that teams with an optimistic ES, that is, made unstable, specific, and external explanations for bad events and stable, global, and internal explanations for good events, won more games in the target season than teams with a more pessimistic ES. The correlations between win percentage in the target season and ES were as follows: CN ($r = -.49$, $p < .05$), CP ($r = .11$, p = ns), and CPCN ($r = .42$, $p < .05$). The correlation between CN and win percentage is comparable to the correlation between win percentages in two consecutive seasons ($r = .45$). Thus, when trying to predict how well a team will do in the next season, one would do as well knowing the team's ES as one would knowing the team's winning percentage from the current season. The relationship between ES and win percentage is depicted graphically in Fig. 10.1.

Using the stepwise regression procedures described in the basketball study, CN remained a significant predictor of performance after partialling out the effect win percentage from the first season [$F(3, 20) = 5.37$, $p < .05$]. CP and CPCN were not significant after controlling for these other variables.

Batting Performance and Explanatory Style

No significant correlations were found between the ability of the entire team to bat under pressure during the target season (as previously defined) and ES. We decided that it may be inappropriate to include the explanatory style of pitchers in this analysis because pitchers in the National League are often replaced by

TABLE 10.4
Means and Reliabilities of Measures: Baseball Study

Measure	Mean	SD	Reliability
	1985 Season		
Explanatory Style			
(with pitchers)			
CN	10.88	0.84	.73
CP	12.52	0.63	.80
CPCN	1.64	1.09	—
(without pitchers)			
CN	10.57	0.62	.74
CP	12.52	0.79	.81
CPCN	1.95	0.99	—
Performance			
Win% (1985)	.500	0.09	—
Win% (1986)	.500	0.07	—
Batting average (overall, 1986)	.253	0.01	—
Batting average (pressure, 1986)	.258	0.02	—
	1986 Season		
Explanatory Style			
(with pitchers)			
CN	11.74	0.68	.68
CP	13.01	0.78	.80
CPCN	1.35	1.44	—
(without pitchers)			
CN	11.87	0.81	.72
CP	12.77	1.56	.83
CPCN	1.35	0.99	—
Performance			
Win% (1986)	.500	0.07	—
Win% (1987)	.500	0.06	—
Batting average (overall, 1987)	.261	0.01	—
Batting average (pressure, 1987)	.258	0.02	—

Note. CN = composite negative explanatory style. CP = composite positive explanatory style. CPCN = CP minus CN. For all measures $n = 12$.

pinch hitters toward the end of the game, especially if that game is close. Thus, we decided to run a separate analysis in which the data from pitchers was removed from the team's ES. In the analysis without pitchers, the correlations improved: CN ($r = -.11$, $p = $ ns), CP ($r = .53$ $p < .05$), and CPCN ($r = .43$, $p < .05$). Furthermore, when the effect of the team's overall batting skill was partialled out (how well the team batted across all situations in the target season), both CP [$F(3,20) = 11.77$, $p < .05$] and CPCN [$F(3,20) = 5.71$, $p < .05$] remained statistically significant. These equations accounted for 55% and 45% of the variance

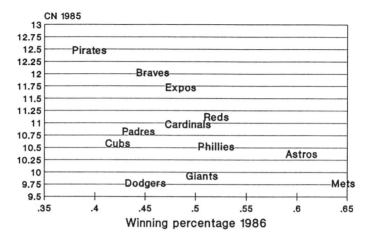

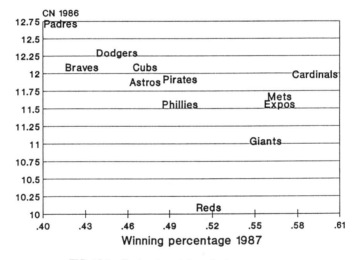

FIG. 10.1.   Explanatory style and win percentage.

respectively. As previously argued, we might expect that the best predictor of batting under pressure would be how a team views bad events and adversity. However, CN did not significantly predict a team's ability to bat under pressure.

Mediators of Explanatory Style

ES was found to predict win percentage in the target season. The question of how ES affects winning percentage needs to be addressed. We know that batting under pressure correlated highly with win percentage in the target year ($r = .57, p < .005$) and both CP and CPCN, as reported previously. Thus, we hypothesized that it may be through batting under pressure that ES leads to winning or losing. To test this, both ES and batting under pressure were entered as independent variables. This regression analysis revealed that although BatPress was a strong predictor of win percentage in the target season [$F(4,19) = 6.12, p < .05$], it could not account for the still significant contribution of CN [$F(4,19) = 4.25, p < .05$]. In summary, ES for good events related to batting under pressure that in turn related to win percentage. The way that teams view bad events also related to win percentage but appears to work through a means other than batting under pressure.

SWIMMING

The baseball and basketball studies presented evidence that pessimistic explanatory styles can lead to future performance deficits for teams, relative to the teams' ability. In addition, there were indications that the effect of ES may be mediated by poor responses to failure or defeat. The swimming studies conducted by Seligman et al. (1990) focused on individual performance and provided additional confirmation of the findings in basketball and baseball. Furthermore, the swimming studies tested the hypothesis that the effect of ES is partially mediated by recovery from defeat.

The subjects in this study were members of the varsity men's and women's swim teams at the University of California at Berkeley during the 1987–1988 season. Twenty-one men and 21 women, many of whom held national or world records in their events, completed the ASQ. This self-report instrument (described in chapter 2) yields the same composite scores as those obtained through the CAVE technique.

In order to determine whether knowing a swimmer's ES provided us with any predictive power over and above coaches' judgments, the coaches rated each swimmer at the beginning of the season on a 1 to 7 scale on how well he or she would perform after a defeat. The coaches were naive to the swimmers' ES scores when these judgments were made. Higher scores indicated better performance relative to ability.

Following each competitive swim during the season, the coach rated each swimmer's performance on a 7-point scale (1 = *much worse than expected*, 4 = *as expected*, 7 = *much better than expected*). Each swim that earned a swimmer a rating of 1, 2, or 3 was counted as a poor swim. Each swimmer also rated his or her performance after each event on the same scale. This rating was discontinued as it was found to be nearly identical to the coach's ratings.

Explanatory Style and Future Performance

Seligman et al. (1990) performed a series of regression analyses to test the prediction that ES would predict future swim performance. In the main analysis, CPCN, sex, and coaches' judgments were simultaneously regressed against percentage of poor swims. The results indicated that each of the predictor variables contributed significantly to the prediction of the percentage of poor swims, over and above the other variables in the model: CPCN ($t = 2.62$, $p < .012$), sex ($t = 2.51$, $p < .016$), and coaches' judgment ($t = 3.28$, $p < .002$).

Response to Simulated Failure

The first study showed that ES and coaches' judgments of swimmers' resilience after defeat predicted how many unexpectedly poor swims the team members would go on to have over the season. Study 1 did not enable the researchers to directly test the mechanism by which ES affects performance. Thus, in order to gain further insight into what mediates the relationship between ES and performance, Seligman et al. (1990) experimentally manipulated defeat. The swimmers were told that they were going to be timed in a trial of their best event (a standard occurrence in swim practice), however, the feedback the swimmers received was manipulated to create the perception of defeat. That is, after the timed trial, the coaches told the swimmers that they swam the trial more slowly than they actually did. The false times were chosen carefully so that they swimmers viewed their performance as a "defeat" and did not doubt the accuracy of the time reported. For 100, 200, 400, and 500 meter events, 1.5, 2, 4, and 5 seconds were added to the actual time. When told of their "slower" times, the swimmers looked disheartened, but did not report suspicion either at the time or during the debriefing at the conclusion of the study.

The dependent variable in this experiment was the coaches' rating on a 1 to 7 scale (described earlier) of how well the swimmer performed in a second timed trial following the rigged defeat (swimmers were given a 30-minute rest before trials to assure a fresh performance). In addition, the ratio of the swimmers' second time over his or her actual first time was computed and used as a dependent variable. Because defeat was the manipulation, the principal independent variable was explanatory style for negative events.

In general, swimmers with an optimistic ES for negative events swam at least as well in their second trial, whereas those with a pessimistic ES for negative events swam worse. Seligman et al. (1990) divided the swimmers into two groups based on a median split of CN scores. The mean ratio of the time after the false feedback to the first time was .995 for the optimistic swimmers as compared to 1.0161 for the pessimistic swimmers ($t = 1.96$, $p < .059$). Whereas this difference may seem small, the authors point out that the absolute differences in many of the cases would be the difference between winning and losing. This pattern of results also held for the coaches' judgments of the swimmers' performances. It is important to note that the coaches' judgments of the first swim were not different for the optimists and the pessimists. The optimists and pessimists did as well as each other initially ($Ms = 3.53$ vs. 3.50). Thus, the effect of ES appeared only after defeat and was specific to ES for negative events; CP and CPCN did not show significant effects on Time 2 performance relative to Time 1.

In order to confirm the results reported earlier, Seligman et al. (1990) performed regression analyses using CN, sex, and coaches' judgments of ability to rebound after defeat to predict second swim times. CN scores, but neither sex nor coaches' judgments, accounted for significant variance in predicting the ratio of times before and after the feedback (CN: $t = 3.06$, $p < .005$). When the difference in coaches' judgments of the two times was used as the dependent variable, CN scores accounted for variance approaching significance ($t = 1.96$, $p < .06$), but neither sex nor coaches' judgments accounted for significant variance.

Thus, three important findings emerged from the two swim studies. First, swimmers with a pessimistic style were more likely to perform below coaches' expectations during the season than swimmers with an optimistic style. Second, after a rigged defeat, the performance of swimmers with a pessimistic explanatory style deteriorated, whereas the performance of optimists did not. Third, ES predicted the swimmers' performance even after coaches' judgments of ability to come back from defeat was taken into account.

DISCUSSION

The studies discussed in this chapter were designed to determine whether explanatory style can predict team and individual athletic achievement. The data generally supported the hypothesis that a pessimistic explanatory style predicts poorer future performance, even after controlling for ability. Also, it appears that the information obtained from ES is in addition to, rather than redundant with, the information players, coaches, and odds makers use when predicting the outcome of competitions.

These studies also indicate that a mechanism of ES is ability to recover from defeat and handle adversity. Athletes and teams with pessimistic styles, perceiving loss to be the result of pervasive and long-lasting causes, do not recover from these setbacks as well as those with a more optimistic style.

Determining Cause and Effect

The studies reported in this chapter went beyond demonstrating a correlational relationship between ES and performance. First, the researchers tried to predict performance in the season following the season in which ES was measured. Second, ability and other known factors contributing to success were controlled either by covarying out performance in the season ES was measured (baseball study), or by handicapping the team using the point spread (basketball study), or by assessing performance relative to expectation (swimming studies). Under each of these conditions, ES continued to predict athletic performance. Nevertheless, these data cannot rule out the possibility of other third variables or of an interactive cascade of ES and failure (Bandura, 1978). Thus, it may be true that poor performance leads to a pessimistic ES that leads to poor performance (see Fig. 10.2).

Evidence for such an interaction comes from the baseball study, in which ES was found to correlate not only with future measures of performance, but also with present ones. An interesting implication of this cycle relates to research techniques. Although it is methodologically important to control for ability, by so doing, one is eliminating at least part of the effect of ES. Ideally, if ES is confounded with how good a team or individual athlete is, it is not ability that one should control, but a measure that is more aligned with raw talent. Unfortunately, it is difficult to find such a measure.

Explanatory Style and Effort

According to the learned helplessness model (Seligman, 1975), failure will be followed by lowered response initiation and ES amplifies this effect. In the domain of sports, where setbacks and losses are common for everyone and where maximal effort is needed for success during a long season, individuals and teams that offer more stable, global, and internal explanations for their failures may become more susceptible to giving up when those failures occur. These deficits, as individuals come to expect failure, may then manifest themselves as a lack of motivation particularly under pressure or after defeat. The baseball player, for example, who views a week of hitless games as the result of a hitch in his swing, will be more inclined to make efforts to correct this problem than the player who believes the same event as evidence that he is getting too old for the game. From the swimming data, it may be that swimmers with an optimistic style responded to the rigged failure by trying harder in the following trial. Thus, the best ES in

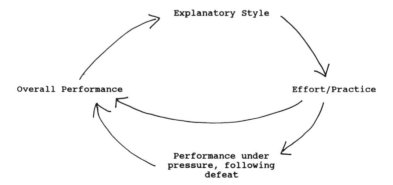

FIG. 10.2. Possible mechanism of explanatory style and athletic performance.

terms of future athletic success is the one that motivates the individual to continue doing whatever he or she does when things are going well, but galvanizes the player when things are not going well.

Limitations

There are limitations with these studies as well. First, there were inconsistencies found as to which ES variable was the best predictor of performance. Previous research found CN to be the most reliable predictor following bad events, and this was found for most of the predictions reported in these studies. However, in the baseball study, a team's ability to bat under pressure was predicted by their style regarding good events, not bad events. Why this is so remains a puzzle. Second, for the baseball and basketball studies, ES was derived from media quotations. It can be argued that this source of information is subject to distortions. After all, much of what is said to the press is self-serving: Bragging, humility, and team spirit all may influence what a player says, regardless of what the player believes. In spite of any distortions, ES did predict future performance. Thus, if distortions do exist in media quotations, it seems clear that what one professes affects how one performs. Finally, the sample sizes used in the baseball and basketball studies were small: 12 teams in the baseball study and only 5 in the basketball study. It is, however, no easy matter to increase the sample size in studies of this nature. Reading and CAVing the sports pages for an entire league takes thousands of hours.

SUMMARY

The relationship of ES and athletic performance was explored in professional baseball and basketball and in high-level collegiate swimming. Overall, teams and athletes with optimistic explanatory styles went to perform better than their competitors with pessimistic styles, especially under pressure or following a defeat. Experimental evidence was presented suggesting that the mechanism of ES is the ability to recover from setbacks. The results of these data underscore the importance of ES theory in achievement settings and suggest that it may be useful to study the role of explanatory style in other group activities.

11
▼▼▼▼▼▼▼

Pessimistic Rumination in American Politics and Society

Harold M. Zullow
Rutgers University

Societies, like individuals, experience hypomanic and depressive periods. Think of America of the 1920s—the bubbly "New Era" of unlimited economic expansion—compared to the 1930s Great Depression. Our leaders, too, go through hypomanic and depressive phases—there was Jimmy Carter, briskly striding down Pennsylvania Avenue after pledging "fresh faith" in his 1977 inaugural, but lamenting America's "crisis in confidence" in his 1979 speech.

Are the same cognitive processes associated with depression among ordinary individuals also associated with depressive outcomes in our collective national life? I examine this in four areas: political elections, the presidency, the economy, and Americans' mental health. The story begins, however, with the study of depression at an individual level—the conditions under which someone with a pessimistic explanatory style is likely to become depressed.

PESSIMISM AND RUMINATION: THE AVAILABILITY OF NEGATIVE THOUGHTS

Content-analysis measures of personality often assume that a disposition is indexed by the availability of disposition-relevant thoughts. For example, Winter's (1989) measure of the power motive in free-form text expresses a score for the number of power images per 1,000 words. Presumably, a highly power-motivated person will more easily call to mind thoughts about impact and influence.

In contrast, the Attributional Style Questionnaire (ASQ) and Content Analysis of Verbatim Explanations (CAVE) measures of explanatory style are qualitative measures of what kind of causal explanations people offer for bad events. They do not tell us how cognitively available these explanations are to an individual. The reformulated learned helplessness model (Abramson, Seligman, & Teasdale, 1978) suggests that importance of a bad event to the individual is a factor affecting whether pessimistic explanations result in helplessness. Importance should operate through increased cognitive availability, if people dwell on what is most important to them.

The availability heuristic is a cognitive bias in which mentally available representations influence our judgments of the probability of events. Imagining a potential bad event increases our subjective estimation of the likelihood of that event (Carroll, 1978; Sherman, Cialdini, Schwartzman, & Reynolds, 1985). Thus, even without a pessimistic explanatory style, we can develop negative expectations about the future simply by worrying about possibilities. Kuhl (1981, 1984) made a related point in his distinction between state- and action-orientation. He argued that dwelling on information about a negative state, rather than action to change the state, can distract from motivated action regardless of one's expectancy.

Peterson and Seligman (1984a) asserted that when bad events happen we ask ourselves why. Is this true? Although attributional search is a common response to bad events, particularly unexpected ones (Clary & Tesser, 1983; Harvey, Harkins, & Kagehiro, 1976; Pittman & Pittman, 1980; Weiner, 1985b; Wong & Weiner, 1981), other responses are possible. Individual difference in state- versus action-orientation, or neuroticism, may influence attributional search.

This is why in predicting risk for depression, we must assess not only the type of causal explanations made, but also the individual's habit of calling bad events to mind—or putting them out of mind. An individual who denies bad events would not ask him or herself "Why has this happened to me?" Ruminating should increase the subjective probability of bad events, which are easily called to mind (availability heuristic). Ruminating about pessimistic causal explanations should further magnify this subjective probability, as bad events are imagined as having long-lasting and pervasive causes. Pessimistic ruminators should be more at risk for depression than pessimists who do not ruminate, thus calling pessimistic explanations to mind.

To test this hypothesis (Zullow, 1984), 134 undergraduates completed the ASQ (Peterson et al., 1982), a questionnaire on ruminating versus action-orientation (Kuhl, 1981), and the Beck Depression Inventory of depressive symptoms (BDI; Beck, Ward, Mendelson, Mock, & Erbaugh, 1961). The rumination questionnaire contains items such as "When a new appliance falls on the floor by accident . . . (a) I concentrate fully on what should be done, (b) I can't stop thinking about how this could happen." Controlling for initial depression, subjects who were ruminative and pessimistic were most depressed 2 to 3 months later.

Not only did the main effect of explanatory style and rumination predict depression, but the interaction as well, controlling for main effects in a simultaneous multiple regression (R^2 for 2 and 3 months' prediction = .32, .33).

Of subjects above the median both on pessimism and rumination, 26% scored above a BDI cutoff for likely clinical depression 2 months later. Only 6% of optimistic ruminators, none of the pessimistic nonruminators, and 3% of the optimistic nonruminators were that depressed 2 months later. Knowing whether a subject ruminates adds important information to explanatory style in predicting depression.

Similarly, Kammer (1983, 1984) found that depressed subjects made more pessimistic explanations and more explanations for failure than nondepressives. Rholes (1989) replicated the finding that ruminating subjects are more at risk for depression than those who are action-oriented.

The Content Analysis Measure of Pessimistic Rumination

To study the consequences of pessimistic rumination at a societal level, and its effects on U.S. politics and leaders (a population not accessible by questionnaire), I developed a content analysis measure. For explanatory style, the CAVE measure already existed, and I adapted it for use in the present studies (Peterson & Seligman, 1984b; Zullow, Oettingen, Peterson, & Seligman, 1988). As the Kuhl rumination questionnaire in conjunction with the ASQ predicted depression among individuals, could the CAVE be used in conjunction with a content analysis measure of rumination to predict depressive outcomes in society and its leaders?

To develop such a measure, subjects who took the Kuhl questionnaires wrote vignettes about how they would cope with hypothetical bad situations. The cognitions that differentiated ruminating subjects' vignettes from action-oriented subjects' were identified, and operationalized in the rating criteria of a manual (Zullow, 1985).

In the content analysis measure of rumination, sentences are rated for the presence or absence of a rumination about a bad event, so the percentage of rumination in a text can range from 0 to 100.

Rumination is rated for: (a) focus on a bad event: the who, what, where, and how of a bad event; (b) explanation for a bad event: the why (here the explanation is not rated for its internality, stability, or globality—merely for its presence in a sentence); and (c) negative emotion—a word is used to indicate the presence of an emotional state, or emotional display (e.g., sad, depressed, angry, crying).

These content-analysis scores are quite reliable. The point-biserial correlations for the sentence-by-sentence ratings of a pair of raters are typically over .85. For the content-analysis ratings of explanatory style, the composite pessimism score (stable + global + internal) typically has a Cronbach's alpha of over .60 or .70. The studies reported here used multiple raters, who were blind to the text's author, and achieved high interrater reliabilities. Pessimism and rumination are usually uncorrelated, or exhibit a low positive correlation. Thus, one can have a pessimistic style without ruminating about bad events, or ruminate about an optimistic view of bad events. The two measures are not redundant, nor are they measuring a broader construct of "negative thinking."

PESSIMISM AND RUMINATION IN AMERICAN POLITICS

Lerner, in *America as a Civilization* (1957), described a value system of "American Exceptionalism." Americans see unlimited horizons for their nation, and believe in a unique mission and destiny. Robinson (1988), in his factor analysis of a nationwide survey of values, confirmed a value system resembling Lerner's construct. I hypothesized that Americans' need for optimism influences their political and economic behavior. A need for optimism should dispose them to elect political candidates who voice confidence in unlimited horizons. More universally, optimistic nonruminators may possess greater interpersonal magnetism than pessimistic ruminators. This would make for a successful candidate in America or any other nation.

Hofstadter (1963), in *Anti-Intellectualism in American Life*, chronicled the history of American voters' disdain for intellectual candidates. Is this disdain stirred in part by the desire for a leader who does not doubt and brood about our ability to control events?

The Presidential Elections Study

To answer this question, Zullow and Seligman (1990a) content-analyzed the nomination acceptance speeches of every Republican and Democratic presidential candidate in the television era. These speeches were broadcast on TV, and quoted widely in the national media since 1948 (Frank, 1988). They represent a standard situation through which all candidates must pass, in which they outline their hopes and fears. They are delivered at a comparable career point: having won the nomination, but with the entire fall campaign ahead to woo the voters.

Table 11.1 shows excerpts from the nomination acceptance speeches of Eisenhower and Stevenson in 1952, rated for pessimism and rumination. Stevenson was far more ruminatively pessimistic, and lost in a landslide. In 9 of 10 elections from 1948 to 1984, the winner's speech was lower in pessimistic rumination (PessRum: the sum of the standardized z scores for pessimism and rumination). The only exception was Nixon's victory over Humphrey in 1968. Humphrey was marginally lower than Nixon in PessRum, and overcame a 16-point deficit in the polls to come within a hair's breadth (0.8%) of winning. The 9-of-10 elections were significantly greater by a binomial test than the 5-of-10 successful predictions expected by chance alone.

TABLE 11.1
Content Analysis of Excerpts From Nomination Acceptance Speeches of 1952

Dwight D. Eisenhower	*Adlai E. Stevenson*
Ladies and gentlemen, you have summoned me on behalf of millions of your fellow Americans to lead a great crusade—for freedom in America and freedom in the world.	I accept your nomination—and your program.
I know something of the solemn responsibility of leading a crusade. I have led one.	I should have preferred to hear those words uttered by a stronger, a wiser, a better man than myself. [Rumination]
I take up this task, therefore, in a spirit of deep obligation.	None of you, my friends, can wholly appreciate what is in my heart. [Rumination]
	I have not sought the honor you have done me.
Mindful of its burdens [Rumination] and of its decisive importance: I accept your summons.	I could not seek it **because I aspired to another office which was the full measure of my ambition.** [Rumination; explanation for negative event: 7-internal, 2-stable, 3-global]
Our aims—the aims of this Republican crusade—are clear: to sweep from office an Administration which has fastened on every one of us the wastefulness, the arrogance and corruption in high places, the heavy burdens and anxieties which are the bitter **fruit of a party too long in power**. [Rumination; explanation for negative event: 1-internal, 3-stable, 6-global]	One does not treat the highest office within the gift of the people of Illinois as an alternative or consolation prize.
The road that leads to November 4th is a fighting road. [Rumination]	I would not seek your nomination for the Presidency **because the burdens of that office stagger the imagination. Its potential for good and evil now and in the years of our lives smothers exultation and converts vanity to prayer.** [Rumination for both sentences; both sentences count as one explanation for a negative event: 1-internal, 7-stable, 6-global]
In that fight I will keep nothing in reserve.	
I have stood before on the eve of battle.	
In this battle to which all of us are now committed, it will be my practice to meet and talk with Americans face to face in every section, every corner, every nook and cranny of this land.	That my heart has been troubled, that I have not sought the nomination, that **I could not seek it in good conscience, that I would not seek it in honest self-appraisal**, is not to say I value it the less. [Rumination; explanation for negative event: 7-internal, 6-stable, 7-global]
Rumination = 3/10 sentences = 30.0%	**Rumination** = 6/9 sentences = 66.7%
Pessimism = (sum internal + sum stable + sum global)/# of explanations = (1 + 3 + 6)/1 = 10.00	**Pessimism** = [(7 + 1 + 7) + (2 + 7 + 6) + (3 + 7 + 7)]/3 = 15.67

Note. Boldfaced text indicates a causal explanation for a bad event.

In three elections, the underdog at the time of the nominating conventions was less ruminatively pessimistic than the odds-on favorite. This happened in 1948, when Harry Truman was more optimistic than Thomas Dewey; 1960, when John F. Kennedy was more optimistic than Richard Nixon; and in 1980, when Ronald Reagan was more optimistic than Jimmy Carter. Each time, the underdog gained support and pulled off an upset victory.

When the overdog was much lower in PessRum than the underdog, he held on to his lead in the polls and even widened it, to win a landslide. This happened in 1952 and 1956 (Eisenhower over Stevenson), 1964 (Johnson over Goldwater), 1972 (Nixon over McGovern), and 1984 (Reagan over Mondale).

The correlation of the difference between the candidates' PessRum scores and the difference in their percentage of the popular vote was significant ($r = .65$, $p < .05$). Also significant was the correlation of the difference in PessRum and the change in the spread between the candidates from the August polls to the November vote ($r = .73$, $p < .02$).

Might these results be due to odds-on favorites and incumbents having an advantage in the polls, that makes them optimistic and unruminative? If so, the correlation between PessRum and winning elections might be an artifact of a relationship between an advantage in the polls and optimism: optimistic candidates correctly perceive an advantage in support that makes them likely victors. However, controlling for the early spread in the polls (at time of nomination) and for incumbency, the correlation between the spread in PessRum and the spread in the popular vote rose to .89 ($p < .01$). The correlation between PessRum and the change in support rose to .88 ($p < .01$). PessRum did not correlate with a handicap in the early polls.

Another third-variable account of the results (Greenstein, 1990; Masters, 1990; Simonton, 1990) holds that an incumbent who presides over a thriving economy will be optimistic based on his rosy re-election prospects, but his optimism is epiphenomenal to winning. To test this, Zullow and Seligman (1990b) used the election-year percentage increase in real per capita disposable income (DI). DI, as Tufte (1978) discovered, correlates with the election outcome. PessRum correlated nonsignificantly (.56, $p < .15$) with this indicator of economic well-being. In a simultaneous multiple regression, PessRum was near-significant as a predictor of the vote spread controlling for DI, while DI was nonsignificant controlling for PessRum. PessRum may thus mediate between economic change and electoral outcome. Candidates' causal explanations for economic conditions may affect voters' explanations, which in turn may affect the vote (Winter, 1990). When Carter blamed the bad economy on "my mistakes" in 1980, voters seemed to agree with him.

A final third-variable account of the results holds that candidates who are congruent with voters' issue positions will be optimistic as a result of the positive reinforcement received from audiences, but it is the issue congruence and not optimism that elicits voter approval (Greenstein, 1990; Masters, 1990; Simonton, 1990).

Rosenstone (1983) asked political scientists to rate the candidates from 1948 to 1980 for congruence with the contemporary electorate. PessRum correlated moderately but nonsignificantly with the absolute difference between candidate and electorate issue positions. However, in a simultaneous multiple regression, PessRum was nearly significant as a predictor of the election when controlling for issue congruence, whereas congruence was not significant controlling for PessRum. Thus, PessRum may moderate between issue congruence and electoral outcome, but is not a mere proxy for congruence. This effect was attributable mainly to the rumination component of PessRum. Candidates may express their ideological bent by ruminating. Their incongruity may be less conspicuous to voters when they do not ruminate about the issues.

There are three mechanisms consistent with the value system of American Exceptionalism that can explain why Americans would vote for optimistic non-ruminators. One is that depressive people are less well-liked and evoke avoidance (Coyne & Gotlib, 1983). This mechanism could be tested by comparing polls of how well voters personally like the candidates. A second is that pessimistic ruminators should be more passive in responding to setbacks. If voters admire vigorous candidates, as exemplars of American Exceptionalism, then the candidate who campaigns more vigorously (even if behind in the polls) should gain support. This mechanism can be tested by whether PessRum correlates with the number of campaign stops a candidate makes each day. The third mechanism is that an optimistic nonruminator should engender more hope in voters, and should match the optimism held by voters for their nation. This can be tested by measuring subjects' reactions to speeches that vary in PessRum.

Are pessimistic ruminators less well-liked than their opponents? The University of Michigan's National Election Studies have queried prospective voters since 1948 on what they like and dislike about the candidates. The number of likes compared to dislikes has strongly predicted the vote (Kelley, 1983). PessRum correlated near-significantly with the predominance of likes over dislikes for the elections through 1976. This effect was attributable to the correlation of rumination with likes ($r = .75, p < .04$).

More activity among optimists is another possible mechanism linking PessRum to the election result. The number of campaign stops per day were culled from candidates' itineraries for 1948 to 1968 (Runyon, Verdini, & Runyon, 1971) and 1980 (West, 1983). PessRum correlated near-significantly with the difference between the candidates in number of stops. This was attributable to the relationship between optimism and peripatetic campaign stops ($r = .76, p < .02$). Truman, Kennedy, and Reagan had the most sizable advantage in campaign stops over their opponents, and all three won upset victories.

In summary, PessRum relates to the economic context (voters' income) and political context (issue positions) in which elections occur. PessRum may mediate between these contextual factors and the election outcome. Candidate activity levels and voter liking of the candidates are also plausible mediators between

PessRum and the election outcome. This is consistent with a voter preference for candidates who exude confidence and dynamism—consistent with Americans' view of their own "manifest destiny."

Election Replication Study

Was PessRum associated with election results before the television era? The nomination acceptance speeches of presidential candidates from 1900 to 1944 were content analyzed for pessimism and rumination (Zullow & Seligman, 1990a). Pessimistic rumination correctly predicted 9 of these 12 elections, the exceptions being the 3 re-elections of Franklin Roosevelt. He presided over an era when ruminating about problems may have been necessary to face the crises of depression and war. PessRum correlated .71 ($p < .005$) with the vote spread for these 12 elections. Controlling for incumbency status (a dummy variable) yielded a correlation of .72, so these results are not attributable to an advantage of incumbency qua incumbency.

Combining the scores for the 1900–1944 and 1948–1984 elections and re-standardizing them for a z sum of pessimism and rumination yielded an overall .61 ($p < .001$) correlation of PessRum and the vote spread. In this century, 11 candidates were nominated more than once. The rank-order correlation between their pessimistic rumination at the time of initial and renomination was .74 ($p < .02$). This is evidence for the general stability over time of PessRum—as must be the case if PessRum (as assessed in the nomination speech) affects the fall election outcome.

The Election Prediction Studies

Knowing that 20th-century U.S. voters prefer optimistic unruminative candidates, can we forecast election outcomes based on PessRum in campaign speeches? In the 1988 presidential primary season, I set out to do just that (Zullow, 1988).

Every candidate has a standard stump speech he or she delivers many times (Dionne, 1988). In 1988, *The New York Times* published stump speeches of the seven Democratic and six Republican candidates for the presidential nomination before the first major contest: the Iowa caucuses. This offered an unprecedented opportunity to predict the presidential nominees.

Michael Dukakis and George Bush, whose speeches were the most optimistic and unruminative in their parties, were predicted far and away to win the nominations. This prediction was made at a time (February 7, 1988) when Dukakis was seen as one of only several potential nominees. Bush was seen as locked in a fight with Robert Dole. The probability of correctly forecasting the Democratic nominee by chance alone was $\frac{1}{7}$ (i.e., there were seven original candidates), and $\frac{1}{6}$ for Republicans. Thus, the joint probability of forecasting both nominees by chance alone was $\frac{1}{42}$ ($p < .025$).

The correlation of PessRum with the number of votes won in the primaries was significant in the predicted direction for the Democrats ($r = -.83, p < .02$) and Republicans ($r = -.84, p < .04$).

Were candidates with an advantage in fundraising and early support more optimistic as a consequence, and their optimism epiphenomenal to winning? Controlling for support in a Gallup poll taken in late January 1988 did not appreciably change the correlation between PessRum and votes won for the Democrats or Republicans. Controlling for fundraising success, as reported by Federal Election Commission, did not change the correlation between PessRum and votes won for the Republicans. It did change the correlation for Democrats (from −.83 to a partial r of −.56, ns). This suggests that campaign funds were either in part: (a) a mechanism through which PessRum affected that voting, (b) a cause leading both to PessRum and losing, or (c) both a and b.

In a post hoc replication of this finding, the stump speeches of the six 1984 Democratic primary candidates were blindly content-analyzed. Walter Mondale's nomination and Gary Hart's emergence as his main challenger were correctly predicted. Alan Cranston—predicted to finish last—was the first to leave the race. PessRum in the stump speech correlated negatively with votes won in the primaries ($r = -.95, p < .005$).

Having successfully predicted the 1988 nomination races, I set out to predict the 1988 fall Senate races and the fall presidential outcome (Zullow, 1988). The advantage of predicting the many Senate races, over predicting the one presidential race, was the law of averages. It is easier to detect a significant relationship with an N of 33 races than an N of 1.

The speeches of both candidates (Democratic and Republican) from 29 of the 33 races were procured. In most cases the announcement of candidacy was analyzed, although in a small minority of the races another campaign or policy speech was used. The announcement speeches were selected to sample the candidates' styles at a comparable point in their campaigns.

The winners of 25 of the 29 races were correctly predicted—a result that differs significantly from the 14.5 expected by chance ($z = 3.72, p < .0001$). The difference in pessimistic rumination correlated significantly with the vote spread between the candidates ($r = .49, p < .008$), in favor of the candidate lower in PessRum. The same was true for the pessimism difference ($r = .37, p < .05$) and rumination difference ($r = .59, p < .0008$). PessRum also correlated with the change in spread between the candidates from the polls 1 month before the election to the time of the election ($r = .45, p < .02$), as did pessimism ($r = .47, p < .02$) and rumination ($r = .50, p < .01$). Candidates who were optimistic but lagged in the public opinion polls were likely to gain support. As a result, of the 12 races regarded as too close to call in advance by the *Congressional Quarterly Weekly Report*, PessRum predicted all but one.

One potential explanation of these results (as with the presidential results) holds that pessimistic rumination simply reflects a candidate's awareness of his or her odds, that unsuccessful fund-raising breeds both pessimism and defeat, but that it is low funds and not pessimism which contributes to the defeat. The Federal Election Commission monitors candidate fund-raising. PessRum correlated significantly with concurrent and later fund-raising, and predicted how much cash the candidates had going into the final days of the campaign. Moreover, in a simultaneous multiple regression controlling for fund-raising, pessimism significantly predicted loss of support between the polls one month beforehand and the actual election. Regression analysis indicates that: (a) fund-raising success may mediate between PessRum and the election outcome, (b) fund-raising success also may affect PessRum, and (c) pessimism predicts last-minute surges in support above and beyond the effect of fund-raising.

The 1988 General Election

Before the 1988 Iowa caucuses, the presidential candidates' stump speeches showed that George Bush and Michael Dukakis were the least pessimistically ruminative in their parties. Direct comparison showed that George Bush was even lower in PessRum than Michael Dukakis. Substituting their stump speech scores into a regression equation for the vote outcome for 1948 to 1984 (based on nomination speeches of those years) yielded a prediction, as of early February 1988, for Bush to defeat Dukakis by a margin of about 7%.

Bush and Dukakis won their nominations, as predicted. When they delivered their acceptance speeches, both were more optimistically unruminative than the 20th-century average for all presidential candidates. In contrast to the stump speeches, this time Dukakis scored even better than Bush. Entering these scores into a regression equation, derived from the study of previous presidential elections, the prediction favored Dukakis by a margin of 3%. This contrasted with the earlier prediction of a Bush victory by 7%.

Another reversal occurred during the fall debates—the advantage in PessRum returned to Bush. This advantage persisted into stump speeches they delivered in the weeks following the debates, as published by *The New York Times*. Figure 11.1 shows the changes in Bush and Dukakis' PessRum during the campaign.

Plugging the average PessRum for Bush and Dukakis during the fall campaign (debates and stump speeches) into the regression equation for predicting the vote, the collapse in Dukakis' style during the autumn translated into a 9.2% expected victory margin for Bush. This prediction, made on the eve of the election, came closer to the actual result (8%) than any of the major national pre-election polls (Zullow, 1988).

In every other year in which debates were televised—1960, 1976, 1980, and 1984—the candidate who was less ruminatively pessimistic in the acceptance speech was also less ruminatively pessimistic on average in the debates. The 1988 election was the first time this was not the case. Dukakis' style in his acceptance speech was his most positive of the year. What happened?

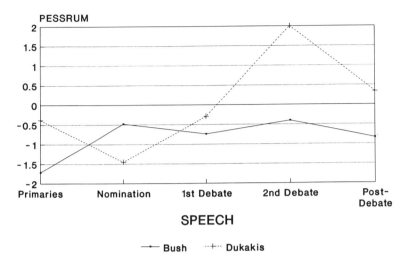

FIG. 11.1.   Bush and Dukakis' pessimistic rumination during the 1988 campaign.

Dukakis hired a special writer for the acceptance speech—Ted Sorenson, who had been John F. Kennedy's speechwriter. The Dukakis staff knew about the present research results, having read about it in the media and requested information (as did Bush's). Their effort to put a good foot forward may have portrayed a positive style that Dukakis was incapable of sustaining. This suggests that if one wants to forecast an election outcome using PessRum, it is best to sample several speeches—especially to include a verbal sample from the fall campaign.

Inaugural Addresses and Presidential Greatness

Tetlock (1981) rated speeches from presidential campaigns, inaugurations, and postinaugural months for integrative complexity: the intellectual complexity with which information is integrated in constructing an argument. He found that presidents are simplistic when they campaign, and shift to complexity immediately upon assuming office—but do not become increasingly complex while in office. This suggests that presidents manage their appearance according to situational demands: simplistic when cultivating voter appeal, complex when tackling the demands of office. This calls to mind the question: Does an optimistic, nonruminating style characterize the presidential as well as campaign phase of a leader's career? Does it predict historical achievements and contemporary popularity as president? Or does a president adapt to the office by shifting toward a pessimistic "realism"?

A president must: (a) convince the public to support policies involving sacrifice, (b) persuade elites of these policies, and (c) manage a governing team. This contrasts with the demands of a campaign. Candidates, not having to worry about managing a government, can raise the public's expectations. As Mondale learned in 1984 when he promised to raise taxes, words of sacrifice do not wash well in a presidential campaign. Thus, although optimistic nonruminators win the presidency, a more problem-focused style of rhetoric may be necessary to exert leadership in office. Burns (1978) characterized a "transformational" leader as one who addresses the nation's wants and needs, acting to bring it closer to its ideals. Optimistic nonruminators might persevere in the face of crisis (Peterson & Seligman, 1984a) and make people feel good, without having the foresight to set a problem-solving agenda before crises occur.

Franklin Roosevelt ruminated in the depths of the Great Depression: "We have nothing to fear but fear itself—nameless, unreasoning terror which paralyzes needed efforts to convert retreat into advance . . . Only a foolish optimist could deny the dark realities of the moment" (Roosevelt, 1933/1965, pp. 235–236). Should this rumination make for a worse presidency than Hoover's unworried contention that the fundamental business conditions of the country were sound? FDR's rhetoric exposed the hazard of denying problems or panicking. It was, I would argue, the rhetoric of transformational leadership: addressing the nation's problems in a way geared toward solving them. In accord with Simonton's (1986) finding that intellect is associated with a great presidency (in historians' judgment), do intellectual ruminators make great presidents even though they do not make successful candidates?

Rumination, I predicted, should be associated with a transformational presidency. The relationship of optimism to a great presidency was not predicted in advance: Optimism might be associated with bold action, but not actions that will be remembered as great. Seligman and Hermann (as cited in Zullow et al., 1988) found optimistic shifts in Lyndon Johnson's press conferences before bold actions in Vietnam—however, those actions are not generally regarded as a legacy of greatness.

The first-term inaugural addresses of presidents who served for more than 2 years (and delivered a formal address) were content-analyzed for explanatory style and rumination. A president's impact on the nation was measured by the Maranell–Simonton (Simonton, 1986) ratings of historical greatness. These were taken from a poll of historians who rated the presidents for prestige, accomplishments, strength of action, and other qualities.

One can also ask: What factors predict a president's popularity with the public? Are they the same as those for electoral success? I predicted that optimistic presidents would be most popular, but rumination might not be a handicap for a president as much as a candidate. To measure presidential popularity, the average Gallup Poll approval rating during a president's tenure (since FDR) was used.

Rumination correlated moderately with presidential greatness, measured by the Maranell–Simonton historians' ratings of greatness. Optimism did not correlate with greatness: There was a nonsignificant tendency for pessimism to correlate with greatness. Pessimistic rumination actually correlated positively (nonsignificant) with greatness.

Does optimism predict presidential popularity though it does not predict greatness? Public approval of the presidents from FDR to Reagan, taken as the average Gallup approval rating during their administrations, correlated significantly with rumination ($r = .72, p < .03$). The change in average popularity from the first half of the administration to the second half also correlated near-significantly, in a positive direction, with rumination ($r = .61, p < .09$). The most ruminative presidents (Roosevelt, Kennedy, and Reagan) lost less popularity during their administrations than other presidents. Optimism did not correlate with public approval of the presidents, in contrast to its correlation with election margins.

This study presents two paradoxes. One is that optimism, which correlates with election victory, does not correlate with public approval of the presidents, nor historical greatness. The second is that rumination, which correlates with election defeat, correlates as strongly (or stronger) in a positive direction with historical greatness, intellectual brilliance, and popularity as president.

How can we resolve this paradox? Further research is needed, but two hypotheses can be hazarded here. One possible resolution draws upon the Expectation/Disillusionment theory of presidential popularity (Sigelman & Knight, 1983, 1985). This states that in the presidential campaign, candidates raise the public's expectations. During an administration, it is hard to live up to the high hopes generated by the campaign. Disillusionment sets in. This could account for why most presidents since World War II have suffered a decline in their public approval rating with time. In accord with this theory of presidential popularity, being optimistic and unruminative during the campaign may raise the public's expectations for a trouble-free administration. Recalling that presidents shift toward greater integrative complexity when inaugurated (Tetlock, 1981), rumination in the inaugural address may prepare the public to anticipate there are problems that the president will tackle. This may adjust the public's expectations to prevent disappointment. Later, I present evidence that public approval of the president is linked to the public's optimism, and that the public's optimism generally rises in election years but falls late in the "honeymoon" year (Zullow, in press).

A second resolution pertains to the paradox that rumination, which correlates strongly with historical greatness, public approval, and intellectual brilliance as president, correlates negatively with election victory. Simonton (1985) found that intellect is—to a point—a predictor of influence in groups. He proposed an inverted U model in which intellect and the verbal and ideational fluency associated with it is curvilinearly linked to leadership. In the campaign, when rhetoric is aimed at the masses, the peak of the inverted U may fall at a lower level of intellect than as president, when the nation's elites also must be persuaded.

Having elevated a person to the presidency, the public may expect him to set a more serious, intelligent tone.

In fact, 20th-century presidents' nomination acceptances have been significantly more optimistic than in the subsequent inaugural address. However, they revert to a significantly more optimistic tone when running for re-election and accepting renomination. Similar to Tetlock's finding on integrative complexity, this suggests that presidents possess the flexibility to shift their outlook according to the self-presentational demands of the situation.

PESSIMISTIC RUMINATION IN U.S. SOCIETY

The Economic Growth Study

Presidential optimism fluctuates according to the situation. Is the same true of U.S. culture and public opinion? History abounds with examples of cultures in which depressions or collapse have followed manias. During the "tulipomania" of the Dutch Gilded Age, speculation drove tulip values up until they became the preferred currency (MacKay, 1852/1980). Exaggerated optimism gave way to a crash in the prices of tulips that sent the Dutch economy into a spin. The Netherlands never again recovered the same level of mercantile and cultural preeminence. We think, too, of the contrast between the United States in the 1920s and the Great Depression of the 1930s.

Do these cases share in common a shift from exaggerated optimism and low rumination to pessimistic rumination? I propose that optimistic, unruminative periods should result in three positive socioeconomic outcomes for their duration: (a) a more salubrious view of economic prospects, that should have a self-fulfilling effect on the economy as consumers spend more, (b) a more approving attitude toward the president, and (c) low rates of suicide. However, as economist Wesley Clare Mitchell (1959) proposed, "errors of optimism" such as excessive borrowing may foster a subsequent pessimistic shift. When Donald Trump built the Taj Mahal casino in Atlantic City in spite of declining casino business, it was an error of optimism that pushed him into further debt. Societies may not be able to sustain waves of extreme mass optimism or pessimism without falling into a disequilibrium from the behavioral consequences. Thus, the short-term effect of unruminative optimism on the economy (over 1–2 years) should be positive, although in the longer term a homeostatic feedback loop may promote greater pessimism and economic contraction.

Katona's (1960, 1980) work demonstrated a link between consumer optimism, consumer spending, and economic growth. Beginning in 1952, the Survey Research Center of the University of Michigan under Katona's guidance conducted periodic nationwide surveys of consumers' optimism about their financial situation and the economy. The resultant Index of Consumer Sentiment (ICS) measures aggregate public optimism. Since 1978, monthly surveys of consumer sentiment have been incorporated in the U.S. Commerce Department's leading indicators of economic activity.

Consumers turn pessimistic an average of 9 months before a recession. The ICS has forewarned us of the last eight recessions, and sounded one false alarm before the minirecession of 1966–1967. The ICS predicts change in durable goods purchases such as cars, that reflects the use of discretionary income and indicates economic turning points in advance. These findings are internationally replicated (Katona & Strumpel, 1978; Praet, 1985; Williams & Defris, 1981), and survey evidence from Germany show that a nation's generalized hopes and fears—not limited to the economy—predict changes in gross national product (GNP; Noelle-Neumann, 1984, 1989).

In a self-fulfilling prophecy, aggregate pessimism may promote the very economic outcomes that are feared. As consumers become worried about the future they spend less, and this leads to an economic downturn. (Consumer spending accounts for two-thirds of GNP.) Why does consumer optimism change? Economists have portrayed it as an epiphenomenal response to economic change (Shapiro, 1972; Vanden Abeele, 1983). Others (Adams & Klein, 1972; Pickering, 1977; Praet, 1985; van Raaij & Gianotten, 1990; Williams & Defris, 1981) have shown that it is only partly predicted by prior economic change.

This is where pessimistic rumination comes in. Ruminating aloud to other people has a contagious effect on their mood (Pennebaker, 1990). If PessRum varies over time on a mass scale, due to cohort differences, current events, Expectation/Disillusionment cycles, or the social learning of defense mechanisms such as denial ("don't worry, be happy"), then everyday social interaction or social channels such as popular culture and media should propagate changes in PessRum. If PessRum contributes to the formation of negative expectancies, then socially and culturally transmitted PessRum should affect consumers' optimism, and thereby affect consumer spending and economic growth.

Hopelessness of individuals predicts suicide attempts (Beck & Weishaar, 1990). Economic downturns also predict increased suicide (Durkheim, 1897/1951; Henry & Short, 1954). As a cognitive disposition toward hopelessness, pessimistic rumination should predict an economic downturn and the suicide associated with it. It should magnify the psychological impact of the downturn on individuals, transforming frustration into despair.

Finally, are changes in pessimistic rumination associated with political change? When PessRum increases, people may vent their frustration on politicians, in accord with frustration-aggression theory (Buss, 1961). Economic downturns correlate with downturns in public approval of the president (Simonton, 1986). Economic change may mediate between PessRum and presidential approval, or PessRum may predict presidential approval above and beyond the effect of the economy.

To test these hypotheses, it was not possible to poll Americans over time to measure their PessRum. It was necessary to measure some proxy for the average

PessRum of Americans—or a factor that contributes to Americans' PessRum. Popular culture and media were used, based on the testable premise that they propagate and reflect changes in pessimistic rumination among the public.

Lyrics of top 40 *Billboard* songs of each year from 1955 to 1989 (Whitburn, 1990), based on nationwide airplay and sales, were content-analyzed. Lyrics for 1,344 (98.5%) of the possible songs were obtained. The captions on 1,827 weekly covers of *Time* magazine from 1955 to 1989 were also rated, to assess changes in rumination in the mass media. Only rumination and not explanatory style was assessed, because the cover of *Time* rarely offers a causal explanation.

The annual rumination score was taken as the average rumination across all songs of that year. The pessimism score was taken as the average pessimism of all causal explanations in songs of that year. The *Time* rumination score for a year was taken as the percentage of weeks in the year in which the cover story caption contained rumination.

The 2-year moving average of PessRum correlated $-.63$ ($p < .0002$) with the moving average of GNP growth in the subsequent 2 years, .46 ($p < .008$) with the occurrence of a recession in the following year (dummy coded 0 for positive real GNP growth and 1 for flat or negative growth), $-.54$ ($p < .002$) with the average of the ICS in the following years, $-.56$ ($p < .001$) with the change in consumers' personal consumption expenditures in the following year, and .54 ($p < .002$) with rumination in *Time* in the following year. Thus, PessRum predicted decreased GNP growth, economic recession, and the hypothesized mediating variables of consumer optimism and spending. It also predicted increased rumination in *Time* magazine, whereas the reverse correlation did not hold. Thus—as with the relationship between PessRum and consumer optimism—PessRum in fantasy-based material predicts the media and public's concern about real-world bad events. Figure 11.2 depicts the relationship between PessRum's moving average and GNP growth in the subsequent year.

The 2-year moving average of PessRum predicted positive GNP growth 5 years later ($r = .53$, $p < .005$), and correlated negatively with its own moving average 4 years later ($r = -.50$, $p < .006$). This suggests a negative feedback effect in which PessRum predicts lower PessRum and higher GNP growth 4 to 5 years later, in contrast to the 1- to 2-year prediction of slowed growth. It is consistent with the possibility that cultural swings in an optimistic or pessimistic direction are self-limiting, and with the finding of an Expectation/Disillusionment cycle of consumer optimism that coincides with the presidential election cycle (Zullow, in press). In the postwar United States, periods of extreme optimism lasting a couple of years or more have been followed by sustained periods of extreme pessimism. This may be a characteristic of the Expectation/Disillusionment cycle—the greater the magnitude of one phase of the cycle, the greater the magnitude of the other phase.

To test a model in which the relationship between PessRum and economic growth is mediated by changes in consumer optimism, followed by changes in

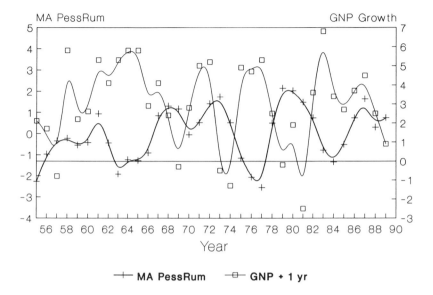

FIG. 11.2. The moving average of pessimistic rumination in popular songs predicts GNP growth in the following year, 1955–1990.

consumer spending, a two-stage least squares model was specified using a set of structural equations, in which:

1. GNP growth is a function of changes in personal consumption expenditures;
2. consumption expenditures are a function of consumer optimism and of changes in optimism;
3. consumer optimism is a function of pessimistic rumination in songs and rumination in *Time*;
4. pessimistic rumination is a lagged function of itself (in a negative feedback relationship); and
5. rumination in *Time* magazine is a function of prior PessRum.

The parameters in this model were at or near significance as hypothesized. PessRum was more significant as a predictor of changes in consumer optimism than the absolute level of consumer optimism, suggesting that PessRum serves best as a leading indicator of changes in the direction of consumer sentiment. The flow chart in Fig. 11.3 depicts the pathways specified in this model.

The changes in pessimistic rumination paralleled and predicted the important changes that have occurred in the economy over the last 35 years. In the late 1950s and early 1960s, increased PessRum predicted the recessions of 1957–1958 and 1960–1961—a period that included the national introspection following the Soviet

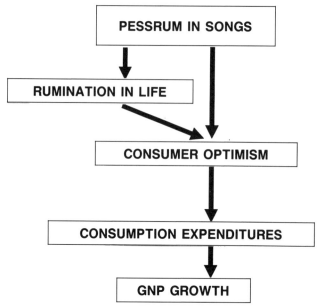

FIG. 11.3. Flow chart of the relationship between pessimistic rumination, consumer optimism, and economic growth.

Union's launch of Sputnik. In the early to mid-1960s, a distinct period of low PessRum set in, auguring the growth years of the 1960s. These were the innocent days of the Kennedy administration and the early Johnson administration. Beginning in 1966 there was an upward trend in PessRum, but only a minirecession at first (in 1966–1967) until the 1969–1970 recession and the stock market crash of 1970. In the early 1970s there was another increase in PessRum, followed by the Great Recession of 1974–1975 and national cynicism over Watergate. The Great Recession saw PessRum fall to another low, that lasted through Jimmy Carter's honeymoon in 1977. The late 1970s, beginning in 1978, saw a huge increase in PessRum, concurrent with the Carter "malaise" days and auguring the recessions of 1980–1982—the worst economic period in the United States since the depression.

During these 35 years, rumination had its ups and downs. It has had distinct and prolonged peaks: from 1966 to 1969, 1971 to 1973, and 1978 to 1980. It has also had distinct troughs, periods of "don't worry, be happy"—notably from 1962 to 1965, 1976 to 1977, and throughout the 1980s. In late 1989, rumination surged to levels not seen since the 1970s—to a record high in *Time* magazine.

Optimism reached high levels from 1955 to 1963, but since 1963 the trend has been a ratcheting up of pessimism. The 1980s began with record pessimism, and continued with greater pessimism than any of the three preceding decades. Then why did the 1980s not continue to be as economically disastrous as the 1970s and early 1980s?

One answer may be the prolonged low levels of rumination in the 1980s. Only at the end of the 1980s (late 1989) did rumination surge as well as pessimism, to a level comparable to that before the Great Recession of 1974–1975.

The collapse of the 1980s "don't worry, be happy" unruminative outlook in 1989, was the first prospective test of PessRum as a predictor of changes in consumer sentiment and economic growth (Zullow, 1991). Although consumer optimism remained at high levels in late 1989, the increased PessRum in popular culture and media indicated risk for a sharp drop in consumer optimism, expenditures, and GNP growth in 1990. What happened in 1990? Consumer pessimism was growing before Saddam Hussein invaded Kuwait, and the optimism of the 1980s collapsed more rapidly thereafter. Consumer spending fell, and we experienced the first recession in 8 years. This was a significant ecological use of content analysis to predict a major event.

To summarize the economy study, a year after increased pessimistic rumination in popular songs, rumination in the media and consumer pessimism follow suit, followed by faltering consumer expenditures and a recession. One key finding is that pessimistic rumination in songs precedes increased rumination in *Time* and increased consumer pessimism. Pessimism in songs then abates while the economy is still in recession, whereas worries about the real world are still evident in *Time* magazine and consumer polls. This suggests a compensatory escape into upbeat fantasies, that may in turn exert a positive influence on expectations for real-world events. Figure 11.4 shows the temporal sequence of the increase in rumination in songs, followed by increased rumination in *Time*, consumer pessimism, and economic recession.

Culturally transmitted fantasies may thus provide a leading indicator to changes in the real-world outlook and behavior of individuals. Kushner (1989) made a similar point in his analysis of changes in suicide rates and methods in the United States.

The Economy–Suicide Connection

Since Durkheim (1897/1951), we have known that economic growth correlates with suicide rates (Horwitz, 1984). We can ask: Is public optimism involved in this relationship? Does hopelessness add to or mediate the effect of an economic recession on the suicide rate? And does it add to or mediate the effect of the economy on public approval of the president?

Using U.S. suicide rates from 1955 to 1986 (incidence per 100,000), the hypothesis that optimism mediates between GNP growth and suicide rates—or contributes independently—was tested using two-stage least squares. The measure of optimism was drawn from the ICS—a question asking whether the economy will be better or worse off in 5 years (to which a "worse off" response presumably reflects a long-term pessimism about real-world events). This was hypothesized to have the most direct relationship to suicide rates, because it bears

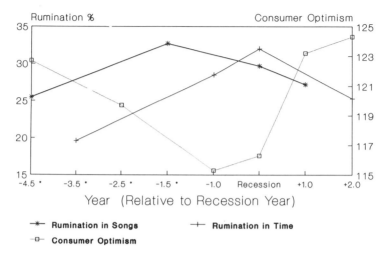

FIG. 11.4. Rumination surges in popular songs before a recession, followed by rumination in *Time* and consumer pessimism.

upon individuals' negative views of the real world. In turn, pessimistic explanatory style and rumination in popular songs were hypothesized to predict long-term economic pessimism.

Economic pessimism strongly predicted concurrent suicide rates, controlling for economic growth. Pessimistic rumination in songs and *Time* magazine, in turn, predicted economic pessimism. The strength of economic pessimism as a predictor of suicide rates suggests that the correlation between economic recession and suicide may be mediated by the pessimistic response of individuals to economic loss.

Pessimism, the Economy, and Presidential Approval Ratings

The economy predicts public approval of the president (Simonton, 1986). Earlier we saw that ruminative presidential rhetoric, which may forestall disappointed public expectations, predicts public approval. Might pessimistic public expectations mediate the economy's impact on public approval?

Consumer optimism about the economy predicted approval of the president better than the actual state of the economy. In fact, actual economic growth did not predict public approval of the president, when controlling for consumer optimism. This result favors the Sigelman and Knight (1983) theory that disappointed expectations are a major factor in decreased public approval of the president. It is also consistent with a frustration-aggression (Buss, 1961) account of presidential approval. When the public has a frustrated view of the future, it takes out that frustration on an available and salient target.

CONCLUSION

Depressive thinking can be quantified for individuals and cultures. In the U.S. culture, which values optimism, political candidates' pessimistic rumination predicts election defeat. Optimistic candidates who do not ruminate about bad events are better liked by voters, are more successful at fund-raising, and stump more vigorously on the campaign trail. They gain support during the campaign even when they start out behind in the polls. It remains to be seen, however, whether optimism is as strongly associated with electoral success in other cultures that may place less emphasis on optimism, such as the more contemplative German culture.

The success of optimistic, nonruminating candidates suggests a mood-enhancing function for elections in the U.S. psyche. The sense of control of having a say in electing a president, and hearing the optimistic rhetoric of presidential candidates, may bolster U.S. voters' own optimism.

In accord with this possibility, polls of consumer optimism since 1950 show a quadrennial peak in optimism during the presidential campaign months (Zullow, in press). Controlling for seasonal variation, Americans are more optimistic during the fall presidential campaign than during the corresponding season in the pre-election and postelection year. Rumination in *Time* magazine also dips in the presidential campaign months. This fluctuation does not appear to result from the boost in disposable income that presidents manipulate to occur just before an election (Tufte, 1978), for a quadrennial peak occurs more so in Americans' optimism for the nation than in their optimism about personal finances, or satisfaction with current finances.

The relationship between Americans' optimism and leaders' optimism remains to be fathomed. To what extent do politicians adapt to the optimism of voters, and to what extent are voters rallied by their leaders' optimism? Winter (1990) found that Americans vote for presidents who match their own psychological motives, and the finding that optimistic candidates win elections at the same time when voters' optimism reaches a peak is yet another example of a leader–situation match. The increase in presidents' pessimism when they are inaugurated also reflects congruence, with the more sobered mood of Americans following the election. This linkage between leader and follower mood is an intriguing area for further research.

The increased pessimism of Americans in postelection years can help explain why most economic recessions in the United States since the 1950s have begun within a year or so after an election. That pessimistic rumination in the U.S. culture predicts important social changes diverse as economic recession, suicide rates, and presidential approval ratings indicates a linkage between the psychological, economic, and political functioning of a nation. It also indicates that societies go through depressive spells in which activity and morale falter. Channels of communication such as popular culture and media, and everyday social interaction, may help propagate a depressive cognitive trend. Homeostatic mechanisms of mood regulation (cf. Parrott & Sabini, 1990) at a cultural level may then prevent depressive trends from perpetuating themselves when the economy sours, and prevent euphoric trends from enduring when the economy soars. Popular culture such as top 40 songs may serve a mood-compensatory function, an escapist role.

For many of the present findings, the intriguing task of exploring the mechanisms remains. Do shifts in pessimistic rumination merely reflect ongoing trends in the economy, constituting an epiphenomenal correlate of other trends such as suicide rates and presidential approval? Because these shifts precede economic changes, and predict suicide rates and presidential approval ratings controlling for economic growth, they do not appear to be a response to economic change.

Explanatory style for bad events, in conjunction with rumination about bad events, has forecasted in advance historical events such as political elections and economic recessions. Accurate predictions were made for the 1988 presidential and senatorial elections, and for an economic recession in 1990 and 1991, based on the pessimistic rumination of candidates and pessimistic rumination in the U.S. culture, respectively.

Optimism is a common link in political, economic, and mental health changes in the United States. Whether this link holds in other countries remains to be seen, but the replication of the optimism/economy link in public opinion surveys from other countries suggests that socioeconomic trends may be linked to optimism cross-culturally. This gives us a potential tool to study the rise and fall of nations from a distance, and across the sweep of history.

12
▼▼▼▼▼▼▼

Explanatory Style in the Context of Culture

Gabriele Oettingen
Max Planck Institute for Human Development and Education

THE CROSS-CULTURAL PERSPECTIVE IN PSYCHOLOGY

The issues addressed in cross-cultural psychology are as diverse as the issues addressed in psychology itself, because they are borrowed from the various fields of psychology (e.g., social, developmental, and personality psychology). Cross-cultural psychology, however, takes a unique perspective. It analyzes psychological phenomena in a cultural context by examining them either between cultures, or within a selected single culture (Berry, 1980a; Triandis 1980).

A jointly held definition of culture is difficult to come by as it is defined in very diverse terms (Kroeber & Kluckhohn, 1952). Marsella (1978) viewed the definition of culture as dependent upon the specific predictions of the investigators, and Segall (1984) even suggested giving up the search for a generally accepted definition of culture. Common to the various definitions is the notion that culture is the manmade part of the human environment (Herskovits, 1948). This manmade part extends to physical objects, which constitute the physical culture (e.g., roads, buildings, tools) and to subjective responses to what is manmade, which constitute the subjective culture (e.g., myths, roles, values, and attitudes; Triandis, 1980). Cross-cultural researchers generally tend to focus on cultures or subcultures that differ substantially in their physical and subjective aspects.

Cultural comparisons are useful for various research purposes. The first is to determine whether or not certain psychological theories are universal. For example, there is evidence that the judgment of facial expression is transcultural (Ekman & Friesen, 1969, 1971; Ekman, Friesen, O'Sullivan et al., 1987). Also, McClelland (1961) claimed universality for his theory of the development of achievement motivation, in which he specified socialization antecedents of achievement motivation. But later, de Vos (1968) in Japan, and LeVine (1966) with three different Nigerian ethnic groups, found only a limited degree of transcultural applicability of McClelland's developmental ideas.

A second approach employs cross-cultural research for the purpose of testing psychological theories. Accordingly, cultures that are high or low on variables critical to the theory of interest are examined. For instance, Witkin and Berry (1975) theorized that interaction styles systematically affect cognitive functioning in terms of perceptual differentiation and organization. They tested this notion by comparing agricultural and fishing/hunting cultures, because these two kinds of cultures are known to organize their social lives quite differently. This approach to cross-cultural psychology is particularly valuable whenever specific variables of a theory cannot be readily manipulated in the laboratory (e.g., cognitive or interpersonal styles), or should not be manipulated for ethical reasons (e.g., anxiety).

A third approach tries to identify specific ecological or cultural factors that shape aspects of psychological functioning. For example, Triandis, Vassiliou, Vassiliou, Tanaka, and Shanmugam (1972) selected cultures in which life events were unpredictable (because of frequent wars, revolutions, floods, tornadoes, etc.) and compared these with cultures characterized by highly predictable life events in terms of people's readiness to value, enjoy, and engage in planning. The findings pointed to "predictability" as a facilitating factor of planning. Referring to principles of reinforcement (i.e., planning is only rewarded in a setting with predictable events), this observation finds an easy (albeit post hoc) explanation.

Theory testing (i.e., the purpose of the second approach) and making inferences on how aspects of a culture influence psychological functioning (i.e., the purpose of the third approach) can also be achieved by analyzing a changing culture over time (Berry, 1980b, 1989; Berry, Poortinga, Segall, & Dasen, 1992; Segall, 1986). For the purpose of theory testing one would look for a culture changing with respect to psychological variables specified in the respective theory. From any changing culture, however, one may make inferences from changes in cultural aspects that preceded (and therefore might have promoted) the observed changes in psychological functioning.

Although each of these approaches has its merits, they are all plagued by methodological problems. A major problem is to ensure that the psychological variables of interest are comprehended and expressed in a similar manner within the cultures under comparison. For instance, if the concept of frustration were of interest, one were to compare cultures in which frustration finds a similar manifestation. Otherwise, one would falsely interpret a qualitatively different expression of frustration across cultures as an indication of differences in the level of frustration. This problem looms large whenever psychological variables that are well-known and widely studied in one culture (e.g., a developed culture) are imposed on another culture (e.g., a developing culture). This approach of trying to compare general principles across different cultures has been labeled *etic* in cross-cultural psychology (Berry, 1969, 1980a; Pike, 1967).

A different line of research—mostly represented by anthropologists and ethologists—studies psychological phenomena by exploring the peculiarities of their expression within a single culture of particular interest or concern. This approach has been labeled *emic*. However, when psychological concepts (e.g., frustration) are understood differently in different cultures, it is no longer very enlightening to compare such concepts across cultures. Each culture stands on its own, and it is the detailed description of individual cultures and the understanding of the intricacies of their functioning that is of primary interest.

EXPLANATORY STYLE

People's causal attributions for positive and negative events are determined by both the situation and the individual. The situation, for example, offers information about covariation (Kelley, 1967; McArthur, 1972). Aspects of the situation that are seen as covarying with the event are prime candidates to be specified as causal factors. More specifically, if the critical event shows low consensus (i.e., few individuals act alike in the same situation), high consistency (i.e., high congruence of behavior in recurring situations) and low distinctiveness (i.e., high congruence of behavior across various situations), attributions to internal (something about the self), stable (it persists or recurs over time), and global (it affects many situations) causal factors are made.

Different individuals develop personal styles of explaining positive and negative events (Peterson & Seligman, 1984a). A specific example of such a style is the tendency to make internal, stable, and global attributions for negative events and external, unstable, and specific attributions for positive events (Abramson, Seligman, & Teasdale, 1978; see chapter 1, this volume). This explanatory style has been linked to depression, because it implies that the future holds an abundance of negative events, whereas positive events are hard to come by (see Brewin, 1985; Peterson & Seligman, 1984a; Sweeney, Anderson, & Bailey, 1986). A closer look reveals, however, that depressive individuals only exhibit a less optimistic explanatory style in comparison to the strong preference of nondepressive individuals for self-serving attributions. Depressive individuals' attributions for positive and negative events are relatively even-handed (i.e., their explanations of positive and negative events are similar on internality, stability, and globality; Raps, Peterson, Reinhard, Abramson, & Seligman, 1982), whereas nondepressive individuals evidence more lop-sidedness (i.e., they explain positive events more by internal, stable, and global factors than negative ones). An extensive discussion of the link between explanatory style and depression is covered in chapter 5, this volume.

The pessimistic explanatory style does not have to encompass all aspects or domains which are of importance to a person's life. For instance, a person may entertain an optimistic explanatory style in the interpersonal realm, but may fail to do so in the achievement domain. In such a case it will be the negative events in the achievement domain only which put the person at risk for depression (Metalsky, Halberstadt, & Abramson, 1987).

In the literature, two different assessment techniques have been employed to measure explanatory style. Most common is the Attributional Style Questionnaire (ASQ; Peterson et al., 1982). This questionnaire requires respondents to generate causes for 12 hypothetical events, 6 positive and 6 negative, and to subsequently rate them on the dimensions of internality, stability, and globality (chapter 2 contains a detailed description of the ASQ). Explanatory style can also be assessed by content analysis of any written or spoken verbal expression that contains causal explanations. This is known as the Content Analysis of Verbatim Explanations (CAVE; Peterson, Luborsky, & Seligman, 1983; Zullow, Oettingen, Peterson, & Seligman, 1988). The CAVE technique allows for the analysis of explanatory style in texts, modern or ancient, written in English or other languages, irrespective of the content domains that are covered. The only prerequisite is that the texts contain identifiable causal attributions for negative and positive events. These causal statements are extracted from the texts and given to independent raters who score them in terms of internality, stability and globality; interrater reliability is high (Zullow et al., 1988). The CAVE technique has been validated in that it yields the typical relationship between pessimistic explanatory style and depression (Peterson, Bettes, & Seligman, 1985; Peterson et al., 1983). Moreover, explanatory style extracted from interview material and open-ended questionnaires significantly correlated with and predicted psychological and physical health (Peterson, Seligman, & Vaillant, 1988; Seligman & Elder, 1986).

Explanatory Style Across Cultures

The analysis of explanatory style across cultures must first deal with the previously described major cross-cultural methodological problem: How can we ensure that the measurement procedures employed actually capture the same concept of optimistic/pessimistic explanatory style across the cultures to be compared? The ASQ procedure (Peterson et al., 1982) entails the problem that the events listed in the questionnaire are rather culture specific (e.g., an unsuccessful date or becoming rich). These events are closely related to the concerns of people who live the American way of life. Therefore, they are appropriate for research conducted in the United States. For comparisons across cultures, however, they create a host of problems: Members of different cultures might not assign the same importance to these events, they might differ in terms of the valence that they attach to them, or may fail to imagine that these events will actually happen to them. Whenever items on the ASQ are experienced as artificial or alien by members of certain cultures, the measurement of explanatory style may not be reliable or valid. When researchers compared intellectual performances across cultures (Berry, 1980a; Brislin, Lonner, & Thorndike, 1973) similar concerns led to the development of so-called culture-free or less culture-bound intelligence tests.

The CAVE technique offers a way around the development of a culture-free ASQ. Because this technique can be used to CAVE all types of texts, it should be possible to select comparable texts from various cultures and thus to determine the prevalence of an optimistic–pessimistic explanatory style. The content of these texts is not alien, because they are produced by these cultures. In addition, the researchers rating the causal statements extracted from these texts do not have to be familiar with the background of the respective culture. Because the raters' task is not to evaluate the content of the causal attributions but, instead to judge them along the structural dimensions of stability, internality, and globality, the CAVE technique is particularly suited for cross-cultural comparisons.

Traditionally, when cross-cultural researchers focus on texts they tend to select folktales, because these are assumed to contain the central values of a culture worthy to be passed on from generation to generation (Brislin, 1980). For example, when McClelland (1961) attempted to demonstrate the prior necessity of achievement motivation for economic development, he content-analyzed stories in children's storybooks or readers in 30 countries with respect to the frequency of achievement themes. He then correlated this variable with measures of economic growth assessed 25 years later (such as per capita income and electrical production per capita). McClelland considered these stories to be "cultural products" that reflected the average level of achievement motivation, and he interpreted the positive correlations observed as support for his hypothesis that economic growth is preceded by high levels of achievement motivation.

In the following study (Oettingen & Morawska, 1990), we set out to demonstrate that CAVing written cultural products such as folktales, songs, proverbs, and prayers allows a reliable and valid assessment of a culture's explanatory style. We chose a culture that has clearly separated domains for two reasons (i.e., the religious and the secular domain). First, we wanted to demonstrate that explanatory style can be coded reliably within each of the different domains. Second, and even more importantly, we formulated hypotheses about the degree of optimism that should be expressed in the writings belonging to these different cultural domains, because support for these hypotheses may then be taken as an indication that explanantory style is assessed validly by the CAVE procedure.

CAVING SECULAR AND RELIGIOUS NARRATIVES: 19TH-CENTURY RUSSIAN JEWRY

We focused on written materials that were part of the Russian Jewish culture at the end of the 19th century and selected popular writings that belonged either to the secular or to the religious domain of this culture (Oettingen & Morawska, 1990). The religious written materials were expected to evidence an optimistic explanatory style, because the Jewish religion promises the arrival of the Messiah, and religion in general serves the function (among other things) of providing relief from a dismal earthly existence by instigating hope for salvation (James, 1902/1961; Marx, 1843–1844/1964). In fact, Gorsuch (1988) reported that religious persons are less anxious, less suicidal, and in better physical and mental health than those who are not religious. The secular writings were expected to be characterized by a less optimistic explanatory style. Secular life for Russian Jews has always been hard (McClelland, 1961). Toward the end of the 19th century they faced an increasingly precarious civil-political situation, such as progroms and anti-Jewish laws (Baron, 1976; Greenberg, 1956).

Written materials were selected in consultation with scholars of Russian Judaism. The religious material consisted of the standard liturgy and prayers (e.g., "Daily Prayers," "Sabbath and Festival Prayers," "High Holiday Prayers" by Birnbaum, 1949, 1951; "Lamentations" by Rosenfeld, 1986, Zlotowitz, 1983) and popular religious stories (Ben-Amos & Mintz, 1970; Buber, 1948, 1975). The secular material included "Yiddish Folk Songs" (Rubin, 1979), "Yiddish Folk Stories" (Howe & Greenberg, 1954; Howe & Wisse, 1979), and "Yiddish Proverbs" (Ayalti, 1949).

Causal statements about events that were clearly good or bad from the point of view of the Jewish culture were extracted. Neutral events and those that had both good and bad elements were discarded. Events included facts (e.g., the Jewish people are oppressed), descriptions (e.g., the Rabbi gave good advice), or emotional expressions (e.g., we have no fear). The extracted units (which included both event and attribution) had to contain a clear causal relationship between the event and the attribution; the explanation was not merely a description or justification of the event. Finally, the causal statements were divided into religious or secular ones on the basis of their content. This amounted to 239 religious statements (the cause referred to God or divine issues) and 380 secular statements (the cause referred to wordly issues, human characteristics, or human action).

The causal statements were then presented in a randomized order to three trained raters who were blind to both the hypotheses and the sources of the statements. The raters scored each statement (using 7-point scales) on the stability, globality, and internality of the causal factor mentioned. Interrater reliability was high for both religious and secular statements on each dimension (all Cronbach alphas > .75). This demonstrates reliability of the CAVE technique, even when it is applied to texts taken from another culture and a different time in history.

As hypothesized, the religious statements were more optimistic than the secular statements. For religious statements we observed optimistic lop-sidedness; positive events were attributed more to stable and global factors than were negative events (t score = 7.6, $p < .001$). The parallel pattern of data was not found for the internal dimension. A simple explanation for this is the fact that the cause referred to in religious statements was generally God. Therefore, positive events could not be attributed more internally than negative events. A less optimistic pattern of attributions emerged for secular statements. Here we observed the so-called even-handed, or pessimistic explanatory pattern. Explanations for both positive and negative events similarly referred to stable and global as well as internal factors. Even-handedness implies less optimism than lop-sidedness and is commonly observed with depressed students, patients, and children (Raps et al., 1982).

Our two hypotheses were thus confirmed. Explanatory style can be measured cross-culturally using the CAVE technique, and religious statements were found to be more optimistic than secular statements. Next, in order to show that our findings were not just specific to the Jewish culture, we attempted a replication.

RUSSIAN ORTHODOX CHRISTIANITY:
A REPLICATION STUDY

Written materials were selected from the religious and secular domains of 19th-century Orthodox Christian peasantry. This culture shared the same geographic location and political system with the Russian Jewry of our first study. The religious materials included "Daily Prayers," "Sunday Prayers," "Festival Prayers," "Russian Lenten" (Holy Trinity Monastery, 1979, 1963, 1973, 1974, 1975; the Holy Transfiguration Monastery, 1974) and religious stories (Holy Trinity Monastery, 1985; see Oettingen & Morawska, 1990, for a detailed list of all stories used). The secular materials were taken from "Russian Folk Songs" (Reeder, 1975), "Russian Fairy Tales" (Gutterman, 1985), and "Russian Proverbs" (Langnas, 1960).

Causal statements from these sources (134 religious and 369 secular) were extracted and scored by three raters along the dimensions of stability, globality, and internality. Again, interrater reliability was high for both religious and secular statements on all three dimensions (all Cronbach alphas > .72). As in the previous study, we found lop-sided explanations in the religious domain for the stable and global dimension ($t = 2.6$, $p < .01$), whereas even-handed explanations were observed in the secular realm. Religious statements were more optimistic than secular statements.

The results of the two studies are remarkably similar. First, there is high interrater reliablity for causal statements of both religious and secular domains. Second, the hypothesis that religious causal statements are more optimistic than secular causal statements was confirmed for both the Russian Jewish culture and the Russian Orthodox Christian culture. This pattern of findings suggests that CAVing solves the central methodological problem in cross-cultural psychology, which is measuring psychological concepts with high reliability and validity at the cultural level.

Explanatory style can be assessed effectively at a cultural level by CAVing. Therefore it now seems possible to explore the question of what aspects of a culture lead to an optimistic explanatory style, and which favor pessimistic explanations. The present studies do not speak to this issue, because explanatory style as assessed in both religious and secular cultural products is similar for Russian Jewry and Orthodox Christianity. The only difference was more optimism in explaining positive events for Jewish religious statements than for Orthodox Christian statements ($t = 4.4$, $p < .001$). It is difficult, however, to pinpoint the features of Russian Jewish and Orthodox Christian cultures responsible for this difference. Possibly the Jews, being a minority in late 19th-century Russia (Baron, 1976; Greenberg, 1956) might have faced even more precarious living conditions than the Orthodox Christian peasants and thus more readily turned to religion for salvation. But a myriad of other features of the two cultures also qualify as potential causes of this difference, these being related to the respective ways religious and secular lives were conducted. Apparently, if one wants to explore features of cultures that affect explanatory style, one must proceed more systematically and select cultures that differ only in the aspect that is expected to make a difference—all other things being equal. At first glance, there does not seem to be a good solution to this methodological demand, but the study to be described next actually comes pretty close.

DO CULTURAL FEATURES SHAPE EXPLANATORY STYLE? A COMPARISON OF EAST AND WEST BERLIN NEWSPAPER REPORTS

In 1984, at the time when this study (Oettingen & Seligman, 1990, Study 2) was conducted, East and West Berlin were still separated by the wall and thus resembled a cultural laboratory: Because East and West Berlin originated from one culture with the same political system before 1945, they were extremely similar on many different physical and subjective cultural features save the variable which split the city apart between 1945 and 1990—the political system. In addition, the ecological (e.g., climate) and biological factors (e.g., gene pool) are shared. This setting was thus ideal to explore the question of whether the political system and its consequences, in this case socialism in East Berlin versus social capitalism in West Berlin, does affect explanatory style. Variables such as dialect, upbringing, weather, and other factors that also might shape the development of explanatory style cannot readily qualify as alternative explanations.

We speculated that the differences in political systems of the East and the West part of the city would be so pervasive and prominent that they would achieve a difference in explanatory style on a cultural level. This would be quite a spectacular product of politics in light of the fact that on an individual level explanatory style is very change-resistant (Burns & Seligman, 1989). We further speculated that, because the East Berlin government needed to build a wall to prevent people from leaving their home city, there should be less optimism about the future in East Berlin than in West Berlin. In a country that suggests that good events recur more often and on a broader basis than bad events (i.e., an optimistic or lop-sided pattern of explanatory style), people should not need to be forced to stay in their home city.

In order to obtain a fair assessment of explanatory style in East and West Berlin, we selected writings related to a domain that was highly valued in the East (GDR) and the West (FRG), namely, sports. More specifically, we analyzed newspaper reports of a representative sports event, the Sarajevo Winter Olympic Games 1984. The GDR and the FRG participated in the Games as separate nations. People of all social strata in both East and West Berlin took great interest in the achievement and the social aspects of the Olympic Games. Also, the Olympic Games were the only topic that was of concern for both countries and extensively covered simultaneously by both the East and the West Berlin newspapers. Finally, in the Olympic Games success and failure were determined by the same rules for both the GDR and the FRG.

Explanatory style was content-analyzed by using a randomly chosen 50% sample of all articles from three East Berlin and three West Berlin newspapers. The events had to be clearly good or bad from the standpoint of the respective nations, and events happening to competitive nations were excluded from the analysis. All statements were then rated by a native German speaker. Again reliability (as assessed by another native German speaker who rated 25% of the statements) was high for each dimension; Cronbach's alphas > .71 (for a detailed description see Oettingen & Seligman, 1990, Study 2).

A strongly lop-sided (optimistic) pattern emerged for causal attributions in the West Berlin reports; positive events were explained more by stable and global factors than negative events ($t = 7.9$, $p < .001$ and $t = 4.0$, $p < .001$, respectively). In contrast, an even-handed (pessimistic) attributional pattern was observed for the causal statements in the East Berlin reports ($ts < 1.2$, ns). The internal dimension, however, showed a lop-sided pattern for both East and West Berlin causal statements ($ts > 4.0$, $ps < .001$), suggesting that reports on both sides of the wall took more credit for their successes than they took blame for their failures.

We were struck by the size of the differences in explanatory style between East and West Berlin Olympic reports. Despite a performance that was clearly in favor of East Berlin (the GDR won 24 medals, whereas the FRG won only 4), explanatory style in East Berlin sports reports were less optimistic than in West Berlin reports. Because the two cities were one before 1945, we can conclude that the differences in political system over the period of 40 years have caused the observed differences in explanatory style. Clearly, Olympic reports in newspapers are only a very small aspect of culture, and thus might not represent the cultural explanatory style. But newspaper reports are a cultural product very much like folktales; they may be assumed to entail the values of the culture for which they are written.

In East Berlin, newspapers were composed and censored in order to promote the party line. Therefore, it was all the more surprising that despite so much success in an area employed to promote the glory of the system (i.e., international sports competitions), the newspaper reports still reflected a rather pessistimic explanatory style. Apparently, explanatory style escaped the censorship and failed to fulfill the task of promoting the system; at least with respect to the stable and global dimensions. Only when it came to taking more credit for positive events than blame for negative events East Berlin Olympic reports managed to benefit their country.

So far, we have demonstrated that East and West Berlin differ in explanatory style as assessed across matched domains (i.e., competitive sports). Our approach is thus in line with any other cross-cultural research that attempts to document effects of cultural variables on psychological functioning. But we can go a step further. Many researchers have hypothesized a negative relation between optimistic explanatory style and depression. The hypothesis has found strong support at the individual level (for a meta-analysis see Sweeney et al., 1986). Because East and West Berlin show differences in terms of optimistic/pessimistic explanatory style, there is the unique opportunity to check whether the classic relationship between explanatory style and depression also holds at the cultural level. Therefore, we set out to assess depression in East and West Berlin hypothesizing that East Berlin would be characterized by higher levels of depression than West Berlin.

EXPLANATORY STYLE AND DEPRESSION AT A CULTURAL LEVEL: A COMPARISON OF EAST AND WEST BERLIN WORKMEN'S DEPRESSIVE AFFECT

Negative expectations about the future stemming from stable and global attributions primarily lead to affective symptoms of depression (Abramson et al., 1978; Abramson, Metalsky, & Alloy, 1989). In addition, a number of cross-cultural studies suggest that in European cultures a dominant symptom of depression is negative affect, whereas in Asian countries depression manifests itself predominantly via somatization (Chang, 1985; Marsella, 1978; Yamamoto, Yeh, Loya, Slawson, & Hurwicz, 1985). Accordingly, we decided to assess depression in East and West Berlin by focusing on negative affect (Oettingen & Seligman, 1990, Study 1).

In 1984–1985, we could not investigate the predominance of depression in East versus West Berlin by handing out depression inventories to randomly sampled individuals, or by consulting official statistics describing the number of patients hospitalized for depression, suicide attempts, or days off from work. Administering questionnaires was strictly forbidden and thus impossible for us. In addition, there was no access to reliable archival data. (Even in 1990 after the fall of the wall it was impossible for us to retrieve relevant data because proper recording of depressive prevalence had been strongly discouraged. For instance, we learned that if the rate of a specific disorder was higher than what was expected by party guidelines, the doctors' diagnoses were attacked as too lenient.) Because of these barriers, we decided to unobtrusively observe behavioral signs consistent with depression in East and in West Berlin. Such unobtrusive procedures are rather time and energy consuming, but they have some advantages. For example, they are better suited than self-report measures in cross-cultural psychology, whenever the topic is socially sensitive or undesirable, taboo, or subject to strong normative pressures (Bochner, 1980). This is certainly true for depression.

With respect to kind of population and setting of observation, ideally, we would want to follow a representative sample of East and West Berliners during most of their daily pursuits. To make the observational method workable, however, we had to limit ourselves to certain sites that are accessible by researchers (e.g., bars, railway stations, parks). We chose bars, because people tend to interact with each other and to stay there for a relatively long period of time. Moreover, a researcher can unobtrusively observe people by taking the role of a patron.

We selected the bars in two typical industrial areas of East and West Berlin that were adjacent, but separated by the wall. Choosing traditional workmen areas guaranteed that the samples of people observed in East and in West Berlin were homogeneous. No foreigners or people of other socioeconomic status (SES) would care to visit these neighborhood bars. Our sample of bars included 31 localities (14 in West Berlin and 17 in East Berlin); workmen met there after work to talk and drink. Thus, the East and West Berlin bars were matched for social class (workmen), kind of work (industry), and gender of the patrons (male), and the observations were made within one single week during the same weather conditions. This matching for socioeconomic background, geographic area, and setting assures that the criteria for recording depression applied equally well for the East and the West Berlin people observed, and thus we avoided that differential manifestations of depression plague our study (see Marsella, 1980).

When observing the patrons of the selected bars, we recorded signs consistent with depressive affect, such as expressiveness versus withdrawal, cheerfulness versus sadness, and confidence versus anxiety in facial and bodily behavior. More specifically, we scored slumped posture as a sign of negative thought (Riskind, 1983) and illustrators (i.e., intentional hand movements illustrating the conversation) as indication of a lack of depressed feelings (Ekman & Friesen, 1974). Also, we scored a mouth with the corners bent down as an expression of sadness; the number of smiles and laughs were scored as indication for no sad feelings (Ekman & Friesen, 1975; Beck, 1967). Finally, we assessed self-adaptors (small adjustment movements, e.g., thumbs down) and protecting the body with one's arms as a sign of insecurity. Interrater reliability for all of these categories as assessed in an independent sample of patrons was high (all $rs > .86$).

The observations were conducted as follows: The observer entered the bar and sat down in a corner. After a while she chose the nearest person whom she could watch without affecting his behavior. She then assessed posture and mouth shape for 10 seconds and thereafter counted the number of illustrators, self-adaptors, smiles, and laughs. To assure independence of the observations, the observed patrons in a given bar were chosen from different groups of people (further, the sizes of the groups were similar in East and West Berlin bars).

Workmen in East Berlin showed more signs consistent with depression than workmen in West Berlin. Fewer East Berliners than West Berliners had bent up mouths, upright postures, and exposed bodies (all χ^2s > 12.0, ps < .001). Moreover, fewer illustrators, smiles, and laughs were counted with patrons of the East Berlin bars as compared to patrons of the West Berlin bars ($Fs \geq 9.5$, $p < .003$). Only the difference in the amount of self-adaptors was not significant.

Taken together, the last two studies reported suggest that the negative relation between an optimistic explanatory style and depression holds even at the cultural level. We found a comparatively more pessimistic explanatory style and more signs of depression on the Eastern side of the wall, and a less pessimistic explanatory style and fewer signs of depression on the Western side of the wall, when comparing matched domains and matched settings. We were able to search for the classic relation between explanatory style and depression on a cultural level, because in our first study we had observed that the socialist system and its consequences had led to a less optimistic explanatory style in the Olympic reports than the social capitalistic system.

POLITICAL SYSTEMS AND EXPLANATORY STYLE

The question remains how the political system differences in East and West Berlin managed to produce differences in explanatory style (and depression). Before we address this issue, we first want to consider how sure we can be that the differences in the political system actually brought about a comparatively more pessimistic explanatory style in East Berlin. After all, the differences in explanatory style were only found in Olympic sport reports, although such reports should reflect the respective cultural voices on a representative and pervasive theme. Clearly, however, more conclusive research is desirable. Because we found that the CAVE technique can successfully be employed on archival or historical material, we can go back to the time of the wall and CAVE reports on other international sports competitions. The only prerequisite is that the GDR and FRG athletes participated and that there was extensive coverage by both East and West Berlin newspapers. If one chooses competitions where the FRG was more successful than the GRD, an even bigger difference in explanatory style between the East and the West Berlin reports should emerge.

Investigations of domains other than sports might also be valuable. For example, in economics the GDR was less successful than the FRG and thus differences in explanatory style should be even more pronounced than those we observed in the Olympic reports. CAVing texts in other domains, however, may pose methodological difficulties because, as noted earlier, there are few topics outside the realm of sports in which both the GDR and the FRG were equally involved and that have been widely covered by both East and West Berlin newspapers. Further, one could try to replicate our findings by comparing the People's Republic of China with Hong Kong, because there also are two different political systems imposed on the same culture. Here the effects of communism and liberal capitalism on the development of explanatory style can be studied.

Finally, there is the possibility to test our hypotheses by looking at the effects of a changing political situation on explanatory style (and depression). Both the European countries and Hong Kong offer a unique opportunity to observe such effects of political systems' rapid change on explanatory style. Interestingly, the change goes in the reverse direction for Eastern Europe and Hong Kong. In Europe a social capitalistic system (e.g., FRG) is replacing a socialistic system (e.g., GDR), while in Asia a communist system (i.e., PRC) will replace the present capitalistic system of Hong Kong. We would hypothesize that while Eastern Europe will become more optimistic, Hong Kong will become more pessimistic after the respective changes.

Let us assume that the observed differences between explanatory style in East and West Berlin can reliably be attributed to differences in the political systems. The question to be answered then is how the socialistic system managed to suppress a lop-sided or optimistic pattern of explanatory style. After the fall of the wall more firsthand information on the system's functioning became available. The descriptions of the people who experienced the working of the system at various positions overlap on the following points (Bierwisch, 1990): The system was pervasive, it tried to be present in nearly every conceivable aspect of human life, extending from personal and intimate life (e.g., marriage, faith, childrearing, hobbies) to the public life (e.g., choice of profession, schooling, party activities). It made itself felt throughout a person's life-span by controlling people in the direction of the party line and its ideology (see also Klien, 1990; Maron, 1992; Waterkamp, 1990). The surveillance was multifaceted; governmental employees officially took part in it, and a still unknown number of people were hired (part time and sometimes by blackmail) to spy on other people for the secret service. All of this was highly effective: In a representative study in the fall of 1990, only 5% of the former GDR citizens said that they were sure nobody used to spy on them (Schöppner, 1991).

The system's economy was less effective. The economy was also strictly controlled by governmental and party officials, but it turned out to be unable to satisfy people's needs. Not only was it difficult or impossible to acquire goods common in West Berlin (e.g., fruits, cars, medicine), the available goods themselves were often of poor quality. The system also managed to ruin large parts of the country's ecology. Finally, it tried to spoil the cultural and scientific life, by forcing researchers and artists either into their ideological closed mindedness or into exile.

It appears, therefore, that positive outcomes were hard to come by in the former GDR. Living conditions were rather grim and if there were successes (e.g., obtaining bricks for one's unfinished house or acquiring fresh fruits), they had to be achieved by the people's own efforts (e.g., successful bargaining or persistent queueing). This is reflected in our observation that positive outcomes in Olympic reports are attributed more to internal factors than negative outcomes. Still, individual successes in daily life should have been rather exceptional (though the criterion for success might have differed between East and West Berlin; see M. Baltes & Carstensen, 1994; Oettingen, 1993). As a consequence, people experienced positive events in a few domains only (e.g., had success with organizing bricks but failed to locate concrete), and, in addition, positive outcomes should not have recurred very reliably (e.g., you did not know where and when fresh fruit was available). Such conditions favor specific and instable attributions for successful outcomes, thus promoting an even-handed explanatory style.

Finally, the socialist ideology prided itself on having promoted the equality of people. The GDR might have pursued this goal by curtailing individual successes. Even exceptional performances (e.g., in science or sports) could be turned into something nonreplicable and unreliable by the totalitarian system of the GDR (e.g., by restricting contacts to colleagues or expelling athletes from the national team). For example, even outstanding scientists in the former GDR could not rely on keeping up the contacts to the international community. The system's officials controlled who could be contacted—when and where (Bierwisch, 1990).

Another doctrine of socialist ideology is its devaluation of religion. As demonstrated in Studies 1 and 2, a lop-sided optimistic explanatory style may flourish in the religious domain, even though the secular domain is characterized by an even-handed explanatory style. This implies that in the socialist system of the GDR people were discouraged from turning to the religious domain as a source of optimism. The fact that the resistance against the system eventually leading to the fall of the wall originated from the people with enduring religious commitments, supports the argument.

EXPLANATORY STYLE AND DEPRESSION
IN THE CONTEXT OF CULTURE

How sure can we be that the negative relation between optimism and depression is present on a cultural level? We chose quite different domains to assess explanatory style and behavioral symptoms of depression (i.e., Olympic newspaper reports and workmen at their leisure in bars) and found the predicted negative relationship. Still, there should be further ways to test our hypotheses.

The first set of evidence might come from signs related to depression in other East Berlin domains, such as the workmen's homes or work places, or else from other populations such as government officials, teachers, or school children (see Frese, Erbe-Heinbokel, Grefe, Rybowiak, & Weike, 1994; Oettingen & Little, 1993; Oettingen, Little, Lindenberger, & Baltes, 1994; Oettingen, in press). Because behavioral observations cannot go back in time and accurate question-naire data or statistics do not seem to be available from the times before the fall of the wall, at first sight the East Berlin versus West Berlin comparison seems no longer fruitful for this purpose. However, this multimethod approach would not resolve the more pressing issue of the causal relationship between explanatory style and depression on a cultural level. Did explanatory style in the East and West Berlin reports affect the workmen's signs of depression or did the signs of depression affect the explanatory style in the reports? Or did the difference in political systems produce both, the differences in explanatory style and the differences in behavior?

An answer to the causal relation between explanatory style and depression on a cultural level might be found by comparing numerous cultures or subcultures, which are high or low on a factor influencing explanatory style. Here, we would be able to use various measures of depression such as official statistics, more extensive observation methods (e.g., via video films) as well as clinically and cross-culturally validated self-report measures. Similar to McClelland's (1961) work on the relationship between childrearing practices and achievement moti-vation one could now test the reformulations of the learned helplessness theory of depression (Abramson, Seligman, & Teasdale, 1978; Abramson, Metalsky, & Alloy, 1989) on a broader cultural level. For example, according to the theory, one would predict that a culture teaching its children a lop-sided explanatory style (e.g., by CAVing children's readers, songs, stories) should be characterized by less prevalence in depression than a culture teaching its children an even-handed explanatory style.

Such a cross-cultural study employing many different countries would also clarify whether the differences in economic wealth rather than in explanatory style are responsible for the comparatively higher levels of depressive signs in East Berlin. For example, one could compare the GDR to countries that have a similar economic stature, but do not share the socialistic system. In addition, comparisons between various socialistic countries that differ in terms of economic prosperity would be revealing.

But one can also explore causal questions without taking a multicultural approach; this leads us back to the East Berlin versus West Berlin comparison. Only recently (in the fall of 1991) we returned to our bars (Oettingen, 1994). About 50% of them still existed unchanged; they were the same neighborhood bars with the same type of clientele. The other 50% were closed or had been reopened after renovation. We did not include these in our observational study, because the clientele had changed, too. We also returned to our West Berlin bars, where about 30% had disappeared or were redecorated and therefore were ex-cluded. Two raters observed signs of depression in the East and the West Berlin patrons using the same category system as we did in 1984. Interrater reliability was as high as before. This puts us in a position to make the same comparison between East and West Berlin workmen as was done in 1984.

Contrary to many West German newspaper reports describing lots of anxiety, insecurity, and hopelessness about the future among the former East Germans (as a response to the change in East Germany's political system), we observed similar frequencies of behavioral signs of depression in East Berlin patrons as compared to West Berlin patrons (except for illustrators which were still more frequent in the East Berlin workmen). The amount of depressive signs on the Western side did not change since 1984; rather, the East Berlin patrons showed fewer signs of depression. As compared to 1984, more East Berlin patrons showed bent up mouths, upright postures, and exposed bodies; moreover, they smiled and laughed more often (all $ps < .001$) and underlined their conversation more often with illustrators ($p < .05$) in 1991 than in 1984. This finding is also revealing with respect to the influence of the poverty/wealth factor on depression, because in 1990, the GDR's economy was going bankrupt.

The decline in depressive signs of East Berlin patrons over recent times points to a unique opportunity of investigating the causal relationship between explanatory style and depression in a straightforward manner. If the notion that pessimistic explanatory style causes depression holds also at the cultural level, we should find a change from even-handedness to lop-sidedness in East Berlin's written cultural products in the times (months or maybe few years) prior to the fall of the wall in the fall of 1989. But even if we obtain such a finding, there still is the possibility that depression faded before explanatory style changed from even-handedness to lop-sidedness. Also, both explanatory style and depression might have danced to the same music (i.e., the change of the political system), or it could even be that the political system changes were a function of explanatory style and depression.

Can such questions be answered through cross-cultural research? In the present historical times we see a possibility. Because all of the Eastern block countries are now in the process of changing their political systems, we can extend our research and keep assessing explanatory style and depression over the upcoming years in various East European countries. Some of these countries will change their systems more effectively and quickly than others. Monitoring the three variables of interest over time—explanatory style, signs of depression, and political system change—would finally provide the data that could answer all of the causal questions raised in this chapter.

13
▼▼▼▼▼▼▼

Explanatory Style and Coronary Heart Disease

Gregory McClellan Buchanan
University of Pennsylvania

The study reported in this chapter concerns the relationship between coronary heart disease (CHD), the Type A behavior pattern (TABP), and pessimistic explanatory style. As part of the Recurrent Coronary Prevention Program (RCPP) 120 men who suffered a first heart attack gave a videotaped interview. These interviews were coded for pessimism using a content analysis of the explanations offered for events in their lives. Within $8\frac{1}{2}$ years, half of these men had died from coronary events. Pessimism at the time of the interview predicted cardiac death independently of initial damage to the heart, TABP, and traditional risk factors.

Cardiovascular disease is the leading cause of death in the United States (Glass, 1977). The disease may be broken down into two components: coronary artery disease (CAD), a condition characterized by lesions of the coronary arteries; and CHD, which has two major manifestations—angina pectoris (severe, recurrent chest pains) and myocardial infarction (MI; "heart attack"). Angina pectoris results when lesioned coronary arteries occlude the blood supply to the heart, resulting in a lack of oxygen known as anoxia or an ischemic attack. If the occlusion is prolonged or complete, actual necrosis of the heart tissue will occur resulting in permanent damage, and possibly death. This is myocardial infarction.

There are numerous physical factors associated with an increased risk of heart disease. Some of the more common factors are aging, cigarette smoking, hypertension, elevated serum cholesterol, diabetes, and being male. It is known that the chances of suffering one of the manifestations of cardiovascular disease are greater when multiple factors are present and when they are more severe (Insull, 1983). These "traditional" risk factors, however, fail to predict many new cases of CHD and CAD, and in most cases the mechanisms by which they lead to disease are unknown.

Beginning in the 1950s, researchers began investigating nonphysical determinants of CHD (Jenkins, 1976). The leading hypothesis that psychological factors contribute to CHD has been the TABP hypothesis. TABP is characterized by an intense desire to achieve, a persistent struggle against time and free-floating hostility. These characteristics are alleged to lead to a state of chronic physiological and psychological arousal that contributes to heart disease (Friedman & Rosenhan, 1974). There have been several successful prospective studies that have linked TABP to subsequent CHD (Friedman et al., 1986: RCPP; Haynes, Feinleib, & Kannel, 1980: The Framingham Heart Study; Rosenhan et al., 1975: The Western Collaborative Group Study). There has also been much controversy over TABP centered around reports of failures to find a relationship between TABP and CHD (e.g., Shekelle et al., 1985: The Multiple Risk Factor Intervention Trial). These failures lead several investigators to suggest that a better definition of TABP is needed to replace the "global" definition originally proposed by Friedman and Rosenhan (e.g., Chesney, Hecker, & Black, 1988; Williams & Barefoot, 1988). This definition should be aimed at determining what, if any, aspects of the syndrome are pathogenic. I propose that pessimism, depression, and a tendency toward helplessness may be the pathogenic components of TABP.

Booth-Kewley and Friedman (1987) reported the results of a meta-analysis that involved both cross-sectional and prospective studies of TABP, "negative emotions," and CHD. A striking finding was reported for depression that prompted the authors to conclude: "When one considers the vast amount of research performed on TABP and the very small amount performed on depression (in relation to CHD), the finding that depression relates about as strongly to the disease as does TABP seems remarkable" (pp. 350–351). Specifically, these authors reported a combined effect size of .204 for depression and CHD from their review of cross-sectional studies and .168 for depression and CHD from prospective studies (both $p < .0001$). The fact that the reported effect size for prospective studies is almost as high as that for cross-sectional studies would suggest that depression may actually contribute to the development of CHD. Not surprisingly, self-reported depression also increases following myocardial infarction (Bruhn, Chandler, & Wolf, 1969), indicating that depression may be a result rather than a contributor to CHD. This reported post-MI increase in depression, however, was found to be predictive of longevity over a 5-year period following the MI. That is, those individuals who became most depressed following their MI died sooner than the less depressed patients (Bruhn et al., 1969). To summarize, depression may be seen as a potential cause of heart disease and as a direct consequence of myocardial infarction with the depth of this consequent depression predicting long-term survival.

There are good reasons for believing that Type A individuals would be particularly susceptible to severe depression. Type A individuals are obsessed with achievement and competitiveness. Unfortunately, it is not always possible to achieve all we want particularly when we have the incessant appetite to achieve that is characteristic of TABP. Thoresen, Friedman, Gill, and Ulmer (1982) noted that "the constant struggling which characterizes TABP leads at times to a state of physical and/or emotional exhaustion, a condition in which one feels helpless and inept, [and] acting in a hostile way . . . appears to serve as a way of reducing these feelings of depression, exhaustion and helplessness" (p. 188). Thus, these authors hypothesize that depression and helplessness result from the impossible struggle Type As subject themselves to. Type A individuals respond to these states with hostility and an increased effort to achieve that results in more depression and helplessness following the next failure. A pernicious circle is thus created.

It is hypothesized that TABP has the potential to leave a person at high risk for helplessness and depression. The hypothesis that Type A individuals are prone to helplessness has been tested. Before discussing helplessness in relation to TABP, however, I briefly review the learned helplessness concept. Seligman (1975) proposed a learned helplessness hypothesis to explain the finding that an organism's response to aversive stimuli depended on its history of success or failure at controlling its environment. Specifically, when exposed to uncontrollable aversive events the organism learns that its efforts to avoid or escape the stressor are essentially futile and thus it gives up. When later placed in a similar situation in which the aversive event is escapable, this same organism will not attempt to escape. That is, it acts as if it is helpless. Further, when it does, by chance, make the appropriate escape response, the organism fails to learn that it has succeeded. Learned helplessness thus consists of a motivational and cognitive deficit (Seligman, Abramson, Semmel, & von Baeyer, 1979).

Glass (1977) investigated learned helplessness in Type A and Type B individuals in the following manner: Subjects were exposed to either a moderate or a highly stressful situation (loud or very loud noise). Half the subjects in each condition could escape the noise, whereas for the remaining subjects the noise was inescapable. Following this training, the Type A and the Type B subjects in all four conditions were given a test phase in which they were exposed to signalled noise bursts that could be escaped. Glass found that following exposure to an uncontrollable highly stressful situation, Type A individuals showed pronounced helplessness deficits in the test phase. These deficits were not apparent following exposure to an uncontrollable moderately stressful situation. In contrast, Type B individuals did show learned helplessness in the moderately stressful situation, but not in the highly stressful situation. Glass hypothesized that this effect was due to the incessant need Type A individuals have to control their environment. Under highly stressful conditions, they persist in their attempts at control (whereas Type B individuals do not) and eventually become exhausted and helpless.

Like depression, helplessness has been related to CHD. Following a study of coronary and noncoronary hospitalized patients, Glass (1977) concluded that TABP and real-life analogues of the experimental helplessness inducing events were more characteristic of coronary patients than of noncoronary hospitalized controls. Not only did these patients possess TABP, they were also more likely to have suffered uncontrollable life events prior to their hospitalization. Although this was a cross-sectional study, Parkes, Benjamin, and Fitzgerald (1969) had earlier reported that helplessness-producing events often precede heart attack. They found that death of a spouse dramatically increased the risk of coronary death in the year following the bereavement.

Recapping, Glass (1977) demonstrated that Type A individuals are particularly susceptible to helplessness and it is hypothesized that they are also particularly susceptible to depression. Further, both helplessness-inducing events and depression have been linked to CHD. It is now necessary to provide an account of the circumstances that allow these uncontrollable aversive events to result in depression and helplessness.

Not all individuals exposed to helplessness-producing circumstances will become helpless. In 1978, Abramson, Seligman, and Teasdale proposed an attributional account of when helplessness will occur (see chapter 1, this volume). They theorized that individuals have an enduring explanatory style that determines how they will interpret the cause of both good and bad events. There are three attributional dimensions: (a) The stable–unstable dimension that is concerned with the permanence or transience of the cause; (b) the global–specific dimension that involves attributing the event to a cause that will affect many areas of the individual's life or just one particular event; and (c) the internal–external dimension that involves attributing the event to something about the individual or to something outside of the individual. Individuals who possess a pessimistic explanatory style—those making stable, global, and internal attributions for negative events and unstable, specific, and external attributions for positive events—have been found to be more susceptible to learned helplessness. Learned helplessness, in turn, has been found to be predictive of depression (see chapter 5, this volume).

There are many parallels between learned helplessness and depression. Miller and Seligman (1975) noted that depressed individuals are less likely to initiate responses than nondepressed people. That is, depressed individuals show a motivational deficit. Likewise, the cognitive deficit found following helplessness training is also characteristic of depression (Miller & Seligman, 1975). Abramson (1978) also noted that helpless individuals who attribute their failure to escape an aversive event to internal factors suffer the same loss of self-esteem seen in depressed patients. Most importantly, Peterson and Seligman (1984a) demonstrated that people who have an explanatory style characterized by internal, stable, and global explanations for bad events are more likely to become depressed following uncontrollable, aversive events.

The study reported here investigated whether high-risk CHD individuals were more likely to die from heart disease if they had a pessimistic explanatory style. Because depression has been found to precede death from CHD, a pessimistic explanatory style (one that precedes depression and amplifies the helplessness response to uncontrollable events) would be expected to increase the likelihood of death. The scenario would thus be as follows: Individuals identified to be at high risk for CHD (on the basis of already having suffered an MI) would be at high risk for depression if they possessed a pessimistic explanatory style and an MI is an uncontrollable negative event. Further, having a pessimistic explanatory style would amplify the depth (global dimension) and increase the duration (stable dimension) of this depression. The more severe this depression, the greater the likelihood of death.

The subjects were 120 men who had volunteered to be control subjects in the RCPP. Initially, 60 subjects for whom death certificates were available (confirming that they had died from coronary events) were chosen and they were matched with another 60 surviving men for age and PEEL index. The PEEL index is a composite measure of coronary functioning following MI that takes into account the site of the infarction and the degree of damage done to the heart (Peel, Semple, Wang, Lancaster, & Dahl, 1962). Videotapes of the subjects' baseline interviews (recorded $8\frac{1}{2}$ years prior to this study) were sent to our offices at the University of Pennsylvania from Stanford. These baseline interviews were the videotaped structured interviews, an alternative to Rosenhan and Friedman's structured interview, used to assess TABP in the RCPP. We were kept blind as to who had died and who had survived.

Explanatory style was assessed using the Content Analysis of Verbatim Explanations (CAVE) technique (see chapter 2, this volume). The CAVE technique, developed by Peterson, Luborsky, and Seligman (1983), allows explanatory style to be assessed from any spoken or written material. Events that have explicit explanations are extracted from the individual's dialogue (in this case, from the videotaped interviews) and are rated on the three dimensions of explanatory style. The raters, eight undergraduate students who were trained in the CAVE procedure, watched the 30-minute tapes in pairs and extracted all event-attribution statements from the tape. These extractions were listed verbatim with the addition of any clarifying background information about the quote in the following format:

Event: I've been under a lot of pressure lately.

Explanation: He (son who is out of work) has moved back home and we don't get along.

Table 13.1 presents several representative event-explanation units from the survivors and the deceased. The event-explanation units were then randomized with units from other individuals and rated by three raters with the additional constraint

TABLE 13.1
Sample Extractions From Deceased and Living Subjects

Deceased Subjects

Event: (Causes of heart attack—question by interviewer.)
Attribution: The way I ate and smoking. I guess when you look down the list of possible causes,
   I had them all.
Event: I feel insecure about my education.
Attribution: My education was limited. My father died when I was 5, and I quit high school in
   the 10th grade.
Event: Drinking too much.
Attribution: It just happens . . . just like different habits.

Living Subjects

Event: It brings on anxious feelings.
Attribution: When I'm away from the doctor for a while.
Event: I don't get irritated by slow drivers (positive event).
Attribution: I'm a patient person.
Event: (Causes of heart attack—question by interviewer.)
Attribution: That day we were at a trade show . . . and I guess I exerted myself a little more than
   most times.

that no rater rated an extraction that they had extracted themselves. Thus, the raters were wholly naive to who said what, the subjects' physical appearance on the videotape, and the health outcome. Each extraction was rated on a 7-point scale along three dimensions (1 = *unstable/specific/external*, 7 = *stable/global/internal*). Scores on these three scales were averaged for each subject across all three raters and across all extractions of a particular valence (good or bad event). This creates six individual variables: internal negative (IN); stable negative (SN); global negative (GN); and internal, stable, and global positive (IP, SP, and GP, respectively). For the individual measures of explanations for negative events, a higher score indicates a more pessimistic response. The reverse is true for individual measures of explanations for positive events. Past research (e.g., Peterson & Seligman, 1984a; Seligman & Schulman, 1986) found that the best predictors from explanatory style are composite measures of the stable, global, and internal dimensions (see chapter 2, this volume, for more details). These are: composite positive (CP), composite negative (CN), and composite positive minus composite negative (CPCN). Additionally, measures of hopefulness (HP—the sum of SP and GP), and hopelessness (HN—the sum of SN and GN) are generated and these scores may be subtracted from one another to yield the HPHN measure. For CN and HN, higher scores indicate more pessimistic responses, whereas for CP, HP, CPCN, and HPHN, lower or negative scores are indicative of pessimism. As Peterson, Villanova, and Raps (1985) noted, studies that have supported the reformulated learned helplessness model have been those that have had more attributions per subject. Ideally, four or five negative events are needed in order to assess a subject's style of explanation (Schulman, Castellon, & Seligman, 1988). Thus, in this study statistical relationships involving explanatory style for negative events were only assessed for subjects with five or more negative events, which resulted in an n of 81. As 23 of the 81 subjects with five or more negative events had no positive event-explanation units, the sample size was 58 for statistical relationships involving attributions for positive events.

Death from CHD was predicted by explanatory style. Individuals who habitually gave stable, global, and internal explanations for bad events were those who were more likely to die in the $8\frac{1}{2}$-year period since their baseline interviews. A significant correlation was found between death and pessimistic scores (see Table 13.2) over and above age and damage to the heart after first heart attack. As seen in Table 13.2, CPCN, the overall composite score for both good and bad events, was significantly related to death ($R = -.215$; $p = .05$) as was HPHN ($R = -.264$; $p = .022$) with HP about good events ($R = -.240$; $p = .032$) and HN about bad events ($R = .190$; $p = .041$) each contributing significantly. A pessimistic (i.e., negative) HPHN score indicates that the individual attributes negative events to stable and global causes (HN), while attributing positive events to unstable and specific causes (HP). Good events are thus seen as transient and local and bad events as chronic and pervasive. The single most predictive dimension was SN—the belief that bad events are permanent ($R = .338$; $p = .001$). When SN ratings are ranked from highest (most pessimistic) to lowest (least pessimistic), 86% of those people in the highest quartile died, whereas 67% of those in the lowest quartile survived. Even more striking is the finding that 15 of the 16 men with the most pessimistic SN scores died, whereas only 5 of the 16 men with the most optimistic SN scores died.

I conclude that a pessimistic explanatory style predicts death from CHD over and above damage to the heart at first infarction and age. But by what mechanisms might pessimism contribute to fatal heart disease? As with Peterson (see chapter 14, this volume) I see three possibilities: First, a pessimistic explanatory style is a precursor to depression, and depression a precursor to CHD. How this link

TABLE 13.2
Point Biserial Correlations Between Death and Individual and
Composite Measures of Explanatory Style

	IN	SN	GN	HN	CN
Death	.007 (.473)	.338 (.002)	.106 (.166)	.190 (.041)	.13 (.224)

	IP	SP	GP	HP	CP
Death	−.148 (.131)	−.099 (.226)	−.214 (.051)	−.240 (.032)	−.223 (.044)

	HPHN	CPCN
Death	−.264 (.022)	−.215 (.050)

Note. Probabilities are given in parentheses and reflect one-tailed tests of significance.

might play out is unclear. It is possible that when under the stress of depression, the adrenal glands produce increased quantities of adrenaline, cortisol, and other "stress" hormones. The net effect of these hormones would be to increase heart rate during periods of stress and a heart that is overtaxed might succumb to disease at a faster rate. Immunosuppression is also a consequence of depression (Schleifer, Keller, Siris, Davis, & Stein, 1985) and a body that cannot fight disease as effectively will be more stressed than a healthy one again taxing the heart and potentially leading to the early development of CHD. It should be noted, however, that although not directly examined in the study reported here, a pessimistic explanatory style predicts poor health over and above health outcome predicted by depression (see chapter 14, this volume, for details of studies demonstrating this effect). So although one path linking explanatory style to CHD may be through depression, there are other possibilities. Individuals who believe that matters are hopeless are more passive and will be less likely to adopt health regimens (Lin & Peterson, 1990; Peterson, 1988). If you believe that nothing you do matters, why give up bacon and eggs? Given that the men in this study had all experienced an MI at some time prior to their interview, they all (one assumes) were given information on how they might change their lifestyles and therefore decrease their risk of further disease. To the extent that pessimism results in passivity, one can imagine the pessimistic subjects not making changes recommended by their cardiologists. This potential link between pessimism, health-related behaviors, and illness is currently under investigation at the University of Pennsylvania (Buchanan, 1994). Finally, pessimistic individuals are also less likely to have high levels of social support, and lack of social support is associated with illness (House, Robbins, & Metzner, 1982).

To the extent that pessimistic explanatory style is a risk factor for cardiac death, it is a modifiable psychological trait (see chapter 15, this volume). The techniques of cognitive therapy applied to depressed individuals reliably change explanatory style from pessimistic to optimistic and thereby relieve depression markedly. It is speculated that these same techniques applied to cardiac patients might prevent further fatal heart disease.

14
▼▼▼▼▼▼▼

Explanatory Style and Health

Christopher Peterson
University of Michigan

Among the most intriguing correlates of explanatory style is physical well-being. Individuals with an optimistic style of explaining bad events, attributing them to external, unstable, and specific causes, tend to experience better health than their pessimistic counterparts, who explain bad events with internal, stable, and global causes. This chapter describes the studies that established this correlation. More recent investigations that attempt to make sense of this link are discussed. The chapter closes with a discussion of questions that remain to be answered regarding this line of work. (For a more extensive discussion of explanatory style and physical health, refer to Peterson & Bossio, 1991.)

ESTABLISHING THE CORRELATION

Investigators began to look at the relationship between explanatory style and physical health in the mid-1980s, spurred by several related influences. The first was simply our desire to explore as widely as possible the potential correlates of explanatory style. As explained in chapter 1 of this volume, explanatory style research from the very beginning focused on depression. Once the relationship of explanatory style to depression had been established (e.g., Peterson & Seligman, 1984a; Sweeney, Anderson, & Bailey, 1986), we began to look elsewhere for possible correlates.

A second influence was our development of the content analysis procedure for measuring explanatory style, the Content Analysis of Verbatim Explanations

(CAVE; see chapter 2, this volume). This operationalization made it possible to ascertain the explanatory style of individuals not amenable to questionnaire investigations, so long as they had left behind some sort of verbal record in which bad events were mentioned. In particular, we saw the opportunity to use the CAVE in longitudinal studies that were already in progress. Explanatory style could be ascertained from verbal material gathered in years past and then be related to more recent characteristics of the subjects in question. Several of the longitudinal studies to which we had access contained measures of morbidity and mortality. One of the reasons for relating explanatory style to measures of physical health was simply that these measures were there.

Finally, a third influence on our research linking explanatory style and health was a series of animal studies implicating the learned helplessness phenomenon in poor functioning of the immune system. Explanatory style was originally proposed as a distal influence on the boundary conditions of helplessness following uncontrollability. Typically, this helplessness was conceived in terms of learning and motivational deficits, but when researchers peered beneath the skin of helpless animals they additionally found physiological consequences of uncontrollability (Maier & Jackson, 1979). Among these consequences was susceptibility to tumor growth (e.g., Laudenslager, Ryan, Drugan, Hyson, & Maier, 1983; Sklar & Anisman, 1979; Visintainer, Volpicelli, & Seligman, 1982). We extrapolated from these animal studies to the hypothesis that explanatory style, because it influences the degree of helplessness following experience with uncontrollable events, should be a risk factor for poor health.

Investigating the influence of any psychological factor on physical health is difficult. Most generally, such studies attempt to span minds and bodies, conceptual realms split apart centuries ago. The attempt to put them together—after altogether different vocabularies have arisen to describe their functioning, and after altogether different scientific disciplines have emerged that make each its respective focus—is fraught with hazard. Skepticism abounds. Indeed, the very attempt to explain physical well-being in psychological terms is dismissed in some quarters as morally questionable: blaming victims for their misfortunes.

The most widely known evidence cited in favor of psychological influences on health comes from isolated case studies, such as Cousins' (1981) storied recovery from a life-threatening disease by mustering his positive emotions. Case studies, however, are scientifically ambiguous because they are unable to isolate causes. Intriguing as case studies may be, they are not useful for the purpose of showing that psychological factors influence health.

Criteria for Studying Psychological Influences on Health

A number of methodological requirements must be satisifed before we are on reasonably firm ground in concluding that psychological factors do indeed influence health (Peterson, Seligman, & Vaillant, 1988). It is fair to say that the vast majority of studies attempting to demonstrate such effects do not meet these requirements, which is why we see such hot debate. Some of the requirements that an ideal study should satisfy are now discussed.

The Research Design Must Be Longitudinal. Although a contemporaneous association between explanatory style and health is consistent with the hypothesis that the former influences the latter, it is a particularly ambiguous piece of information. It is just as plausible—and perhaps more so—that someone's good or bad health influences how the world is seen, including the causes of events. Or perhaps a third variable influences both one's psychological state and one's physical well-being (cf. Salovey & Birnbaum, 1989). If the psychological influences on health are to be discerned, they must be teased apart over time.

Relatedly, the time span must be sufficient for these influences to take place. It is not entirely clear just what time frame is appropriate, but with regard to explanatory style, it is doubtful that the influence takes place within mere hours or days. It may well take weeks, months, or even years to develop. What this means is that researchers must use a range of longitudinal designs, and take "negative results" with more than the usual grain of salt, because they may simply mean that the wrong time frame has been chosen.

The Health Status of Individual Research Subjects Must Be Known at the Time the Study Begins and When It Ends. Physical health (or the absence of it) can be a highly stable individual difference. To argue that a psychological factor such as explanatory style influences health is to propose that it accounts for *changes* in health over time, for better or worse. Obviously, this is only possible if the researcher can track these changes over time.

On the face of it, the operationalization of physical health seems straightforward. Upon closer examination, it becomes clear that there is no single meaning of good or bad health and thus no single measure that suffices for all purposes. Our strategy for measuring health has been twofold. First, we have tried to be sure that our measures are not confounded by the psychological characteristic we are trying to correlate with health. Second, we have tried to determine the relationship between explanatory style and health across a variety of health measures. This is simply a special case of the multimethod research strategy long followed within psychology (Campbell & Fiske, 1959), here applied to physical well-being.

A Sufficient Number of Research Participants Must Be Studied. Explanatory style research is often plagued by sample sizes that do not give sufficient power to detect relationships that are actually present (Peterson, Villanova, & Raps, 1985; Robins, 1988). Perhaps the problem here has been the application of explanatory style to clinical phenomena and the consequent goal of investigators to make clinical sense of findings, that is, interpreting them vis-à-vis particular individuals. Be that as it may, the fact remains that correlations with explanatory style are usually in the familiar .30 range (see chapter 1, this volume), which means that these correlations cannot be consistently detected unless the sample size approaches or even better exceeds $n = 100$. To the degree that a researcher wishes to examine several variables simultaneously, sample sizes must be correspondingly increased.

We concede that these criteria are idealizations, to be approached in particular investigations but perhaps never fully achieved. Nevertheless, we believe that our research program into explanatory style and health is highly satisfactory on such methodological grounds. We have measured health and illness in several ways and then shown in longitudinal designs with sufficient numbers of subjects that pessimistic explanatory style foreshadows poor health. Two of these studies are described in some detail; note that the thrust of their findings has been replicated in several other studies (see Peterson & Bossio, 1991, chapter 2).

A 35-Year Longitudinal Study of Explanatory Style and Health

The Harvard Study of Adult Development began in 1937 when the William T. Grant Foundation funded a project to study the functioning of physically and emotionally healthy individuals (see Vaillant, 1977, for details). The sample was drawn from members of the Harvard classes of 1942 to 1944. Potential research subjects were first screened on the basis of academic success (40% of the entire student body was excluded), then on the basis of physical and psychological health (another 30% was excluded), and finally on the basis of nominations by college deans of the most independent and accomplished individuals. In all, 268 men were included in the final sample.

Each subject, while an undergraduate, took an extensive physical examination and completed numerous personality and intelligence tests. After graduation, the subjects completed annual questionnaires asking about their employment, family, and health. Regular physical examinations of each subject were conducted by his own doctor. Only 10 men withdrew from the study during their college years, and 2 more after graduation.

The Harvard Study of Adult Development satisfies most of our criteria for an ideal study of how psychological states might influence physical well-being. It is longitudinal. It employs good measures of physical health (i.e., physician examinations). It has a large number of research participants.

The study also allowed us to ascertain the explanatory style of the research participants when they were young (Peterson, Seligman, & Vaillant, 1988). Among the many questionnaires completed by subjects was one to which they responded in 1946 that asked about difficult wartime experiences:

> What difficult personal situations did you encounter (we want details), were they in combat or not, or did they occur in relations with superiors or men under you?

Were these battles you had to fight within yourself? How successful or unsuccessful in your own opinion were you in these situations? How were they related to your work or health? What physical or mental symptoms did you experience at such times?

The answers to this question were more essays than brief statements, and causal explanations for bad events abounded within them.

We chose an arbitrary subset of 99 subjects, and we read through their responses on the lookout for causal explanations of bad events. For the 99 men, we found 1,102 bad events and causal explanations (an average of 11.1 per subject). These causal explanations were rated according to their internality (vs. externality), stability (vs. instability), and globality (vs. specificity) by four judges. Then we combined the ratings by averaging across the judges, across the three rating dimensions, and finally across the different events explained by a particular research subject. What resulted were scores that placed each subject someplace along the dimension ranging from an extremely optimistic explanatory style to an extremely pessimistic one.

We now turn to how the physical health of the research participants was ascertained. At eight times in each subject's life—at ages 25 (approximately when the 1946 questionnaire was completed), 30, 35, 40, 45, 50, 55, and 60, his personal physician completed a thorough physical examination and forwarded the results to a research internist at the Harvard Study. In light of the examination results, the internist then rated each subject's global health:

1 = good health, normal
2 = multiple minor complaints, mild back trouble, prostatitis, gout, kidney stones, single joint problems, chronic ear problems
3 = probably irreversible chronic illness without disability; illness that will not fully remit and will probably progress—like treated hypertension, emphysema with cor pulmonae, diabetes
4 = probably irreversible chronic illness with disability—for example, myocardial infarction with angina, disabling back trouble, hypertension *and* extreme obesity, diabetes *and* severe arthritis, multiple sclerosis
5 = deceased

For most of the subjects from age 50 on, the research internist also had available blood and urine tests, an electrocardiogram, and a chest X-ray.

One more pertinent measure must be described. In 1945, an overall rating was made by an examining psychiatrist who attempted to predict the individual's likelihood of encountering emotional difficulties at some point in the future. Emotional soundness was important to know in order for us to be able to rule out the possibility that an underlying emotional difficulty might cause both a pessimistic explanatory style and poor physical health.

As we would expect, the health of subjects on the whole worsened as they became older. However, what also happened was that the range of health scores increased as well, meaning that that there was an ever-increasing difference between the most and least healthy of our subjects. Although all of the subjects started out extremely healthy, given the stringent selection criteria, some nonetheless became quite sickly as they aged. Indeed, of the 99 men we studied, 13 died before age 60. What made the difference between those with a good outcome and those without? Was explanatory style relevant?

Overall, men who used optimistic explanations for bad events at age 25 were healthier later in life than men who favored pessimistic explanations. This correlation held even when their initial physical and emotional soundness were held constant statistically. More specifically, explanatory style was unrelated to health at ages 30–40, but thereafter a relationship emerged, reaching its most robust level at age 45 (partial $r = .37$, $p < .001$), nearly two decades after the time that explanatory style was assessed. Thereafter, the relation between optimism and health fell off somewhat.

We also looked at how explanatory style (at age 25) was associated with changes in health status from one age to another. This allowed us to determine where an optimistic explanatory style starts to have benefits (and a pessimistic explanatory style costs). To some degree, a pessimistic explanatory style was associated with a worsening of health from ages 35 to 40. But the link became abundantly clear between ages 40 and 45 (partial $r = .42$, $p < .001$). Here, those with an optimistic explanatory style as young men maintained their health, in contrast to those with a pessimistic explanatory style. These latter individuals showed a marked deterioration in their health.

The major shortcoming of this study is that its sample was originally chosen not to be representative of the population as a whole. Our subjects were initially healthy, often wealthy, successful men, mostly from the northeastern United States. This hardly detracts from the value of the study as a demonstration, but it leaves unanswered questions about boundary conditions. Does the relationship between explanatory style and health hold for all people in all circumstances? Our next step was to establish more broadly the link between explanatory style and physical health.

A Study of Explanatory Style and the Common Cold

Our second investigation of the relationship between explanatory style and physical health therefore drew subjects from a different population, used a different time frame, employed a different measure of explanatory style, and chose two different criteria for good versus poor health (Peterson, 1988). The study began during the fall of 1984, what we refer to as Time 1. Our subjects were 172 undergraduates enrolled at Virginia Tech. They completed a version of the Attributional Style Questionnaire (ASQ; Peterson & Villanova, 1988) and a measure we called the Illness Scale, a questionnaire that asked them to describe all the illnesses they had experienced during the previous 30 days (Suls & Mullen, 1981). For each illness described, subjects reported the date that the symptoms were first noticed and the date that they were last present. The degree of illness was then calculated as the number of different days during the month that at least one symptom was present. To control for possible tendencies to complain by some of our subjects, we also administered the Beck Depression Inventory (BDI) as a measure of depressive symptoms (Beck, 1967).

At Time 2—1 month later—our subjects were asked to return and to again complete the Illness Scale. Of the original 172 subjects, 170 (99%) indeed did so. At Time 2, they described illnesses occurring since Time 1, when their explanatory style had been ascertained. As in the Harvard Study, our interest was in the relationship between explanatory style at the early point in time and health at the later point.

Finally, we contacted our subjects by letter 1 year later (Time 3). Enclosing a stamped envelope addressed to us, we asked:

> Would you please indicate in the space below the number of times you have visited a physician since last Thanksgiving for diagnosis and/or treatment of an illness? Do not include routine checkups or visits because of an injury (like a broken leg).

We assumed that the worse someone's health, the more frequently he or she would visit a doctor. Of the original 172 subjects, we heard back at Time 3 from 146 (86%). Again, we wanted to see the relationship between explanatory style and subsequent health.

College students with a pessimistic explanatory style—when compared with their more optimistic peers—indeed experienced more days of illness in the subsequent month ($r = .27$, $p < .005$) and made more doctor visits in the subsequent year ($r = .20$, $p < .05$). These results held even when their initial health status and depression were held constant statistically.

The magnitudes of these relationships were somewhat less than those found in the Harvard Study, perhaps because a shorter time frame was involved. Nonetheless, these findings become more impressive when recast to compare the health status of those subjects who are among the least optimistic with those who are among the most optimistic. When we compared the subjects whose ASQ scores were in the highest quartile (most pessimistic) with those whose scores were in the lowest quartile (most optimistic), we found a more than 2:1 difference in terms of days of illness (8.56 vs. 3.70) and more than a 3:1 difference in terms of number of doctor visits (3.56 vs. .95).

Subjects at Times 1 and 2 described exclusively infectious diseases, usually colds or the flu. Although subjects at Time 3 were not asked to describe why they had visited a physician, some of them did so. Again, every illness mentioned was infectious in nature. These results may tell us something that the Harvard

Study did not: what sort of illness pessimistic explanatory style predisposes. This finding hints at a possible path between explanatory style and health, one that involves how the body responds to infection. However, because our college student subjects were more likely to develop colds or the flu as opposed to other sorts of illness, this hint may be a misleading one.

Again, this study is not ideal. As in the Harvard Study of Adult Development, the research subjects did not comprise a cross-section of the population. College students on the average are healthier, more intelligent, and more privileged than those in the general population. The common cold is not to be confused with cancer and heart disease, and perhaps college students—who usually live in such close proximity to one another—are at great risk for the sniffles. However, with the converging results, we begin to have more confidence in the link between explanatory style and health.

MAKING SENSE OF THE CORRELATION

Our results, however tantalizing, are merely descriptive. They do not tell us how optimistic explanatory style translates itself into good health or pessimistic explanatory style into poor health. So, our current research goal has been to map out the various routes between explanatory style and health. Given the likely complexity of psychological influences on health, we suspect that no single mechanism will fully explain the correlation between explanatory style and health. Indeed, our working assumption has been that there exist several pathways between explanatory style and health, cross-cutting and mutually influencing one another (Peterson & Seligman, 1987).

This discussion is not simply one of idle academic interest. If a psychological state indeed influences health, then we can start to ask if changing this state will have an impact on health. It seems unlikely that anyone would be rescued from death's door by changing his or her explanatory style. But it is not so far-fetched to think that the deliberate encouraging of an optimistic way of explaining events, started early in life, might later pay dividends in terms of increased quantity and quality of life. And it is not far-fetched to think that the acquisition of an optimistic exoplanatory might help a person recover more quickly and more fully from a less than fatal illness. Indeed, we know already that cognitive therapy can change explanatory style from pessimistic to optimistic (Seligman et al., 1988). If such changes can be maintained, there is good reason to suppose that they will lead eventually to improved health.

Biological Pathways

Of late, learned helplessness research with animals has been extended to look at the physiological effects of uncontrollability. Obtained findings imply that uncontrollability may compromise the immune system. Granted the established correlation between explanatory style and health among people, we can turn to these animal studies to make sense of the correlation. The animal studies suggest a rather straightforward series of biological events (Rosenhan & Seligman, 1989):

1. Uncontrollable events lead to increased endorphins.
2. Increased endorphins interfere with the functioning of the immune system.
3. A less-than-robust immune system is not as able to fight off infection.
4. Illness becomes more likely.

If we assume that people with a pessimistic explanatory style experience more uncontrollability, then we can conclude that they are more likely to experience this chain of events. This is a reasonable assumption, because individuals with a pessimistic view of things not only catastrophize bad events but also experience more of them in the first place as a result of being poor problem solvers (Alloy, Peterson, Abramson, & Seligman, 1984).

Several comments should be made about this possible biological pathway between explanatory style and health. On the cautious side, the studies giving rise to these conclusions have been done with animals exposed to uncontrollable shocks. There may be asymmetries in generalizing these results to people experiencing difficult life events. Also, some of these studies have proven difficult to replicate, suggesting at the very least that the hypothesized links are fragile ones possibly depending on subtle aspects of the experimental procedure. More generally, the entire field of psychoneuroimmunology is very much in its infancy, and legitimate debate takes place with regard to how the immune system works and what indices should be used to gauge its functioning (Melnechuk, 1985). We have glibly spoken of the immune system as a whole, but in point of fact, the relevant research is much more analytic and always focuses on a particular aspect of immune functioning operationalized in a specific way.

On the other hand, this pathway is a plausible one, and some of the links indeed have been established with people. For example, we already know that uncontrollable bad events, such as the death of one's spouse, depresses the immune system (Kiecolt-Glaser & Glaser, 1987). We know that the more uncontrollable events someone experiences, the more likely he or she is to fall ill (Rabkin & Struening, 1976). We know that a pessimistic explanatory style is linked with poor immune functioning (Seligman, 1987).

It would be a mistake, however, to think that the biological story is complete once the immune system has been implicated. It is also conceivable that a biological pathway somehow runs through the autonomic nervous system. Perhaps those with a pessimistic explanatiory style are more likely to be aroused: generally anxious and tense. Indeed, studies suggest that explanatory style correlates not only with symptoms of depression but also with those of anxiety (e.g., Nezu, Nezu, & Nezu, 1986). And there are hints that explanatory style is related to cardiac problems (see chapter 13, this volume).

Emotional Pathways

Probably the most well-established correlate of explanatory style is depression (Sweeney, Anderson, & Bailey, 1986). And one of the concomitants of depression, according to recent research, is immunosupression (e.g., Schleifer, Keller, Siris, Davis, & Stein, 1985). It makes sense, therefore, to suggest that one of the routes between explanatory style and physical well-being runs through depression. Despite the plausibility of this mechanism, we do not want it to be the only one linking explanatory style and poor health. If it were, our research program on physical health would be a mere footnote to our research program on depression (Peterson & Seligman, 1984a). This is why we have taken pains, in the two studies described in this chapter, to show that explanatory style affects physical health above and beyond any effect that it might have on depression.

But given that explanatory style influences health in ways other than through depression, it then makes sense to add that depression is nonetheless one of the possible mediators. Or to be more exact, let us say that dysphoria is one of the plausible mechanisms. In a quantitative literature review of studies bearing on the notion of the "disease-prone personality," Friedman and Booth-Kewley (1987) found ample evidence linking a variety of negative emotional states—depression, anxiety, and anger—to a variety of physical ailments. They found no evidence of specificity. In other words, negative psychological states were equally associated with poor health in a variety of forms.

Psychosomatic medicine as pioneered by Alexander (1939, 1950) sought links between specific emotional conflicts and specific diseases. These links were interpreted on two levels, physiologically and symbolically. Research evidence for them has been scant, except in the case of linking hostility to heart disease (e.g., Matthews, 1982). The current wisdom seems to be that we should not expect specific links between emotional states and illness. We conclude that the emotional pathway between explanatory style and poor health entails a wide range of negative feelings.

Behavioral Pathways

We sometimes wonder why people are more intrigued by the biological and emotional pathways discussed earlier than by what is the most obvious one of all: particular health-promoting behaviors that a person does or does not perform. Then we think about our own exercise and diet programs, and groan, and remember that a behavioral route between explanatory style and health necessarily entails hard work. Would it not be nice if good health were simply a matter of wearing a smiley button in order to feel happier and thus to live forever after?

But it is not that simple. The link between particular behaviors and one's mortality has been definitively established by epidemiologists. To the degree that someone eats and drinks sensibly, exercises moderately, and sleeps regularly, then one lives longer (Belloc, 1973; Belloc & Breslow, 1972). By some estimates, the majority of people's physical illnesses are contributed to importantly by their lifestyle—that is, behavior. It is therefore clear that explanatory style, as a distal influence on helplessness, should be relevant to behavior, affecting whether someone initiates goal-directed actions in the first place and sustains them in the long run.

In a series of studies, we have looked specifically at the relationship between explanatory style and health-relevant behavior. Our findings support this analysis. Individuals with a pessimistic explanatory style do not do the sorts of things that lead to long-term well-being. Unlike their more optimistic counterparts, they smoke, drink, and refrain from exercise (Peterson, 1988). When they happen to fall ill, they respond in a passive and helpless manner (Lin & Peterson, 1990). In contrast, individuals with a more optimistic explanatory style take active steps in order to feel better (Peterson, Colvin, & Lin, 1992).

There is an apparent puzzle here. We have already noted that pessimistic individuals visit doctors more frequently than optimistic individuals, but now we are saying that optimists are more likely to respond to illness with active means, which of course include visiting a physician. Can both of these conclusions be true? Yes. If an optimist and a pessimist are both ill, the optimist is more likely to seek and follow medical advice. However, over time, pessimists are more likely to fall ill and thus have more reason to visit their doctor.

In one of our studies, the majority of our subjects who happened to fall ill had colds (Peterson et al., 1992). We ascertained the relationship between taking active steps in order to feel better and whether one actually did feel better the following week. There was no link evident. In other words, it made no difference in the short run, if one is suffering from a cold, whether one rests more, increases fluid intake, and the like.

But does this mean that behavior has nothing to do with health? Of course not, because the epidemiological evidence here is indisputable. What it does mean is that the links between behavior and health are distant and somewhat subtle. They must be accepted on faith, as it were, and not because they are immediately self-evident. And this explains why people with a pessimistic ex-planatory style do not engage in health-promoting activities. They see no point. Their fatalism overrides their abstract knowledge. In contrast, the optimistic individual believes that what he or she does in the present will have an effect in the future.

Interpersonal Pathways

Other people are good for us. Those who find themselves in supportive relation-ships with others are healthier and live longer (e.g., House, Robbins, & Metzner, 1982). The explanations for these effects are fully as complex as those accounting for the link between explanatory style and health, so let us merely take the beneficial effects of other people as a given and ask what explanatory style has to do with social relationships.

Those with a pessimistic explanatory style are more likely to experience loneliness (Anderson & Arnoult, 1985), which means that we have yet another plausible path linking explanatory style and poor health. Just what is it about a pessimistic explanatory style that leads to loneliness? Here we enter speculative territory, but among the possibilities is that the pessimistic individual initiates fewer attempts to be friends with others. And once in a relationship, this person probably turns others off. Gotlib and Beatty (1985), for example, did an experiment in which they showed subjects brief descriptions of other people, exactly the same except for how these other people explained the causes of bad events. Some used pessimistic explanations, whereas others used more efficacious ones. Then the subjects were asked to note their reactions to these people. Sure enough, the pessimistic individuals were responded to more negatively than were the optimistic individuals. We imagine that as such scenarios unfold again and again in real life, the eventual result is alienation and therefore increased risk for illness. Laugh and the world laughs with you; cry and you cry all alone . . . and perhaps fall ill as a result!

Cultural Pathways

A final topic is the possible link between the optimisn inherent in a culture and the physical health of individuals in that culture. I coin the term *collective optimism* to describe the shared belief of people in a group that the causes of bad events that befall them are external and circumscribed (Peterson & Bossio, 1991). This definition intentionally parallels our notion of an individual's optimistic explanatory style. *Collective pessimism* is obviously the group equivalent of an individual's pessimistic explanatory style. What are the consequences of collective optimism? We hypothesize that collective optimism benefits a group just as an optimistic explanatory style benefits the individual. It should be associated with perseverance, achievement, and good morale.

In a preliminary study exploring these possibilities, we administered questionnaires to 150 people who were members of groups ranging from social cliques to service organizations to work teams (Peterson & Jacobs, 1989). We asked them about rate each group's collective optimism versus pessimism, as just defined, and also to indicate how the group responded to setbacks and disappointments. Our results showed that group members make distinctions with respect to the collective optimism or pessimism of groups and further that the more optimistic groups are those with higher morale, greater cohesiveness, lower turnover of members, and greater willingness to take on new projects and goals. We are currently planning further studies in which we actually observe groups in action, rather than relying on the reports of group members.

How do collective optimism and pessimism pertain to physical health? Let us turn to the provocative argument advanced by epidemiologist Sagan (1987).

Although he did not use the term *collective optimism*, Sagan theorized extensively about the notion, linking it explicitly to health. He proposed that the dramatic increase in people's life expectancy over the last few centuries is not the result of medical breakthroughs or public health programs. Instead, the increased longevity of people today is due to their psychological makeup. Compared to their ancestors centuries ago, people nowadays are more resilient and resourceful. They are better educated. They have more meaningful relationships. They have a better articulated sense of self, one characterized by agency and efficacy. These characteristics—which are paraphrased versions of our concept of an optimistic explanatory style—presumably make for healthier people.

Sagan's evidence is historical. He identified those periods in which people's life expectancy showed dramatic increases, and then argued that these jumps do not occur in lockstep with innovations in health practices and services. Rather, they closely lag revisions in how society views the individual. Other theorists have observed that the conception of the *self* indeed varies greatly across historical periods (e.g., Baumeister, 1986), but Sagan was the first to link this variation to culutral differences in longevity.

In Europe during the Middle Ages, for instance, the modern idea of individuality was for the most part absent. One was born into a role, and one stayed in that role. The same has been true historically in small tribal groups. Individuality was not part of the human agenda until relatively recently. Sagan proposed that once people started to think of themselves as individual entities with an effect on the world, they became healthier and thus increased their life expectancy.

Sagan's ideas converge with our conclusions about what happens at the level of individuals. Indeed, individual optimism is legitimized (or not) at the societal level. During its existence, the United States has been an extremely optimistic nation. If and when this societal optimism wanes, then so too will individual optimism. Will the health of our nation take a turn for the worse? Sagan made the dire prediction that this is exactly what will happen if and when contemporary Americans become alienated and disenfranchised. Poverty, malnutrition, and the epidemic of drug abuse may threaten our nation not just in obvious biological ways, but also psychologically, by undercutting efficacy and resilience.

UNANSWERED QUESTIONS

The studies in our research program all point to the same conclusion: optimistic thinking is associated with good health, and pessimistic thinking is associated with poor health. There doubtlessly exist numerous mechanisms responsible for these effects, and our work leaves unanswered several important questions.

First, we are not sure if explanatory style affects the onset of illness, its course once it begins, or both. Different processes may be implicated depending on the answer to this question. Different sorts of psychological interventions may be needed depending on the answer.

Second, we do not know if the relationship between explanatory style and health is specific to a particular type of illness or not. We saw in the studies of college students that colds and the flu seem to be influenced by explanatory style, but this does not mean that other illnesses are not. In the Harvard Study of Adult Development, illness was operationalized in nonspecific terms. The men in this study suffered from a variety of physical problems. So, we suspect a nonspecific link, but we are not entirely sure. There could be one primary problem associated with pessimistic explanatory style, from which other illnesses stem.

Third, we do not know how men and women might differ with respect to explanatory style and its relationship to good health. A familiar finding from epidemiology is that women have more illnesses but men die at a younger age (Verbrugge, 1989). Stated another way, the illnesses of women are not as likely to be fatal as the illnesses of men. Does explanatory style have anything to do with this pattern?

At least on the face of it, we would think that explanatory style is not able to explain both findings. Perhaps it can explain neither. If there is a gender difference in explanatory style, either women are more optimistic than men, or vice versa. Which ever gender is more optimistic should have fewer illnesses and should live longer. At the present time, we cannot even say whether men and women differ with respect to explanatory style. There is no definitive evidence from our research that men and women differ in their explanatory styles, which may mean that optimism and pessimism have nothing to do with gender differences in morbidity and mortality.

Fourth, we do not know if explanatory style can be changed so that it has an effect on health. We have mentioned the finding that cognitive therapy can make someone's explanatory style more optimistic. What we do not yet understand is the effects of such an intervention on health. Is a "born-again" optimist as able to reap the benefits of positive thinking as someone who has explained events optimistically all along? If our hypothesized mechanisms linking explanatory style and health prove operative, an optimistic explanatory style, whenever it is achieved, should be beneficial. But these mechanisms are mundane processes, not miraculous events. Whatever effects they produce take place over time, perhaps years or even decades. One must undertake health-promoting interventions with a long view and modest expectations. And one should supplement explanatory style change by intervening as well at points closer to good health— such as, by changing one's diet and exercise habits. Needless to say, one can change one's behavior most readily by changing how one thinks, which means that behavior change and explanatory style change might mutually support one another and thus should be pursued in tandem.

We raise these unanswered questions to be honest about the state of our knowledge. We should not overstate what we know about explanatory style and health. We think that the association between thinking "good" and feeling "well" is a valid one, but we need to do a great deal more work in order to make sense of it and use it to guide interventions.

15

▼▼▼▼▼▼▼

Afterword:
The Future of the Field

Gregory McClellan Buchanan
Martin E. P. Seligman
University of Pennsylvania

The chapters in this volume present the extensive literature on explanatory style. Topics have ranged from predicting performance in college swimmers (chapter 10) to death from coronary heart disease (chapter 13). From subtypes of depression (chapter 7) to victory in presidential elections (chapter 11). The field of explanatory style clearly spans a huge segment of personal and social experience. The field is also expanding in many different directions and the future is filled with promise. Perhaps the most exciting aspect of current research is the programs designed to alter explanatory style and so prevent some of the problems that pessimistic explanatory style brings in its wake. The implications of this work are far reaching: the prevention of depression, anxiety, ill health, and the establishment of psychological well-being and the ability to achieve and persevere. Before discussing this recent work, we review some of the major topics of this volume and clarify some of the questions we believe remain unanswered.

Where does our explanatory style come from? Explanatory style is a relatively stable personality trait—indeed its stability has been demonstrated over five decades (Burns & Seligman, 1989). It also appears to be in place, and to remain consistent, by about age 9 (Nolen-Hoeksema, Girgus, & Seligman, 1986; see chapter 4, this volume). Yet its origins are still somewhat mysterious. Environmental causes acting on the individual such as modeling, performance feedback and, recently, interpersonal trust have been implicated (Eisner, 1992; see chapter 3, this volume). There is also evidence that aspects of the environment (e.g., the political system) can influence the explanatory style of an entire society (Oettingen & Seligman, 1990; see chapter 12, this volume). Hints of a genetic component—a much higher concordance rate for monozygotic twins than for dizygotic twins—have also been reported (Schulman, Keith, & Seligman, 1991). Uncontrollable negative events themselves, the stressors in the diathesis-stress model discussed throughout this volume, may also contribute to the development of our explanatory style (Nolen-Hoeksema, 1991). At the risk of being anesthetic, we suspect that the explanatory style we develop is likely to be multiply determined—an interaction between biological factors such as temperament and disposition, culture, and major environmental events, particularly failure and success.

By what mechanism does explanatory style influence the wide variety of outcomes discussed in this volume? The relationship between pessimism and poor physical health, for example, is not proposed to be a strictly causal one. Rather, possessing a pessimistic explanatory style is a risk factor for later ill health in just the same sense that smoking is a risk factor for lung cancer. But what are the intervening steps? How does explanatory style influence molar performance? Mental health? Endurance? Resilience? Neurotransmitter changes? Much current research is aimed at answering these questions.

Is explanatory style specific to certain types of psychopathology or does possessing a pessimistic explanatory style leave one at risk for a host of mental illnesses? The theoretical model presented by Abramson, Metalsky, and Alloy (1989; chapter 7, this volume) indicates that pessimism should specifically predict a subtype of depression dubbed "hopelessness depression." This subtype, characterized by retarded initiation of voluntary responses, sad affect, early insomnia, and increased suicidal ideation has not, as yet, been segregated into a clinical syndrome. But evidence to date indicates that it does exist and that it may be particularly related to an insidious explanatory style. We eagerly await further validation of this theory.

What about anxiety? The high comorbidity between anxiety and mood disorders, coupled with the fact that both types of pathology are characterized by maladaptive cognitions, suggests that there might be a specific explanatory style for anxiety disorders. There is evidence that a pessimistic explanatory style may be a risk factor for social phobia and agoraphobia (Heimberg et al., 1989), whereas a distinct pattern of explanatory style might characterize posttraumatic stress disorder (Mikulincer & Solomon, 1988; see chapter 8, this volume). Presently, there is a pressing need for more longitudinal studies that include appropriate nondepressed and nonanxious control groups and take measures of explanatory style premorbidly before the exact nature of these relationships can be teased out.

Are there specific physical health outcomes that stem from specific explanatory styles, or is pessimism globally bad for health? Infectious illnesses, by way of a compromised immune system, have been predicted from explanatory style scores (Peterson, 1988). So too has death from coronary heart disease (Buchanan, 1989) and longevity in general (Peterson, Seligman, & Vaillant, 1988; see chapters 13 and 14, this volume). Is there one physical parameter involved here (e.g., increased endorphinergic action) or are there many? Is pessimism's effect on health-risk and health-preventative behaviors an intervening factor in the production of poor health? If we had a better idea of the mechanism by which pessimism produces worse health—immune system, poor health habits, more bad life events, less social support—the answer to such questions might fall out directly.

What of the model itself? Explanatory style research was born from experiments on learned helplessness (Seligman, 1974, 1975) that then led to the development of the reformulated theory (Abramson, Seligman, & Teasdale, 1978) with pessimistic causal explanations as a risk factor for helplessness deficits (see chapter 1, this volume). Yet much of the research has often ignored some of the variables in this model. The model originally stated that a pessimistic explanatory style was a risk factor if the individual was exposed to uncontrollable, negative events, such as failure and rejection. But many of the prospective studies linking explanatory style to depression, anxiety, achievement, and physical health have not assessed the presence or absence of these events. In fact, a good prospective study investigating the interaction between negative life events and pessimism in a clinically depressed population is still needed.

Part of the reason for the failure to assess such events is the likelihood that objective events are a much less proximal cause than the perception that something bad has happened. The link between objective bad events and the perception of loss is very loose. Many, perhaps most, instances of the perception of loss occur without a major negative event setting it off. And many objective bad events do not set off the perception of loss. Refinement is needed in the assessment of bad events, loss, and hassle to make the independent variable better capture the perception of loss.

Recently there has been a return to the notion of diathesis-stress, particularly in the model proposed by Abramson et al. (chapter 7, this volume). Robins and Hayes (chapter 5, this volume) point out that prospective studies of explanatory style and depression have been more supportive of the model if the diathesis-stress component was examined. But the relationship may be more complicated than that initially proposed. For example, Oettingen (chapter 12, this volume) hypothesizes that it was the increased frequency of uncontrollable negative events under communism that led to the increased pessimistic explanatory style found in East Berlin. Similarly, Nolen-Hoeksema and Girgus (chapter 4, this volume) note that an early childhood experience with a negative event (such as depression) may predispose one to develop a pessimistic outlook. That is, these events may first act as the stress in the diathesis-stress model and then they may go on to influence the development of the diathesis itself. To complicate matters further, possessing a pessimistic explanatory style may increase the number of negative life events one experiences (Robins & Hayes; see chapter 5, this volume). That is, the diathesis leads to increased stress and the stress can produce the diathesis!

This is not to indicate that the reasoning is circular, but that the two major variables mutually interact. But what are we to make of this? It is essential that future research examine both explanatory style and negative life events in a prospective manner, and that a clearer theory of their mutual influence emerge.

We can also wonder about the uses of the individual dimensions of explanatory style. Internality, stability, and globality are not the only ways to slice the explanatory pie. With respect to these individual dimensions, there has been a movement away from the theory. The theory stated that the specific components will be related to specific aspects of depression, but we do not think that the investigation of the specific properties of the separate dimensions has yet been adequate. Theoretically and empirically it is permissible to use composite measures of explanatory style (see chapters 1 and 2, this volume) but can we gain anything from individual measures? It would be very useful to see more studies of the relative predictive power of the individual dimensions, compared to the composite, in turn compared to alternative dimensions for parsing explanatory style.

We also need to think more about people's explanations for positive events. The learned helplessness and reformulated models have little to say about positive events, and they are not routinely reported in the literature. Yet there are reasons to believe that they may be of some importance. For example, Mineka et al. (chapter 8, this volume) discuss how reactions to positive events may differentiate between those who become depressed and those who become anxious. Although explanations for positive events can be assessed with the ASQ and the CAVE techniques, they have few theoretical underpinnings and are often found to be less predictive than explanations for negative events. Perhaps it is time to rethink what positive events mean to us.

PREVENTION AND CHANGE IN EXPLANATORY STYLE

Seligman was with Jonas Salk on the 30th anniversary of the first trials of the Salk vaccine. When Seligman asked Salk what he would be doing today if he were a young scientist, he replied without hesitation, "I'd still do immunization, but I'd do it psychologically rather than biologically. That's a task for the poets of biology."

There are three "poets of biology" who have been doing just this: Lisa Jaycox, Jane Gillham, and Karen Reivich, all graduate students at the University of Pennsylvania. They have been using the techniques of cognitive therapy in a preventive mode on children at risk for depression, asking if depression can be prevented. Their results are very promising and with their kind permission, we want to end the chapter about the future of the field by describing their results briefly.

Can we buffer children against depression by teaching them cognitive techniques? They use the term *prevention* to refer to two related concepts: (a) enduring relief—long after the end of the treatment—among those experiencing depressive symptoms at the start of intervention, and (b) the subsequent nonoccurrence of expected depressive symptoms that would otherwise have occurred in those who were not depressed at the outset (Gillham, Reivich, Jaycox, & Seligman, 1993; Jaycox, Reivich, Gillham, & Seligman, 1993).

They identified normal 10- to 11-year-old school children as "at risk" based on two factors: their current level of depressive symptoms and their perception of parental conflict. They used current level of symptoms because children who exhibit depressive symptoms currently are much more likely to exhibit them in the future, and they used perceptions of parental conflict because parental conflict predicts increased depressive symptoms in children (Seligman, 1991).

The 18-hour program included two main components: a cognitive component and a social problem-solving component. The cognitive component was based largely on theories and techniques of Beck (1967, 1976), Ellis (1962), and Seligman (1991). They focused on explanatory style because it is an active ingredient in successful outcome of cognitive therapy with depressed adults (DeRubeis et al., 1990; Seligman, Castellon et al., 1988).

The social problem-solving component targeted conduct problems and interpersonal problems that are often associated with depression in children. They taught children perspective taking, peer group entry skills, and techniques for coping with parental conflict. They also taught children to set goals, to generate multiple solutions, and to make decisions by weighing pros and cons of each option.

They found evidence that the program prevented depressive symptoms. Overall, children in the prevention group reported markedly fewer depressive symptoms on the Children's Depression Inventory (CDI) at 12-, 18-, and 24-month follow-up assessments. Children in the prevention group were also less likely than controls to report moderate or severe depressive symptoms. At the 12-month follow-up, 29% of the children in the control group had CDI scores greater than or equal to 15 (the cutoff for "moderate" depression). Only 7.4% of the prevention group had CDI scores at or above this level. At the 18-month follow-up, these percentages were 33% and 12%, respectively. At the 24-month follow-up, 44% of the controls had CDI scores greater or equal to 15, whereas only 22% of the prevention group had scores at or above this level.

There was evidence that the program produced enduring relief of depressive symptoms in children initially reporting depressive symptoms. The results were analyzed separately for those children with pre-CDI scores greater or equal to the sample mean (9.56). The initially symptomatic children in the prevention group reported an average of fewer depressive symptoms than controls at 12, 18, and 24 months. There was also evidence that the program prevented depressive symptoms in children with few or no initial symptoms. Initially asymptomatic children from the prevention group reported fewer depressive symptoms than controls at 12-, 18-, and 24-month follow-ups. Initially asymptomatic children in the prevention group were also less likely than controls to report moderate to severe levels of symptoms. At the 12-month follow-up, 22% of the children in the control group had CDI scores greater than or equal to 15. Only 3% of children in the prevention group had CDI scores at or above this level. At the 18-month follow-up, these percentages were 30% and 7%, respectively. At the 24-month follow-up, 27% of children in the control group and 20% of children in the prevention group had scores at or above this level.

The program also improved children's explanatory style. Children who participated in the prevention program had a more optimistic explanatory style for negative events (CN) than controls. Changes in explanatory style (CN) were significantly correlated with changes in depressive symptoms over the 2-year period. The program had a particularly strong effect on the negative stable dimension of explanatory style, the dimension focused on in the explanatory style training.

Perhaps most surprising are the effects of the prevention program over time. First there existed a significant linear effect for time, indicating that depressive symptoms increased in both groups as the children got older over the 2-year follow-up. But there was also a significant interaction of time with condition, indicating that the control group showed a greater increase in depressive symptoms than the prevention group. So it appears that the prevention effect on depressive symptoms grew over time.

This study fills us with optimism about the future of the field. We believe that the next decade will see the development of prevention programs in just those domains where explanatory style has been shown to be a risk factor. Such a program is currently in place at the University of Pennsylvania. Freshmen identified to be at risk for future depression (on the basis of their explanatory style) complete an 8-session cognitive therapy program (targeted at preventing episodes of depression), or serve as controls. We speculate that changing explanatory style from pessimistic to optimistic in preventive programs such as this may decrease the rate of depression and anxiety, increase success at school, work, and on the playing field, and even, perhaps, improve physical health.

References

Abramson, L. Y. (1978). *Universal versus personal helplessness*. Unpublished doctoral dissertation, University of Pennsylvania.

Abramson, L. Y., Dykman, B. M., & Needles, D. J. (1991). Attributional style and theory: Let no one tear them asunder. *Psychological Inquiry, 2*, 11–13.

Abramson, L. Y., Garber, J., Edwards, N. B., & Seligman, M. E. P. (1978). Expectancy changes in depression and schizophrenia. *Journal of Abnormal Psychology, 87*, 49–74.

Abramson, L. Y., Metalsky, G. I., & Alloy, L. B. (1988). The hopelessness theory of depression: Does the research test the theory? In L. Y. Abramson (Ed.), *Social cognition and clinical psychology: A synthesis* (pp. 33–65). New York: Guilford.

Abramson, L. Y., Metalsky, G. I., & Alloy, L. B. (1989). Hopelessness depression: A theory-based subtype of depression. *Psychological Review, 96*, 358–372.

Abramson, L. Y., Seligman, M. E. P., & Teasdale, J. D. (1978). Learned helplessness in humans: Critique and reformulation. *Journal of Abnormal Psychology, 87*, 49–74.

Ackermann, R., & DeRubeis, R. J. (1991). Is depressive realism real? *Clinical Psychology Review, 11*, 565–584.

Adams, F. G., & Klein, L. R. (1972). Anticipations variables in macro-economic models. In B. Strumpel, J. N. Morgan, & E. Zahn (Eds.), *Human behavior in economic affairs: Essays in honor of George Katona* (pp. 69–93). San Francisco, CA: Jossey-Bass.

Adler, A. (1964). Inferiority feelings and defiance and obedience. In H. L. Ansbacher & R. R. Ansbacher (Eds.), *The individual psychology of Alfred Adler*. New York: Harper. (Original work published 1910).

Adler, A. (1927). *The theory and practice of individual psychology*. New York: Harcourt Brace.

Alden, L. (1987). Attributional responses of anxious individuals to different patterns of social feedback: Nothing succeeds like improvement. *Journal of Personality and Social Psychology, 52*, 100–106.

Alexander, F. (1939). Emotional factors in essential hypertension. *Psychosomatic Medicine, 1*, 139–152.

Alexander, F. (1950). *Psychosomatic medicine: Its principles and applications*. New York: Norton.

Allgood-Merten, B., Lewinsohn, P. M., & Hops, H. (1990). Sex differences and adolescent depression. *Journal of Abnormal Psychology, 99,* 55–63.

Alloy, L. B. (1982). The role of perceptions and attributions for response-outcome noncontingency in learned helplessness: A commentary and discussion. *Journal of Personality, 50,* 443–479.

Alloy, L. B., & Abramson, L. Y. (1979). Judgment of contingency in depressed and nondepressed students: Sadder but wiser? *Journal of Experimental Psychology: General, 108,* 441–485.

Alloy, L. B., & Abramson, L. Y. (1988). Depressive realism: Four theoretical perspectives. In L. B. Alloy (Ed.), *Cognitive processes in depression* (pp. 223–265). New York: Guilford.

Alloy, L. B., & Ahrens, A. (1987). Depression and pessimism for the future: Biased use of statistically relevant information in predictions for self versus others. *Journal of Personality and Social Psychology, 52,* 366–378.

Alloy, L. B., Albright, J. S., Abramson, L. Y., & Dykman, B. M. (1990). Depressive realism and nondepressive optimistic illusions: The role of the self. In R. E. Ingram (Ed.), *Contemporary psychological approaches to depression* (pp. 71–86). New York: Plenum.

Alloy, L. B., Albright, J. S., Fresco, D. M., & Whitehouse, W. G. (1992a). *Stability of cognitive styles across the mood swings of DSM-III(R) cyclothymics, dysthymics, and hypomanics: A longitudinal study in a college sample.* Unpublished manuscript, Temple University, Philadelphia, PA.

Alloy, L. B., Albright, J. S., Fresco, D. M., & Whitehouse, W. G. (1992b). *Predicting depressive and hypomanic symptoms in students with subsyndromal mood disorders: The interaction of cognitive styles and life events.* Unpublished manuscript, Temple University, Philadelphia, PA.

Alloy, L. B., & Clements, C. M. (1991, August). *The hopelessness theory of depression: Test of the symptom component in late adolescents.* Paper presented at the American Psychological Association Meeting, San Francisco, CA.

Alloy, L. B., Hartlage, S., & Abramson, L. Y. (1988). Testing the cognitive diathesis-stress theories of depression: Issues of research design, conceptualization and assessment. In L. B. Alloy (Ed.), *Cognitive processes in depression* (pp. 31–73). New York: Guilford.

Alloy, L. B., & Just, N. (1992, May). *Attributional style and variability of depressive symptoms: A prospective behavioral high risk paradigm.* Paper presented at the Midwestern Psychological Association Meeting, Chicago, IL.

Alloy, L. B., Kayne, N. T., Romer, D., & Crocker, J. (1992). *Predicting depressive reactions in the classroom: A test of a cognitive diathesis stress theory of depression with causal modeling techniques.* Unpublished manuscript, Temple University, Philadelphia, PA.

Alloy, L. B., Kelly, K. A., Mineka, S., & Clements, C. M. (1990). Comorbidity in anxiety and depressive disorders: A helplessness/hopelessness perspective. In J. D. Maser & C. R. Cloninger (Eds.), *Comorbidity in anxiety and mood disorders* (pp. 499–544). Washington, DC: American Psychiatric Press.

Alloy, L. B., Lipman, A. J., & Abramson, L. Y. (1992). Attributional style as a vulnerability factor for depression: Validation by past history of mood disorders. *Cognitive Therapy and Research, 16,* 391–407.

Alloy, L. B., Peterson, C., Abramson, L. Y., & Seligman, M. E. P. (1984). Attributional style and the generality of learned helplessness. *Journal of Personality and Social Psychology, 46,* 681–687.

Allport, G. W. (1942). *The use of personal documents in psychological science.* New York: Social Science Research Council.

American Psychiatric Association. (1980). *Diagnostic and statistical manual of mental disorders* (3rd ed.). Washington, DC: Author.

Anderson, C. A., & Arnoult, L. H. (1985). Attributional style and everyday problems in living: Depression, loneliness, and shyness. *Social Cognition, 3,* 16–35.

Anderson, C. A., Horowitz, L. M., & French, R. D. (1983). Attributional style of lonely and depressed people. *Journal of Personality and Social Psychology, 45,* 127–136.

Anderson, J. C., Williams, S., McGee, R., & Silva, P. A. (1987). DSM-III disorders in preadolescent children. *Archives of General Psychiatry, 44,* 69–76.

Angst, J., Vollrath, M., Merikangas, K. R., & Ernst, C. (1990). Comorbidity of anxiety and depression in the Zurich cohort study of young adults. In J. D. Maser & C. R. Cloninger (Eds.), *Comorbidity in anxiety and mood disorders* (pp. 123–138). Washington, DC: American Psychiatric Press.

Arieti, S., & Bemporad, J. R. (1980). The psychological organization of depression. *American Journal of Psychiatry, 137*, 1360–1365.

Arkin, R. M., & Maruyama, G. M. (1979). Attribution, affect, and college exam performance. *Journal of Educational Psychology, 71*, 85–93.

Arntz, A., Gerlsma, C., & Albersnagel, F. A. (1985). Attributional style questioned: Psychometric evaluation of the ASQ in Dutch adolescents. *Advances in Behaviour Research and Therapy, 7*, 55–89.

Asarnow, J. R., & Bates, S. (1988). Depression in child psychiatric inpatients: Cognitive and attributional patterns. *Journal of Abnormal Child Psychology, 16*, 601–615.

Asarnow, J. R., Carlson, G. A., & Guthrie, D. (1987). Coping strategies, self-perceptions, hopelessness, and perceived family environments in depressed and suicidal children. *Journal of Consulting and Clinical Psychology, 55*, 361–366.

Atkinson, J. W. (1957). Motivational determinants of risk-taking behavior. *Psychological Review, 64*, 359–372.

Atkinson, J. W. (1958). *Motives in fantasy action and society.* Princeton, NJ: Van Nostrand.

Atlas, G. D., & Peterson, C. (1990). Explanatory style and gambling: How pessimists respond to lost wagers. *Behaviour Research and Therapy, 28*, 523–529.

Ayalti, H. J. (Ed.). (1949). *Yiddish Proverbs.* New York: Schocken Books.

Baltes, M. M., & Carstensen, L. L. (1994). *The process of succesful aging.* Unpublished manuscript, Free University of Berlin.

Bandura, A. (1969). *Principles of behavior modification.* New York: Holt, Rinehart & Winston.

Bandura, A. (1973). *Aggression: A social learning analysis.* Englewood Cliffs, NJ: Prentice-Hall.

Bandura, A. (1977a). Self-efficacy: Toward a unifying theory of behavioral change. *Psychological Review, 84*, 191–215.

Bandura, A. (1977b). *Social learning theory.* Englewood Cliffs, NJ: Prentice-Hall.

Bandura, A. (1978). The self system in reciprocal determinism. *American Psychologist, 33*, 344–358.

Bandura, A. (1982). Self-efficacy mechanism in human agency. *American Psychologist, 37*, 122–147.

Bandura, A. (1986). *Social foundations of thought and action: A social-cognitive theory.* Englewood Cliffs, NJ: Prentice-Hall.

Bandura, A., & Walters, R. (1963). *Social learning and personality development.* New York: Holt, Rinehart & Winston.

Barber, J. P., & DeRubeis, R. J. (1989). On second thought: Where the action is in cognitive therapy for depression. *Cognitive Therapy and Research, 13*, 441–457.

Barlow, D. H. (1985). Dimensions of anxiety disorders. In A. Tuma & J. Maser (Eds.), *Anxiety and the anxiety disorders* (pp. 479–500). Hillsdale, NJ: Lawrence Erlbaum Associates.

Barlow, D. H. (1988). *Anxiety and its disorders: The nature and treatment of anxiety and panic.* New York: Guilford.

Barlow, D. H. (1991). Disorders of emotion. *Psychological Inquiry, 2*, 58–71.

Barlow, D. H., DiNardo, P. A., Vermilyea, B. B., Vermilyea, J. A., & Blanchard, E. B. (1986). Co-morbidity and depression among the anxiety disorders: Issues in diagnosis and classification. *Journal of Nervous and Mental Disease, 174*, 63–72.

Barnett, P. A., & Gotlib, I. H. (1988). Psychosocial functioning and depression: Distinguishing among antecedents, concomitants, and consequences. *Psychological Bulletin, 104*, 97–126.

Baron, R. M., & Kenny, D. A. (1986). The moderator–mediator variable distinction in social psychological research: Conceptual, strategic, and statistical considerations. *Journal of Personality and Social Psychology, 51*, 1173–1182.

Baron, S. (1976). *The Russian Jew under tsar and Soviets.* New York: MacMillan.

Basow, S. A. (1986). *Gender stereotypes: Traditions and alternatives* (2nd ed.). Monterey, CA: Brooks/Cole.

Baumeister, R. F. (1986). *Identity: Cultural change and the struggle for self.* New York: Oxford.

Beck, A. T. (1967). *Depression: Clinical, experimental, and theoretical aspects.* New York: Harper & Row.

Beck, A. T. (1970). Cognitive therapy: Nature and relation to behavior therapy. *Behavior Therapy, 1,* 184–200.

Beck, A. T. (1976). *Cognitive therapy and the emotional disorders.* New York: International Universities Press.

Beck, A. T. (1983). Cognitive therapy of depression: New perspectives. In P. Clayton & J. Barrett (Eds.), *Treatment of depression: Old controversies and new approaches* (pp. 265–290). New York: Raven.

Beck, A. T. (1984). Cognition and therapy. *Archives of General Psychiatry, 41,* 1112–1114.

Beck, A. T., & Clark, D. A. (1988). Anxiety and depression: An information processing perspective. *Anxiety Research, 1,* 23–36.

Beck, A. T., & Emery, G. (1985). *Anxiety disorders and phobias: A cognitive perspective.* New York: Basic Books.

Beck, A. T., Kovacs, M., & Weissman, A. N. (1975). Hopelessness and suicidal behavior: An overview. *Journal of the American Medical Association, 234,* 1146–1149.

Beck, A. T., Riskind, J. H., Brown, G., & Steer, R. A. (1988). Levels of hopelessness in DSM-III disorders: A partial test of content-specificity in depression. *Cognitive Therapy and Research, 12,* 459–469.

Beck, A. T., Rush, A. J., Shaw, B. F., & Emery, G. (1979). *Cognitive therapy of depression: A treatment manual.* New York: Guilford.

Beck, A. T., Ward, C. H., Mendelson, M., Mock, J., & Erbaugh, J. (1961). An inventory for measuring depression. *Archives of General Psychiatry, 4,* 561–571.

Beck, A. T., & Weishaar, M. E. (1990). Suicide risk assessment and prediction. *Crisis, 11,* 22–30.

Beck, A. T., Weissman, A. N., Lester, D., & Trexler, L. (1974). The measurement of pessimism: The Hopelessness Scale. *Journal of Consulting and Clinical Psychology, 42,* 861–865.

Belloc, N. B. (1973). Relationship of health practices and mortality. *Preventive Medicine, 2,* 67–81.

Belloc, N. B., & Breslow, L. (1972). Relationship of physical health status and family practices. *Preventive Medicine, 1,* 409–421.

Ben-Amos, D., & Mintz, J. (Eds.). (1970). *In praise of the Baal Shem Tov.* New York: Schocken Books.

Benfield, C. Y., Palmer, D. J., Pfefferbaum, B., & Stowe, M. L. (1988). A comparison of depressed and nondepressed disturbed children on measures of attributional style, hopelessness, life stress, and temperament. *Journal of Abnormal Child Psychology, 16,* 397–410.

Berndt, S. M., Berndt, D. J., & Kaiser, C. F. (1982). Attributional styles for helplessness and depression: The importance of sex and situational context. *Sex Roles, 8,* 433–441.

Berry, J. W. (1969). On cross-cultural comparability. *International Journal of Psychology, 4,* 119–128.

Berry, J. W. (1980a). Introduction to methodology. In H. C. Triandis & J. W. Berry (Eds.), *Handbook of cross-cultural psychology: Vol. 2. Methodology* (pp. 1–28). Boston, MA: Allyn & Bacon.

Berry, J. W. (1980b). Social and cultural change. In H. C. Triandis & R. W. Brislin (Eds.), *Handbook of cross-cultural psychology: Vol. 5. Social psychology* (pp. 211–279). Boston, MA: Allyn & Bacon.

Berry, J. W. (1989). Psychology of acculturation. In J. J. Berman (Ed.), *Nebraska Symposium on Motivation* (Vol. 37, pp. 201–234). Lincoln: University of Nebraska Press.

Berry, J. W., Poortinga, Y. H., Segall, M. H., & Dasen, P. R. (1992). *Cross-cultural psychology: Research and applications.* New York: Cambridge University Press.

Bierwisch, M. (1990). Wissenschaft im realen Sozialismus [Science in real socialism. *Coursebook*]. *Kursbuch, 101,* 112–123.

Birnbaum, P. (1949). *Daily prayer book: Ha-siddur ha-shalem.* New York: Hebrew Publishing Co.

Birnbaum, P. (1951). *High holiday prayer book.* New York: Hebrew Publishing Co.

Blackburn, I. M., & Bishop, S. (1983). Changes in cognition with pharmacotherapy and cognitive therapy. *British Journal of Psychiatry, 143*, 609–617.

Blackburn, I. M., Eunson, K. M., & Bishop, S. (1986). A two-year naturalistic follow-up of depressed patients treated with cognitive therapy, pharmacotherapy and a combination of both. *Journal of Affective Disorders, 10*, 67–75.

Blaney, P. H. (1986). Affect and memory: A review. *Psychological Bulletin, 99*, 229–246.

Blaney, P. H., Behar, V., & Head, R. (1980). Two measures of depressive cognitions: Their association with depression and with each other. *Journal of Abnormal Psychology, 89*, 678–682.

Blatt, S. J., Quinlan, D. M., Chevron, E. S., McDonald, C., & Zuroff, D. (1982). Dependency and self-criticism: Psychological dimensions of depression. *Journal of Consulting and Clinical Psychology, 50*, 113–124.

Blumberg, S. H., & Izard, C. E. (1985). Affective and cognitive characteristics of depression in 10-year and 11-year-old children. *Journal of Personality and Social Psychology, 49*, 194–202.

Bochner, S. (1980). Unobtrusive methods in cross-cultural experimentation. In H. C. Triandis & J. W. Berry (Eds.), *Handbook of cross-cultural psychology: Vol. 2. Methodology* (pp. 319–387). Boston, MA: Allyn & Bacon.

Bolles, R. C. (1972). Reinforcement, expectancy, and learning. *Psychological Review, 79*, 394–409.

Bonner, R. L., & Rich, A. R. (1988). Negative life stress, social problem-solving, self-appraisal, and hopelessness: Implications for suicide research. *Cognitive Therapy and Research, 12*, 549–556.

Booth-Kewley, S., & Friedman, H. S. (1987). Psychological predictors of heart disease: A quantitative review. *Psychological Bulletin, 101*, 343–362.

Bower, G. H. (1981). Mood and memory. *American Psychologist, 36*, 129–148.

Bowlby, J. (1973). *Attachment and loss: Vol. 2. Separation: Anxiety and anger.* New York: Basic Books.

Bowlby, J. (1977). The making and breaking of affectional bonds: I. Aetiology and psychopathology in the light of attachment theory. *British Journal of Psychiatry, 130*, 201–210.

Bowlby, J. (1980). *Attachment and loss: Vol. 3. Loss: Sadness and depression.* New York: Basic Books.

Brewin, C. R. (1985). Depression and causal attributions: What is their relation? *Psychological Bulletin, 98*, 297–309.

Brewin, C. R. (1988). *Cognitive foundations of clinical psychology.* Hillsdale, NJ: Lawrence Erlbaum Associates.

Brewin, C. R., & Furnham, A. (1986). Attributional versus preattributional variables in self-esteem and depression: A comparison and test of learned helplessness theory. *Journal of Personality and Social Psychology, 50*, 1013–1020.

Brewin, C. R., & Furnham, A. (1987). Dependency, self-criticism, and depressive attributional style. *British Journal of Clinical Psychology, 26*, 225–226.

Brislin, R. W. (1980). Translation and content analysis of oral and written materials. In H. C. Triandis & J. W. Berry (Eds.), *Handbook of cross-cultural psychology: Vol. 2. Methodology* (pp. 389–444). Boston, MA: Allyn & Bacon.

Brislin, R. W., Lonner, W. J., & Thorndike, R. M. (1973). *Cross-cultural research methods.* New York: Wiley.

Broadbeck, C., & Michelson, L. (1987). Problem-solving skills and attributional styles of agoraphobics. *Cognitive Therapy and Research, 11*, 593–610.

Brown, G. W., & Harris, T. O. (1978). *Social origins of depression: A study of psychiatric disorder in women.* New York: Free Press.

Brown, J. A. C. (1964). *Freud and the post-Freudians.* New York: Penguin.

Brown, J. D., & Siegel, J. M. (1988). Attributions for negative life events and depression: The role of perceived control. *Journal of Personality and Social Psychology, 54*, 316–322.

Brown, J. D., & Silberschatz, G. (1989). Dependency, self criticism, and depressive attributional style. *Journal of Abnormal Psychology, 98*, 187–188.

Bruhn, J. G., Chandler, B., & Wolf, S. (1969). A psychological study of survivors and non-survivors of myocardial infarction. *Psychosomatic Medicine, 31,* 8–19.

Buber, M. (Ed.) (1948). *Tales of Hasidim: The late masters.* New York: Schocken Books.

Buber, M. (Ed.) (1975). *Tales of Hasidim: The early masters.* New York: Schocken Books.

Buchanan, G. M. (1989). *Pessimism predicts death from coronary heart disease.* Unpublished master's thesis, University of Pennsylvania.

Buchanan, G. M. (1994). *Health related behaviors in optimistic and pessimistic college students.* Research in progress, University of Pennsylvania.

Bukstel, L. H., & Kilmann, P. R. (1980). Psychological effects of imprisonment on confined individuals. *Psychological Bulletin, 88,* 469–493.

Burns, J. M. (1978). *Leadership.* New York: Harper & Row.

Burns, M. O., & Seligman, M. E. P. (1989). Explanatory style across the life span: Evidence for stability over 52 years. *Journal of Personality and Social Psychology, 56,* 471–477.

Buss, A. (1961). *The psychology of aggression.* New York: Wiley.

Butler, L., Miezitis, S., Friedman, R., & Cole, E. (1980). The effect of two school-based intervention programs on depressive symptoms in preadolescents. *American Educational Research Journal, 17,* 110–119.

Campbell, D. T., & Fiske, D. W. (1959). Convergent and discriminant validity by the multitrait-multimethod matrix. *Psychological Bulletin, 56,* 81–105.

Carroll, J. S. (1978). The effect of imagining an event on expectations for the event: An interpretation in terms of the availability heuristic. *Journal of Personality and Social Psychology, 36,* 1501–1511.

Carver, C. S. (1989). How should multi-faceted personality constructs be tested? Issues illustrated by self-monitoring, attributional style, and hardiness. *Journal of Personality and Social Psychology, 56,* 577–585.

Carver, C. S., & Gaines, J. G. (1987). Optimism, pessimism, and postpartum depression. *Cognitive Therapy and Research, 11,* 449–462.

Carver, C. S., Ganellen, R. J., & Behar-Mitrani, V. (1985). Depression and cognitive style: Comparisons Between measures. *Journal of Personality and Social Psychology, 49,* 722–728.

Chang, W. C. (1985). A cross-cultural study of depressive symptomatology. *Culture, Medicine and Psychiatry, 9,* 295–317.

Chesney, M. A., Hecker, M. H. L., & Black, G. W. (1988). Coronary prone components of Type A behavior in the Western Collaborative Group Study: A new methodology. In B. K. Houston & C. R. Snyder (Eds.), *Type A behavior pattern: Research, theory and intervention* (pp. 168–188). New York: Wiley.

Clark, A. (1983). Hypothetical constructs, circular reasoning, and criteria. *The Journal of Mind and Behavior, 4,* 1–12.

Clark, L. A. (1989). The anxiety and depressive disorders: Descriptive psychopathology and differential diagnosis. In P. C. Kendall & D. Watson (Eds.), *Anxiety and depression: Distinctive and overlapping features* (pp. 83–129). New York: Academic.

Clark, L. A., & Watson, D. (1991a). Theoretical and empirical issues in differentiating depression from anxiety. In J. Becker & A. Kleinman (Eds.), *Psychosocial aspects of mood disorders* (pp. 39–65). Hillsdale, NJ: Lawrence Erlbaum Associates.

Clark, L. A., & Watson, D. (1991b). Tripartite model of anxiety and depression: Psychometric evidence and taxonomic implications. *Journal of Abnormal Psychology, 100,* 316–336.

Clark, L. A., Watson, D., & Mineka, S. (1994). Temperament, personality and the mood and anxiety disorders [Special issue]. *Journal of Abnormal Psychology, 103,* 103–116.

Clary, E. G., & Tesser, A. (1983). Reactions to unexpected events: The naive scientist and interpretive activity. *Personality and Social Psychology Bulletin, 9,* 609–620.

Clements, C. M., & Alloy, L. B. (1990). *Depression, depression proneness and self and other evaluation: Perceiving the self when you believe you are another and others when you believe they are the self.* Unpublished manuscript, Temple University, Philadelphia, PA.

Cochran, S. D., & Hammen, C. L. (1985). Perceptions of stressful life events and depression: A test of attributional models. *Journal of Personality and Social Psychology, 48*, 1562–1571.

Coopersmith, S. (1987). *Self-esteem inventories*. Palo Alto, CA: Consulting Psychologists Press.

Costello, C. G. (1972). Depression: Loss of reinforcers or loss of reinforcer effectiveness? *Behavior Therapy, 3*, 240–247.

Cousins, N. (1981). *The anatomy of an illness*. New York: Norton.

Cox, D. R. (1972). Regression models with life tables (with discussion). *Journal of the Royal Statistical Society of Britain, 34*, 187–220.

Coyne, J. C., & Gotlib, I. H. (1983). The role of cognition in depression: A critical appraisal. *Psychological Bulletin, 94*, 472–505.

Crandall, V. J. (1963). Achievement. In H. W. Stevenson (Ed.), *National society for the study of education yearbook: Part I. Child psychology* (pp. 416–459). Chicago: University of Chicago Press.

Crocker, J., Alloy, L. B., & Kayne, N. T. (1988). Attributional style, depression, and perceptions of consensus for events. *Journal of Personality and Social Psychology, 54*, 840–846.

Cronbach, L. J. (1951). Coefficient alpha and the internal structure of tests. *Psychometrika, 15*, 297–334.

Cronbach, L. J. (1957). The two disciplines of scientific psychology. *American Psychologist, 12*, 671–684.

Crosby, F. J. (1982). *Relative deprivation and working women*. Oxford, England: Oxford University Press.

Curry, J. F., & Craighead, W. E. (1990). Attributional style in clinically depressed and conduct disordered adolescents. *Journal of Consulting and Clinical Psychology, 58*, 757–764.

Cutler, S., & Nolen-Hoeksema, S. (1991). Accounting for sex differences in depression through female victimization: Childhood sexual abuse. *Sex Roles, 24*, 425–438.

Cutrona, C. E. (1983). Causal attributions and perinatal depression. *Journal of Abnormal Psychology, 92*, 161–172.

Cutrona, C. E., Russell, D., & Jones, R. D. (1984). Cross situational consistency in causal attributions: Does attributional style exist? *Journal of Personality and Social Psychology, 47*, 1043–1058.

Davidson, R. J., Abramson, L. Y., Tomarken, A. J., & Wheeler, R. E. (1992). *Asymmetrical anterior temporal brain activity predicts beliefs about the causes of negative life events*. Unpublished manuscript, University of Wisconsin, Madison, WI.

de Vos, G. (1968). Achievement and innovation in culture and personality. In E. Norbeck, D. Price-Williams, & W. McCord (Eds.), *The study of personality: An interdisciplinary appraisal* (pp. 348–370). New York: Holt, Rinehart & Winston.

Deaux, K., & Taynor, J. (1973). Evaluation of male and female ability: Bias works two ways. *Psychological Reports, 32*, 261–262.

Derry, P. A. & Stone, G. L. (1979). Effects of cognitive-adjunct treatments on assertiveness. *Cognitive Therapy and Research, 3*, 213–221.

DeRubeis, R. J., Evans, M. D., Hollon, S. D., Garvey, M. J., Grove, W. M., & Tuason, V. B. (1990). How does cognitive therapy work? Cognitive change and symptom change in cognitive therapy and pharmacotherapy for depression. *Journal of Consulting and Clinical Psychology, 58*, 862–869.

DeRubeis, R. J., Hollon, S. D., Evans, M. D., & Bemis, K. M. (1982). Can psychotherapies for depression be discriminated? A systematic investigation of cognitive therapy and interpersonal psychotherapy. *Journal of Consulting and Clinical Psychology, 50*, 744–756.

DeRubeis, R. J., Hollon, S. D., Evans, M. D., Garvey, M. J., Grove, W. M., & Tuason, V. B. (1989). *Active components and mechanisms in cognitive therapy and pharmacotherapy for depression: Part III. Processes of change in the CPT Project*. Manuscript submitted for publication.

DeVellis, B., & Blalock, S. (1992). Illness attributions and hopelessness depression: The role of hopelessness expectancy. *Journal of Abnormal Psychology, 101*, 257–264.

Diener, C. I., & Dweck, C. S. (1978). An analysis of learned helplessness: Continuous changes in performance, strategy, and achievement conditions following failure. *Journal of Personality and Social Psychology, 36,* 451–462.

Diener, C. I. and Dweck, C. S. (1980). An analysis of learned helplessness: Part II. The processing of success. *Journal of Personality and Social Psychology, 39,* 940–952.

DiNardo, P. A., & Barlow, D. H. (1990). Syndrome and symptom co-occurrence in the anxiety disorders. In J. D. Maser & C. R. Cloninger (Eds.), *Comorbidity in anxiety and mood disorders* (pp. 205–230). Washington, DC: American Psychiatric Press.

Dionne, E. J., Jr. (1988, January 4). Stump speeches. *New York Times,* p. 12.

Dobson, K. S. (1985). The relationship between anxiety and depression. *Clinical Psychology Review, 5,* 307–324.

Dornbusch, S. M., Carlsmith, J. M., Duncan, P. D., Gross, R. T., Martin, J. A., Ritter, P. L., & Siegel-Gorelick, B. (1984). Sexual maturation, social class, and the desire to be thin among adolescent females. *Developmental and Behavioral Pediatrics, 5,* 308–314.

Dowd, E. T., Claiborn, C. D., & Milne, C. R. (1985). Anxiety, attributional style, and perceived coping ability. *Cognitive Therapy and Research, 9,* 575–582.

Durkheim, E. (1951). *Suicide.* New York: Free Press. (Original work published 1897)

Dweck, C. S. (1975). The role of expectations and attributions in the alleviation of learned helplessness. *Journal of Personality and Social Psychology, 31,* 674–685.

Dweck, C. S., Davidson, W., Nelson, S., & Enna, B. (1978). Sex differences in learned helplessness: Part II. The contingencies of evaluative feedback in the classroom; and Part III. An experimental analysis. *Developmental Psychology, 14,* 268–276.

Dweck, C. S., & Elliott, E. S. (1983). Achievement motivation. In P. Mussen & E. M. Hetherington (Eds.), *Handbook of child psychology* (Vol. 4, pp. 643–691). New York: Wiley.

Dweck, C. S., & Gilliard, D. (1975). Expectancy statements as determinants of reactions to failure: Sex differences in persistence and expectancy change. *Journal of Personality and Social Psychology, 32,* 1077–1084.

Dweck, C. S., & Goetz, T. E. (1978). Attributions and learned helplessness. In J. H. Harvey, W. Ickes, & R. F. Kidd (Eds.), *New directions in attribution research* (Vol. 2, pp. 157–179). Hillsdale, NJ: Lawrence Erlbaum Associates.

Dweck, C. S., & Licht, B. G. (1980). Learned helplessness and intellectual achievement. In J. Garber & M. E. P. Seligman (Eds.), *Human helplessness: Theory and application* (pp. 197–221). New York: Academic.

Dweck, C. S., & Reppucci, N. D. (1973). Learned helplessness and reinforcement responsibility in children. *Journal of Personality and Social Psychology, 25,* 109–116.

Dweck, C. S., & Wortman, C. B. (1982). Learned helplessness, anxiety, and achievement motivation. In H. W. Krohne & L. Laux (Eds.), *Achievement, stress, and anxiety* (pp. 93–125). Washington, DC: Hemisphere.

Dykman, B. M., Abramson, L. Y., Alloy, L. B., & Hartlage, S. (1989). Processing of ambiguous and unambiguous feedback by depressed and nondepressed college students: Schematic biases and their implications for depressive realism. *Journal of Personality and Social Psychology, 56,* 431–445.

Eaves, G., & Rush, A. J. (1984). Cognitive patterns in symptomatic and remitted unipolar major depressives. *Journal of Abnormal Psychology, 93,* 31–40.

Eccles, J. (1983). Expectancies, values, and academic behaviors. In J. T. Spence (Ed.), *Achievement and achievement motives* (pp. 75–146). San Francisco: Freeman.

Eccles, J., Adler, T., & Meece, J. L. (1984). Sex differences in achievement: A test of alternate theories. *Journal of Personality and Social Psychology, 46,* 26–43.

Eisner, J. P. (1992). *Interpersonal trust in close relationships: The construct and its role in friendship formation.* Unpublished doctoral dissertation, University of Pennsylvania.

Ekman, P., & Friesen, W. V. (1969). The repertoire of nonverbal behavior: Categories, usage, and coding. *Semiotica, 1,* 49–98.

Ekman, P., & Friesen, W. V. (1971). Constants across cultures in the face and emotion. *Journal of Personality and Social Psychology, 17*, 124–129.

Ekman, P., & Friesen, W. V. (1974). Nonverbal behavior and psychopathology. In R. J. Friedman & M. M. Katz (Eds.), *The psychology of depression: Contemporary theory and research* (pp. 203–232). Washington, DC: Winston & Sons.

Ekman, P., & Friesen, W. V. (1975). *Unmasking the face: A guide to recognizing emotions from facial expressions.* Englewood Cliffs, NJ: Prentice-Hall.

Ekman, P., Friesen, W. V., O'Sullivan, M., Chan, A., Diacoyanni-Tarlatzis, I., Heider, K., Krause, R., LeCompte, W. A., Pitcairn, T., Ricci-Bitti, P. E., Scherer, K., & Tomita, M. (1987). Universals and cultural differences in the judgements of facial expressions of emotion. *Journal of Personality and Social Psychology, 53*, 712–717.

Elig, L. W., & Frieze, I. H. (1979). Measuring causal attributions for success and failure. *Journal of Personality and Social Psychology, 37*, 621–634.

Elkin, I., Shea, M. T., Watkins, J. T., Imber, S. D., Sotsky, S. M., Collins, J. F., Glass, D. R., Pilkonis, P. A., Leber, W. R., Docherty, J. P., Fiester, S. J., & Parloff, M. B. (1989). NIMH Treatment of Depression Collaborative Research Program: Part I. General effectiveness of treatments. *Archives of General Psychiatry, 46*, 971–982.

Ellis, A. (1962). *Reason and emotion in psychotherapy.* New York: Lyle Stuart.

Ellis, A. (1977). The basic clinical theory of rational-emotive therapy. In A. Ellis & R. Grieger (Eds.), *Handbook of rational-emotive therapy.* New York: Springer.

Emmelkamp, P. M. G. (1982). *Phobic and obsessive-compulsive disorders: Theory, research, and practice.* New York: Plenum.

Erikson, E. H. (1950). *Childhood and society.* New York: Norton.

Evans, M. D., Hollon, S. D., DeRubeis, R. J., Piasecki, J. M., Garvey, M. J., Grove, W. M., & Tuason, V. B. (1992). Differential relapse following cognitive therapy, pharmacotherapy, and combined cognitive-pharmacotherapy for depression. *Archives of General Psychiatry, 49*, 802–808.

Eysenck, H. J., & Eysenck, S. B. G. (1968). *Manual for the Eysenck Personality Inventory.* San Diego, CA: Educational Testing Service.

Feather, N. T. (1983). Some correlates of attributional style: Depressive symptoms, self-esteem, and Protestant ethic values. *Personality and Social Psychology Bulletin, 9*, 125–135.

Feather, N. T., & Barber, J. G. (1983). Depressive reactions and unemployment. *Journal of Abnormal Psychology, 92*, 185–195.

Feather, N. T., & Simon, J. G. (1975). Reactions to male and female success and failure in sex-linked cultures. *Journal of Personality and Social Psychology, 31*, 20–31.

Finlay-Jones, R., & Brown, G. W. (1981). Types of stressful life events and the onset of anxiety and depressive disorders. *Psychological Medicine, 11*, 803–815.

Firth, J., & Brewin, C. R. (1982). Attributions and recovery from depression: A preliminary study using cross-lagged correlation and analysis. *British Journal of Clinical Psychology, 21*, 229–230.

Firth, M. (1982). Sex discrimination in job opportunities for women. *Sex Roles, 8*, 891–901.

Fisher, L. M., & Wilson, G. T. (1985). A study of the psychology of agoraphobia. *Behaviour Research and Therapy, 23*, 97–107.

Flett, G. L., Pliner, P., & Blankstein, K. R. (1989). Depression and components of attributional complexity. *Journal of Personality and Social Psychology, 56*, 757–764.

Follette, V. M., & Jacobson, N. S. (1987). Importance of attributions as a predictor of how people cope with failure. *Journal of Personality and Social Psychology, 52*, 1205–1211.

Frank, R. (1988, April 17). 1948: Live . . . from Philadelphia . . . its the National Conventions. *New York Times Magazine*, pp. 62–65.

Frese, M., Erbe-Heinbokel, M., Grefe, J., Rybowiak, V., & Weike, A. (1994). "Mir ist est lieber, wenn ich genau gesagt bekomme, was ich tun muss": Probleme der Akzeptanz von Verantwortung und Handlugsspielraum in Ost und West ["I would rather be told exactly what I have to do at work": Problems of acceptance of responsiblity and control in East and West]. *Zeitschrift fuer Arbeits-Organisationspsycholgie, 38*, 22–33.

Freud, S. (1959). Inhibitions, symptoms, and anxiety. In J. Strachey (Ed. & Trans.), *The standard edition of the complete psychological works of Sigmund Freud* (Vol. 20, pp. 75–175). London: Hogarth Press. (Original work published 1926)

Friedlander, S., Traylor, J. A., & Weiss, D. S. (1986). Depressive symptoms and attributional style in children. *Personality and Social Psychology Bulletin, 12*, 442–453.

Friedman, H. S., & Booth-Kewley, S. (1987). The "disease-prone personality": A meta-analytic view of the concept. *American Psychologist, 42*, 539–555.

Friedman, M., & Rosenhan, R. H. (1974). *Type A behavior and your heart*. New York: Knopf.

Friedman, M., Thoresen, C. E., Gill, J. K., Ulmer, D. K., Powell, L. H., Price, V. A., Brown, B. B., Thompson, L., Rabin, D. D., Breall, W. S., Bourg, E., Levy, R., & Dixon, T. (1986). Alteration of Type A behavior and its effects of cardiac recurrences in post myocardial infarction patients: Summary results of the Recurrent Coronary Prevention Project. *American Heart Journal, 112*, 653–665.

Frieze, I. H., & Snyder, H. N. (1980). Children's beliefs about the causes of success and failure in school settings. *Journal of Educational Psychology, 72*, 186–196.

Funder, D. C., & Ozer, D. J. (1983). Behavior as a function of the situation. *Journal of Personality and Social Psychology, 44*, 107–112.

Ganellen, R. J. (1988). Specificity of attributions and overgeneralization in depression and anxiety. *Journal of Abnormal Psychology, 97*, 83–86.

Garber, J. & Hollon, S. D. (1991). What can specificity designs say about causality in psychopathology research? *Psychological Bulletin, 110*, 129–136.

Garber, J., Miller, S. M., & Abramson, L. Y. (1980). On the distinction between anxiety and depression: Perceived control, certainty, and probability of goal attainment. In J. Garber & M. E. P. Seligman (Eds.), *Human helplessness: Theory and Implications* (pp. 131–169). New York: Academic.

Garland, H. (1984). Relation of effort-performance expectancy to performance in goal-setting experiments. *Journal of Applied Psychology, 69*, 79–84.

Gill, D. L., Ruder, M. K., & Gross, J. B. (1982). Open-ended attributions in team competition. *Journal of Sport Psychology, 4*, 159–169.

Gillham, J. E., Reivich, K. J., Jaycox, L. H., & Seligman, M. E. P. (1993). *Prevention of depression in school children: 2 year follow-up*. Manuscript submitted for publication, University of Pennsylvania.

Girgus, J. S., Nolen-Hoeksema, S., & Seligman, M. E. P. (1989, August). *Why do sex differences in depression emerge during adolescence?* Paper presented at the meetings of the American Psychological Association, New Orleans.

Gitelson, B., Petersen, A. C., & Tobin-Richards, M. H. (1982). Adolescents' expectancies of success, self-evaluations, and attributions about performance on spatial and verbal tasks. *Sex Roles, 8*, 411–419.

Glass, D. C. (1977). *Behavior patterns, stress and coronary disease*. Hillsdale, NJ: Lawrence Erlbaum Associates.

Golin, S., Sweeney, P. D., & Schaeffer, D. E. (1981). The causality of causal attributions in depression: A cross-lagged panel correlational analysis. *Journal of Abnormal Psychology, 90*, 14–22.

Gong-Guy, E., & Hammen, C. L. (1980). Causal perceptions of stressful events in depressed and nondepressed outpatients. *Journal of Abnormal Psychology, 89*, 662–669.

Gorsuch, R. L. (1988). Psychology of religion. *Annual Review of Psychology, 39*, 201–221.

Gotlib, I. H., & Beatty, M. E. (1985). Negative responses to depression: The role of attributional style. *Cognitive Therapy and Research, 9*, 91–103.

Gotlib, I. H., & Cane, D. B. (1989). Self-report assessment of depression and anxiety. In P. C. Kendall & D. Watson (Eds.), *Anxiety and depression: Distinctive and overlapping features* (pp. 173–184). New York: Academic.

Greenberg, L. (1956). *The Jews in Russia*. New Haven, CT: Yale University Press.

Greenstein, F. I. (1990). Proximate and remote antecedents of political choice. *Psychological Inquiry, 1*, 62–63.

Gutterman, N. (1985). *Russian fairy tales.* New York: Pantheon.

Haack, L. J., Metalsky, G. I., Dykman, B. M., & Abramson, L. Y. (1992). *Use of current situational information and depressive inference: Do depressed students make unwarranted causal inferences?* Unpublished manuscript, University of Wisconsin, Madison.

Halberstadt, L. J., Mukherji, B. R., Metalsky, G. I., Dykman, B. M., & Abramson, L. Y. (1984). *Cognitive style and severity of depression.* Unpublished manuscript, University of Wisconsin, Madison.

Hamilton, E. W., & Abramson, L. Y. (1983). Cognitive patterns and major depressive disorder: A longitudinal study in a hospital setting. *Journal of Abnormal Psychology, 92*, 173–184.

Hamilton, J. A., Alagna, S. W., King, L. S., & Lloyd, C. (1987). The emotional consequences of gender-based abuse in the workplace: New counseling programs for sex discrimination. *Women and Therapy, 6*, 155–182.

Hammen, C. L. (1985). Predicting depression: A cognitive-behavioral perspective. In P. C. Kendall (Ed.), *Advances in cognitive-behavioral research and therapy* (Vol. 4, pp. 30–71). New York: Academic.

Hammen, C. L., Adrian, C., & Hiroto, D. (1988). A longitudinal test of the attributional vulnerability model in children at risk for depression. *British Journal of Clinical Psychology, 27*, 37–46.

Hammen, C. L., & Cochran, S. D. (1981). Cognitive correlates of life stress and depression in college students. *Journal of Abnormal Psychology, 90*, 23–27.

Hammen, C. L., & deMayo, R. (1982). Cognitive correlates of teacher stress and depressive symptoms: Implications for attributional models of depression. *Journal of Abnormal Psychology, 91*, 96–101.

Hammen, C. L., Krantz, S. E., & Cochran, S. D. (1981). Relationships between depression and causal attributions about stressful life events. *Cognitive Therapy and Research, 5*, 351–358.

Hammen, C. L., Marks, T., Mayol, A., & deMayo, R. (1985). Depressive self-schemas, life stress, and vulnerability to depression. *Journal of Abnormal Psychology, 94*, 308–319.

Hammen, C. L., & Mayol, A. (1982). Depression and cognitive characteristics of stressful life-event types. *Journal of Abnormal Psychology, 91*, 165–174.

Harter, S. (1983). Developmental perspectives on the self-system. In P. H. Mussen (Ed.), *Handbook of child development* (Vol. 4, pp. 275–385). New York: Wiley.

Harvey, J. H., Harkins, S. G., & Kagehiro, D. K. (1976). Cognitive tuning and the attribution of causality. *Journal of Personality and Social Psychology, 34*, 708–715.

Harvey, J. H., Ickes, W., & Kidd, R. F. (Eds.). (1976). *New directions in attribution research* (Vol. 1). Hillsdale, NJ: Lawrence Erlbaum Associates.

Harvey, J. H., Ickes, W., & Kidd, R. F. (Eds.). (1978). *New directions in attribution research* (Vol. 2). Hillsdale, NJ: Lawrence Erlbaum Associates.

Harvey, J. H., Ickes, W., & Kidd, R. F. (Eds.). (1981). *New directions in attribution research* (Vol. 3). Hillsdale, NJ: Lawrence Erlbaum Associates.

Haynes, S. G., Feinleib, M., & Kannel, W. B. (1980). The relationship of psychosocial factors to coronary heart disease in the Framingham Study: Part III. Eight year incidence of coronary heart disease. *American Journal of Epidemiology, 111*, 37–58.

Heider, F. (1958). *The psychology of interpersonal relationships.* New York: Wiley.

Heilman, M. E., & Guzzo, R. A. (1978). The perceived cause of work success as a mediator of sex discrimination in organizations. *Organizational Behavior and Human Performance, 21*, 346–357.

Heimberg, R. G., Klosko, J. C., Dodge, C. S., Shadick, R., Becker, R. E., & Barlow, D. H. (1989). Anxiety disorders, depression, and attributional style: A further test of the specificity of depressive attributions. *Cognitive Therapy and Research, 13*, 21–36.

Heimberg, R. G., Vermilyea, J. A., Dodge, C. S., Becker, R. E., & Barlow, D. H. (1987). Attributional style, depression, and anxiety: An evaluation of the specifity of depressive attributions. *Cognitive Therapy and Research, 11*, 537–550.

Henry, A. F., & Short, J. F. (1954). *Suicide and homicide: Some economic, sociological, and psychological aspects of aggression.* New York: Free Press.

Heppner, P. P., Baumgardner, A., & Jackson, J. (1985). Problem-solving self appraisal, depression, and attributional style: Are they related? *Cognitive Therapy and Research, 9,* 105–113.

Herskovits, M. J. (1948). *Man and his works: The science of cultural anthropology.* New York: Knopf.

Hill, A. B., & Kemp-Wheeler, S. M. (1986). Personality, life events, and subclinical depression in students. *Personality and Individual Differences, 7,* 469–478.

Hiroto, D. S., & Seligman, M. E. P. (1975). Generality of learned helplessness in man. *Journal of Personality and Social Psychology, 31,* 311–327.

Hoffart, A., & Martinsen, E. W. (1990). Agoraphobia, depression, mental health locus of control, and attributional styles. *Cognitive Therapy and Research, 14,* 343–351.

Hofstadter, R. (1963). *Anti-intellectualism in American life.* New York: Vintage.

Hogan, R., deSoto, C. N., & Solano, C. (1977). Traits, tests, and personality research. *American Psychologist, 32,* 255–264.

Hollon, S. D. (1990). Cognitive therapy and pharmacotherapy for depression. *Psychiatric Annals, 20,* 249–258.

Hollon, S. D., DeRubeis, R. J., & Evans, M. D. (1987). Causal mediation of change in treatment for depression: Discriminating between nonspecificity and noncausality. *Psychological Bulletin, 102,* 139–149.

Hollon, S. D., DeRubeis, R. J., Evans, M. D., Wiemer, M. J., Garvey, M. J., Grove, W. M., & Tuason, V. B. (1992). Cognitive therapy and pharmacotherapy for depression: Singly and in combination. *Archives of General Psychiatry, 49,* 774–781.

Hollon, S. D., Evans, M. D., & DeRubeis, R. J. (1990). Cognitive mediation of relapse prevention following treatment for depression: Implications of differential risk. In R. E. Ingram (Ed.), *Contemporary psychological approaches to depression* (pp. 117–136). New York: Guilford.

Hollon, S. D., & Garber, J. (1980). A cognitive-expectancy theory of therapy for helplessness and depression. In J. Garber & M. E. P. Seligman (Eds.), *Human helplessness: Theory and applications* (pp. 173–195). New York: Academic.

Hollon, S. D., & Kendall, P. C. (1980). Cognitive self-statements in depression: Development of an automatic thoughts questionnaire. *Cognitive Therapy and Research, 4,* 383–396.

Hollon, S. D., & Kriss, M. R. (1984). Cognitive factors in clinical research and practice. *Clinical Psychology Review, 4,* 35–76.

Hollon, S. D., Shelton, R. C., & Loosen, P. T. (1991). Cognitive therapy and pharmacotherapy for depression. *Journal of Consulting and Clinical Psychology, 59,* 88–99.

Holsti, O. R. (1968). Content analysis. In G. Lindzey & E. Aronson (Eds.), *Handbook of social psychology* (Vol. 2, pp. 596–644). Reading, MA: Addison-Wesley.

Holy Transfiguration Monastery. (1974). *The Psalter according to the seventy.* Boston, MA: Author.

Holy Trinity Monastery. (1963, 1973, 1974, 1975). *Russian Orthodox calendar.* Cambridge, England: Cambridge University Press.

Holy Trinity Monastery. (1979). *Prayer book.* Jordanville, NY: Author.

Holy Trinity Monastery. (1985). *Orthodox life* (Vol. 35). Jordanville, NY: Author.

Horwitz, A. V. (1984). The economy and social pathology. *Annual Review of Sociology, 10,* 95–119.

House, J. S., Robbins, C., & Metzner, H. L. (1982). The association of social relationships and activities with mortality: Predictive evidence from the Tecumseh Community Health Study. *American Journal of Epidemiology, 116,* 123–140.

Howe, I., & Greenberg, E. (Eds.). (1954). *A treasury of Yiddish stories.* New York: Schocken Books.

Howe, I., & Wisse, R (Eds.). (1979). *The best of Sholom Aleichem.* Washington, DC: New Republic.

Ickes, W., & Layden, M. A. (1978). Attributional styles. In J. H. Harvey, W. Ickes, & R. F. Kidd (Eds.), *New directions in attribution research* (Vol. 2, pp. 119–192). Hillsdale, NJ: Lawrence Erlbaum Associates.

Imber, S. D., Pilkonis, P. A., Sotsky, S. M., Elkin, I., Watkins, J. T., Collins, J. F., Shea, M. T., Leber, W. R., & Glass, D. R. (1990). Mode-specific effects among three treatments for depression. *Journal of Consulting and Clinical Psychology, 58*, 352–359.

Ingram, R. E., Kendall, P. C., Smith, T. W., Donnell, C., & Ronan, K. (1987). Cognitive specificity in emotional distress. *Journal of Personality and Social Psychology, 53*, 734–742.

Insull, W. (1983). *Coronary Risk Handbook*. New York: American Heart Association.

Iso-Ahola, S. E. (1977). Immediate attributional effects of success and failure in the field: Testing some laboratory hypotheses. *Journal of Abnormal and Social Psychology, 68*, 447–452.

Jaenicke, C., Hammen, C. L., Zupan, B., Hiroto, D., Gordon, D., Adrian, C., & Burge, D. (1987). Cognitive vulnerability in children at risk for depression. *Journal of Abnormal Child Psychology, 15*, 559–572.

James, W. (1961). *The varieties of religious experience: A study in human nature*. New York: Collier Books. (Original work published 1902)

Janoff-Bulman, R. (1979). Characterological versus behavioral self-blame: Inquiries into depression and rape. *Journal of Personality and Social Psychology, 37*, 1798–1809.

Jaycox, L. H., Reivich, K. J., Gillham, J. E., & Seligman, M. E. P. (1993). *Prevention of depression in school children*. Manuscript submitted for publication, University of Pennsylvania.

Jemmott, J. B. & Locke, S. E. (1984). Psychosocial factors, immunologic mediation, and human susceptibility to infectious disease: How much do we know? *Psychological Bulletin, 95*, 78–108.

Jenkins, C. D. (1976). Recent evidence supporting psychological and social risk factors in coronary disease. *New England Journal of Medicine, 294*, 1033–1038.

Johnson, J. E., Petzel, T. P., & Munic, D. (1986). An examination of the relative contribution of depression versus global psychopathology to depressive attributional style in a clinical population. *Journal of Social and Clinical Psychology, 4*, 107–113.

Johnson, J. G., & Miller, S. M. (1990). Attributional, life-event, and affective predictors of onset of depression, anxiety, and negative attributional style. *Cognitive Therapy and Research, 14*, 417–430.

Johnson, J. M., Petzel, T. P., & Johnson, J. E. (1991). Attributions of shy persons in affiliation and achievement situations. *Journal of Psychology, 125*, 51–58.

Jones, E. E., & Davis, K. E. (1965). From acts to dispositions: The attribution process in person perception. In L. Berkowitz (Ed.), *Advances in experimental social psychology* (Vol. 2, pp. 219–266). New York: Academic.

Kamen, L. P. (1989). *Learned helplessness, cognitive dissonance, and cell-mediated immunity*. Unpublished doctoral dissertation, University of Pennsylvania.

Kamen, L. P. & Seligman, M. E. P. (1986). *Explanatory style predicts college grade point average*. Unpublished manuscript.

Kamen-Siegel, L. P., Rodin, J., Seligman, M. E. P., & Dwyer, J. (1991). Explanatory style and cell-mediated immunity in elderly men and women. *Health Psychology, 10*, 229–235.

Kammer, D. (1983). Depression, attributional style, and failure generalization. *Cognitive Therapy and Research, 4*, 383–395.

Kammer, D. (1984). Attributional style processing differences in depressed and nondepressed individuals. *Motivation and Emotion, 8*, 211–220.

Kashani, J. H., Cantwell, D. P., Shekim, W. O., & Reid, J. C. (1982). Major depressive disorder in children admitted to an inpatient community mental health center. *American Journal of Psychiatry, 139*, 671–672.

Kaslow, N. J., Rehm, L. P., Pollack, S. L., & Siegel, A. W. (1988). Attributional style and self-control behavior in depressed and nondepressed children and their parents. *Journal of Abnormal Child Psychology, 16*, 163–175.

Kaslow, N. J., Rehm, L. P., & Siegel, A. W. (1984). Social-cognitive and cognitive correlates of depression in children. *Journal of Abnormal Child Psychology, 12*, 605–620.

Kaslow, N. J., Tannenbaum, R. L., & Seligman, M. E. P. (1978). *The KASTAN: A children's attributional style questionnaire*. Unpublished manuscript, University of Pennsylvania.

Katona, G. (1960). *The powerful consumer: Psychological studies of the American economy.* New York: McGraw-Hill.

Katona, G. (1980). *Essays on behavioral economics.* Ann Arbor, MI: Institute for Social Research.

Katona, G., & Strumpel, B. (1978). *A new economic era.* New York: Elsevier.

Kazdin, A. E., French, N. H., Unis, A. S., Esveldt-Dawson, K., & Sherick, R. B. (1983). Hopelessness, depression, and suicidal intent among psychiatrically disturbed inpatient children. *Journal of Consulting and Clinical Psychology, 51,* 504–510.

Kelley, H. H. (1967). Attribution theory in social psychology. In C. Levine (Ed.), *Nebraska Symposium on Motivation* (Vol. 15, pp. 192–238). Lincoln, NK: University of Nebraska Press.

Kelley, H. H. (1973). The process of causal attribution. *American Psychologist, 28,* 107–128.

Kelley, S., Jr. (1983). *Interpreting elections.* Princeton, NJ: Princeton University Press.

Kenardy, J., Evans, L., & Oei, T. P. S. (1990). Attributional style and panic disorder. *Journal of Behaviour Therapy and Experimental Psychiatry, 21,* 9–13.

Kendall, P. C., & Hollon, S. D. (1981). Assessing self-referent speech: Methods in the measurement of self-statements. In P. C. Kendall & S. D. Hollon (Eds.), *Assessment strategies for cognitive-behavioral interventions* (pp. 88–118). New York: Academic.

Kendall, P. C., & Watson, D. (Eds.). (1989). *Anxiety and depression: Distinctive and overlapping features.* New York: Academic.

Kendall, P. C. Williams, L., Pechacek, T. F., Graham, L. E., Shisslak, C., & Herzoff, N. (1979). Cognitive-behavioral and patient education interventions in cardiac catherization procedures: The Palo Alto medical psychology project. *Journal of Consulting and Clinical Psychology, 47,* 49–58.

Kendell, R. E. (1968). *The classification of depression illness.* London: Oxford University Press.

Kendell, R. E. (1974). The stability of psychiatric diagnoses. *British Journal of Psychiatry, 124,* 352–356.

Kiecolt-Glaser, J. K., & Glaser, R. (1987). Psychosocial moderators of immune function. *Annals of Behavioral Medicine, 9,* 16–20.

Kim, R. S., & Alloy, L. B. (1992). *Differential activation of clinical disorders by self-focused attention.* Unpublished manuscript, Temple University, Philadelphia, PA.

Klein, D. C., Fencil-Morse, E. & Seligman, M. E. P. (1976). Learned helplessness, depression, and the attribution of failure. *Journal of Personality and Social Psychology, 33,* 508–516.

Klein, D. F. (1974). Endogenomorphic depression: Conceptual and terminological revision. *Archives of General Psychiatry, 31,* 447–454.

Klerman, G. L. (1978). The evolution of a scientific nosology. In J. C. Shershow (Ed.), *Schizophrenia: Science and practice.* Cambridge, MA: Harvard University Press.

Klien, F. (1990). *Lueg Vaterland. Erziehung in der DDR [The Fatherland. Education in the GDR].* Muenchen: Kindler.

Kovacs, M. (1985). The Children's Depression Inventory (CDI). *Psychopharmacology Bulletin, 21,* 995–1124.

Kovacs, M., & Beck, A. T. (1977). An empirical-clinical approach toward a definition of childhood depression. In J. G. Schulterbrandt & A. Askin (Eds.), *Depression in childhood: Diagnosis, treatment and conceptual issues* (pp. 1–27). New York: Raven.

Kovacs, M., & Beck, A. T. (1978a). Maladaptive cognitive structures in depression. *American Journal of Psychiatry, 135,* 525–533.

Kovacs, M., & Beck, A. T. (1978b). Maladaptive cognitive structures in depression. *Archives of General Psychiatry, 38,* 33–39.

Kovacs, M., & Beck, A. T. (1979). Cognitive-affective processes in depression. In C. E. Izard (Ed.), *Emotions in personality and psychopathology* (pp. 417–442). New York: Plenum.

Kovacs, M., Feinberg, T. L., Crouse–Novak, M. A., Paulauskas, S. L., & Finkelstein, R. (1984). Depressive disorders in children. Part I. A longitudinal prospective study of characteristics and recovery. *Archives of General Psychiatry, 41,* 229–237.

Kovacs, M., Rush, A. T., Beck, A. T., & Hollon, S. D. (1981). Depressed outpatients treated with cognitive therapy or pharmacotherapy: A one-year follow-up. *Archives of General Psychiatry, 38*, 33–39.

Krantz, S. E. (1985). When depressive cognitions reflect negative realities. *Cognitive Therapy and Research, 9*, 595–610.

Krantz, S. E., & Rude, S. (1984). Depressive attributions: Selection of different causes or assignment of dimensional meanings? *Journal of Personality and Social Psychology, 47*, 193–203.

Krippendorf, K. (1980). *Content analysis*. Beverly Hills, CA: Sage.

Kroeber, A. L., & Kluckhohn, C. (1952). *Culture: A critical review of concepts and definitions* (Vol. 47). Cambridge, MA: Peabody Museum.

Kuhl, J. (1981). Motivational and functional helplessness: The moderating effect of state versus action orientation. *Journal of Personality and Social Psychology, 40*, 155–170.

Kuhl, J. (1984). Volitional aspects of achievement motivation and learned helplessness: Toward a comprehensive theory of action control. In B. A. Maher (Ed.), *Progress in experimental personality research* (Vol. 13, pp. 99–171). New York: Academic.

Kuiper, N. A. (1978). Depression and causal attributions for success and failure. *Journal of Personality and Social Psychology, 3*, 236–246.

Kushner, H. I. (1989). *Self-destruction in the promised land: A psychocultural biology of American suicide*. New Brunswick, NJ: Rutgers University Press.

Langer, E. J. (1978). Rethinking the role of thought in social interaction. In J. H. Harvey, W. Ickes, & R. F. Kidd (Eds.), *New directions in attribution research* (Vol. 2, pp. 35–58). Hillsdale, NJ: Lawrence Erlbaum Associates.

Langer, E. J. (1989). *Mindfulness*. Reading, MA: Addison-Wesley.

Langnas, I. (1960). *1200 Russian proverbs*. New York: Philosophical Library.

Larzelere, R. E., & Huston, T. L. (1980). The Dyadic Trust Scale: Toward understanding interpersonal trust in close relationships. *Journal of Marriage and the Family, 42*, 595–604.

Laudenslager, M. L., Ryan, S. M., Drugan, R. C., Hyson, R. L., & Maier, S. F. (1983). Coping and immunosuppression: Inescapable but not escapable shock suppresses lymphocyte proliferation. *Science, 221*, 568–570.

Lazarus, R. J., & Launier, R. (1978). Stress-related transactions between person and environment. In L. Pervin & M. Lewis (Eds.), *Internal and external determinants of behavior*. New York: Plenum.

Lefcourt, H. M. (1976). *Locus of control*. Hillsdale, NJ: Lawrence Erlbaum Associates.

Lefkowitz, M. M., & Burton, N. (1978). Childhood depression: A critique of the concept. *Psychological Bulletin, 85*, 716–726.

Leon, G. R., Kendall, P. C., & Garber, J. (1980). Depression in children: Parent, teacher, and child perspectives. *Journal of Abnormal Child Psychology, 8*, 221–235.

Lerner, M. (1957). *America as a civilization: Life and thought in the United States today*. New York: Simon & Schuster.

Lerner, R. M., & Karabenick, S. A. (1974). Physical attractiveness, body attitudes, and self-concept in late adolescents. *Journal of Youth and Adolescence, 3*, 307–316.

LeVine, R. A. (1966). *Dreams and deeds: Achievement motivation in Nigeria*. Chicago: University of Chicago Press.

Lewin, K. (1935). *A dynamic theory of personality*. New York: McGraw-Hill.

Lewin, K. (1951). *Field theory in social science: Selected theoretical papers*. New York: Harper.

Lewinsohn, P. M. (1987). The coping-with-depression course. In R. F. Munoz (Ed.), *Depression prevention: Research directions* (pp. 159–170). New York: Hemisphere.

Lewinsohn, P. M., Steinmetz, J. L., Larson, D. W., & Franklin, J. (1981). Depression-related cognitions: Antecedent or consequence? *Journal of Abnormal Psychology, 90*, 213–219.

Life Insurance Marketing Research Association. (1983). *The manpower and production survey*. Hartford, CT: Author.

Life Insurance Marketing Research Association. (1984). *The Career Profile*. Hartford, CT: Author.

Lin, E. H., & Peterson, C. (1990). Pessimistic explanatory style and response to illness. *Behavior Therapy and Research, 28,* 243–248.

Lipman, A. J., & Alloy, L. B. (1992). *Social support, adaptive inferential feedback, and depression: Empirical test of an expanded hopelessness theory of depression.* Unpublished manuscript, Temple University, Philadelphia, PA.

Lloyd, C., Zisook, S., Click, M., Jr., & Jaffe, K. E. (1981). Life events and response to antidepressants. *Journal of Human Stress, 7,* 2–15.

Locke, E. A., Motowidlo, S. J., & Bobko, P. (1986). Using self-efficacy theory to resolve the conflict between goal-setting theory and expectancy theory in organizational behavior and industrial/organizational psychology. *Journal of Social and Clinical Psychology, 4,* 328–338.

Locke, E. A., Shaw, K. N., Saari, L. M., & Latham, G. P. (1981). Goal setting and task performance. *Psychological Bulletin, 90,* 125–152.

Luborsky, L. (1984). *Principles of psychoanalytic psychotherapy: A manual for Supportive/Expressive treatment.* New York: Basic Books.

Luten, A. G., Ralph, J., & Mineka, S. (1994). *Pessimistic attributional style: Is it specific to depression vs. anxiety vs. negative affect?* Manuscript submitted for publication, Northwestern University, Evanston, IL.

Maccoby, E. E., & Jacklin, C. N. (1974). *The psychology of sex differences,* Stanford, CA: Stanford University Press.

MacKay, C. (1980). *Memoirs of extraordinary popular delusions and the madness of crowds.* Toronto, Canada: Coles. (Original work published 1852)

Maier, S. F., & Jackson, R. L. (1979). Learned helplessness: All of us were right (and wrong)—Inescapable shock has multiple effects. In G. H. Bower (Ed.), *The psychology of learning and motivation* (Vol. 13, pp. 155–218). New York: Academic.

Maier, S. F., & Seligman, M. E. P. (1976). Learned helplessness: Theory and evidence. *Journal of Experimental Psychology: General, 105,* 3–46.

Manly, P. C., McMahon, R. J., Bradley, C. F., & Davidson, P. O. (1982). Depressive attributional style and depression following child birth. *Journal of Abnormal Psychology, 91,* 245–254.

Maron, M. (1992). Zonophobie [GDR phobia]. *Kursbuch, 109,* 91–96.

Marsella, A. J. (1978). Cross-cultural research on severe mental disorders: Issues and findings [*Proceedings of the Scandanavian Psychiatric Society*]. *Acta Psychiatrica Scandinavica, 78,* 7–22.

Marsella, A. J. (1980). Depressive experience and disorder across cultures. In H. C. Triandis & J. G. Draguns (Eds.), *Handbook of cross-cultural psychology. Psychopathology* (Vol. 6, pp. 237–289). Boston, MA: Allyn & Bacon.

Marx, K. (1964). Zur Kritik der Hegelschen Rechtsphilosophie [On the critique of Hegelian legal philosophy]. In S. Landshut (Ed.), *Die Fruehschriften* (pp. 207–224). Stuttgart, DDR: Kroener. (Original work published 1843–1844)

Maser, J. D., & Cloninger, C. R. (Eds.). (1990). *Comorbidity in anxiety and mood disorders.* Washington, DC: American Psychiatric Press.

Masters, R. D. (1990). Candidate rhetoric, political leadership, and electoral success: The broader context of "pessimistic rumination". *Psychological Inquiry, 1,* 65–68.

Matthews, K. A. (1982). Psychological perspectives on the Type A behavior pattern. *Psychological Bulletin, 91,* 293–323.

Mavissakalian, M., Michelson, L., Greenwald, D., Kornblith, S., & Greenwald, M. (1983). Cognitive-behavioral treatment of agoraphobia: Paradoxical intention vs. self-statement training. *Behavior Research Therapy, 21,* 75–86.

McArthur, L. A. (1972). The how and what of why: Some determinants and consequences of causal attribution. *Journal of Personality and Social Psychology, 22,* 171–193.

McCarthy, M. (1990). The thin ideal, depression and eating disorders in women. *Behavior Research and Therapy, 28,* 205–215.

McCauley, E., & Gross, J. B. (1983). Perceptions of causality in sport: An application of the causal dimension scale. *Journal of Sport Psychology, 5,* 72–76.

McCauley, E., Mitchell, J. R., Burke, P., & Moss, S. (1988). Cognitive attributes of depression in children and adolescents. *Journal of Consulting and Clinical Psychology, 56*, 903–908.

McClelland, D. C. (1961). *The achieving society*. Princeton, NJ: Van Nostrand.

McClelland, D. C., Atkinson, J. W., Clark, R. A., & Lowell, E. L. (1953). *The achievement motive*. New York: Appleton-Century-Crofts.

McCormick, R. A., Taber, J. I., & Kruedelbach, N. (1989). The relationship between attributional style and post-traumatic stress disorder in addicted patients. *Journal of Traumatic Stress, 2*, 477–487.

McLemore, C. W., & Benjamin, L. S. (1979). Whatever happened to interpersonal diagnosis? A psychosocial alternative to DSM-III. *American Psychologist, 34*, 17–34.

Melnechuk, T. (1985). Why has psychoneuroimmunology been controversial? *Advances, 2*, 22–38.

Merikangas, K. R. (1990). Comorbidity for anxiety and depression: Review of family and genetic studies. In J. D. Maser & C. R. Cloninger (Eds.), *Comorbidity in anxiety and mood disorders* (pp. 331–348). Washington, DC: American Psychiatric Press.

Metalsky, G. I., & Abramson, L. Y. (1981). Attributional styles: Toward a framework for conceptualization and assessment. In P. C. Kendall & S. D. Hollon (Eds.), *Cognitive-behavioral interventions: Assessment methods* (pp. 13–58). New York: Academic.

Metalsky, G. I., Abramson, L. Y., Seligman, M. E. P., Semmel, A., & Peterson, C. (1982). Attributional styles and life events in the classroom: Vulnerability and invulnerability to depressive mood reactions. *Journal of Personality and Social Psychology, 43*, 612–617.

Metalsky, G. I., Halberstadt, L. J., & Abramson, L. Y. (1987). Vulnerability to depressive mood reactions: Toward a more powerful test of the diathesis-stress and causal mediation components of the reformulated theory of depression. *Journal of Personality and Social Psychology, 52*, 386–393.

Metalsky, G. I., & Joiner, T. E., Jr. (1992). Vulnerability to depressive symptomatology: A perspective test of the diathesis-stress and causal mediation components of the hopelessness theory of depression. *Journal of Personality and Social Psychology, 63*, 667–675.

Metalsky, G. I., Joiner, T. E., Jr., Hardin, T. S., & Abramson, L. Y. (1993). Depressive reactions to failure in a naturalistic setting: A test of the hopelessness and self-esteem theories of depression. *Journal of Abnormal Psychology, 102*, 101–109.

Meyers, A. W., & Craighead, W. E. (1984). *Cognitive behavior therapy with children*. New York: Plenum.

Mikulincer, M., & Solomon, Z. (1988). Attributional style and combat-related post-traumatic stress disorder. *Journal of Abnormal Psychology, 97*, 308–313.

Miller, D. T., & Moretti, M. M. (1988). The causal attributions of depressives: Self-serving or self-disserving? In L. B. Alloy (Ed.), *Cognitive processes in depression* (pp. 266–286). New York: Guilford.

Miller, D. T., & Ross, M. (1975). Self-serving biases in the attribution of causality: Fact or fiction? *Psychological Bulletin, 82*, 213–225.

Miller, I. W., Klee, S. H., & Norman, W. H. (1982). Depressed and nondepressed inpatients' cognitions of hypothetical events, experimental tasks, and stressful life events. *Journal of Abnormal Psychology, 91*, 78–81.

Miller, I. W., & Norman, W. H. (1979). Learned helplessness in humans: A review and attribution theory model. *Psychological Bulletin, 86*, 93–119.

Miller, J. G. (1984). Culture and the development of everyday social explanation. *Journal of Personality and Social Psychology, 46*, 961–978.

Miller, W. R., & Seligman, M. E. P. (1975). Depression and learned helplessness in man. *Journal of Abnormal Psychology, 84*, 228–238.

Mineka, S., Cook, M., & Miller, S. (1984). Fear conditioned with escapable and inescapable shock: Effects of a feedback stimulus. *Journal of Experimental Psychology: Animal Behavior Processes, 10*, 307–323.

Mineka, S., Gunnar, M., & Champoux, M. (1986). Control and early socioemotional development: Infant rhesus monkeys reared in controllable versus uncontrollable environments. *Child Development, 57,* 1241–1256.

Mineka, S., & Kelly, K. A. (1989). The relationship between anxiety, lack of control and loss of control. In A. Steptoe & A. Appels (Eds.), *Stress, personal control and health* (pp. 163–192). New York: Wiley.

Minkoff, K., Bergman, E., Beck, A. T., & Beck, R. (1973). Hopelessness, depression and attempted suicide. *American Journal of Psychiatry, 130,* 455–459.

Miranda, J., & Persons, J. B. (1988). Dysfunctional attitudes are mood-state dependent. *Journal of Abnormal Psychology, 97,* 76–79.

Miranda, J, Persons, J. B., & Byers, C. N. (1990). Endorsement of dysfunctional beliefs depends on current mood state. *Journal of Abnormal Psychology, 99,* 237–241.

Mitchell, W. C. (1959). *Business cycles and their causes.* Berkeley, CA: University of California Press.

Mowrer, D. H., & Viek, P. (1948). An experimental analogue of fear from a sense of helplessness. *Journal of Abnormal and Social Psychology, 43,* 193–200.

Munoz, R. F., Ying, Y. W., Armas, R., Chan, F., & Gurza, R. (1987). The San Francisco Depression Prevention Research Project: A randomized trial with medical outpatients. In R. F. Munoz (Ed.), *Depression prevention: Research directions* (pp. 199–215). Washington, DC: Hemisphere.

Needles, D. J., & Abramson, L. Y. (1990). Positive life events, attributional style, and hopefulness: Testing a model of recovery from depression. *Journal of Abnormal Psychology, 99,* 156–165.

Needles, D. J., & Abramson, L. Y. (1992). *Cognitive and affective consequences of rumination and distraction in response to a depressed mood.* Unpublished manuscript, University of Wisconsin, Madison.

Nezu, A. M., Kalmar, K., Ronan, G. F., & Clarijo, A. (1986). Attributional correlates of depression: An interactional model including problem solving. *Behavior Therapy, 17,* 50–56.

Nezu, A. M., Nezu, C. M., & Nezu, V. A. (1986). Depression, general distress, and causal attributions among university students. *Journal of Abnormal Psychology, 95,* 184–186.

Nicholls, J. G. (1975). Causal attributions and other achievement-related cognitions: Effects of task outcomes, attainment value, and sex. *Journal of Personality and Social Psychology, 31,* 379–389.

Nisbett, R., & Ross, L. (1980). *Human inference: Strategies and shortcomings of social judgment.* Englewood Cliffs, NJ: Prentice-Hall.

Noelle-Neumann, E. (1984). *The spiral of silence: Public opinion—our social skin.* Chicago, IL: University of Chicago Press.

Noelle-Neumann, E. (1989). The public as prophet: Findings from continuous survey research and their importance for early diagnosis of economic growth. *International Journal of Public Opinion Research, 1,* 136–150.

Nolen-Hoeksema, S. (1987). Sex differences in unipolar depression: Evidence and theory. *Psychological Bulletin, 101,* 259–282.

Nolen-Hoeksema, S. (1990). *Sex differences in depression.* Stanford, CA: Stanford University Press.

Nolen-Hoeksema, S. (1991). Responses to depression and their effects on the duration of depressive episodes. *Journal of Abnormal Psychology, 100,* 569–582.

Nolen-Hoeksema, S., Girgus, J. S., & Seligman, M. E. P. (1986). Learned helplessness in children: A longitudinal study of depression, achievement, and explanatory style. *Journal of Personality and Social Psychology, 51,* 435–442.

Nolen-Hoeksema, S., Girgus, J. S., & Seligman, M. E. P. (1991). Sex differences in depression and explanatory style in children. *Journal of Youth and Adolescence, 20,* 233–245.

Nolen-Hoeksema, S., Girgus, J. S., & Seligman, M. E. P. (1992). Predictors and consequences of childhood depressive symptoms: A five-year longitudinal study. *Journal of Abnormal Psychology, 101,* 405–422.

O'Hara, M. W., Neunaber, D. J., & Zekoski, E. M. (1984). Prospective study of postpartum depression: Prevalence, course, and predictive factors. *Journal of Abnormal Psychology, 93,* 158–171.

O'Hara, M. W., Rehm, L. P., & Campbell, S. B. (1982). Predicting depressive symptomatology: Cognitive-behavioral models and postpartum depression. *Journal of Abnormal Psychology, 91*, 457–461.

Oettingen, G. (Ed.). (1993). Deutschland Ost und Deutschland West. [Germany East and Germany West] [Special Issue]. *Zeitschrift fuer Sozialpsychologie, 24.*

Oettingen, G. (1994). Attributionsstil und expressives Verhalten in Ost- und West-Berlin [Explanatory style and expressive behavior in East and West Berlin]. In G. Trommsdorff (Ed.), *Psycholgische Aspekte des soziopolitischen Wandels in Ostdeutschland* (pp. 144–153). Berlin: De Gruyter.

Oettingen, G. (in press). Cross-cultural perspectives on self-efficacy beliefs. In A. Bandura (Ed.), *Self-efficacy in adaptation of youth to changing societies.* Cambridge, UK: Cambridge University Press.

Oettingen, G. & Little, T. D. (1993). Intelligenz und Selbstwirksamkeitsurteile bei Ost- und Westberliner Schulkindern [Intelligence and performance-related self-efficacy beliefs in East and West Berlin school children]. *Zeitschrift fuer Sozialpsychologie, 24*, 186–197.

Oettingen, G., Little, T. D., Lindenberger, U., & Baltes, P. B. (1994). Causality, agency, and control beliefs in East versus West Berlin children: A natural experiment on the role of context. *Journal of Personality and Social Psychology, 66*, 579–595.

Oettingen, G., & Morawska, E. T. (1990). *Explanatory style in religious vs. secular domains in Russian Judaism vs. Orthodox Christianity.* Unpublished manuscript, University of Pennsylvania.

Oettingen, G., & Seligman, M. E. P. (1990). Pessimism and behavioural signs of depression in East versus West Berlin. *European Journal of Social Psychology, 20*, 207–220.

Olinger, L. J., Kuiper, N. A., & Shaw, B. F. (1987). Dysfunctional attitudes and stressful life events: An interactive model of depression. *Cognitive Therapy and Research, 11*, 25–40.

Overmier, J. B., & Seligman, M. E. P. (1967). Effects of inescapable shock upon subsequent escape and avoidance learning. *Journal of Comparative and Physiological Psychology, 63*, 23–33.

Panzarella-Tse, C., Alloy, L. B., & Lipman, A. J. (1992). *Social support, hopelessness, and depression: On the mechanisms for the social support-reduced depression link.* Unpublished manuscript, Temple University, Philadelphia, PA.

Parkes, C. M., Benjamin, B., & Fitzgerald, R. G. (1969). Broken heart: A statistical study of increased mortality among widowers. *British Medical Journal, 1*, 740–743.

Parrot, G., & Sabini, J. (1990). Mood and memory under natural conditions: Evidence for mood-incongruent recall. *Journal of Personality and Social Psychology, 59*, 321–336.

Parsons, J. E., Meece, J. L., Adler, T. F., & Kaczala, C. M. (1982). Sex differences in attributional patterns and learned helplessness? *Sex Roles, 8*, 421–432.

Paul, G., Girgus, J. S., Nolen-Hoeksema, S., & Seligman, M. E. P. (1989, April). *Precursors of deficits in children's academic achievement.* Paper presented at the meetings of the Eastern Psychological Association, Philadelphia, PA.

Peel, A., Semple, T., Wang, I., Lancaster, W. M., & Dahl, J. L. G. (1962). A coronary prognostic index for grading the severity of infarctions. *British Heart Journal, 24*, 745–750.

Pennebaker, J. W. (1990). *Opening up: The healing power of confinding in others.* New York: Morrow.

Pepper, S. C. (1942). *World hypotheses.* Berkeley, CA: University of California Press.

Persons, J. B., & Rao, P. A. (1985). Longitudinal study of cognitions, life events, and depression in psychiatric inpatients. *Journal of Abnormal Psychology, 94*, 51–63.

Petersen, A. C. (1979). Female pubertal development. In M. Sugar (Ed.), *Female adolescent development* (pp. 23–46). New York: Brunner/Mazel.

Petersen, A. C., Sarigiani, P. A., & Kennedy, R. E. (1991). Adolescent depression: Why more girls? *Journal of Youth and Adolescence, 20*, 247–271.

Peterson, C. (1988). Explanatory style as a risk factor for illness. *Cognitive Therapy and Research, 12*, 117–130.

Peterson, C. (1991). The meaning and measurement of explanatory style. *Psychological Inquiry, 2*, 1–10.

Peterson, C. (1992). *Personality* (2nd ed.). Fort Worth, TX: Harcourt Brace Jovanovich.

Peterson, C., & Barrett, L. (1987). Explanatory style and academic performance among university freshmen. *Journal of Personality and Social Psychology, 53*, 603–607.

Peterson, C., Bettes, B. A., & Seligman, M. E. P. (1985). Depressive symptoms and unprompted causal attributions: Content analysis. *Behaviour Research and Therapy, 23*, 379–382.

Peterson, C., & Bossio, L. M. (1991). *Health and optimism.* New York: Free Press.

Peterson, C., Colvin, D., & Lin, E. H. (1992). Explanatory style and helplessness. *Social Behavior and Personality, 20*, 1–14.

Peterson, C., & Jacobs, J. (1989). *Collective optimism and group performance.* Unpublished manuscript, University of Michigan, Ann Arbor.

Peterson, C., Luborsky, L., & Seligman, M. E. P. (1983). Attributions and depressive mood shifts: A case study using the symptom-context method. *Journal of Abnormal Psychology, 92*, 96–103.

Peterson, C., Maier, S. F., & Seligman, M. E. P. (1993). *Learned helplessness: A theory for the age of personal control.* New York: Oxford.

Peterson, C., Schulman, P., Castellon, C., & Seligman, M. E. P. (1992). The explanatory style scoring manual. In C. P. Smith (Ed.), *Handbook of thematic analysis* (pp. 383–392). New York: Cambridge University Press.

Peterson, C., Schwartz, S. M., & Seligman, M. E. P. (1981). Self-blame and depressive symptoms. *Journal of Personality and Social Psychology, 41*, 253–259.

Peterson, C. & Seligman, M. E. P. (1981). Helplessness and attributional style in depression. *Tiddsskrift for Norsk Psykologforening, 18*, 3–18; 53–59.

Peterson, C., & Seligman, M. E. P. (1984a). Causal explanations as a risk factor for depression: Theory and evidence. *Psychological Review, 91*, 347–374.

Peterson, C., & Seligman, M. E. P. (1984b). *Content analysis of verbatim explanations: The CAVE technique for assessing explanatory style.* Unpublished manuscript, Virginia Polytechnic Institute and State University.

Peterson, C., & Seligman, M. E. P. (1985). The learned helplessness model of depression: Current status of theory and research. In E. E. Beckham & W. R. Leber (Eds.), *Handbook of depression: Treatment, assessment, and research* (pp. 914–939). Homewood, IL: Dorsey.

Peterson, C., & Seligman, M. E. P. (1987). Explanatory style and illness. *Journal of Personality, 55*, 237–265.

Peterson, C., Seligman, M. E. P., & Vaillant, G. E. (1988). Pessimistic explanatory style is a risk factor for physical illness: A thirty-five year longitudinal study. *Journal of Personality and Social Psychology, 55*, 23–27.

Peterson, C. Semmel, A., von Baeyer, C., Abramson, L. Y., Metalsky, G. I., & Seligman, M. E. P. (1982). The Attributional Style Questionnaire. *Cognitive Therapy and Research, 6*, 287–299.

Peterson, C., & Stunkard, A. J. (1989). Personal control and health promotion. *Social Science and Medicine, 28*, 819–828.

Peterson, C., & Stunkard, A. J. (1992). Cognates of personal control: Locus of control, self-efficacy, and explanatory style. *Applied and Preventive Psychology, 1*, 111–117.

Peterson, C., & Villanova, P. (1988). An Expanded Attributional Style Questionnaire. *Journal of Abnormal Psychology, 97*, 87–89.

Peterson, C., Villanova, P., & Raps, C. S. (1985). Depression and attributions: Factors responsible for inconsistent results in the published literature. *Journal of Abnormal Psychology, 94*, 165–168.

Petrie, K., & Chamberlain, K. (1983). Hopelessness and social desirability as moderator variables in predicting suicidal behavior. *Journal of Consulting and Clinical Psychology, 51*, 485–487.

Phares, E. J. (1976). *Locus of control in personality.* Morristown, NJ: General Learning Press.

Pickering, J. F. (1977). *The acquisition of consumer durables.* London: Associated Business Programmes.

Pike, K. L. (1967). *Language in relation to a united theory of the structure of human behavior.* The Hague, Netherlands: Mouton.

Pittman, T. S., & Pittman, N. L. (1980). Deprivation of control and the attribution process. *Journal of Personality and Social Psychology, 39*, 377–389.

Praet, P. (1985). Endogenizing consumers' expectations in four major European Community countries. *Journal of Economic Psychology, 6*, 255–269.

Puig-Antich, J. (1986). Psychobiological markers: Effects of age and puberty. In M. Rutter, C. E. Izard, & P. B. Read (Eds.), *Depression in young people* (pp. 341–382). New York: Guilford.

Rabkin, J. G., & Struening, E. L. (1976). Life events, stress, and illness. *Science, 194*, 1013–1020.

Ralph, J. A., & Mineka, S. (1993, May). *The interaction of attributional style and life stress: Does it predict change in depression, anxiety, or positive/negative affectivity?* Poster presented at Midwestern Psychological Association, Chicago, IL.

Raps, C. S., Peterson, C., Reinhard, K. E., Abramson, L. Y., & Seligman, M. E. P. (1982). Attributional style among depressed patients. *Journal of Abnormal Psychology, 91*, 102–108.

Reeder, R. (1975). *Down along the mother Volga.* Philadelphia: University of Pennsylvania Press.

Reivich, K. J., & Seligman, M. E. P. (1991). *The forced-choice Attributional Style Questionnaire.* Unpublished data, University of Pennsylvania, Philadelphia.

Rempel, J. K., Holmes, J. G., & Zanna, M. P. (1985). Trust in close relationships. *Journal of Personality and Social Psychology, 49*, 95–112.

Reynolds, W. M., & Coats, K. I. (1986). A comparison of cognitive-behavioral therapy and relaxation training for the treatment of depression in adolescents. *Journal of Consulting and Clinical Psychology, 54*, 653–660.

Rholes, W. S. (1989). Action control as a vulnerability factor in depressed mood. *Cognitive Therapy and Research, 13*, 263–274.

Rholes, W. S., Riskind, J. H., & Neville, B. (1985). The relationship of cognitions and hopelessness to depression and anxiety. *Social Cognition, 3*, 36–50.

Rie, H. E. (1966). Depression in childhood: A survey of some pertinent contributions. *Journal of the American Academy of Child Psychiatry, 5*, 653–683.

Riskind, J. H. (1983). Nonverbal expressions and the accessibility of life experience memories: A congruence hypothesis. *Social Cognition, 2*, 62–86.

Riskind, J. H., Castellon, C. S., & Beck, A. T. (1989). Spontaneous causal explanations in unipolar depression and generalized anxiety: Content analysis of dysfunctional-thought diaries. *Cognitive Therapy and Research, 13*, 97–108.

Riskind, J. H., & Rholes, W. S. (1984). Cognitive accessibility and the capacity of cognitions to predict future depression: A theoretical note. *Cognitive Therapy and Research, 8*, 1–12.

Riskind, J. H., Rholes, W. S., Brannon, A. M., & Burdick, C. A. (1987). Attributions and expectations: A confluence of vulnerabilities in mild depression in a college student population. *Journal of Personality and Social Psychology, 53*, 349–354.

Rizley, R. (1978). Depression and distortion in the attribution of causality. *Journal of Abnormal Psychology, 37*, 32–48.

Roberts, G. C. (1977). Win–loss causal attributions of little league players. In. J. Salmela (Ed.), *Canadian Symposium for Psychomotor Learning and Sport Psychology* (pp. 116–138). Ithaca NY: Movement.

Robins, C. J. (1988). Attributions and depression: Why is the literature so inconsistent? *Journal of Personality and Social Psychology, 54*, 880–889.

Robins, C. J. (1994). *Personality diathesis—stress models of depression: The roles of personality-event domain matching and gender.* Manuscript submitted for publication, Duke University, Durham, NC.

Robins, C. J., & Block, P. (1989). Cognitive theories of depression viewed from a diathesis-stress perspective: Evaluations of the models of Beck and of Abramson, Seligman, and Teasdale. *Cognitive Therapy and Research, 13*, 297–313.

Robins, C. J., & Hinkley, K. (1989). Social-cognitive processing and depressive symptoms in children: A comparison of measures. *Journal of Abnormal Child Psychology, 17*, 29–36.

Robinson, M. J. (1988). Can values save George Bush? *Public Opinion, 11*, 11–13; 59–60.

Roosevelt, F. D. (1965). First inaugural address. In *Inaugural addresses of the Presidents of the United States* (pp. 235–239). Washington, DC: U.S. Government Printing Office. (Original work published 1933)

Rose, D. T., & Abramson, L. Y. (1992). Developmental predictors of depressive cognitive style: Research and theory. In C. Cicchetti & S. Toth (Eds.), *Rochester Symposium on Developmental Psychopathology* (Vol. 4, pp. 323–349). Rochester, NY: University of Rochester Press.

Rose, D. T., Abramson, L. Y., Hodulik, C., Leff, G., & Halberstadt, L. J. (in press). Heterogeneity of cognitive style among depressed inpatients. *Journal of Abnormal Psychology.*

Rose, D. T., Leff, G., Halberstadt, L. J., Hodulik, C., & Abramson, L. Y. (1992). *Heterogeneity of cognitive style among inpatient depressives: A search for "negative cognition" depressives.* Unpublished manuscript, University of Wisconsin, Madison.

Rosenfeld, A., Rev. (1986). *Tisha B'Av Compendium. Tephilot and Kinot.* New York: The Judaica Press.

Rosenhan, D. L., & Seligman, M. E. P. (1989). *Abnormal Psychology* (2nd ed.). New York: Norton.

Rosenhan, R. H., Brand, R. J., Jenkins, C. D., Friedman, M., Straus, R., & Wurm, M. (1975). Coronary heart disease in the Western Collaborative Group Study: Final follow-up experience of eight and a half years. *Journal of the American Medical Association, 233,* 872–877.

Rosenstone, S. J. (1983). *Forecasting presidential elections.* New Haven, CT: Yale University Press.

Rosenthal, R. (1990). How are we doing in soft psychology? *American Psychologist, 45,* 775–777.

Rosenthal, R., & Rubin, D. B. (1982). A simple, general purpose display of magnitude of experimental effect. *Journal of Educational Psychology, 74,* 166–169.

Rotenberg, K. J. (1980). "A promise kept, a promise broken": Developmental bases of trust. *Child Development, 51,* 614–617.

Roth, S. (1980). A revised model of learned helplessness in humans. *Journal of Personality, 48,* 103–133.

Rothwell, N., & Williams, J. M. G. (1983). Attributional style and life events. *British Journal of Clinical Psychology, 22,* 139–140.

Rotter, J. B. (1954). *Social learning and clinical psychology.* Englewood Cliffs, NJ: Prentice-Hall.

Rotter, J. B. (1966). Generalized expectancies for internal versus external control of reinforcement. *Psychological Monographs, 81,* 1–28.

Rubin, R. (Ed.). (1979). *Voices of the people: The story of Yiddish folksong.* Philadelphia, PA: The Jewish Publication Society of America.

Ruehlman, L. S., West, S. G., & Pasahow, R. J. (1985). Depression and evaluative schemata. *Journal of Personality, 53,* 46–92.

Runyan, W. K. (1982). *Life histories and psychobiography.* New York: Oxford.

Runyon, J., Verdini, J., & Runyon, S. (1971). *Source book of American presidential campaign and election statistics, 1948–1968.* New York: Ungar.

Rush, A. J., Weissenburger, J., & Eaves, G. (1986). Do thinking patterns predict depressive symptoms? *Cognitive Therapy and Research, 10,* 225–236.

Russell, D. (1982). The causal dimension scale: A measure of how individuals perceive causes. *Journal of Personality and Social Psychology, 42,* 1137–1145.

Sackheim, H. A., & Wegner, A. Z. (1986). Attributional patterns in depression and euthymia. *Archives of General Psychiatry, 43,* 553–560.

Sacks, C. H., & Bugental, D. B. (1987). Attributions as moderators of affective and behavioral responses to social failure. *Journal of Personality and Social Psychology, 53,* 939–947.

Sagan, L. A. (1987). *The health of nations: True causes of sickness and well-being.* New York: Basic Books.

Salovey, P., & Birnbaum, D. (1989). Influence of mood on health-relevant cognitions. *Journal of Personality and Social Psychology, 57,* 539–551.

Scheier, M. F., & Carver, C. S. (1985). Optimism, coping, and health: Assessment and implications of generalized outcome expectancies. *Health Psychology, 4,* 219–247.

Schleifer, S. J., Keller, S. E., Siris, S. G., Davis, K. L., & Stein, M. (1985). Depression and immunity. *Archives of General Psychiatry, 42*, 129–133.

Schöppner, K. P. (1991). Mit Gestrigen in die zukunft [With the past in the future]. *Spiegel Spezial, 1*, 30–38.

Schulman, P., Castellon, C., & Seligman, M. E. P. (1988). *Guidelines for extracting and rating spontaneous explanations.* Unpublished manuscript, University of Pennsylvania.

Schulman, P., Castellon, C., & Seligman, M. E. P. (1989). Assessing explanatory style: The Content analysis of verbatim explanations and the Attributional Style Questionnaire. *Behavior Research and Therapy, 27*, 505–512.

Schulman, P., Keith, D., Seligman, M. E. P. (1991). Is optimism heritable? A study of twins. *Behavior Research and Therapy, 31*, 569–574.

Schulman, P., Seligman, M. E. P., & Amsterdam, D. (1987). The Attributional Style Questionnaire is not transparent. *Behavior Research and Therapy, 25*, 391–395.

Schulman, P., Seligman, M. E. P., Kamen, L. P., Butler, R. P., Oran, D., Priest, R. F., & Burke, W. P. (1990). *Explanatory style as a predictor of achievement in several domains.* Unpublished manuscript, University of Pennsylvania.

Schulman, P., & Seligman, M. E. P. (1986). Explanatory style predicts productivity among life insurance sales agents. *Journal of Personality and Social Psychology, 50*, 832–838.

Schwartz, R. M., & Gottman, J. M. (1976). Toward a task analysis of assertive behavior. *Journal of Consulting and Clinical Psychology, 44*, 910–920.

Segall, M. H. (1984). More than we need to know about culture, but are afraid to ask. *Journal of Cross-Cultural Psychology, 15*, 153–162.

Segall, M. H. (1986). Culture and behavior: Psychology in global perspective. *Annual Review of Psychology, 37*, 523–564.

Seligman, M. E. P. (1974). Depression and learned helplessness. In R. J. Friedman & M. M. Katz (Eds.), *The psychology of depression: Contemporary theory and research* (pp. 83–113). Washington, DC: Winston.

Seligman, M. E. P. (1975). *Helplessness: On depression, development, and death.* San Francisco, CA: Freeman.

Seligman, M. E. P. (1978). Comment and integration. *Journal of Abnormal Psychology, 87*, 165–179.

Seligman, M. E. P. (1981). Behavioral and cognitive therapy for depression from a learned helplessness point of view. In L. P. Rehm (Ed.), *Behavior therapy for depression: Present status and future directions* (pp. 33–71). New York: Academic.

Seligman, M. E. P. (1987). *Predicting depression, poor health, and presidential elections: A science and public policy seminar.* Washington, DC: Federation of Behavioral, Psychological, and Cognitive Sciences.

Seligman, M. E. P. (1991). *Learned optimism.* New York: Knopf.

Seligman, M. E. P., Abramson, L. Y., Semmel, A., & von Baeyer, C. (1979). Depressive attributional style. *Journal of Abnormal Psychology, 88*, 242–247.

Seligman, M. E. P., Castellon, C., Cacciola, J., Schulman, P., Luborsky, L., Ollove, M., & Downing, R. (1988). Explanatory style change during cognitive therapy for unipolar depression. *Journal of Abnormal Psychology, 97*, 13–18.

Seligman, M. E. P., & Elder, G. H. (1986). Learned helplessness and life-span development. In A. B. Sorensen, F. E. Weinert, & L. R. Sherrod (Eds.), *Human development and the life course: Multidisciplinary perspectives* (pp. 377–428). Hillsdale, NJ: Lawrence Erlbaum Associates.

Seligman, M. E. P., & Maier, S. F. (1967). Failure to escape traumatic shock. *Journal of Experimental Psychology, 74*, 1–9.

Seligman, M. E. P., Nolen-Hoeksema, S., Thornton, K. M., & Thornton, N. (1990). Explanatory style as a mechanism of disappointing athletic performance. *Psychological Science, 1*, 143–146.

Seligman, M. E. P., Peterson, C., Kaslow, N. J., Tannenbaum, R. L., Alloy, L. B., & Abramson, L. Y. (1984). Attributional style and depressive symptoms in children. *Journal of Abnormal Psychology, 93*, 235–238.

Seligman, M. E. P., & Schulman, P. (1986). Explanatory style as a predictor of productivity and quitting among life insurance sales agents. *Journal of Personality and Social Psychology, 50,* 832–838.

Sellers, R. M., & Peterson, C. (1993). Explanatory style and coping with controllable events by student-athletes. *Cognition and Emotion, 7,* 431–441.

Shapiro, H. T. (1972). The Index of Consumer Sentiment and economic forecasting: A reappraisal. In B. Strumpel, J. N. Morgan, & E. Zahn (Eds.), *Human behavior in economic affairs: Essays in honor of George Katona* (pp. 373–396). San Francisco, CA: Jossey-Bass.

Shekelle, R. B., Hulley, S., Neaton, J., Billings, J., Borhani, N., Gerace, T., Jacobs, D., Lasser, N., Mittlemark, M., Stamler, J., & the Multiple Risk Factor Intervention Trial Research Group (1985). The Multiple Risk Factor Intervention Trial behavioral pattern study: Part II. Type A behavior pattern and incidence of coronary heart disease. *American Journal of Epidemiology, 122,* 559–570.

Sherman, S. J., Cialdini, R. B., Schwartzman, D. F., & Reynolds, R. D. (1985). Imagining can heighten or lower the percieved likelihood of contracting a disease: The mediating effect of ease of imagery. *Personality and Social Psychology Bulletin, 11,* 118–127.

Sigelman, L., & Knight, K. (1983). Why does presidential popularity decline? A test of the Expectation/Disillusion theory. *Public Opinion Quarterly, 49,* 310–324.

Sigelman, L., & Knight, K. (1985). Expectation/Disillusion and presidential popularity: The Reagan experience. *Public Opinion Quarterly, 49,* 209–213.

Simmons, R. G., & Blyth, D. A. (1987). *Moving into adolescence: The impact of pubertal change and school context.* New York: Aldine DeGruyter.

Simmons, R. G., Blyth, D. A., Van Cleave, E. F., & Bush, D. M. (1979). Entry into early adolescence: The impact of school structure, puberty, and early dating on self-esteem. *American Sociological Review, 44,* 948–967.

Simons, A. D., Garfield, S. L., & Murphy, G. E. (1984). The process of change in cognitive therapy and pharmacotherapy for depression. *Archives of General Psychiatry, 41,* 45–51.

Simons, A. D., Murphy, G. E., Levine, J. L., & Wetzel, R. D. (1986). Cognitive therapy and pharmacotherapy for depression: Sustained improvement over one year. *Archives of General Psychiatry, 43,* 43–48.

Simonton, D. K. (1981). The library laboratory: Archival data in personality and social psychology. In L. Wheeler (Ed.), *Review of personality and social psychology* (Vol. 2, pp. 217–243). Beverly Hills, CA: Sage.

Simonton, D. K. (1985). Intelligence and personal influence in groups: Four nonlinear models. *Psychological review, 92,* 532–547.

Simonton, D. K. (1986). *Why presidents succeed: A political psychology of leadership.* New Haven, CT: Yale University Press.

Simonton, D. K. (1990). Some optimistic thoughts on the pessimistic-rumination thesis. *Psychological Inquiry, 1,* 73–75.

Siwoff, S., Hirdt, S., & Hirdt, P. (1985). *The 1985 Elias Baseball Analyst.* New York: Collier Books.

Siwoff, S., Hirdt, S., & Hirdt, P. (1986). *The 1986 Elias Baseball Analyst.* New York: Collier Books.

Siwoff, S., Hirdt, S., & Hirdt, P. (1987). *The 1987 Elias Baseball Analyst.* New York: Collier Books.

Skinner, H. A. (1981). Toward the integration of classification theory and methods. *Journal of Abnormal Psychology, 90,* 68–87.

Sklar, L. S., & Anisman, H. (1979). Stress and coping factors influence tumor growth. *Science, 205,* 513–515.

Smucker, M. R., Craighead, W. E., Craighead, L. W., & Green, B. J. (1986). Normative and reliability data for the Children's Depression Inventory. *Journal of Abnormal Child Psychology, 14,* 25–40.

Spink, K. S. (1978). Win–loss causal attributions of high school basketball players. *Canadian Journal of Applied Sport Sciences, 3,* 195–201.

Spink, K. S., & Roberts, G. C. (1980). Ambiguity of outcome and causal attributions. *Journal of Sport Psychology, 2,* 237–244.

Stark, K. D. (1990). *The treatment of depression during childhood: A school based program.* New York: Guilford.

Stark, K. D., Reynolds, W. M., & Kaslow, N. J. (1987). A comparsion of the relative efficacy of self-control therapy and a behavioral problem-solving therapy for depression in children. *Journal of Abnormal Child Psychology, 15*, 91–113.

Stoltz, R. F., & Galassi, J. P. (1989). Internal attributions and types of depression in college students: The learned helplessness model revisted. *Journal of Counseling Psychology, 36*, 316–321.

Suls, J., & Mullen, B. (1981). Life events, perceived control, and illness: The role of uncertainty. *Journal of Human Stress, 7*, 30–34.

Sweeney, P. D., Anderson, K., & Bailey, S. (1986). Attributional style in depression: A meta-analytic review. *Journal of Personality and Social Psychology, 50*, 974–991.

Sweeney, P. D., Shaeffer, D., & Golin, S. (1982). Attributions about self and others in depression. *Personality and Social Psychology Bulletin, 8*, 37–42.

Taylor, S. E., & Brown, J. D. (1988). Illusion and well-being: A social psychological perspective on mental health. *Psychological Bulletin, 103*, 193–210.

Taylor, S. E., & Fiske, S. T. (1978). Salience, attention, and attribution: Top of the head phenomena. In L. Berkowitz (Ed.), *Advances in experimental social psychology* (Vol. 11, pp. 249–288). New York: Academic.

Taynor, J., & Deaux, K. (1973). When women are more deserving than men: Equity, attribution and perceived sex differences. *Journal of Personality and Social Psychology, 28*, 360–367.

Tellegen, A. (1985). Structures of mood and personality and their relevance to assessing anxiety, with an emphasis on self-report. In A. H. Tuma & J. D. Maser (Eds.), *Anxiety and the anxiety disorders* (pp. 681–706). Hillsdale, NJ: Lawrence Erlbaum Associates.

Tennen, H., & Herzberger, S. (1986). Attributional Style Questionnaire. In D. J. Keyser & R. C. Sweetland (Eds.), *Test critiques* (Vol. 4, pp. 20–30). Kansas City, KS: Test Corporation of America.

Tennen, H., & Herzberger, S. (1987). Depression, self-esteem, and the absence of self-protective attributional biases. *Journal of Personality and Social Psychology, 52*, 72–80.

Tennen, H., Herzberger, S., & Nelson, H. F. (1987). Depressive attributional style: The role of self-esteem. *Journal of Personality, 55*, 631–660.

Tetlock, P. E. (1981). Pre- to post-election shifts in presidential rhetoric: Impression management or cognitive adjustment? *Journal of Personality and Social Psychology, 41*, 207–212.

Thoresen, C. E., Friedman, M., Gill, J. K., & Ulmer, D. K. (1982). The Recurrent Coronary Prevention Project. Some preliminary findings. *Acta Medica Scandinavia, 660*, 172–192.

Tiger, L. (1979). *Optimism: The biology of hope.* New York: Simon & Schuster.

Triandis, H. C. (1980). Introduction to "Handbook of cross cultural psychology". In H. C. Triandis & W. W. Lambert (Eds.), *Handbook of cross-cultural psychology: Vol 1. Perspectives* (pp. 1–14). Boston, MA: Allyn & Bacon.

Triandis, H. C., Vassiliou, V., Vassiliou, G., Tanaka, Y., & Shanmugam, A. V. (Eds.). (1972). *The analysis of subjective culture.* New York: Wiley.

Tufte, E. R. (1978). *Political control of the economy.* Princeton, NJ: Princeton University Press.

Tversky, M. & Kahneman, D. (1981). The framing of decisions and the psychology of choice. *Science, 211*, 453–458.

Vaihinger, H. (1911). *The psychology of "as if": A system of the theoretical, practical, and religious fictions of mankind.* New York: Harcourt, Brace, & World.

Vaillant, G. E. (1977). *Adaptation to life.* Boston, MA: Little, Brown.

van den Berg, J. H. (1983). *The changing nature of man.* New York: Norton.

van Raaij, W. F., & Gianotten, H. J. (1990). Consumer confidence, expenditure, saving, and credit. *Journal of Economic Psychology, 11*, 269–290.

Vanden Abeele, P. (1983). The Index of Consumer Sentiment: Predictability and predictive power in the EEC. *Journal of Economic Psychology 3*, 1–17.

Vega, W. A., Valle, R. Kolody, B., & Hough, R. (1987). The Hispanic Social Network Prevention Intervention Study: A community-based randomized trial. In R. F. Munoz (Ed.), *Depression prevention: Research directions* (pp. 217–231). Washington, DC: Hemisphere.

Verbrugge, L. M. (1989). Recent, present, and future health of American adults. *Annual Review of Public Health, 10*, 333–361.

Viney, L. L. (1983). The assessment of psychological states through content analysis of verbal communications. *Psychological Bulletin, 94*, 542–563.

Visintainer, M., Volpicelli, J. R., & Seligman, M. E. P. (1982). Tumor rejection in rats after inescapable or escapable shock. *Science, 216*, 437–439.

Vroom, V. (1964). *Work and motivation*. New York: Wiley.

Wallston, B. S., & O'Leary, V. E. (1981). Sex makes a difference: Differential perceptions of women and men. In L. Wheeler (Ed.), *Review of personality and social psychology* (pp. 9–41). Beverly Hills, CA: Sage.

Waterkamp, D. (1990). Erziehung in der Schule [Education in the school]. In Bundesministerium fuer innerdeutsche Beziehungen (Ed.), *Vergleich von Bildung und Erziehung in der Bundesrepublik Deutschlan und in der Deutschen Demokratischen Republik* (pp. 261–277). Koeln: Wissenschaft und Politik.

Watson, D., Clark, L. A., & Carey, G. (1988). Positive and negative affectivity and their relation to anxiety and depressive disorders. *Journal of Abnormal Psychology, 97*, 346–353.

Watson, D., & Friend, R. (1969). Measurement of social-evaluative anxiety. *Journal of Consulting and Clinical Psychology, 33*, 448–457.

Weiner, B. (Ed.). (1974). *Achievement motivation and attribution theory*. Morristown, NJ: General Learning Press.

Weiner, B. (1978). Achievement strivings. In H. London & J. E. Exner (Eds.), *Dimensions of personality* (pp. 1–36). New York: Wiley.

Weiner, B. (1979). A theory of motivation for some classroom experiences, *Journal of Educational Psychology, 71*, 3–25.

Weiner, B. (1985a). An attributional theory of achievement motivation and emotion. *Psychological Review, 92*, 548–573.

Weiner, B. (1985b). "Spontaneous" causal thinking. *Psychological Bulletin, 97*, 74–84.

Weiner, B. (1986). *An attributional theory of motivation and emotion*. New York: Springer-Verlag.

Weiner, B. (1990). Searching for the roots of applied attribution theory. In S. Graham & V. S. Folkes (Eds.), *Attribution theory: Applications to achievement, mental health, and interpersonal conflict* (pp. 1–13). Hillsdale, NJ: Lawrence Erlbaum Associates.

Weissman, A. N. (1979). The dysfunctional attitude scale: A validation study. (Doctoral dissertation, University of Pennsylvania, 1978.) *Dissertation Abstracts International, 40*, 1389B–1390B.

Weissman, A. N., & Beck, A. T. (1978, November). *Development and validation of the dysfunctional attitudes scale: A preliminary investigation*. Paper presented at the annual meeting of the American Educational Research Association, Toronto, Canada.

Weissman, A. N., & Beck, A. T. (1979, July). *The Dysfunctional Attitude Scale*. Paper presented at the annual meeting of the American Psychological Association, New York.

Weissman, M. M. (1990). Evidence for comorbidity of anxiety and depression: Family and genetic studies of children. *Anxiety and depression: Distinctive and overlapping features* (pp. 349–366). New York: Academic.

Weissman, M. M., & Klerman, G. L. (1977). Sex differences in the epidemiology of depression. *Archives of General Psychiatry, 34*, 98–111.

Weissman, M. M., Leaf, P. J., Tischler, G. L., Blazer, D. G., Karno, M., Bruce, M. L., & Florio, L. P. (1988). Affective disorders in five United States communities. *Psychological Medicine, 18*, 141–153.

Weisz, J. R., Rothbaum, F. M., & Blackburn, T. C. (1984). Standing out and standing in: The psychology of control in America and Japan. *American Pscyhologist, 39*, 955–969.

West, D. M. (1983). Press coverage in the 1980 presidential campaign. *Social Science Quarterly, 64*, 624–633.

Whiffen, V. E. (1988). Vulnerability to postpartum depression: A prospective multivariate study. *Journal of Abnormal Psychology, 97*, 467–474.

Whitburn, J. (1990). *Billboard top 1000 singles 1955–1989*. Milwaukee, WI: Hal Leonard.

White, R. W. (1959). Motivation reconsidered: The concept of competence. *Psychological Review, 66*, 297–333.

Williams, J. M. G. (1985). Attributional formulation of depression as a diathesis-stress model: Metalsky et al. reconsidered. *Journal of Personality and Social Psychology, 48*, 1572–1575.

Williams, R. A., & Defris, L. V. (1981). The roles of inflation and consumer sentiment in explaining Australian consumption and savings patterns. *Journal of Economic Psychology, 1*, 105–120.

Williams, R. B., Jr., & Barefoot, J. C. (1988). Coronary prone behavior: The emerging role of the hostility complex. In B. K. Houston & C. R. Snyder (Eds.), *Type A behavior pattern: Research, theory and intervention* (pp. 189–211). New York: Wiley.

Willner, P., Wilkes, M., & Orwin, A. (1990). Attributional style and perceived stress in endogenous and reactive depression. *Journal of Affective Disorders, 18*, 281–287.

Winter, D. G. (1989). *Manual for scoring motive imagery in running text*. Unpublished manuscript, University of Michigan, Ann Arbor.

Winter, D. G. (1990). Leadership, presidential elections, and pessimistic rumination. *Psychological Inquiry, 1*, 77–79.

Wise, E. H., & Barnes, D. R. (1986). The relationship among life events, dysfunctional attitudes, and depression. *Cognitive Therapy and Research, 10*, 257–266.

Witkin, H. A., & Berry, J. W. (1975). Psychological differentiation in cross-cultural perspective. *Journal of Cross-Cultural Psychology, 6*, 4–87.

Wong, P. T. P., & Weiner, B. (1981). When people ask "why" questions, and the heuristics of attribution search. *Journal of Personality and Social Psychology, 40*, 649–663.

Wortman, C. B., & Brehm, J. W. (1975). Response to uncontrollable outcomes: An integration of reactance theory and the learned helplessness model. In L. Berkowitz (Ed.), *Advances in experimental psychology* (Vol. 8, pp. 277–336). New York: Academic.

Wortman, C. B., & Dintzer, L. (1978). Is an attributional analysis of the learned helplessness phenomenon viable? A critique of the Abramson-Seligman-Teasdale reformulation. *Journal of Abnormal Psychology, 87*, 75–80.

Wrightsman, L. S. (1981). Personal documents as data in conceptualizing adult personality development. *Personality and Social Psychology Bulletin, 7*, 367–385.

Yamamoto, J., Yeh, E. K., Loya, F., Slawson, P., & Hurwicz, M. L. (1985). Are American psychiatric outpatients more depressed than Chinese outpatients? *American Journal of Psychiatry, 142*, 1347–1351.

Young, J., & Beck, A. T. (1980). *The development of the Cognitive Therapy Scale*. Unpublished manuscript, Center for Cognitive Therapy, Philadelphia, PA.

Zautra, A. J., Guenther, R. T., & Chartier, G. M. (1985). Attributions for real and hypothetical events: Their relation to self-esteem and depression. *Journal of Abnormal Psychology, 94*, 530–540.

Zautra, A. J., & Reich, J. W. (1983). Life events and perceptions of life quality: Developments in a two-factor approach. *Journal of Communications Psychology, 11*, 121–132.

Zimmerman, M., Coryell, W., & Corenthal, C. (1984). Attributional style, the dexamethasone suppression test, and the diagnosis of melancholia in depressed inpatients. *Journal of Abnormal Psychology, 93*, 373–377.

Zimmerman, M., Coryell, W., Corenthal, C., & Wilson, S. (1986). Dysfunctional attitudes and attributional style in healthy controls and patients with schizophrenia, psychotic depression, and nonpsychotic depression. *Journal of Abnormal Psychology, 95*, 403–405.

Zlotowitz, R. M. (1983). *Megillas Eichah Lamentations*. Brooklyn, NY: Mesorah.

Zubin, H. E., & Spring, B. (1977). Vulnerability: A new view of schizophrenia. *Journal of Abnormal Psychology, 86*, 103–126.

Zullow, H. M. (1984). *The interaction of rumination and explanatory style in depression.* Unpublished master's thesis, University of Pennsylvania.

Zullow, H. M. (1985). *Manual for rating action styles.* Unpublished manuscript, University of Pennsylvania.

Zullow, H. M. (1988). The hopeful edge: A new tool for forecasting elections. *The Polling Report, 4,* 4–6.

Zullow, H. M. (1991). Pessimistic rumination in popular songs and newsmagazines predicts economic recession via decreased consumer optimism and spending. *Journal of Economic Psychology, 12,* 501–526.

Zullow, H. M. (in press). American exceptionalism and the quadrenial peak in optimism. In A. Miller & B. Gronbeck (Eds.), *Presidential elections and American self-images.* Boulder, CO: Westview.

Zullow, H. M., Oettingen, G., Peterson, C., & Seligman, M. E. P. (1988). Pessimistic explanatory style in the historical record: CAVing LBJ, presidential candidates, and East versus West Berlin. *American Psychologist, 43,* 673–682.

Zullow, H. M., & Seligman, M. E. P. (1990a). Pessimistic rumination predicts defeat of presidential candidates, 1900 to 1984. *Psychological Inquiry, 1,* 52–61.

Zullow, H. M., & Seligman, M. E. P. (1990b). Author's reply. *Psychological Inquiry, 1,* 90–91.

Author Index

Subject Index